Thank you for choosing a SAGE product!
If you have any comment, observation or feedback,
I would like to personally hear from you.

Please write to me at **contactceo@sagepub.in**

Vivek Mehra, Managing Director and CEO, SAGE India.

Bulk Sales

SAGE India offers special discounts
for purchase of books in bulk.
We also make available special imprints
and excerpts from our books on demand.

For orders and enquiries, write to us at

Marketing Department
SAGE Publications India Pvt Ltd
B1/I-1, Mohan Cooperative Industrial Area
Mathura Road, Post Bag 7
New Delhi 110044, India

E-mail us at **marketing@sagepub.in**

Get to know more about SAGE

Be invited to SAGE events, get on our mailing list.
Write today to **marketing@sagepub.in**

This book is also available as an e-book.

HIGHER
EDUCATION
IN FEDERAL
COUNTRIES

SAGE Studies in Higher Education

Higher Education has become an important player in the global economy and has a dynamic and growing role in every society. Massification, differentiation, human resource development, knowledge development and transfer, internationalization and privatization are key characteristics of the global higher education landscape, although they manifest themselves in different ways depending on the type of institution, country and/or region of the world. Traditional divisions—such as those between North and South, developed and underdeveloped economies, universities and vocational schools, and so on—are no longer adequate to describe the dynamic and complex patterns of postsecondary education worldwide. *SAGE Studies in Higher Education* provides cogent discussion, analysis and debate of key themes in global higher education.

Series Editors

Philip G. Altbach
Research Professor and
Founding Director
Center for International
Higher Education
Boston College, USA

Hans de Wit
Director
Center for International
Higher Education
Boston College, USA

Laura Rumbley
Associate Director
Center for International
Higher Education
Campion Hall, Boston College,
USA

Simon Marginson
Professor of International
Higher Education
UCL Institute of Education
University College London, UK

Claire Callender
Professor of Higher Education
Studies
UCL Institute of Education and
Birkbeck University of London,
UK

HIGHER EDUCATION IN FEDERAL COUNTRIES

A Comparative Study

Edited by
Martin Carnoy
Isak Froumin
Oleg Leshukov
Simon Marginson

Los Angeles | London | New Delhi
Singapore | Washington DC | Melbourne

First published in 2018 by

SAGE Publications India Pvt Ltd
B1/I-1 Mohan Cooperative Industrial Area
Mathura Road, New Delhi 110 044, India
www.sagepub.in

SAGE Publications Inc
2455 Teller Road
Thousand Oaks, California 91320, USA

SAGE Publications Ltd
1 Oliver's Yard, 55 City Road
London EC1Y 1SP, United Kingdom

SAGE Publications Asia-Pacific Pte Ltd
3 Church Street
#10-04 Samsung Hub
Singapore 049483

Published by Vivek Mehra for SAGE Publications India Pvt Ltd, typeset in 10.5/13 pt Bembo by Zaza Eunice, Hosur, Tamil Nadu, India and printed at Chaman Enterprises, New Delhi.

Library of Congress Cataloging-in-Publication Data

Name: Carnoy, Martin, editor.
Title: Higher education in federal countries: a comparative study/edited
  by Martin Carnoy, Isak Froumin, Oleg Leshukov and Simon Marginson.
Description: Thousand Oaks, California, USA: SAGE Publications India Pvt,
  Ltd, 2018. | Includes bibliographical references and index.
Identifiers: LCCN 2018005262 | ISBN 9789352806713 (print (hb)) |
  ISBN 9789352806720 (e-pub 2.0) | ISBN 9789352806737 (e-book)
Subjects: LCSH: Higher education and state—Case studies. | Federal
  government—Case studies. | Central–local government relations—Case
  studies.
Classification: LCC LC171 .H547 2018 | DDC 378—dc23 LC record available at https://lccn.loc.
gov/2018005262

ISBN: 978-93-528-0671-3 (HB)

SAGE Team: Rajesh Dey, Alekha Chandra Jena, Kumar Indra Mishra and Ritu Chopra

Contents

List of Tables

List of Figures

List of Abbreviations

AICTE	All-India Council for Technical Education
ANMEB	National Accord for the Modernization of Basic and Teachers' Education
ANU	Australian National University
ARWU	Academic Ranking of World Universities
AUC	Australian Universities Commission
BEOG	basic educational opportunities grant
BLK	*Bund-Länder-Kommission für Bildungsplanung und Forschungsförderung*
CABE	Central Advisory Board of Education
CBSE	Central Board of Secondary Education
CEO	chief executive officer
CHEA	Council for Higher Education Accreditation
CHT	Canada Health Transfer
CICIC	Canadian Information Centre for International Credentials
CIHR	Canadian Institutes of Health Research
CMEC	Council of Ministers of Education, Canada
CNPq	National Research Council
CONACYT	National Council for Science and Technology
CSLP	Canada Student Loans Program
CST	Canada Social Transfer
DAAD	*Deutscher Academic Exchange Service*
DFG	*Deutsche Forschungsgemeinschaft*
ECS	Education Commission of the States
EOGs	educational opportunity grants
ERA	Excellent Research for Australia
EU	European Union
FHs	*Fachhochschulen*

FIES	Fund for Student Financing
FIMPES	Federation of Mexican Private Higher Education Institutions
FOMES	Fund for the Modernization of Higher Education
GDP	Gross Domestic Product
GSL	guaranteed student loans
GST	Goods and Services Tax
GWK	*Gemeinsame Wissenschaftskonferenz*
HBCU	historically black colleges and universities
HEA	Higher Education Act
HEFA	Higher Education Finance Agency
HEI	higher education institution
HEP	*Hochschulerneuerungsprogramm*
HRG	*Hochschulrahmengesetz*
HSE	Higher School of Economics
ICSSR	Indian Council of Social Science Research
IGC	General Course Index
IIM	Indian Institute of Management
IIT	Indian Institute of Technology
IPN	National Polytechnic Institute
ISCED	International Standard Classification of Education
ITAM	Mexican Autonomous Technological Institute
ITESM	Monterrey Technological Institute of Superior Studies
JEE	Joint Entrance Examination
KMK	*Ständige Konferenz der Kultusminister der Länder in der Bundesrepublik Deutschland*
MAT	Management Aptitude Test
MCI	Medical Council of India
MHRD	Ministry of Human Resource Development
MoES	Ministry of Education and Science
NAAC	National Assessment and Accreditation Council
NBA	National Board of Accreditation
NCLB	No Child Left Behind
NCTE	National Council for Teacher Education
NDEA	National Defense Education Act

NEET	National Entrance Eligibility Test
NET	National Eligibility Test
NIT	National Institute of Technology
NSERC	Natural Sciences and Engineering Research Council
NSF	National Science Foundation
OBC	other backward classes
OECD	Organization for Economic Co-operation and Development
OOP	out-of-province
PAN	National Action Party
PEI	Prince Edward Island
PISA	Program for International Student Assessment
PPP	purchasing power parity
PRI	Partido Revolucionario Institucional (Institutional Revolutionary Party)
PROMEP	Program for the Improvement of the Professorship
RDA	regionally decentralized authoritarian
RUSA	Rashtriya Uchchatar Shiksha Abhiyan
RVOE	Official Recognition of Educational Validity
SEP	Public Education Secretariat
SES	Undersecretariat for Higher Education
SHEEO	State Higher Education Executive Officers Association
SINAES	National System of Higher Education Evaluation
SNI	National Researchers System
SNTE	National Union of Education Workers
SSHRC	Social Sciences and Humanities Research Council of Canada
STEM	science, technology, engineering and mathematics
TAFE	Technical and Further Education
TEQSA	Tertiary Education Quality and Standards Agency
TFF	Territorial Formula Financing
UAM	Autonomous Metropolitan University
UGC	University Grants Commission
UIs	intercultural universities
UNAM	National Autonomous University of Mexico

UPEAS	public universities with solidarity support
UPN	National Pedagogical University
VET	Vocational Education and Training
WCU	world-class universities
WR	*Wissenschaftsrat*
WRK	*Westdeutsche Rektorenkonferenz*

Preface

The idea for this book emerged from discussion in Beijing during the preparation of a book on the expansion of higher education in BRIC countries that was written by an American–Brazil–Chinese–Russian–Indian team (Carnoy et al. 2013). We noted that China and Russia had different approaches to the issue of the university development and governance at provincial (regional) level. While Russia had decided to maintain all of the public universities inherited from the Soviet Union under direct central responsibility, the Chinese government had devolved responsibility for the majority of public universities to provincial governments. This minor discovery initiated an active discussion on what might be the optimal model for governing a national system of higher education in a big and diverse country in which the regions play a significant role. In the course of this discussion, we touched on the further examples of India and the United States. We realized that from a scholarly viewpoint, it would be very interesting to look at this issue more systematically and in comparative perspective. At the same time, we felt that such a study might be useful for administrators who needed to find effective ways of managing the organization of a large public sector of higher education.

Until now, studies of higher education systems level have not paid much attention to questions of multilayer structure and governance. The most recent scholarly publication of significance that discussed this issue from a comparative perspective was derived from a symposium that took place in 1991 (Brown, Cazalis and Jasmin 1991). This provided important information about seven federal countries, with an emphasis on issues related to legal frameworks. However, in the more than a quarter of a century since that study was published, federal systems have evolved and changed.

The conjunction of federalism and higher education is especially important for those countries that are required to adjust their governance system to meet the challenges of higher education expansion and growing global competition. Russia is one such country. The central government continues its search for an optimal model of federal–regional relationships in the different sectors. Hence, this study received enthusiastic support in Russia. The National Research University Higher School of Economics (HSE) awarded a specific research grant for the conduct of a comparative study and the preparation of a book.

Over the last five years, the Institute of Education of HSE in cooperation with leading foreign social scientists has maintained a research agenda that has been focused on the transformation of education systems in terms of massification, access to education and institutional differentiation. Perhaps, however, the importance of regional variations has been underestimated. In this book, we treat the regional level of higher education systems as a specific object of analysis. In this perspective, a national higher education system can be described as a set of regional educational subsystems, each with specific developmental paths, albeit affected by the whole national system.

The first plan for the research was presented by Isak Froumin in November 2012 during a conference in Peking University. An editorial group consisting of Isak Froumin, Martin Carnoy, Simon Marginson and Oleg Leshukov began by choosing case study countries and inviting research teams. The main selection criteria for the cases were (a) a high level of heterogeneity of regional development, (b) a relatively large scale of country and higher education system, and (c) the division of responsibility for higher education between national and regional levels of power. Using these criteria, the main cases selected were Australia, Brazil, Canada, India, Germany, Mexico, Russia and the Unites States. China was added because although it is formally a unitary rather than federal country, it meets criteria (a) to (c).

The resulting research group consisted of highly qualified and distinguished experts from each country: S. Marginson (University College London, United Kingdom), R. Verhine and L. Dantas (Federal University of Bahia, Brazil), G. Jones and C. Noumi (University of Toronto, Canada), Jandhyala B. G. Tilak (National University of Educational Planning and Administration, India), U. Teichler (University of Kassel, Germany), I. Ordorika, R. Rodríguez-Gómez and M. Lloyd (Universidad Nacional Autónoma de México, Mexico), I. Froumin and O. Leshukov (National Research University HSE, Russia), M. Carnoy, A. L. Antonio and C. R. Nelson (Stanford University, United States of America) and R. Wang and P. Yang (Peking University, China).

It was agreed that each case study must include at least three main parts; these are as follows:

1. The overall context of national–regional relationships and federalism
2. National–regional relationships in higher education, in terms of legal, economic and other aspects
3. An evaluation of the implications of the country's model of national–regional relationships for the higher education sector, including the effects on regional higher education systems

The inquiry is focused on higher education at Level 5A (degree programmes) in terms of the UNESCO/OECD definition; Level 5B varies considerably between countries.

During the course of the project, there were several meetings of the editorial group. There was also a general workshop involving the participants, held in autumn 2014 under the auspices of the HSE Institute of Education and the Russian Association of Higher Education Researchers. The title of the workshop was 'Higher Education Federalism: Governance and Development of Higher Education in "Federal Type" Systems'. Participants discussed first drafts of most of the chapters and reworked the general framework of the project.

Preliminary results of the project were presented at two international research events—the 2015 Summer School on 'Higher Education Finance and the State' organized by China Institute for Education Finance Research (Peking University) and the HSE Institute of Education in Peking; and the 2016 conference of the Comparative and International Education Society (CIES) in Vancouver.

REFERENCES

Brown, D., Cazalis, P., and Jasmin, G. eds. 1991. *Higher Education in Federal Systems: Proceedings of an International Colloquium Held at Queen's University.* Ottawa, Canada: Renouf Publishing.

Carnoy, M., Loyalka, P., Dobryakova, M. S., Dossani, R., Froumin, I., Kuhns, K., Tilak, J. B. G., and Rong, W. 2013. *University Expansion in a Changing Global Economy: Triumph of the BRICs?* Stanford: Stanford University Press.

Acknowledgements

The authors are grateful to the Rector of National Research University HSE, Yaroslav Kuzminov, for his support of the project. We thank the Moscow office of the World Bank for funding some stages of the project.

Also we would like to thank Philip Altbach for valuable advice at the first stage, and again in relation to publishing issues. We are pleased to be the first book published in the new series of *SAGE Studies in Higher Education* led by Philip.

We appreciate the contribution of the team at the HSE Institute of Education and Russian Association of Higher Education Researchers that organized the project workshop in 2014. We acknowledge the engagement of representatives of the Ministry of Education and Science of the Russian Federation, who participated in some project discussions at the workshop. It is pleasing to note that some of the results of the project have been used to inform policy recommendations in relation to the development of regional higher education systems in Russia.

Thanks also go to the Lemann Center for Educational Entrepreneurship and Innovation in Brazil at the Graduate School of Education, Stanford, which supported the contributions of Martin Carnoy and Robert Verhine, and the ESRC/HEFCE Centre for Global Higher Education at the Institute of Education at University College London, where Simon Marginson is based.

Chapter 1

Introduction
Higher Education in Federal Countries

Simon Marginson and Martin Carnoy

INTRODUCTION

We live in one world. Ideas and money circle that world in microseconds. Yet we are still divided into nation-state units with firm boundaries between them. There are also boundaries within countries that are not quite as firm and fixed. Some nation-states with jurisdiction over large geographic territories use partly decentralized federal systems of government, or something like formal federalism, for historically grounded reasons of size. Other nation-states have developed in countries with potent regional traditions that underpin federal structures from the bottom up. Federalism is a system of government in which sovereignty is shared between a central governing authority and constituent political units such as states or provinces. The arrangement is mostly defined in a constitution that spells out the respective rights and obligations, though not all federally shaped countries give federalism a full constitutional form.

Focus of the Book

In this book, our focus is on what happens with *higher education* in federal systems. How has federalism shaped the evolution of higher learning, credentialing and research? What are the special problems, challenges and advantages of higher education within a federal setting? Do the different federal systems of higher education have something to learn from each other?

Why does it matter what happens to higher education in federal systems? Because higher education matters. Higher education has become centrally important to families and societies all over the world. Worldwide participation in higher education has doubled in the last two decades. In 55 countries, age cohort participation exceeds 50 per cent (Marginson 2016a, 2016b; World Bank 2016). Most national governments see higher education as a primary instrument of nation-building and economic capacity (Carnoy et al. 2013). Research universities are seen to form national elites, drive industry innovation and shape national cultures. Governments want 'world-class universities' with sufficient capacity in science and technology for the institution to figure in global university rankings (ARWU 2015; Hazelkorn 2015).

Yet, in most federal countries, public institutions of higher education answer not just to national government but also to the provinces or states. Higher education is 'one of those areas in which both levels of government have had an interest' (Watts 1992, 12). Some universities emerged before their present national federations were formed; for example, in Germany, India, Mexico, Russia, Australia and the United States. In a smaller world, their founding public identities were primarily local/municipal and state/provincial. They were also semi-autonomous, like all universities. Once federations were formed as institutions with a public remit, they became national as well. There is ongoing potential for tension between the four kinds of identity in play: national, provincial/state, local and university. What are the effects on institutions, researchers, stakeholders and students? What kinds of state or provincial sub-systems of higher education are sustained in a more national and global world? Are they instruments of federal rule or their own master? What are the implications for financing, access, quality and inequality between regions? Do multiple layers of government help or hinder?

To explore these questions, for this book, we selected nine countries with federalist, or in the case of China quasi-federalist, political systems: Australia, Brazil, Canada, China, Germany, India, Mexico, Russia and the United States. A sample of the many federalist countries in the world, they embody a wide range of political arrangements between local and central government, and contrasting traditions in higher education.

In these countries, in which government, political culture and the education system are all products of history, federalism has changed over time, changes that have often affected higher education. On the whole, the role of national government in higher education has strengthened, especially in educational financing, but every case is different. There are countries with a stable balance between national and state/provincial elements in higher education, and others where the respective roles of national and state/provincial government seem to fluctuate. At the same time, higher education in federal countries has been shaped by the mega-trends affecting the sector everywhere, including growth in educational participation or 'massification', globalization and international competition in higher education and, in many systems, market reforms and business models. Again, these mega-trends intersect with federalism in varying ways. The historical record suggests that federal systems are often adaptive in the face of historical trends—some scholars refer to 'pragmatic' federalism (Hollander and Patapan 2007). This adaptability can be associated with tendencies to centralization, decentralization, or a mix of the two.

The Chapters

Higher Education in Federal Countries largely consists of national case study chapters, prepared by leading scholars of higher education policy in each country. These chapters provide many insights into the differing political cultures, modes of federalism and higher education systems. All the authors address the same questions but with varying emphases. As well as a welcome diversity in academic approach, the variations indicate real world differences between modes of federalism, ranging from the constitutional and legal mode, the financial and economic mode, the macro-political mode and mixes of all three.

The remainder of this introductory chapter proceeds as follows. First, we discuss factors that govern variations between federal systems of government in the case study countries, summarized in Table 1.1: differences in state traditions, political culture and mode of federalism. Second, we shift the focus to higher education, noting common worldwide tendencies. Third, we open the discussion about what happens when changing higher education systems intersect with state tradition and mode of federalism. This intersection is explored in more depth in each country chapter. Table 1.2 summarizes federal relations in higher education in the nine case study countries. What stands out in the table is the heterogeneity of modes of federalism and the broad range of possible effects in higher education. It is also interesting that on a nation-by-nation basis, federal systems are more diverse than are higher education systems—degree structures and the forms of the research university are partly converging.

The case studies in this book have two implications for scholarship. The first implication will be especially interesting for scholars of federalism. Because higher education—especially the research university—has much in common but federal systems are more diverse, the comparison of federated higher education systems says something about comparative federalism. The second implication will interest scholars of higher education. The case studies show that to understand higher education in the nine countries, it is necessary to consider the particularities of its federated character in each case. It is also helpful to draw out general lessons about federated systems in higher education from across the cases, a discussion begins at the end of this chapter.

STATE TRADITION AND POLITICAL CULTURE

The nine studies presented in this book demonstrate great variation in how power is shared between the central government and constituent elements in federal systems in general and in higher education. These variations have three sets of roots. First, there are ongoing differences between nations in political culture and the role of the state, which can be profoundly important, shaping distinctive approaches to government, power sharing and education. Second, there are differences between nations in the mode of federal or quasi-federal relations—in the legal shape of federalism, norms of autonomy, location of decisions according to level of government, approach to equity between the

Table 1.1 *Modes of Federalism, Nine Countries**

Countries	State Political Culture	Foundational Federal Relations	Commitment to Subsidiarity Principle	Equity in Relations Between States	Means of National Coordination/Control
United States	Limited liberal	Federation, strong states	Significant local traditions	High state inequality	Legal
Canada	Limited liberal	Federation, strong states	Significant local traditions	Provincial inequality	Legal
Australia	Limited liberal	Federation	Limited	State inequality minimized	Legal and fiscal (taxing power)
Germany	Social market (limited liberal)	Confederation/ federation	Profound in the political culture	Homogeneity of life conditions	Inter-government negotiation
Russia	Comprehensive, Russian	Unitary with token federalism	Rare, contingent	High regional inequality	Political, fiscal, intervention
China	Comprehensive, East Asian	Unitary	Devolution but not subsidiarity	High provincial inequality	Political, fiscal domination
India	Post-colonial	Unitary with federal features	Limited, conjunctural	High state inequality	Political, legal, intervention
Mexico	Post-colonial	Fluctuates, some decentralization	Limited, conjunctural	High state inequality	Political, fiscal, intervention
Brazil	Post-colonial	Tripartite federation	Limited, conjunctural	High state inequality	Political, intervention

Source: Compiled by editors (Simon Marginson and Oleg Leshukov).
Note: * For explanation of terminology, see text.

Table 1.2 *Federalism in Higher Education, Nine Countries**

Countries	Legal/Constitutional Responsibility	Real Political Control	Public Financing	Private Sector	Heterogeneity in Higher Education System
United States	States	Shared, largely state, stable	Shared, national research and loans	Largely deregulated	High stratification, high diversity
Canada	Provinces	Shared, largely provincial, stable	Shared, national research, student	Provincial regulation	Mid stratification, mid diversity
Australia	States in most matters	National, stable	National, less than 5% state	Nationally regulated	High stratification, low diversity
Germany	*Länder* (states)	Shared, negotiated	Shared, national is growing	Small, *Länder* regulated	Low stratification, binary diversity
Russia	National and regions	National (with contingent gaps)	National, less than 5% regional	National has main role	High stratification, high diversity
China	National, partly devolved	National, stable	Shared, national research and WCU	Nationally regulated	High stratification, mid diversity
India	National	Fluctuates, complex	Shared, largely state	Large, mostly state regulated	High stratification, mid diversity
Mexico	National, recent decentralization	Fluctuates, mixed	Shared	Moderate, state regulated	High stratification, mid diversity
Brazil	National and states	Mixed, primarily national	Shared	Large, national regulation	High stratification, high diversity

Source: Compiled by editors (Simon Marginson and Oleg Leshukov).
Note: * For discussion of entries, see text.

states/provinces and the means of national coordination and control. Third, both political culture and mode of federalism may change over time, especially through major shocks such as wars and economic depressions. The first two causes of variation are now discussed. The third, historical transformation, is addressed in the country chapters.

In relation to state types and political cultures, there are three broad groupings of countries in this study: First, the limited liberal states, Australia, Canada and the United States, with Germany as a social market cousin; second, countries with a tradition of comprehensive states—China and Russia; third, post-colonial states—Brazil, India and Mexico—still forming their state traditions as they build government, economy and education, influenced by both limited liberal approaches and comprehensive state models, and also touched by in-country regional traditions, especially in India, where the pre-colonial political culture was primarily regional rather than national.

Limited Liberal States

The Anglo-American limited liberal states are embedded in the political tradition of John Locke (1690/1967) and Adam Smith (1776/1969). Political culture turns on a zero-sum distinction between public and private. The sphere of government is separated from and variously opposed to the economic market, to civil society and to the sphere of the individual or the family, each of which is defined as a realm of freedom. Much of politics turns on the legitimacy or otherwise of government action. Anti-statism is a principal theme of critical politics, especially in the United States. In higher education, the state/university boundary is watched closely. University autonomy and academic freedom are core concerns. With limited liberal states framed by the arbitrary distinctions of public versus private and state versus market/civil society, codes of law play a central role in defining and policing those distinctions. In the first instance, federalism is legal and constitutional in form, though ongoing federal relations are also shaped in the economic departments of government.

In limited liberal states, the interface between state and economy is pivotal, for example in economic agencies such as the British Treasury and the Federal Reserve or Department of the Treasury in the United

States. However, the relationship between government and the capitalist economy is not symmetrical. While there is some potential for social democratic policy, there is a prima facie bias in favour of conducting social activities through economic markets. Even state intervention is often presented within a rhetoric of deregulation and market primacy. It is difficult for limited liberal states, unitary or federal, to interfere with the freedom to trade, and they tolerate corporate interference in national politics and economic decisions through political funding and policy lobbying (Stiglitz 2013). Contrary to beliefs cherished in limited liberal states, they are not inherently more democratic than other states. However, the evolution of electoral democracy was facilitated by the capacity of these states to demarcate shared power, as Locke advised, between law, economy, state bureaucracy and democratic politics. Democracy cannot overthrow industrial or financial capital, but nor is it entirely reducible to capital. In this context, federalism is another structural form in the mosaic of legally separated authorities.

That mosaic is nevertheless structured as a hierarchy with a command and control centre, potent in action. Self-limits of limited liberal government should not be overstated. Anglo-American states synergize closely with the legal system and successfully enforce conformity in public security and economic regulation. While both the public good and governmental responsibility are more narrowly defined than in North-western and Central Europe, or in China or Russia, autonomous public universities are expected to follow policy agendas in all three limited liberal countries. This is more obvious in Australia and the United Kingdom, with their more centralized polities and more uniform political economies. In the United States and Canada, the cultural pressure to confirm with policy is more informal but it is there.

Germany

Germany shares with the Anglo-American countries the centrality of the rule of law and the demarcation of state and market. Relations between national and state (*Länder*) governments are closely defined in the legal-constitutional sense. But, in social market countries, governments have a larger role in providing for the conditions of life, and 'the state' is less of a political negative, than in the Anglo-American countries; and federalism in Germany is less hierarchical, with more scope for bottom-up determination. While the limited liberal countries position higher education institutions somewhere between state and civil society, with the American universities the closest to civil society, higher education is seen as an autonomous sector of state in Germany.

Comprehensive States

In comprehensive states, government exercises authority in a holistic manner. At most, it takes full responsibility for the prosperity, health and orderly functioning of society and economy. In comprehensive states such as China and Russia, the boundaries between state, economy and society are more porous than they are in limited liberal states. (In Nordic Finland, a social democratic variant of the comprehensive state tradition not included in this book, 'state' and 'society' are identical.) Centralized authority is irreducible. The comprehensive state by definition cannot partition itself; government is in command vis-à-vis the economy, although its agendas are often advanced through the bureaucratic state rather than the formal political leadership, and there is a natural limit to state or provincial independence. The comprehensive state does not necessarily direct everything from above or programme society in detail or habitually intervene in many spheres. Nor is it necessarily associated with authoritarian rule. Comprehensive states are associated with both electoral democracy and one-party regimes. However, the law tends to be subordinate to the state not vice versa.

In the East Asian and Russian variant of the comprehensive state, there are fewer barriers to state action, including intervention in market exchange and civil matters, and the sphere of private life and property is less absolute than in the limited liberal state. Comprehensive states have well-developed forms of devolution, but the provinces derive their authority from the centre, and federal relations and state/provincial autonomy, such as university autonomy, are shaped from above and evolve largely through politics and policy rather than the legal framework.

From the foundation of imperial rule in the Qin (221–206 BCE) and Han (206 BCE–220 CE) dynasties, China's government was unitary, except in the interregnums when the state was disordered and fragmented. The unitary model patterned all of the East Asian nations

shaped by Chinese Civilization (Gernet 2002). The pattern of devolution is a thousand years old. After the Tang Dynasty (618–907 CE)
declined when it lost control of its military leaders in the borderlands,
the Song Dynasty (960–1279 CE) concluded that what was needed was
not more intensive control from the centre but more effective devolution (Blockmans and de Weerdt 2016). It evolved sophisticated systems
of devolved local/regional decision-making in which central control
was maintained. The central government managed common systems
(including language, units of measure, financial exchange, taxation,
land and property) and retained the scope to intervene anywhere to
secure order and prosperity. Otherwise, the provinces governed their
own affairs. The Song Dynasty built the capacity of the provinces by
expanding and training the local governing elite while retaining control
over personnel selection and promotion. The provincial elite remained
'tied to broader networks of peers and continued to cultivate an interest
in matters of empire-wide significance. Localization and the consolidation of unified imperial rule appeared to be positively correlated'
(Blockmans and de Weerdt 2016, 311). This established a stable and
enduring relationship between national centre and provinces.

There is significant continuity in the political culture of China, more
than is often realized. In the present party-state regime, higher education is understood as proceeding from the state and is subject to high
priority central intervention, yet research universities have a regulated
autonomy in finance and education. Like provincial leaders, university
presidents, socialized in common as members of the Communist Party
of China, enjoy substantial local agency, although the exercise of central
control tends to oscillate fluidly between restriction and relaxation, as it
always has been in China (Blockmans and de Weerdt 2016, 311)—the
counterpart of the more legalistic government/university tensions over
autonomy in limited liberal states.

Established political cultures are resilient and reproductive. Russia
has a long history of broad ruling mandates and state-driven economic
development. In that most general sense, there is continuity between
central authority under Tsarism, in the Soviet time and the present
(Hosking 2012). Russia today is constitutionally a federal system, but,
in practice, it operates as a unitary system. At first, after the collapse of
the Soviet Union in 1991, when the market sphere expanded and the

state partly retreated from providing for the welfare of the population (Izyumov 2010), there was decentralization to self-determining regions. It appeared the comprehensive state tradition had been modified. But it soon became apparent that the authority and potential scope of the state was little diminished. After the year 2000, the Russian centre reconsolidated power vis-à-vis the regions, which were historically less autonomous than their counterparts in China. The federal system in Russia, with uneven levels of regional autonomy, is also less consistent than provincial decentralization in China. All Russian higher education is positioned under national control yet, in parts of the country, regional government and institutions enjoy surprising scope to manage their own affairs. There are places to hide and even to flourish in a geography as large and heterogeneous as Russia's, in which some localities are declining and others have substantial resources, and in a government bureaucracy that has become more regionally heterogeneous.

Post-colonial States

Since national independence was achieved, Brazil, India and Mexico have undergone fluctuations in the respective roles of the state, market and civil society, and in the degree of practical autonomy of higher education institutions. The role of the state is shaped by a mix of indigenous and colonial traditions; by globalization; by neo-imperial relations—a diminishing problem for India but a continuing burden for Mexico, with its history of economic and political intervention by its powerful neighbour to the North—and by the ebb and flow of political forces. All three have yet to evolve their own reproductive state tradition. All three have been affected by both the limited liberal and the comprehensive state models, in varying ways.

In the three post-colonial states, the turn to a more comprehensive role of government is mostly associated with both national centralization and a degree of authoritarianism, like Russia in that respect but unlike, say, Denmark or Finland. For example, in Mexico, under the Partido Revolucionario Institucional (PRI), in office for more than six decades, the constituent regional states were highly subordinated to the central government, mainly through the party apparatuses. Correspondingly, periods of greater decentralization in Mexico and

Brazil were associated in the 1990s with the breakdown of one-party rule in Mexico and with greater democracy in Brazil. In India, the national government enjoyed clear constitutional primacy after independence in 1947 but the 1990s witnessed wide-scale devolution to the regional states, strengthening their authority and responsibility in higher education and other sectors. In the case of India, the move from national primacy to regional autonomy was accompanied by neoliberal financial deregulation—an explicit move towards the limited liberal state—rather than political democratization. In Brazil, especially, and also India, recent policies on expanding student participation and building world-class universities (WCUs) have been associated with some reassertion of the nation within federalism in higher education.

TYPES OF FEDERALISM

In addition to political culture and state tradition, the federal ordering of governance is affected by four questions. The first question is what kinds of territory—national only, national and in-country regional, regional only—had a prior legal-political existence, an independent starting position in federal governance. The second question is what level of government—national or regional—is the most suitable for making decisions about the matter concerned. The third question is whether there should be distributional equity between the in-country regions, in which domains equity might apply, and how equity is defined, measured and regulated. The fourth question is the means of national coordination in the federal system, particularly how national control or influence are secured—whether through legal and constitutional rules, ongoing spending and taxing power or selective political interventions.

Table 1.1 summarizes the types of federalism in the nine countries in this book. No doubt, all of the judgements in the simplified table are open to discussion and dispute.

Founding Federal Relations

In the previous cross-national study of federal arrangements in higher education, Watts (1992) highlights the importance of foundations prior to federation. In *unitary* systems, only one level of government—the national level—had an independent legal-political existence prior to the formalization of intergovernmental arrangements. In-country regional—state or provincial—and local governments derive their power solely from that of the central government and are legally and politically subordinated to it. China and, in practice, Russia have a unitary political form that decisively limits the potential of states or provinces. However, variations in intergovernmental relations are expressed not only in constitutional structures (independence/non-independence) but also in political structures (autonomy/non-autonomy); and, as discussed, there is often significant provincial autonomy in China. For this reason, China is understood in this book as a quasi-federal country, despite the lack of a constitutional federation of the type found in Russia.

The opposite of the unitary constitutional form is a *confederal* system, in which only the in-country state/provincial entities had a prior existence. The central government may be granted powers, but it is subject to the constituent units of the confederation and derives its powers solely from them. In this book, Germany is closest to that kind of federal arrangement, but the position of the federal government in Germany has evolved sufficiently to ensure its authority is balanced with that of the *Länder*—so finely balanced that, as described in the country chapter, relations between the federal government and the *Länder* shifted back and forth several times in the four decades between the end of World War II and reunification of the country in 1990, and changed again after the reunification. Each shift in intergovernmental relations has been expressed in the financing and management of the higher education system.

Between these two constitutional forms are systems that Watts describes as classically *federal*, in which both levels of government have a prior existence.

> Neither the central nor the constituent units of government are subordinate to the other. Neither level of government derives its authority from the other. Both derive their coordinate, that is, non-subordinate, authority from a contract embodied in a constitution and in that sense are of equal constitutional status. (Watts 1992, 7)

Canada, Australia and the United States are examples of this kind of federation. The dual character of governmental origins permits considerable variation in the relationship. Regional states in the United States have much power relative to the federal government. They collect their own tax revenues—income, sales and property taxes—and, under the US Constitution, have extensive legislative authority. In Australia, regional states have less income-raising power because the federal government dominates taxation. As the country chapter shows, this fiscal imbalance has become associated with a federal takeover of higher education policy.

When there is more than one centre of power, as in both federal or confederal systems, there is always a potential for disagreement between states/provinces and the central government on the rights and obligations of regions vis-à-vis the centre. In unitary systems, central control is readily used to sort disagreements, although authoritarian approaches may undermine local consent.

Level of Government in Decision-making

In a multilevel political system, decisions and their implementation should be managed by the appropriate level(s) of government: The question is how to determine the appropriate level. European law has developed the principle of subsidiarity, defined in the Article 5 of the Treaty on European Union (EU), which 'aims to ensure that decisions are taken as closely as possible to the citizen' (EU 2016). The EU only makes the decision if the area falls within its exclusive competence or if the action at national, in-country regional or local level is ineffective. When the same principle of subsidiarity is applied within national higher education systems in federal countries, matters are devolved down as far as possible. Decisions are made by individual universities unless they have a relational dimension and must be made at state/provincial level. Systemic decisions are made at the state/provincial level unless better made at national level. This approach suggests a major role for the states or provinces in the system ordering of higher education. The potential advantage of federalist systems is that state/provincial government are more likely to be in touch with local constituencies and better at allocating resources to needs.

In the case studies in this book, German federalism, followed by Canada, is closest to this approach. However, nearly all higher education systems work with the subsidiarity principle to some extent.

Systems of governance and management everywhere turn on devolved authority.

There are also limits to reliance on local decision-making. Localities and in-country regions gain from belonging to a larger entity. Consistent legal and financial arrangements maximize freedom of movement within the nation. Common cross-regional infrastructure and systems (e.g., in transport and communications) are essential. Standardized nomenclature and structures for university titles and degrees benefit all. Regions can share the cost of common provision, especially in defence and other functions with an international interface. Regions benefit from economies of scale in larger markets and national economic management, including the brokering of relations between localities and in-country regions with differing resources and specializations. National governments can manage equity and ensure that poorer regions benefit from the success of richer ones. These nationally ordered factors cannot be achieved effectively on a spontaneous basis from state/provincial level or through cross-state policy borrowing alone.

The question of the appropriate level of government is easy to resolve when, in the matter concerned, one level of government is clearly more effective. However, there is a grey area: Matters where effective decisions can be made at either state/provincial or national level but, for the public good, decisions may still need to be made at national level, despite subsidiarity.

Equity Within Federalism

All federal or quasi-federal nations collect data comparing the economic and social position of the different regions. Such data often includes rates of educational participation. However, interregional equity has more than one meaning and is more important in some countries than others.

Federal and quasi-federal systems vary in the extent to which they engage in policies and programmes designed to equalize the conditions of life between the different states or provinces, for example, by providing additional resources to states or provinces where unit costs per person are relatively high or unit resources are low. Such conditions of life may include access to higher education or expenditure on higher education. For example, in Australian government, an important principle of federal government is 'fiscal equalization'—funding arrangements that compensate poorer states and states where the cost of services is high because of geographical dispersion or low population density (Mathews 1981). Germany also aims to provide equivalent conditions of life according to national standards. The poorer states of Mexico receive compensatory national government funding, although regional disparities remain large. On the other hand, in the United States, where there are marked differences between the states in the union and regions within states in wealth, income and service provision (including access to research universities), national government is not expected to equalize resources or service provision (Bentele 2013). While regional inequalities are part of policy discussion in China and Russia, those inequalities continue, including significant disparities in the provision of degree level and research university education. In China, there are striking differences between primarily urban and primarily rural provinces (Gustafsson and Nivorozhkina 2011; Treiman 2012).

Second, most federal nations also consider a different and more limited notion of equity—equality in the public resources provided on a per capita basis. There is a potential tension between the goal of equal per capita treatment and the goals of equal conditions of life and raising the disadvantaged, both of which require unequal treatment by the central government. Wealthy regions that oppose the redistributive sharing of income and resources with poorer regions tend to prefer the more limited notion of equity. Governments vary in the extent to which their taxing and spending, including federal redistribution, reduce market-generated inequalities. OECD data indicate that the German government significantly modifies market-generated income inequality, while, in the English-speaking countries, there is less redistribution. The United States and Mexico are at the bottom of the OECD group in terms of tax-spend redistributive effects (OECD 2015), and this affects the poorer states where low-income families are concentrated.

Equity goals also have other functions within federal systems. Some national governments have policies designed to advance particular disadvantaged groups, for example, through access to higher education. In India and, more recently, Brazil, national laws dictate that a proportion of public university places must be reserved for the members of disadvantaged groups. In Brazil, this applies only in federal public universities, but the federal government also subsidizes private universities for admitting disadvantaged students. In the United States, the federal government has intervened to prevent discrimination against African–Americans but has been inconsistent in supporting state-initiated affirmative action admissions. In Mexico, indigenous groups seek national resources to compensate for discriminatory treatment within the states. These policy moves to create greater equity again tend to shift power from the states to the centre.

Means of National Control or Influence

An important variation between federal systems is the mode(s) of coordination, control and influence used to manage relations between the national and state/provincial levels.

In all formally federal systems, the constitutional and legal structure plays a role in intergovernmental alignment and coordination and often conditions the potentials for action. Some legal structures specify a division of responsibility between the different levels of government for social programmes such as higher education. In the United States and Canada, the legal structure decisively limits the potentials of the federal government in regulating higher education at systemic and institutional levels. Canada has no national minister for higher education. However, in federal systems, law is not the only game in town. National constitutions are slow to change and can become obsolete over time, and legal reform often follows practical developments rather than leading them. In some cases, such as Russia and Australia, the legal structure has become partly decoupled from the economics and politics of federalism. In both countries, the national government is stronger than its formal constitutional position would suggest, with more authority in higher education and research than might be expected—in Russia, because the centralized tradition of the comprehensive state overcame the post-Soviet federal reform; in Australia, because the taxation power secured by the federal government in World War II (Macintyre 2015) laid the basis for a national takeover of higher education finance and policy. In India, the legal structure again often lags behind federalism in the political and financial spheres.

As this suggests, a second form of coordination and intergovernmental alignment and control lies in the financial relationship between levels of government. Where the national government enjoys the main control over government revenues and/or redistributes public financing between the branches of government, it is in a strong position to dictate policy in higher education. However, there are many possible financial arrangements with varied implications for control. When the national government controls most of the government revenues but formal responsibility for government functions lies primarily at the decentralized level—the 'vertical fiscal imbalance' discussed in the chapter on Australia—over time, there is a tendency to the accumulation of both powers and functions at national level. The same imbalance is found in China, where it is both a cause and an effect of national political control. In the contrasting cases of Canada and Germany, the fiscal capacities of each level of government are more closely aligned to the division of responsibility. Federalism in higher education is more stable with less potential for contestation. In the United States, the states have more financial autonomy than in Australia, but growing state budget incapacity, plus ongoing national concerns about comparative international performance in education may be paving the way for a new federal intervention (see the US chapter).

The third method of intergovernmental alignment and control—'coordination' is probably the wrong term here—is selective policy and/or financial intervention by national government. For example, large-scale national infrastructure programmes, triggering complimentary activities by regional or local governments and the private sector shape patterns of regional economic development and interregional inequalities. For example, a national programme to create 'world-class universities' promotes universities in certain cities and regions. Selective interventions, without a formal commitment to ongoing changes in the federal system, may be essential to deal with specific local problems. They are also potentially disruptive of federal relations. Selective intervention is more likely to be favoured by comprehensive or postcolonial states rather than limited liberal states and favoured by national governments in unitary systems rather than in federal or confederal systems. However, all governments are capable of policies of this kind.

THE CHANGING FEDERAL LANDSCAPE IN HIGHER EDUCATION

As noted, three broad tendencies currently affect higher education systems across the world: the continuing growth of social participation in higher education (massification), globalization and marketization (Carnoy et al. 2013). These tendencies are contextually contingent rather than uniform: They are articulated by national factors, are manifested differently from country to country and felt more strongly in some countries than others. In federalized nations, the tendencies to massification, globalization and marketization are affected by multilayered federal systems, and these tendencies can also affect the evolution of federalism in higher education. In the country chapters, it can be difficult to disentangle changes associated with federalism from changes driven by growth, global engagement and the politics of neoliberal reform.

Massification

Of the three tendencies, massification is the most universal (Baker 2011; Trow 1973). With more than one-third of all young people now entering some kind of 'tertiary education', meaning a full-time post-school programme of two years or more, 'higher education' in the North American sense, and age-group participation increasing at 1 per cent a year, in another generation half of all young people will enter tertiary education. 'High participation' systems with more than 50 per cent of the age cohort (Cantwell, Marginson and Smolentseva, forthcoming; Marginson 2016b) have spread from high-income to middle-income countries. In almost every country, except the poorest, the rate of participation is advancing, in some with extraordinary rapidity. Enrolment growth is especially marked in emerging China, India and Indonesia, all large countries with federal or quasi-federal governmental structures (World Bank 2016).

On the whole, massification is associated with more stratified systems with a larger 'stretch' in resources and social esteem between elite universities and other institutions. High participation systems are more socially inclusive but more socially unequal, in that competition for entry to elite universities is more intense and crowded out by middle-class families. Despite the greater vertical diversity between institutions, there is no tendency to greater horizontal diversity of mission or type. Instead, the large comprehensive and often growing multipurpose research 'multiversity' (Kerr 1963/2001) is increasingly dominant in institutional form. Single purpose and non-university institutions have lost ground. Larger massified higher education systems need more sophisticated multilevel coordination, including their federal governance. Massifying institutions not only take in more of society in terms of students, they engage with a more extensive group of stakeholders (Cantwell et al., forthcoming, Chapters 3–6).

Massification creates complexities and tensions in the relations between states/provinces and national authorities. In all the systems in this book, it has forced state and provincial governments beyond their capacity—no nation can finance high participation higher education entirely at state or provincial level—thereby promoting a growing role for the nation in financing, bringing with it greater national power in policy and regulation. The extent of this process varies by country. In most federal countries, massification is also been associated with a tendency to marketization. As demand for higher education has expanded worldwide and governments have counted the financial costs of the social pressure for expansion, in some countries (e.g., Australia and the United States), they have increased tuition fees, and, in others (e.g., Brazil, India and, to some extent, Mexico), they have relied on the expansion of privately provided higher education financed largely by tuition. Fee-based places, regulated by national government, have also played an adjunct role in the growth of participation in Russia and China in both public and private sectors.

Massification is accompanied by increased political pressure for greater equity in higher education, as disadvantaged groups complete secondary schooling but find access to higher education—especially more prestigious institutions—blocked by academic and financial barriers. As noted, political demands for greater equity, expressed as national movements, can trigger increased central government legislation, financing and power. Massification also generates issues about quality and its management. Although in most federal countries the formal decision to expand higher education is made at state or provincial level, the growing role of national government raises questions about the degree national authorities should hold locally based and controlled institutions accountable. Who should define the terms of accountability?

Who should be the regulator and what should they regulate? In systems where the private sector is playing a key role in growth, which level of government should monitor and guarantee its standards?

Globalization

There is a large literature on the implications of globalization, the tendency to worldwide global convergence and integration, in higher education and research (e.g., King, Marginson and Naidoo 2011, 2013). Globalization advances, constrains and also relativizes the nation-state (Carnoy and Rhoten 2002, 3–4). It triggers both direct global effects and, more indirectly, the autonomous responses of nations and institutions.

The most important direct impacts of globalization are in relation to knowledge. Research has become a worldwide system. The world knowledge bank published in global journals or otherwise accessed through the Internet is now the principal source of industry innovations. All nations want to build their capacity to access and use global science. Also, global comparisons and rankings of research universities are watched everywhere by national policymakers (Hazelkorn 2015). Most nations want to grow their ranked 'world-class universities' as a signifier of innovation power and national prestige. This is a priority in China and Russia, talked about (in more desultory fashion) in India and Australia and the focus of the Excellence Initiative in Germany. The last programme has so strengthened the role of the federal (national) government that constitutional provisions were changed in 2014 to facilitate central involvement.

The indirect effects of globalization include convergences of system and institutional design, cross-border policy borrowing and policies designed to lift national competitiveness in higher education and science, policies often again referenced to global ranking. These policies include the enhanced international mobility of students and faculty, cross-border campuses, partnership-based international centres and programmes, international benchmarking with foreign partners to lift standards at home and, in some countries, higher education as a commercial export industry. Australia, Canada and China place a high priority on internationalization, and the United States (especially) and Germany have broad international networks and influence higher education in other parts of the world. Brazil and, to a lesser extent, India are becoming more globally active.

All else being equal, international programmes and relations affect federal governance in two ways. First, some institutions engage cross-border agents directly, bypassing both national and state/provincial government, perhaps generating new resources while strengthening institutional independence. Second, international activity often boosts national government in relation to the states or provinces. Internationalization policies are more effectively pursued from the central pivot. The cross-border mobility of people, services and money entails national immigration and trade regulation. Offshore university activity often entails collaboration with national diplomatic missions. In Canada, the provinces support a single national office responsible for international student recruitment into Canadian institutions. In Australia, the national trade department promotes student recruitment, and international education is supervised by national legislation. When in 2008–2010 there were problems at state level in managing international student safety, and in urban student housing, the states were signed up to a combined intergovernmental international student strategy that was orchestrated by national government agencies.

Marketization

Marketization refers to the policy implementation of business models and quasi market systems, especially enhanced competition and mixed public/private educational financing. It has been a central strategy of government in the limited liberal states since the second half of the 1980s and, to some degree, has spread to most higher education systems. Market models were especially influential in the reforms to higher education in 1990s in post-Soviet countries, and they have affected policy and practice in China and the post-colonial states in this book. The market model has little sway in Germany. All *Länder* have free tuition. Competition between universities plays a moderate role, largely in research. However, all countries favour business-like reforms to augment efficiency and public accountability, and output targets, transparency and performance management have growing roles. Marketization can be implemented at either levels—the national and the state/provincial. Unlike massification and globalization, it does not contain a prima facie tendency to grow the role of national government, but market reform is often shaped by economic units attached to national finance or education ministries. Germany is unusual in that student tuition is entirely a *Länder*-level matter. Even in the decentralized United States, the national (federal) government governs tuition financing and student support via loans and grants.

Taken together, massification, globalization and marketization make higher education more central to national self-interest and strengthen the role of national government within federated systems. Higher education has become installed in the strategies of economic ministries. With the knowledge made by university researchers seen as essential to national defence, economic growth, health care and ecology, an arms race in innovation has developed, with the scorecard set by national R&D spending as a proportion of GDP, the annual output of science papers and university rankings. The increasing funding needed to finance such research can only come from national governments. The level of participation in education is another zone of international competition (Carnoy and Rhoten 2002, 5), and most governments set national targets. Further, as noted, equity in participation can only be effectively addressed on a system wide basis. However, this tendency towards national government and the rate of change varies from country to country and institution to institution. The tendency is strong in Australia, China and Brazil, partially apparent in Canada, Russia, India and Mexico, and least apparent in Germany and the United States. However, in most of the federal countries in this book, the expanding role of national government has not eliminated the state/provincial factor, merely shifted the balance. The federal landscape for higher education institutions remains complex and has the potential to throw up a broad range of issues in future. The increased weight of national government does not eliminate issues arising from shared national and state/provincial government and funding.

These issues can be fundamental, falling along the fault line of differences about the purpose and role of higher education. National governments often emphasize macroeconomic policy and global competitiveness. Elite universities are concerned about global city elite formation, national culture and global science. State and provincial administration often focus on social access and local economic needs. One example is the tension between regional development and 'world-class university' policy in Russia. How can federalist countries bind their decentralized universities to the national project? How do state and provincial governments pursue coherent policy agendas when they are continually overdetermined at national level? Does the university mediate national/regional tensions, or is that a matter for government? Which government?

Sometimes the differences between national values and regional/local values are too sharp to finesse. For example, in 1962, the US national government sent US marshals to escort a black student, James Meredith, into the University of Mississippi under a federal court order to racially integrate the university. The University and State of Mississippi opposed the federal order. Which level of government should prevail in such circumstances? More generally, what arrangements between national and regional governments are optimal in shaping the growth and character of higher education? Do federal systems generate differing outcomes from those in centrally financed and run systems? Does more centralized funding bind university systems more closely with not just national policies but national values? As the removal of segregation after James Meredith shows, public universities across the United States have been drawn closer towards national values in policy domains, such as race relations, minority access and gender rights, but the process has been protracted and uneven across the country and is still contested.

DEVELOPMENTS IN EACH COUNTRY

Developments in each country are now compared (for more details, see the country chapters). Federal relations in higher education are summarized in Table 1.2.

In the Limited Liberal States

In the limited liberal states, as elsewhere, central government has expanded its role within the federal system, using its greater taxation and fiscal power. However, the cases vary.

In Australia, after World War II, the growth and modernization of higher education became associated with national government takeover of the erstwhile role of the states in funding, policy and system development, although the constitutional basis for national control was (and remains) weak. Federal fiscal imbalance played a key role; the states/provinces simply could not finance expansion and modernization, including infrastructure, enrolment growth and research. Private sector-based expansion was not considered; in fact, the small private higher education sector is now subsidized, accredited and regulated at national level. Once a unified national system was established by 1990, national government implemented a neoliberal quasi market with competition between institutions for public and private resources and research prestige, tuition charges and entrepreneurial international education. It may seem surprising that federal Australia's higher education became as decisively organized as a unitary national sector rather than evolving as a federal system parallel to higher education in the other limited liberal states.

Canadian higher education remains resolutely provincial in funding and accountability, with the national role growing but largely confined to research funding and international students. For Canadian research universities, the existence of dual political masters and funding sources may provide strategic advantages, for example, in giving university leaders greater flexibility in raising and allocating resources. There is less governmental focus on inter-institutional competition and entrepreneurship in Australia and much less in US higher education.

The 1950s–1960s in the United States witnessed a major expansion in federal funding of university research and development, and the large public and private universities awarding PhD degrees shifted from a primarily teaching function to a primarily research function. With tuition increasing rapidly, the federal government became the lender or donor of last resort for student loans and scholarships. These two financial roles gave the central authorities increasing power to regulate public and private institutions. It is ironic, and a sign of the potency of the states within federation, that the national (federal) government still has a limited direct say in university policies. Public universities still answer to regional state mandates, although state financing has steadily declined as a proportion of total funding, in some universities, to below 10 per cent. State university systems are supervised by state-appointed boards of trustees and answer to state governors and legislatures. State laws traditionally govern admissions policies and set tuition, although, as noted, the federal judiciary intervened in the 1960s to force desegregation of public and private universities in the South. Further, accreditation of higher education institutions is in the hands of private non-profit organizations answering to the Council for Higher Education Accreditation (CHEA), which is independent of both levels of government. Expanded national funding does not necessarily generate expanded national power in linear fashion.

One outcome of the highly decentralized federal systems in the United States and Canada is that there is much variation among states/ provinces in the percentage of students at two and four year institutions, in the respective roles of public and private institutions, and, in the United States, in the public–private funding of public institutions (Mettler 2014). In comparison, the Australian system is both more equally resourced across the country and more homogeneous in institutional mission, with the comprehensive research university dominant across the country. However, in all limited liberal states, heightened competition is increasing the vertical differentials between institutions, and there is a danger of decline in the quality and status of mass institutions. In the United States, this danger is differentiated, articulated through inequalities in state budgetary capacity.

Germany

The chapter on Germany indicates that federalism in higher education is relatively stable with good congruence between the two levels of government. In contrast with Australia, and the comprehensive and post-colonial states, in Germany, relations between national and state level government take the form of a negotiated partnership of equals rather than a hierarchy enforced by law or economic power. Despite a drift towards greater central government power, the *Länder* retains considerable control over institutions and the delivery of social services. Nevertheless, as in all the countries in this book, the growing influence of national government in Germany in higher education reform and regulation has been joined to increased financial support from the central government for research and need-based student aid, partly because of policy emphasis on increased social participation in universities and the Excellence Initiative in research.

The situation in Germany is more complex in that Germany is part of the EU and participates in the Bologna Process of homogenizing higher education structures and requirements across all countries and programmes. German *Länder* has implemented the process in their jurisdictions, although the rules were set outside the *Länder*. Meta-national formations such as the EU have the potential to interact directly with in-country regions within a federal system, changing in-country balances and enhancing regional autonomy. Of the other countries in this study, externally fostered effects in internal regions have also affected India, Brazil and Mexico—mostly international development aid or the economic intervention of international companies.

In the Comprehensive States

Russia and China share similar ambitions in higher education but are at different points in system development. China is more advanced in research and in governmental capacity, while Russia is nominally wealthier and has more extensive participation and infrastructure. Despite the gesture to decentralization in the 1990s, Russian federalism has reverted to strong central control, and whereas China's provinces have much responsibility and some autonomy in public policy, decisive power in higher education is concentrated in the central (national) government. Both countries, especially China, have moved away from the Soviet system model of a small number of multidisciplinary universities combined with specialized higher education institutions under different branches of government, linked to industry policy. Russia has also partly set aside the Soviet-era regional division of labour in industry and education, leaving some regions and institutions in an uncertain position. Each country faces the challenge of creating more effective devolution and better regional provision, while elevating national scientific capacity.

In China, the fault line between national and provincial levels of government plays a key role in structuring the national system of higher education. National government provides selective support for research universities and research institutes while delegating responsibility for most higher education provision to the provincial authorities with lesser financial capacity. In contrast, Russia retains more direct control over the regions. Though both national governments have policy levers that can supplement regional efforts, each is focusing its main effort on institutions at the top of the system with designated national significance. Both governments want a layer of globally ranked research universities comparable to those of the Anglosphere. For almost two decades, China has invested systematically on a large and growing scale in science and university infrastructure and is well ahead of Russia where global science has stagnated (Marginson 2015).

China is also building participation in higher education and will exceed its objective of 40 per cent enrolment in four- and three-year institutions by 2020. Russia has long had one of the highest levels of higher education participation in the world, but it is concerned about the quality of many institutions, which is uneven by region. China has proceeded much further than Russia in reforms at the regional level, including the reorganization and consolidation of the institutional structure. The chapter on Russia asks why. Perhaps, despite greater centralization since 2000 and national control of public finances, some regions have a residual capacity to retard the centrally driven reorganization of higher education, and where regional autonomy is a positive force, when local administration fosters effective relations between government, institutions and stakeholders, this can happen despite rather than because of national government. In China, regional provision, participation and research capacity are highly uneven across the country but the situation is more coherent and transparent than it is in Russia. If national government in China sets out to modify regional educational imbalances systematically, it is likely to make progress. But this would depend on the implementation of a new policy on regional development as a whole.

Every country distributes resources unequally between elite and non-elite public institutions. In Russia and China, these inequalities threaten to become entrenched as part of a drive for national legitimacy through WCUs and further institutionalized by the national/provincial divide and the ongoing superiority of national government in power and money. The elite institutions are dominated by students from socially advantaged backgrounds who do best in academic tests for entry, so that the enhanced stratification of higher education enhances social stratification. In these two large countries, stratification also takes a spatial form based on mobility. Regional institutions educate students in lower status institutions for primarily local employment. The only antidote to this growing inequality is policies that will lift the quality of second- and third-tier institutions in a sustained manner. If present policies in China and Russia continue, this is unlikely with the possible exception of wealthy regions where local resources are concentrated.

In both China and Russia, governments justify their WCU emphasis by the externalities that flow from research and well-trained graduates. However, when all student participation takes place in institutions fostering knowledge and skill at advanced levels, the externalities are more broadly distributed, as in Germany, Canada and the United States (where provision is highly stratified, but non–elite four-year state universities offer low-cost higher education of adequate quality at mass level). In China and Russia, this would mean reworking the division of labour between levels of government so as to supplement regional funding in the provinces with national funding.

In the Post-colonial States

In Brazil, India and Mexico, the expansion of higher education is accomplished by a complex combination of national, regional/state and private resources and institutions. In these three countries, the national government has direct financial and political control of autonomous federal (central) universities, many of which are elite institutions. State/ provincial governments finance and exert bureaucratic control over regional-level public universities, some of which are also elite, with varying financial help from the central government. A small number of students attend costly elite private universities. A much larger percentage of students are in private universities and colleges of questionable quality, largely designed to generate private rents for their owners. Both private financing and private sector enrolments have grown rapidly. The private sector now enrols the majority of students in India and Brazil and one-third in Mexico.

In each country, national- and regional-level governments search for the right formula that will enable them to achieve an array of financial and political goals through system expansion and control. For example, on one hand government allows low-quality private higher education to absorb an increasing fraction of students so that the public sector does not have to spend as much on higher education provision (goals is to expand but save public money). On the other hand, government wants to enhance social equity between low- and high-income students (goals is to make participation meaningful, equalize society). In the outcome, low-quality expansion on the cheap has largely taken priority over equity, although policy rhetoric has an egalitarian flavour.

Unlike other nations in this book, none of the post-colonial states provide mass public higher education at scale, except in isolated pockets. In all three, the expansion of participation will continue, but the present developmental model seems decisively limited. As in all nations that rely on private institutions to absorb rapidly increasing demand, as private higher education has expanded, it has become clear that higher education does not function as a textbook economic market. Deregulated market competition in itself is unable to establish a dynamic of continuous improvements in teaching and learning, and government funding and close regulation of private sectors are crucial, as shown by the successful cases of Japan and South Korea. All else being equal, the expansion of for-profit private higher education at scale must decrease the quality of higher education, as shown by the case of the United States (Mettler 2014). The main goal of for-profit private higher education is to extract surplus from student families, not to deliver high quality learning. In addition, private higher education may be less effective than public institutions in developing the skills for participation in democratic societies. India, Brazil and Mexico are plagued by market-based diploma mills and low-capacity private colleges. The divide between higher quality public universities dominated by the social elite and lower-tier private institutions appears to be increasing. Reworking the political contract between national and regional levels of government is one medium for the implementation of reform agendas.

The focus on the private sector appears to have greatly decentralized these higher education systems. In India and Mexico, private institutions are largely regulated at the state/provincial level. These institutions have their own boards of directors, often family-based, independent of public bureaucracies. Given their lack of fiscal capacity, the states/ provinces tend to encourage privatization. Thus, devolution of control over the private sector facilitates a continuing dynamic of private sector decentralization within governmental decentralization, pulling the system further from national supervision. The situation is different in Brazil, where the federal government regulates the private institutions. By increasing the fraction of enrolment in private higher education, it augments its power relative to the states/provinces, even while the growth of the private sector decentralizes control of higher education from the central institutions of public sector as a whole. In all three countries, the national government has taken the lead in accreditation and evaluation. These processes are ostensibly designed to monitor, control and improve educational quality in the decentralized private sector. As the chapter on Brazil explains, the Brazilian government has established a national higher education evaluation system primarily aimed at measuring the quality of private providers, although public universities must participate. This form of supervision is a centralizing device, but it has yet to demonstrate that it can sustain improvement in mass higher education. The outcome is that all three post-colonial states have an arm of government—state/provincial governments in India and Mexico, national government in Brazil—with a vested interest in private sector expansion, while neither market competition nor government supervision has installed a reliable process of quality improvement. However, Brazil's framework does create the potential to regulate the private sector more closely.

CONCLUSIONS

Federation was originally a device for achieving a limited unity between formerly separated territories, as in Germany and post-colonial India, or alternately, for managing a space too large to be administered by direct rule, as in Russia and China. In large settler nations with forward moving frontiers, such as the United States, Canada, Australia, Brazil and Mexico, both were involved. The United States was originally composed of post-colonial states that jealously guarded their original identities. The nation was extended by national government grants of statehood in new territories but in doing so, it replicated the old autarkic state form. However, while federal structures always bear the marks of their origins, they also adapt and evolve.

The Nation as Modernizer

The evolution of transport, communications, information systems, finance and organizational design and standardized government administration have much augmented the capacity of national governments to supervise large territories. State/provincial bureaucratic networks, local warlords and closed units have not disappeared but are now more vulnerable to new brooms. Since World War II, in most countries, national regimes have been the modernizing and reforming agent vis-à-vis states/provinces. The move to national power, in higher education and other sectors, tends to be associated with larger infrastructure, improved people capacity (more skills, higher levels of training) and more advanced academic programmes (e.g., graduate education and doctoral research), although not necessarily greater diversity of programme. Reformist national governments attempt to achieve these objectives through direct investment, changing regional leadership and reform programmes designed to secure the more effective use of resources. Not all national governments are positioned effectively to do this; and lack of coordination between the national and state/provincial levels is a key issue in Mexico, India and Brazil, and often also in Russia. There are also instances (e.g., Mexico) where state bureaucracy duplicates and overlaps with national administration, diminishing the autonomy of higher education institutions.

In the country examples in this book, the development of higher education has been achieved on one of two pathways. On the first pathway, public higher education, most often managed by states/provinces but with some federal institutions and considerable federal funding, has been the main vehicle for bringing in millions of new students and upgrading institutions. On the second pathway, private education has been the main means of expanding mass access. On both pathways, higher education systems have become more stratified, partly through nationally driven WCU agendas, with the quantitative expansion in lower-tier institutions. In India, Brazil, Mexico, China, Russia, the United States and Australia, lower-tier institutions do not receive adequate support. Their quality is lowest in those countries that ask private institutions to carry expansion. Generally, private sectors are less accessible to national regulation and improvement, especially when they are predominantly managed at the regional state/provincial level.

Everywhere there is the danger that undue national emphasis on WCUs will undermine state or provincial mass higher education, in either sector. Nevertheless, and while the private sector can grow rapidly, the public sector is associated with better institutions. If the public sector is the principal mass education provider, it can be upgraded in future. This means that of the emerging federal giants, China is better placed than India and Brazil. Relying on private higher education to improve the quality of higher education system through market mechanisms is not working.

The State/Province as Democratizer

Nations are normally the key to large strong higher education systems. The United States might appear as the great exception because of state control over public higher education and the importance of the private Ivy League universities and elite liberal arts colleges. But it is impossible to imagine contemporary US higher education without the federal research grants that created the 'multiversity' (Kerr 1963/2001) and the federal subsidy of participation via student loans. There is a similar story in Canada. In Germany, the real exception, the *Länder* cooperates closely to achieve collective national leadership and a commonality of standards across the country.

China is a classic case of a country that has used national government to create systematically a high participation system that includes leading research universities. It is doing so at remarkable speed, although with some gaps. India, Brazil and Mexico have yet to pass through the national construction phase and are unlikely to do so if the national/ regional settings are not changed. Russia needs to remake the role of the national government in order to modernize and reform its higher education system, but its political culture suggests that this is possible.

Australia is a classic case of a transition from regional power to national power that was integral to modernization and reform. It built a nationally led and funded elite/mass system of higher education and research between the late 1950s and the mid-1970s, and a globalized high participation system in the late-1980s and after. The role of the states was almost eliminated, despite their constitutional primacy in education. This system is remarkable for its degrees of centralization and uniformity and the level of control exercised by financial instruments. Given the modest level of public funding, the country is a high achiever in research, with 19 universities in the ARWU (2015) top 500, and a potent attractor of international students. Yet the reformed Australian system has reached a policy impasse. Where does government go from here? Average institutional size is large; there is little more to be gained from mergers or economies of scale. The system is highly competitive, new public managed at every level, with little scope to squeeze out more performance from modest resources. Market reforms to introduce a subsidized private sector have had no discernible effect on quality in the mainstream research universities, which are unaffected by marginal providers. Australia's impasse indicates a larger dilemma for advocates of an increasingly national role in federated countries. Arguably, 'nationalization' is not a timeless principle but a temporary expedient to improve systems and outcomes. Once the gains to be made from supplementing or subordinating the states/provinces have been obtained, the question of what to do with the decentralized structures returns. For states and provinces, and local government, have virtues of subsidiarity that larger formations cannot replicate.

This suggests that after nation-driven modernization, the next step is to bring the modernized states/provinces back into the picture so policies and decisions can be framed closer to the point of implementation. This would enable higher institutions to better fulfil policy agendas related to community and stakeholder engagement and expand their contributions to local regions, cities and industry. These agendas are much discussed but often with little effect.

Of the nine national higher education systems that are discussed in this book, the one that is closest to a healthy, stable balance between national and state/provincial government—a balance not fraught by federal fiscal overhang or free-wheeling national interventions—is Germany, followed by Canada. Both have a healthy broad-based capacity, high participation (especially in Canada), very strong research university sectors, good second sectors (especially in Germany) and mass higher education of adequate quality. In these two systems, federalism in higher education is not a weakness but a clear-cut strength. In the case of the United States, where there is a strong public university tradition with stakeholder presence and democratic local engagement, the decentralizing side of federalism would be more positive if state budgets were boosted. In China, the quasi-federal system would work better if there was equalization between the regions, greater scope for regional initiative, and a better alignment between on one hand the centre–province division of responsibility and on the other, the centre–province division of political and financial power. Arguably, in the other five countries, federalism in higher education seems to be more negative than positive. Australia, Russia, Brazil, India and Mexico have yet to find effective ways to turn multilevel educational government into an asset.

REFERENCES

Academic Ranking of World Universities, ARWU. 2015. *2015 Academic Ranking of World Universities*. Shanghai Jiao Tong University. Available at http://www.shanghairanking.com

Baker, D. 2011. 'Forward and Backward, Horizontal and Vertical: Transformation of Occupational Credentialing in the Schooled Society'. *Research in Social Stratification and Mobility* 29 (1): 5–29.

Bentele, K. 2013. 'Distinct Paths to Higher Inequality? A Qualitative Comparative Analysis of Rising Earnings Inequality Among US States, 1980–2010'. *Research in Social Stratification and Mobility* 34: 30–57.

Blockmans, W., and de Weerdt, H. 2016. 'The Diverging Legacies of Classical Empires in China and Europe'. *European Review* 24 (2): 306–324.

Cantwell, B., Marginson, S., and Smolentseva, A. forthcoming. *High Participation Systems of Higher Education*. Oxford: Oxford University Press.

Carnoy, M., Loyalka, P., Dobryakova, M., Dossani, R., Froumin, I., Kuhns, K., Tilak, J. B. G., and Rong W. 2013. *University Expansion in a Changing Global Economy: Triumph of the BRICs?* Stanford: Stanford University Press.

Carnoy, M., and Rhoten, D. 2002. 'What Does Globalization Mean for Educational Change? A Comparative Approach'. *Comparative Education Review* 46 (1): 1–9.

European Union, EU. 2016. 'The Principle of Subsidiarity'. In *Access to European Law*. Available at http://eur-lex.europa.eu/legal-content/EN/TXT/?uri=URISERV%3Aai0017

Gernet, J. 2002. *A History of Chinese Civilization*, 3rd edition. Cambridge: Cambridge University Press.

Gustafsson, B., Shi, L., and Nivorozhkina, L. 2011. 'Why are Household Incomes More Unequally Distributed in China than in Russia?' *Cambridge Journal of Economics* 35 (5): 897–920.

Hazelkorn, E. 2015. *Rankings and the Reshaping of Higher Education: The Battle for World-class Excellence*, 2nd Edition. Houndmills: Palgrave Macmillan.

Hollander, R., and Patapan, H. 2007. 'Pragmatic Federalism: Australian Federalism from Hawke to Howard'. *Australian Journal of Public Administration* 66 (3): 280–297.

Hosking, G. 2012. *Russia and the Russians: From Earliest Times to the Present.* London: Penguin.

Izyumov, A. 2010. 'Human Costs of Post-communist Transition: Public Policies and Private Response'. *Review of Social Economy* 68 (1): 93–125.

Kerr, C. 1963/2001. *The Uses of the University*, 1st edition. Cambridge, MA: Harvard University Press.

King, R., Marginson, S., and Naidoo, R., eds. 2011. *Handbook of Higher Education and Globalization.* Cheltenham: Edward Elgar.

———. 2013. *The Globalization of Higher Education.* Cheltenham: Edward Elgar.

Locke, J. 1689/1967. *Two Treatises of Government*, edited by P. Laslett. Cambridge: Cambridge University Press.

Macintyre, S. 2015. *Australia's Boldest Experiment: War and Reconstruction in the 1940s.* Sydney: NewSouth Publishing.

Marginson, S. 2015. 'The Role of the State in University Science: Russia and China Compared'. *International Organisations Research Journal* 10 (1). Originally published in Russia. Available at http://papers.ssrn.com/sol3/papers.cfm?abstract_id=2700278

———. 2016a. 'High Participation Systems of Higher Education'. *The Journal of Higher Education* 87 (2): 243–270.

———. 2016b. 'The Worldwide Trend to High Participation Higher Education: Dynamics of Social Stratification in Inclusive Systems'. *Higher Education* 72 (4): 413–435.

———. 2016c. *The Dream is Over: The Crisis of Clark Kerr's Californian Idea of Higher Education.* Berkeley, CA: University of California Press.

Mathews, R. 1981. 'The Development of Australian Fiscal Federalism'. In *Advisory Commission on Intergovernmental Relations (ACIR), Studies in Comparative Federalism: Australia*, 1–26. Washington, DC: ACIR.

Mettler, S. 2014. *Degrees of Inequality: How the Politics of Higher Education Sabotaged the American Dream.* New York, NY: Basic Books.

Organisation for Economic Cooperation and Development, OECD. 2015. *Data on Income Distribution and Poverty.* Available at http://stats.oecd.org/Index.aspx?DataSetCode=IDD

Smith, A. 1776/1979. *The Wealth of Nations.* Harmondsworth: Penguin.

Stiglitz, J. 2013. *The Price of Inequality.* London: Penguin.

Treiman, D. 2012. 'The "Difference Between Heaven and Earth": Urban–Rural Disparities in Well-being in China'. *Research in Social Stratification and Mobility* 30 (1): 33–47.

Trow, M. 1973. *Problems in the Transition from Elite to Mass Higher Education.* Berkeley, CA: Carnegie Commission on Higher Education.

Watts, R. 1992. 'The Federal Context for Higher Education'. In *Higher Education in Federal Systems: Proceedings of an International Colloquium Held at Queen's University, May 1991*, edited by D. Brown, P. Cazalis, and G. Jasmin, 3–26. Ottawa: Renouf Publishing.

World Bank. 2016. Data and Statistics. Available at http://data.worldbank.org/indicator/all

Chapter 2

The United States of America
Changes and Challenges in a Highly Decentralized System

Anthony Lising Antonio, Martin Carnoy
and C. Rose Nelson

INTRODUCTION

The United States' federal system of government is one in which the federal Constitution gives member states enormous legislative powers. States have the right to raise their own revenue by taxing individuals and businesses, both directly (property taxes, income taxes) and indirectly (sales taxes) and to spend this revenue largely as the voters of the states determine. States are prohibited from taxing commerce between states or to levy duties on exports and imports. These are taxation powers left to the federal government. Indeed, such excise taxes were the main source of revenue for the federal government until 1913, when, with the passage of the 16th amendment to the Constitution, the federal government was given the power to tax income of individuals and businesses.[1]

---

[1] Federal revenue from taxes is spent in the states, but not equally. Poorer, more rural states receive, on average, more money back in government spending than their residents pay federal taxes; richer, Northeastern states, some more urbanized Midwestern states, and California and Texas, get less back than their residents pay.

In addition, legislation in the United States, as in some federal countries such as Germany and Canada, but not like in most other countries of the world, assigns responsibility for providing all levels of education to the states rather than the federal government. As Martin Trow (1991, 69) writes, '… this reflects the deep suspicion of central government reflected in the separation of powers in the [US] Constitution'.

We show in this chapter that it is in this context of asymmetric power to legislate, tax, and spend on education by the states that the US university system developed in the nineteenth and early twentieth century. The federal government assisted this process, but had limited influence on its size and shape. Nevertheless, we also suggest that by the middle of the twentieth century, this relation changed. With the enormous growth of federal revenues and spending during and after World War II, the role of the federal government increased in two important ways.

The first was through federal funding of research and development in a relatively small group of universities. Federal spending on R&D has been mainly on basic science and technology, stimulated by the growth of military spending during the Cold War and its aftermath but also through major support of R&D in medicine and medically related research. Although states also supported university R&D, federal funding has been 15–20 times larger.

The second was as a major source of student financial aid through grants and loans. Through the GI Bill after World War II and through the federal grant and loan programme after 1972, the federal government promoted access to higher education for low- and middle-income students. However, through the student loan programme, the federal government is now in a much more complex relationship with state governments and with the private higher education sector, especially with for-profit private universities. Student loans were never intended to become a means to shifting the cost of higher education from the public sector to students and their families. Yet, we suggest, in this chapter, that as states have reduced their support for public higher education and relied increasingly on tuition to fund universities and colleges, federal student loans are, in effect, becoming crucial to the financing of the

---

Most federal revenues are spent in the states on defence, social security payments and Medicare and Medicaid.

public system. The loan programme is also paying a similar key role in the expansion of private higher education, including, most recently, of for-profit universities. Unlike the proactive influence on universities of federal funding for R&D, the enormous growth of the federal student loan programme has been largely reactive, especially in recent years, and has cast the federal government into the unusual and politically uncomfortable role of being the banker of the higher education system.

We argue that these federal R&D funding and student financial aid roles have been influential, and that other federal interventions through the judicial system, such as racial integration of higher education and affirmative action, have also had major effects on otherwise relatively autonomous public and private institutions.[2] That said, the functioning of most US higher education institutions, at least until now, has depended almost entirely on conditions and regulations in states rather than on the federal government. And, even then, the development of higher education in the United States has been '... untidy, uncoordinated from the center, without national (or even state) standards for the admission of students, the appointment of academic staff, or the awarding of degrees' (Trow 1991, 70). The bottom line is that with all its financial influence over the way that particularly research universities developed in the second half of the twentieth century, the direct (legal) power of the federal government over the larger US higher education system is highly limited. At best, it can use its considerable financial clout, either through its R&D spending or, in the broader higher education system, through accountability concerning student loans to shape universities' and states' behaviour.

We therefore focus heavily in this chapter on variations among states in how university education is financed and in how financing and the operations of higher education are changing over time. We show that these changes have been great in the past 30 years. We also suggest that mainly because of rapidly increasing costs of university education and reliance on increased tuition to pay those costs, there is a growing possibility for the federal government to be called upon to regulate the 'quality' of higher education and to regulate university costs.

---

[2] All other federal supports for universities have been minor, constituting less than 3 per cent of funding even for public universities.

THE US UNIVERSITY SYSTEM BEFORE WORLD WAR II

Higher education in the United States began in colonial times as a 'copy' of England's Oxbridge College model (Thelin and Gasman 2010), but evolved after independence into a unique system that was almost entirely under the control of the states and, until the late nineteenth century, largely private. Like higher education in other countries, US colleges long served primarily to form elites, but sooner than elsewhere, also incorporated non-elites, mainly because the competition to attract students to the many small colleges springing up in the nineteenth century meant accepting almost anyone who could afford to pay. Most colleges, including public, state-funded institutions, had difficulties raising money. This competition also resulted in various religious dominations starting their own institutions, and, after the Civil War, the appearance of a number of colleges exclusively for women or blacks—even, by the end of the nineteenth century, publicly funded state colleges for blacks.

Undergraduate education remained the mainstay of US colleges and universities until after World War II, and institutions—including state universities—tended to be small, rarely exceeding 5,000 students. Nevertheless, in the 1870s, Johns Hopkins, a wealthy businessman, founded the first US research university, modelled on Germany's Humboldt University, where research, graduate education and undergraduate education all took place in one institution. Another private university founded in this period, the University of Chicago, followed this same model, but Clark University (1887) in Massachusetts became the first all graduate research university in the United States.

The federal role in higher education before World War II was very limited but important. As we noted earlier, the limited role is reflected by the absence of any provision for education on behalf of the government in the Constitution. Indeed, a federal department of education was not created until 1953. A number of state universities had been founded beginning at the end of the eighteenth century and mainly in the South, where private educational institutions were less developed—the University of North Carolina was the first to hold classes, in 1795—and in the new western territories, Ohio University was established in 1804. Nevertheless, pushed by a movement to promote higher-level training in agriculture and engineering (mechanic arts), the US Congress passed the Morrill Land-Grant College Act of 1862, which granted states areas of federal land that they could sell to raise money to finance higher education institutions that would focus on teaching these practical skills. The first state legislatures to accept the conditions of the Morrill Act were Iowa and Kansas in 1862 and 1863. Subsequently most states took advantage of the Act to finance existing or new colleges. Michigan State and Pennsylvania State, for example, had been founded in the 1850s as state land-grant colleges and subsequently were designated as federal land-grant colleges in 1863. The Morrill Act also benefitted a few existing private institutions, such as Rutgers (which later became a state university), Cornell and the Massachusetts Institute of Technology, both of which had earlier received grants of state land.

The second Morrill Act of 1890 extended federal grants to the former Confederate States, this time in the form of cash rather than land, although the institutions were still given legal standing as land-grant colleges or universities. To qualify, the states had to show that race was not an issue in admissions or to designate a separate land-grant institution that would serve students of colour. As a result, a number of today's historically black colleges and universities received funding under the Act. Southern states did not voluntarily create land-grant institutions for black; rather, the federal government refused to make funding available to states that did not provide higher education to blacks (Thelin and Gasman 2010).

In addition, starting in 1887 with the Hatch Act, Congress funded agricultural experiment stations and agricultural research under the direction of the land-grant universities, and with the Smith-Lever Act of 1914, began federal funding of agriculture extension services to disseminate the innovations of the land-grant universities by sending university extension agents to almost every county in every state. The funding formulas for these and additional land-grant bills required states to provide matching funds to incentivize larger and regular state appropriations for public higher education. In some states, the money available for research and extension exceeded the income from the original land grants.

Even so, it was not until the turn of the century that states—especially in the Mid-west and West—began to embrace and financially support through taxation the idea of a great university as a symbol of state pride. Applied research, a utilitarian and comprehensive curriculum, not to mention the public appeal of spectator sports and the availability of federal funds for such fields as agriculture and engineering, led to the growth and maturation of the state university. (Thelin and Gasman 2010, 11)

University enrolment grew relatively rapidly after World War I in both private and state institutions, but beyond the funds from the Morrill Act and for agricultural research, the expansion was driven mainly by increased state funding and by increased demand, continuing even during the Depression years, thanks to high unemployment. Demand came mainly from a 13-fold increase in secondary school enrolment, from 500 thousand in 1900 to almost 6.6 million in 1940. An important feature of the response to this increased demand for higher education was the increased stratification of the higher education system. Junior colleges emerged as a new type of institution by 1915. Enrolment also increased in two-year state normal schools and teachers' colleges, driven by an immigration-fuelled growth in primary school (grades 1–8) population from 14 million to 22 million in 30 years.

To summarize, the development of the US higher education system from its beginnings in the seventeenth and eighteenth centuries until the second half of the nineteenth century was entirely in the hands of private philanthropists, various religious denominations and, after independence, the states—the latter particularly in the South and the new settlements in what is now the Mid-west. In the middle of the nineteenth century, the federal government began to play a role in fostering the growth of higher education—specifically to help state public universities generate income to train students in practical skills that would contribute to agricultural and industrial development. The federal government also provided funding for agricultural research, and by the end of the eighteenth century, used its funding lever to force Southern states to create access to public college for black students—this in an era of legalized segregation. The federal government therefore set the stage in the nineteenth century for its much-expanded role after 1945 in all these areas—promoting the expansion of enrolment, basic research and enforcing equal access for discriminated against minority groups.

POST-WAR FEDERALISM: THE GROWTH OF FEDERAL INFLUENCE AND THE EMERGENCE OF TIERED STATE PUBLIC HIGHER EDUCATION SYSTEMS

The contemporary federal role, as we recognize it today, developed relatively quickly following the end of World War II. Federal post-war policies designed to bring the country into peacetime quickly included a role for higher education as the primary institution for civilian training of returning military servicemen. Goals for post-war prosperity and growth were soon superseded by the Cold War with the USSR, which again prompted federal involvement and investment in higher education for the purposes of conducting research to forward national interests in science, technology, heath and defence. By the early 1970s, the federal government was contributing significantly to higher education through direct student support and sponsored research programmes. Enrolments more than quadrupled from 1950 to 1980 to a total of about 12 million students (Thelin 2011), and federal contributions to institutions, though just 13 per cent of public institutions' total revenue, totalled over $5.5 billion (Snyder and Hoffman 2003).

The Servicemen's Readjustment Act, known commonly as the GI Bill, was passed in 1944. The bill laid out a path for readjustment by offering veterans federally subsidized home loans, small business loans and through funds for tuition and living expenses, a college education. By 1946, over one million veterans were enrolled in colleges under the GI Bill, accounting for just under one half of all enrolments (Bennett 1996). The policy was deliberately hands off. Funds were directed to students; students could use the funds to attend any federally approved institution. Further, the government chose not to play a direct role in designating approved institutions, allowing regional accreditation associations to certify institutions (Thelin 2011). In the three decades following 1945, the entire higher education system expanded, including institutions (55% growth to 2,747 institutions) and enrolments (over 560% growth from 2.2 million students in 1950 to about 12 million students in 1980, see Cohen 1998).

President Harry Truman envisioned a stronger federal role in higher education policy, and, in 1947, his appointed Commission on Higher Education delivered their report, 'Higher Education for Democracy'. The report marked the first federal policy statement on higher education, arguing for the increased investment in higher education to further national interests in the social sphere, defence and national security. Although the Truman Commission proposed stronger federal investment to grow the system, reduce financial barriers to college and eliminate educational discrimination based on race, sex and religion, federal policy was not immediately responsive to the report (Gilbert and Heller 2013). In fact, federal support for higher education began to decline after peaking at about $1.9 billion in 1949 (Heller 2002). State governments, however, began to take up the issue of financial aid and the development of two-year community colleges outlined in the report.

In 1957, the USSR successfully launched the world's first artificial satellite, Sputnik. Sputnik spurred the space race against the Soviets and with it, increased federal attention to undergraduate and graduate training in the sciences and higher education as a site for scientific research and development. Federal action included greater commitments to research agencies such as the National Institutes of Health, the National Science Foundation (NSF) and the US Atomic Energy Commission, the founding of the National Aeronautics and Space Agency, and the passage of the National Defense Education Act (NDEA). The NDEA, signed into law in 1958, provided one billion dollars to support teaching, learning, and research in science and mathematics, including the establishment of the first federal student loan programme, directed to low-income students (Gilbert and Heller 2013).

Sputnik and the succeeding Cold War induced a substantial increase of federal spending directed to higher education institutions for research and development. Between 1958 and 1968, universities conducted half of the nation's basic research, up from 33 per cent in 1958. In terms of gross national product, academic research more than doubled from 0.10 per cent to 0.25 per cent of GDP, and the proportion coming from federal sources, from 0.05 per cent to 0.17 per cent of GDP. Annual federal contributions to academic research grew from $1 billion to $5 billion—constant 1988 dollars—(Bloch 1989). As in the past, federal monies passed straight to institutions. States did not receive research funds designated for higher education.

The decision by Washington to direct the bulk of basic and applied research activities to higher education institutions led to the development of the dominant research university form as we know it today

(Thelin 2011). Scientific research conducted in the national interest was performed by college faculty and graduate students, within institutions that not only conducted research but also trained future scientists. Not regionally nor strictly politically directed, obtaining federal research funding was a competitive undertaking. Consequently, a relatively small number of institutions developed the capacity, talent and infrastructure to win successfully larger and more numerous research grants. Out of these conditions emerged the prestigious research universities. In 1960, just six universities received the majority of federal research funds (Kerr 1963), and, by the early 1970s, about half the federal funds for basic research were awarded to the nation's top 25 research universities (Gumport 2011). Gumport further notes that graduate training grew dramatically with these investments in university research. For example, doctoral conferrals increased from 6,000 in 1950 to 10,000 in 1960 and 30,000 in 1970.

Federal policy and support for higher education in post-war America initially did little to address the extreme racial segregation of students. While the Morrill Land-Grant Acts provided postsecondary access for African–Americans in the form of historically black colleges and universities (HBCUs), the 'separate but equal' approach by the government maintained a segregated system of institutions. As late as 1950, approximately 90 per cent of African–American college students attended HBCUs, and many institutions—public and private—still prohibited blacks from enrolling (Fleming 1985). Progress towards desegregation did not materialize until a decade later, with the passage of the historic Civil Rights Act of 1964. The statute enforced desegregation in higher education institutions by withholding federal funds from any institution that discriminated or otherwise excluded from participation any person on the basis of race, sex or national origin and, more importantly, by establishing a federal agency charged with enforcement and ensuring compliance with non-discrimination law (Stefkovich and Leas 1994). In the higher education sector, compliance included the recruitment of black, Asian–American, Hispanic and Native American students and race-conscious admission policies ('affirmative action'). By 1976, the proportion of African-American college students attending HBCUs had dropped dramatically to 18 per cent (Hoffman, Snyder and Sonnenberg 1996).

While civil rights legislation and executive enforcement of anti-discrimination practices have been credited with increasing educational access and reducing racial segregation, particularly among African–Americans in the 1960s and 1970s, subsequent federal action in the judicial system has continually challenged this policy direction. Federal Court rulings in the 1970s (*University of California v. Bakke, 1978*), 1990s (*Hopwood v. Texas, 1996*), 2000s (*Gratz v. Bollinger and Grutter v. Bollinger, 2003*) and most recently in 2013 (*Fisher v. Texas*) have challenged the constitutionality of affirmative action practices in higher education admissions. The policy has been thus far been upheld, but the cases have increased the legal scrutiny on institutions (Schmidt 2013).

Federal funding for higher education expanded in the 1960s and 1970s, with the Higher Education Act (HEA) of 1965 creating formal structures for federal student aid. The HEA emphasized equal educational opportunity with need-based grants and guaranteed student loans or GSL (St. John 2003).

Title IV of the HEA created two new programmes: educational opportunity grants (EOGs) and low-interest insured loans. The EOG, later renamed the Pell grant, provided funds to low-income undergraduate students who lacked the means to afford a postsecondary education. Initially, institutions received funds under the EOG programme to distribute to eligible students with high need. Students could receive EOG funds for up to four years. Eligibility depended on four criteria: enrolment as a full-time student, demonstration of academic or creative promise, exceptional financial need and inability to afford attendance without the EOG. The GSL programme promoted development of state and non-profit student loan insurance programmes, created a federal loan insurance programme and established student loan interest subsidization programmes for enrolled students. Loan insurance limited the risk for agencies granting student loans, allowing individuals from a wider range of backgrounds to benefit from the programme. Unlike other federal aid programmes linked to an individual campus, the GSL programme provided funds directly to students, allowing them to transfer from one school to another without loss of loan aid. College work-study programmes, initially created as part of the Economic Opportunity Act of 1964, became more focused under the HEA, emphasizing the goal of providing work opportunities for low-income students and shifting oversight to the Department of Health, Education and Welfare, connecting it with other financial aid programmes.

Even before the emergence of human capital theory at the end of the 1950s, the federal government was promoting the idea that college was an investment in an individual's economic productivity and, through the individual, in the nation's aggregate productivity. This was represented by the movement in federal policy towards individual rather than institutional subsidies for enrolment, a policy strategy successfully implemented with the GI Bill (St. John 2003). The Higher Education Amendments of 1972 expanded on Title IV programmes, with additional emphasis on equal opportunity. The initial EOG programme expanded, providing basic grants to all eligible students and supplemental grants to students with exceptional financial need. Unlike its predecessor, the basic educational opportunities grant (BEOG) programme provided funds to students directly, allowing for portability between programmes and guaranteeing a minimum amount of aid regardless of school attended (St. John 2003). Supplemental grants remained connected to individual institutions and were distributed at the discretion of that institution. With financial aid resources no longer limited to a specific campus, individual student college choices increased (Thelin 2011). The new grant structure encouraged colleges and universities to identify and enrol low-income students, as all students meeting eligibility criteria received aid under the amended HEA. The 1972 amendments increased student loan insurance guarantees from a minimum of 80 per cent of the principal balance to 100 per cent of the principal balance plus interest, slowly supporting the growth of student loan programmes.[3] Beyond student aid programmes administered at the federal level, the 1972 amendments promoted development of state-level financial aid programmes through matching funds. In 1970, less than half of states provided financial assistance for college; by 1980, aid programmes existed in nearly every state (Brint and Karabel 1989) at a level of about $1.15B (Clotfelter 1991). This

---

[3] The federal student loan programme went through several iterations, until 2010 divided into direct loans from the federal government and loans from private banks guaranteed by the federal government and, after 2010, only as loans directly from the federal government. Losses on federal student loans are very low because such loans cannot be discharged through bankruptcy. Almost all students qualify for student loans, and undergraduate students are eligible for loans that are interest free until they leave their studies or graduate. The federal government makes a substantial profit (negative subsidy) on these loans, even though many of them are low-interest and, in theory, subsidized.

represents a greater than five-fold increase in state funding from prior to HEA in 1965 to 1980. The broader combination of new resources provided greater opportunities for institutions as well as potential students.

Increases in federal student financial aid programmes fuelled postsecondary enrolment growth. In particular, community colleges gained broader access to federal funds via the BEOG programme, as they no longer competed directly with four-year institutions (Thelin 2011). Even in states with minimal or no tuition, students struggled to remain enrolled due to other costs of attendance. Access to BEOG funds allowed more students to attend the programme of their choice. Community colleges were significant beneficiaries of these grants.

In addition to student financial aid, the 1972 amendments increased availability of state grants for postsecondary occupational education. Limited to institutions focused on sub-professional career education, the programme encouraged states to develop and expand community colleges (Brint and Karabel 1989). Reduced demand for workers with academic degrees and student concerns about underemployment in the early 1970s additionally contributed to development of new occupational training programmes (Brint and Karabel 1989).

With greater availability of federal funds and increased policy emphasis on equal educational opportunity, states expanded educational offerings after high school, contributing to the development of a tiered public postsecondary structure. In 1970, community colleges enrolled over 1.6 million students nationally, approximately 24 per cent of undergraduate students; by 1980, community college enrolment increased to over 4.5 million students, representing over 41 per cent of undergraduate students (Brint and Karabel 1989). Community colleges actively recruited minority and economically disadvantaged students eligible for new financial aid programmes. By the end of the 1970s, minority students were disproportionately represented in community colleges; this educational stratification mirrored broader societal trends. Non-traditional enrolments at community colleges expanded with the increased focus on vocational education. Many non-traditional students began taking courses on an as-needed basis, focusing on personal interests or job requirements rather than preparing to transfer to another institution or completion of a structured academic programme. Marginal students interested in attending college found a pathway to access through a combination of increased federal financial aid availability and open access community colleges. As enrolment grew, so did needs for remedial coursework. Community colleges shifted to accommodate the needs of students, increasing availability of basic reading, writing and mathematics courses for students lacking adequate preparation for college-level coursework (Brint and Karabel 1989).

The enrolment boom and subsequent creation of new community colleges, arguably driven by the increasing aspirations and ability to pay for higher education, and triggered by federal financial aid policy, allowed more students to attend, but with increased focus on vocational programmes. The vocational focus diverted students from traditional academic programmes and discouraged transfer to four-year colleges and universities (Brint and Karabel 1989). Federal policy was not directive with regard to the specific institutional structure of the system, allowing states and institutions to respond to the increasing demand on their own terms. State universities voiced increased concern about declining quality of community college transfers and lower percentages of students applying to transfer (Thelin 2011). Two-year and four-year colleges began focusing on distinct missions, with availability of federal funds guiding community colleges towards the creation of vocational programmes while four-year colleges and universities increasingly concentrated on research and preparing students for professional careers.

Although, on average, a high fraction of high school students who attend college in the United States attend college in their home state, US higher education is also marked by a significant degree of student mobility from state to state. Student mobility in the past has always been high in the north-eastern states because of geographic proximity, but mobility has spread to other states. The outmigration of college freshmen from their state to another state for college in 1998 varied from 8 per cent (North Carolina and Mississippi) to more than 50 per cent (Connecticut, Vermont and New Hampshire). The average was about 20 per cent (Mak and Moncur 2003). Net migration also varies by state. Not surprisingly, '… migration flows decrease with the distance between the origin and destination, increase if states are adjacent to one another, and increase (decrease) [into states] if the origin is surrounded by states with few (many) higher education opportunities' (Cooke and Boyle 2011, 207). Student migration also flows towards states with public universities whose students have high SAT scores and from states with higher in-state costs of attendance towards states with lower out-of-state student tuition (Cooke and Boyle 2011). The fact that federal student loans go to individual students, regardless of the state/university to which they pay tuition, is a stimulus to interstate student movement. On the other hand, many states offer residents scholarships that must be used in the state and are not offered to non-residents.

It is notable that the role of the federal government in higher education—a decentralized approach allowing for state control, student mobility and institutional autonomy—remained largely limited to the funding of university research and student aid programmes in the post-war era. The federal role in education vis-à-vis local control has been continually debated, however, since the Reagan Era of the 1980s. This is most clearly evident by the standards and accountability movement in elementary and secondary education originating in that era, a movement which has brought great deliberation, and greater federal control, to education policy in that sector (McDonnell 2005). The substantially greater autonomy of the higher education sector has thus far limited the repercussions of this movement, but there are signs of a changing approach in Washington.

DEMOGRAPHICS AND ENROLMENT GROWTH IN THE US STATES, 1970-2012

As shown in the previous section, the expansion of the US higher education system post–World War II was massive and was characterized by considerable stratification into various types of public options—large state research universities, second-tier four-year institutions, many with graduate education and community colleges offering associate degrees. Since the 1990s, there has also been an expansion of private higher education. Enrolment in non-profit private higher education institutions has grown more slowly than in the public sector. However, enrolment in for-profit four-year and two-year institutions has increased rapidly since the late 1990s, mainly because of online offerings (see Figure 2.1).

Thus, *the first important feature of enrolment expansion* is the more rapid growth of two-year institutions. In 1970, 73 per cent of higher education students were in four-year institutions and 59 per cent were

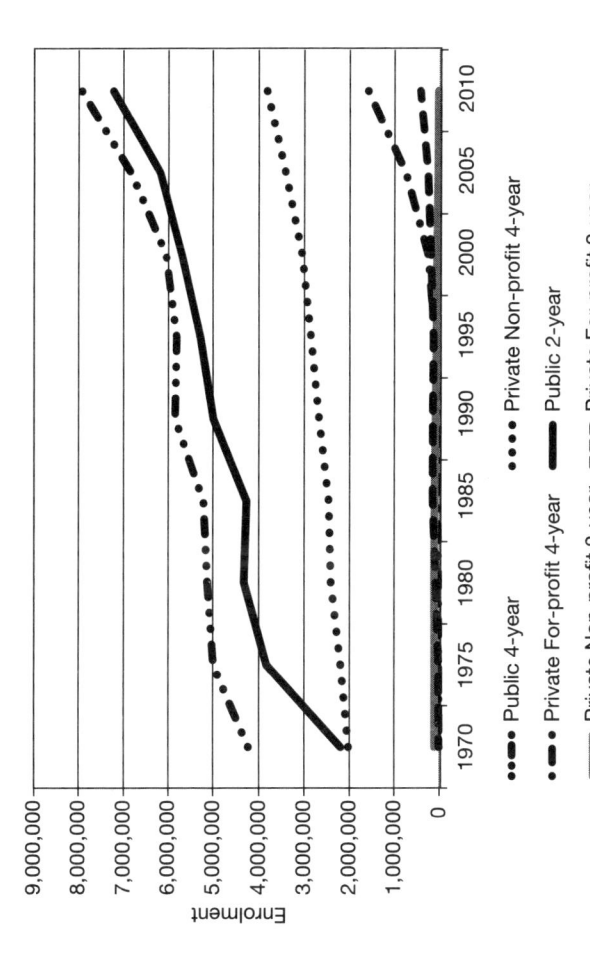

Figure 2.1 *Enrolment Growth, by Type of Institution, 1970–2010*

Source: National Center of Educational Statistics, *Digest of Educational Statistics, 2012*, Table 230.

in public institutions; by 2010, only 63 per cent were in four-year institutions, but 68 per cent in public institutions. The major growth after 1970 was in two-year enrolment, from 27 to 37 per cent of total enrolment, which remained at 94–95 per cent in public institutions.

The second important feature of enrolment expansion is that different segments of the population formed the basis of increasing enrolment in different periods. The main source of enrolment growth in 1970–1990 was females, who entered higher education in large numbers starting in the 1960s, but accelerating after 1970, first white females in the 1970s and 1980s, then minority females after the mid-1980s (Figure 2.2). By 2010, female enrolment greatly exceeded male enrolment overall. Black enrolment in higher education began to increase rapidly in the mid-1980s, especially black females, whose increasing rate of enrolment paralleled white females. Yet, black males also closed the gap with white males in the rate of higher education enrolment in the 2000s (Figure 2.2). This was quickly followed by increased enrolment rates among Hispanics—first females, then males (Figure 2.3).

Since Hispanics are a rapidly growing proportion of the US population, this increased enrolment rate (plus the increased enrolment rate among blacks) constituted most of the increase in absolute enrolment in US higher education. When we add the growing (but smaller in absolute size) Asian-origin population, with their very high college enrolment rate, this forms the increasingly minoritization of US higher education since 1990. Nevertheless, this minoritization is highly stratified. Hispanics especially are concentrated in two-year institutions and Asians and, to a lesser extent, African-Americans are in four-year institutions.

The third important feature of this period is the increase (1980–late 1990s) and subsequent decline in the internationalization of US higher education at undergraduate level as US higher education expanded rapidly in the 2000s. The percentage of international students in US institutions remains low—even if we were to assume that all the international students attended four-year institutions, it would still be less than 4 per cent. To the contrary, at the graduate level in science, technology, engineering and mathematics (STEM) fields, internationalization continues to increase in the 2000s, albeit at a slower rate (Figure 2.4). The phenomenon of internationalization of US STEM education at the graduate level has been fuelled by the influx of students

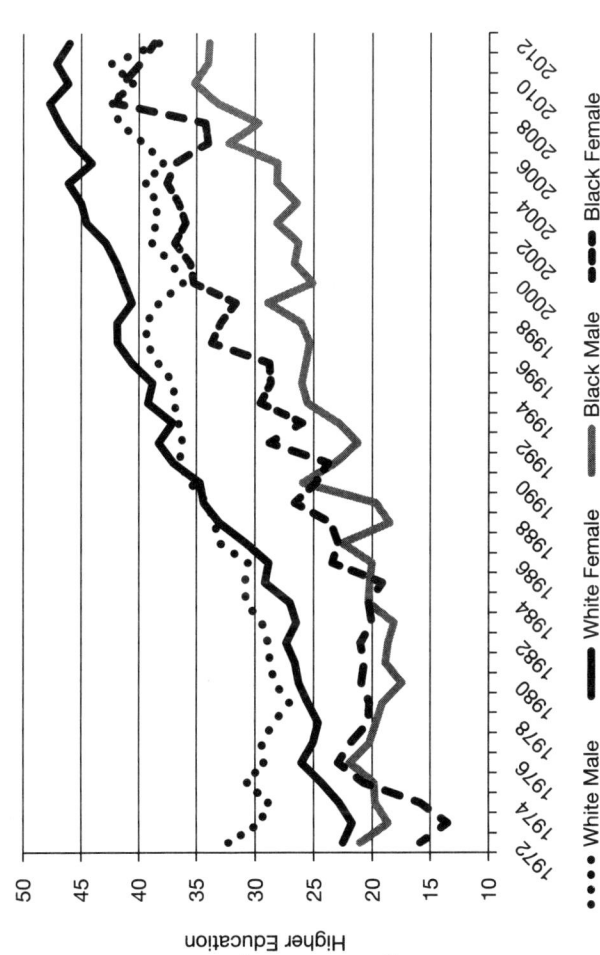

Figure 2.2 United States: Percentage of 18- to 24-year-olds Enrolled in Higher Education, by Race, 1972–2012

Source: National Center of Educational Statistics, Digest of Educational Statistics, 2013, Table 302.60.

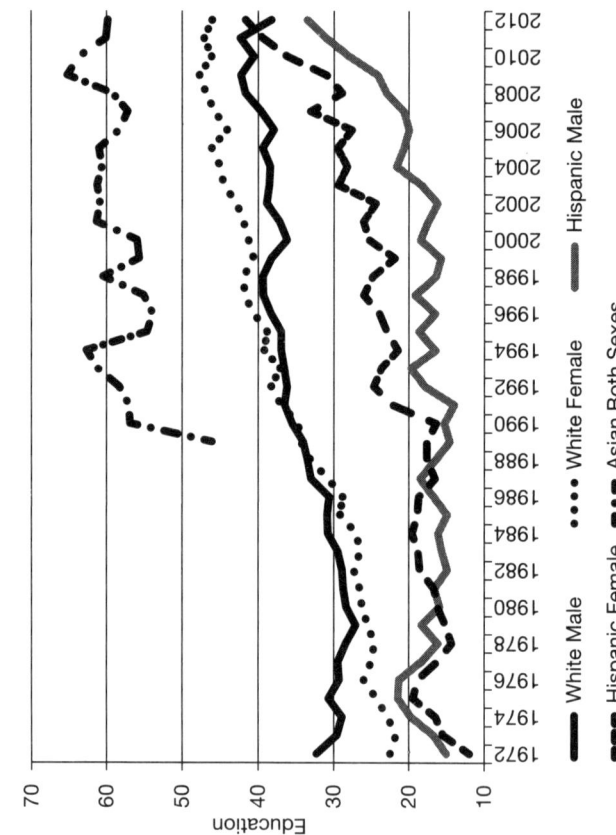

Figure 2.3 *United States: Percentage of 18- to 24-year-olds Enrolled in Higher Education, by Ethnicity, 1972–2012*

Source: National Center of Educational Statistics. Digest of Educational Statistics, 2013, Table 302.60.

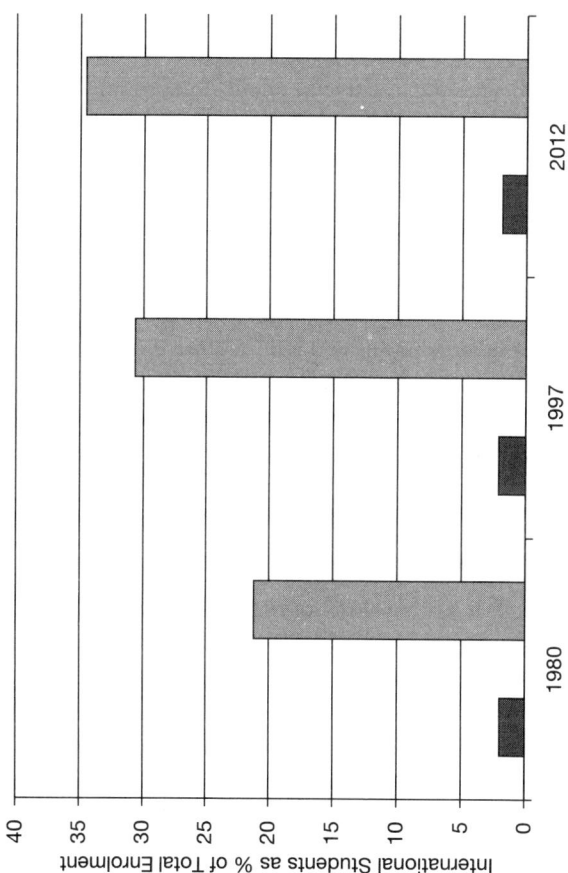

Figure 2.4 *United States: Proportion of International Students at the Undergraduate Level and at the Graduate Level in STEM Fields, 1980–2012.*

Source: NSF, Science and Engineering Indicators, 2002 and 2012.

from East and South Asia since the 1990s and the lack of sufficient US-born graduate students to undertake STEM research and fill US academic jobs in STEM fields (Carnoy 1998, 2014). A high percentage of international STEM doctoral graduates (66%), particularly those from China and India (85 and 82%, respectively) remain in the United States to work mainly in the high-tech sector (NSF 2016, Table 3–27).

The fourth important feature of the higher education expansion after 1970 is that its pattern varies considerably among states. The variation occurs in (a) the rate of expansion relative to population growth, (b) the mix of four-year and two-year institutions and (c) the public–private mix of institutions through which the expansion took place. There is also variation among states in minoritization, but this is largely the result of variation in changes in population composition.

Table 2.1 shows the rate of enrolment expansion by state in 1970–2011 and 1984–2011. The enrolment growth rates (percentage per annum) are shown as unadjusted and adjusted for the increase in population growth of the 18–24 years old age group in each state. We show both periods—1970–2011 and 1984–2011—because 1984 is the first year for which we have data on enrolment by state divided into four-year and two-year institutions. Beginning in 1984, we also have enrolment data by state on four-year and two-year institutions divided into whether these institutions are public or private.

The results indicate that net enrolment growth was highest in both periods in a group of states led by Iowa, West Virginia, Kentucky, Arkansas, Georgia, Virginia, Minnesota and, particularly since 1984, Arizona. The states with the lowest net enrolment growth vary more in the two periods, but California, the District of Columbia, Massachusetts, Washington and Oklahoma have expanded their higher education systems at much slower rates than other states. The situation of DC is somewhat unusual, since the District is surrounded by Maryland and Virginia, and the latter has had very high enrolment growth, so most DC high school students are attending college in neighbouring states. However, California, the nation's most populous state, has expanded its higher education very slowly.

Table 2.1 also shows that states vary greatly in the proportion of students enrolled in higher education that attend two-year institutions

Table 2.1 *Total Enrolment in Higher Education and Percentage in Two-year Institutions, by State 1970–2011*

State	Total Enrolment Growth, 1970–2011	Total Enrolment Growth, 1984–2011	Net Total Enrolment Growth, 1970–2011	Net Total Enrolment Growth, 1984–2011	% Enrolment in Two-year Institutions, 1984	% Enrolment in Two-year Institutions, 2011	% Enrolment in Two-year Institutions, 2011/1984
Alabama	2.77	2.09	2.38	2.29	28.6	26.6	0.93
Alaska	3.23	2.11	2.07	1.30	43.0	3.4	0.08
Arizona	4.96	6.06	2.25	4.17	40.5	21.1	0.52
Arkansas	3.06	2.89	2.39	2.80	17.2	30.0	1.75
California	1.87	2.11	0.72	1.45	47.7	48.7	1.02
Colorado	2.69	2.98	1.38	2.39	20.9	24.5	1.17
Connecticut	1.18	1.25	1.23	1.75	20.8	21.5	1.03
Delaware	1.98	2.09	1.14	1.76	21.0	20.9	0.99
District of Columbia	0.38	0.77	0.95	1.23	0.0	0.0	1.00
Florida	3.93	3.88	1.75	2.41	42.4	10.7	0.25
Georgia	3.72	3.85	2.45	2.82	21.0	24.5	1.16
Hawaii	1.9	1.56	1.48	1.80	35.4	32.9	0.93
Idaho	2.37	2.98	0.83	2.17	26.9	14.9	0.55

(Continued)

Table 2.1 (Continued)

State	Total Enrolment Growth, 1970–2011	Total Enrolment Growth, 1984–2011	Net Total Enrolment Growth, 1970–2011	Net Total Enrolment Growth, 1984–2011	% Enrolment in Two-year Institutions, 1984	% Enrolment in Two-year Institutions, 2011	% Enrolment in Two-year Institutions, 2011/1984
Illinois	1.67	1.48	1.69	2.09	37.3	35.2	0.94
Indiana	2.13	2.29	1.99	2.66	14.2	19.6	1.38
Iowa	3.04	3.10	3.09	3.84	25.8	23.6	0.92
Kansas	1.84	1.70	1.70	2.06	23.7	34.3	1.45
Kentucky	2.7	2.51	2.57	3.04	21.4	30.8	1.44
Louisiana	1.94	1.28	1.83	2.00	8.1	28.0	3.45
Maine	1.85	1.39	1.83	2.03	11.5	21.7	1.88
Maryland	2.3	2.08	1.87	2.03	33.8	33.3	0.99
Massachusetts	1.26	0.90	1.25	1.37	18.1	16.3	0.90
Michigan	1.37	1.13	1.54	1.90	35.8	29.1	0.81
Minnesota	2.58	2.54	2.28	2.88	20.9	26.3	1.25
Mississippi	2.18	1.93	1.84	2.23	37.6	44.4	1.18
Missouri	2.24	2.42	1.97	2.66	19.0	24.3	1.28
Montana	1.44	1.50	0.98	1.72	8.1	15.0	1.86

Nebraska	1.87	1.63	1.72	2.06	18.6	27.9	1.50
Nevada	5.46	5.08	1.69	2.17	33.3	12.1	0.36
New Hampshire	2.39	1.44	1.48	1.34	15.0	13.6	0.91
New Jersey	1.77	1.89	1.73	2.28	31.6	36.3	1.15
New Mexico	3.13	3.25	1.91	2.75	15.8	44.8	2.84
New York	1.21	1.20	1.26	1.47	27.1	24.6	0.91
North Carolina	3.03	2.32	2.18	1.83	34.5	35.4	1.02
North Dakota	1.4	1.23	1.15	1.70	20.6	10.1	0.49
Ohio	1.65	1.47	1.96	2.29	24.0	25.6	1.07
Oklahoma	1.81	1.28	1.24	1.39	26.9	27.1	1.01
Oregon	1.85	2.36	0.89	2.04	37.2	38.6	1.04
Pennsylvania	1.6	1.58	1.66	2.14	22.5	18.9	0.84
Rhode Island	1.5	1.69	1.55	1.90	12.9	12.3	0.95
South Carolina	3.27	2.22	2.51	1.98	29.7	35.1	1.18
South Dakota	1.48	1.76	1.32	2.21	1.9	12.9	6.91
Tennessee	2.35	2.18	1.73	2.11	23.0	25.7	1.12

(Continued)

Table 2.1 (*Continued*)

State	Total Enrolment Growth, 1970–2011	Total Enrolment Growth, 1984–2011	Net Total Enrolment Growth, 1970–2011	Net Total Enrolment Growth, 1984–2011	% Enrolment in Two-year Institutions, 1984	% Enrolment in Two-year Institutions, 2011	% Enrolment in Two-year Institutions, 2011/1984
Texas	3.13	2.32	1.58	1.40	32.8	39.8	1.21
Utah	2.91	3.36	0.92	1.98	18.0	13.0	0.72
Vermont	1.75	1.42	1.26	1.65	12.9	7.9	0.61
Virginia	3.36	2.95	2.69	2.64	27.0	28.1	1.04
Washington	1.74	2.03	0.67	1.43	44.0	36.3	0.82
West Virginia	2.33	2.44	2.71	3.60	12.6	15.3	1.22
Wisconsin	1.53	1.15	1.35	1.63	25.2	23.1	0.92
Wyoming	2.26	1.82	1.29	2.43	45.5	58.7	1.29

Source: National Center of Educational Statistics, Digest of Educational Statistics, 1974, 1986, 2012.

and in the relative expansion or contraction of the proportion of two-year enrolment in the almost 30 years since 1984. Some states, such as California, Oregon, Washington, Texas and Mississippi, enrol a very high fraction of their students in two-year institutions and have maintained those percentages over a long period of time. With the increase in the fraction of disadvantaged minority population finishing high school in most US states in 1984–2011, we would have assumed that many states would have increased the proportion of students in two-year institutions; yet, this is not universally the case, for example, Florida has greatly expanded enrolment in four-year public institutions.

There are some 'distorted' cases, such as Arizona, the site of University of Phoenix, whose hundreds of thousands of online students, non-existent in 1984, are counted as all being in Arizona in 2011. If we omit the students in Arizona's four-year private for-profit institutions in 2011, the proportion of Arizona's students attending two-year institutions increases from 40 to 50 per cent in 1984–2011, staying at the high levels reached throughout the Southwest (California, Arizona, New Mexico and Texas) and suggesting the Hispanic 18–24 years old population is being absorbed into these states' higher education systems mainly through enrolment in two-year institutions. However, this appears less true of Texas than California (Carnoy 2010).

The fifth feature of enrolment expansion is the variation across states in the role of private higher education. Most private enrolment is in four-year institutions, but the fraction of students enrolled in private four-year institutions in states varies greatly. The highest rates of enrolment in private colleges and universities is in the Northeast—Massachusetts, Connecticut, New Hampshire, Vermont, New York, Rhode Island and Pennsylvania. As discussed, these are the states where higher education developed early and mainly as private institutions. At the other end of the spectrum are many of the southern mid-western and western states, whose higher education systems developed around public land-grant colleges. Nevertheless, many of these show considerable expansion of private four-year education, at least, partly through the growth of enrolment in for-profit institutions, which have shown the sharpest growth in four-year enrolment—almost entirely post-2000 with the advent of online education.

Table 2.2 shows the proportion of students enrolled in private institutions in 1970, 1984 and 2011. Most states increased the percentage of

Table 2.2 *Enrolment in Private Higher Education Institutions, States 1970–2011 (%)*

State	% Enrolment in Private Institutions, 1970	% Enrolment in Private Institutions, 1984	% Enrolment in Private Institutions, 2011	% Enrolment in Private Institutions, 2011/1970	% Four-year Enrolment in Private For-profit, 2011	% Two-year Enrolment in Private For-profit 2011	% Hispanic Enrolment in Primary and Secondary School, 1986
Alabama	15.7	13.8	19.8	1.27	12.7	5.0	0.1
Alaska	12.0	4.4	10.8	0.90	7.2	47.9	1.7
Arizona	2.0	9.7	61.9	30.56	74.1	10.3	26.4
Arkansas	10.1	17.3	12.7	1.26	2.3	0.6	0.4
California	10.4	16.0	23.5	2.26	11.0	9.2	27.5
Colorado	12.0	13.4	28.7	2.39	19.8	16.8	13.7
Connecticut	41.6	40.9	40.7	0.98	4.0	0.9	8.9
Delaware	16.3	11.5	24.8	1.52	0.6	0.0	2.5
D. of Columbia	86.2	87.3	95.0	1.10	4.2	0.0	3.9
Florida	19.0	24.1	32.8	1.73	12.4	42.7	9.5
Georgia	19.3	26.3	26.7	1.38	13.7	8.0	0.6
Hawaii	9.7	12.1	26.5	2.73	5.1	7.1	2.2

Idaho	21.3	22.3	29.4	1.38	3.4	5.2	4.9
Illinois	30.5	28.4	38.8	1.27	12.0	3.6	9.2
Indiana	29.4	25.7	28.5	0.97	6.0	9.3	1.7
Iowa	37.3	29.0	54.2	1.45	48.1	1.0	0.9
Kansas	14.1	11.8	13.5	0.96	1.5	3.0	4.4
Kentucky	21.9	23.8	22.7	1.04	8.8	5.1	0.1
Louisiana	16.2	14.5	16.3	1.00	2.4	10.6	0.8
Maine	28.3	35.9	33.7	1.19	1.4	3.5	0.2
Maryland	20.5	15.4	19.3	0.94	2.7	3.3	1.7
Massachusetts	62.4	60.2	59.8	0.96	1.2	2.9	6
Michigan	13.2	18.5	19.5	1.48	2.1	1.1	1.8
Minnesota	18.9	25.1	39.9	2.11	28.1	2.5	0.9
Mississippi	12.2	10.7	10.7	0.88	0.4	3.1	0.1
Missouri	27.9	31.4	42.4	1.52	8.6	10.9	0.7
Montana	9.4	9.1	9.4	0.99	0.0	0.0	0.9
Nebraska	23.2	20.4	27.4	1.18	2.2	2.4	2.4

(Continued)

Table 2.2 (Continued)

State	% Enrolment in Private Institutions, 1970	% Enrolment in Private Institutions, 1984	% Enrolment in Private Institutions, 2011	% Enrolment in Private Institutions, 2011/1970	% Four-year Enrolment in Private For-profit, 2011	% Two-year Enrolment in Private For-profit 2011	% Hispanic Enrolment in Primary and Secondary School, 1986
Nevada	0.8	0.9	17.1	22.22	8.9	45.5	7.5
New Hampshire	45.9	49.4	44.1	0.96	5.0	0.0	0.5
New Jersey	33.0	22.3	20.6	0.62	2.6	1.6	10.7
New Mexico	7.6	3.2	9.2	1.22	11.8	4.0	45.1
New York	43.7	45.4	46.3	1.06	3.4	7.9	12.3
North Carolina	28.3	22.8	22.2	0.78	3.9	2.2	0.4
North Dakota	4.3	8.0	12.7	2.97	2.0	0.0	1.1
Ohio	25.4	27.0	27.9	1.10	3.1	16.3	1
Oklahoma	16.5	15.3	16.8	1.01	3.8	8.6	1.6
Oregon	11.8	15.5	19.4	1.64	3.9	5.0	3.9

State						
Pennsylvania	43.3	44.0	46.4	1.07	2.8	27.3	1.8
Rhode Island	44.3	54.8	61.1	1.38	15.5	0.0	3.7
South Carolina	31.8	22.4	17.3	0.54	0.0	3.7	0.2
South Dakota	22.5	26.5	19.7	0.87	7.0	0.0	0.6
Tennessee	26.8	27.9	33.6	1.25	6.2	14.5	0.2
Texas	17.3	13.4	15.2	0.88	4.0	6.6	32.5
Utah	37.3	36.1	38.6	1.03	6.5	5.9	3
Vermont	43.4	44.1	43.2	0.99	1.4	0.0	0.2
Virginia	19.0	16.4	31.1	1.64	11.3	7.7	1
Washington	13.6	14.9	16.6	1.22	3.3	4.5	3.8
West Virginia	14.1	15.1	31.4	2.23	23.6	14.8	0.1
Wisconsin	5.8	14.4	22.3	3.88	4.4	1.9	1.9
Wyoming	0.0	0.0	6.3	N/A	1.1	10.0	5.9

Source: National Center of Educational Statistics, *Digest of Educational Statistics*, 1974, 1986, 2012.

students in private institutions in this period, but a significant number (15) did not. The table also shows the percentage of students enrolled in a for-profit four-year institution. Again, the proportion of students in for-profit institutions varies greatly across states, although these proportions can be misleading, since much of for-profit higher educa-tion is now online. Students can be anywhere in the United States, not necessarily, in, say, Arizona, where the University of Phoenix head-quarters are located; yet, in educational statistics, Phoenix's students are all counted as in Arizona.

The general increase in the proportion of students who attend two-year institutions, the rapid increase in enrolment in private four-year institutions and the increasing minoritization of higher education are all possible indicators of why some states increased enrolment more rapidly than others in the past three or four decades. We used the variation across states to 'test' which of these factors may explain the variation in higher education growth across states. Specifically, we estimated a model in which total enrolment growth is a function of the change in the percentage of students in two-year institutions, the percentage of students in the state enrolled in higher education who were not non-Hispanic whites in 1988 (the first year for which we could obtain these data), the percentage of students in four-year institutions who were enrolled in a for-profit in 2011, and the percentage of students in two-year institutions who were enrolled in a for-profit in 2011. Data on students attending private for-profit institutions have only been available for the past few years, so the proportion in 2011 is a good indicator of the rapid growth of enrolment in for-profits in the past 10 years.

The results of our estimates are reported in Table 2.3. They suggest that the degree to which students in a state enrol in private for-profit institutions—particularly four-year for-profit higher education—and the expansion of two-year institutions are important correlates of the variation in net enrolment growth in the United States in the past 30 years. These same factors are important correlates of the expansion over the past 40 years, but, as is logical, the recent growth of for-profit higher education has a smaller effect on enrolment increases over the longer period of time. The percentage of minorities in a state's educa-tion system (both the percentage of all minorities in higher educa in 1988 and the percentage of Hispanics in primary and secondary school

Table 2.3 Estimated Higher Education Enrolment Growth, 1970–2011 and 1984–2011

Variable	Change in Enrolment in Two-year Institutions, 1984–2011	Change in Total HE Enrolment, 1970–2011	Change in Total HE Enrolment, 1984–2011	Change in Total HE Enrolment, 1984–2011
Hispanic in Schools, 1986 (%)	0.0055* (0.0029)	–	–	–0.0002*** (0.0001)
Change in Enrolment in two-year Institutions,	–	0.0125** (0.0049)	0.0103** (0.0042)	0.0140*** (0.0042)
Four-year Enrolment in For-profit Institutions, 2011 (%)	–	0.0147** (0.0057)	0.0330*** (0.0050)	0.0353*** (0.0047)
Two-year Enrolment in For-profit Institutions, 2011 (%)	–	0.0186** (0.0082)	0.0107 (0.0072)	0.0153** (0.0070)
Constant	1.1141*** (0.0298)	0.9998*** (0.0059)	1.0060*** (0.0051)	1.0022** (0.0050)
Adjusted R^2	0.069	0.300	0.587	0.643
Number of Observations	51	51	51	51

Source: Tables 2.1 and 2.2, above.

Notes: *=$p<0.10$; **=$p<0.05$; ***=$p<0.01$.

in 1986—we only show results for the latter) has a positive relation with the increase in enrolment in two-year institutions, but, once we control for the expansion in two-year institutions, the Hispanic student population in primary and secondary schools is negatively related to total enrolment growth in higher education. Thus, the percentage of younger minorities in the state is positively indirectly related to total higher education enrolment growth but negatively directly related to total enrolment growth, which is not a surprising result, given that Hispanic enrolment has played an important role in overall enrolment expansion after 1990, but mainly through enrolment in two-year institutions.

HIGHER EDUCATION GOVERNANCE AND THE STATES

The vast and rapid growth of students and institutions, beginning in post-war America and continuing through the current period demanded greater governmental involvement to manage this growth. As an exclusively private and state-sponsored enterprise, the governance of higher education systems and institutions was not centrally controlled in Washington, but left to the state governments and lay governing boards.

The early history of higher education governance was modelled after traditional private corporations. Lay boards or trustees typically held authority over lands and other fiscal matters of the college, while board-appointed presidents were solely responsible for all other matters including the nature of the curriculum and the hiring of faculty. The strength of the private sector set precedence for governance such that public institutions that emerged later adopted similar structures with lay boards made up of businessmen rather than the clergy of the church-sponsored colonial colleges (Cohen 1998). Part of this imprint derived from private sector governance was the role of governing boards as insulating bodies between state government and the university. The University of California, for example, was founded in 1868 with a Board of Regents governance structure and constitutional autonomy from legislative control. This form of individual boards for single institutions, and its attendant institutional autonomy, dominated higher education until the massification period beginning in the 1960s.

Enrolment growth in the decades after World War II surfaced a number of concerns at the state level. Within individual states, there was conflict over resources among institutions, concern for the waste and the duplication of services and a perceived need to monitor the addition and growth of new institutions (Richardson et al. 1998). Prior to 1940, the majority of states had no state-level boards or councils to guide or regulate public higher education. By 1979, all states had installed some form of governing board for their public and sometimes their private institutions (Carnegie Council on Policy Studies 1976). Thus, the state role in higher education after World War II effectively evolved from primarily the provider of resources to relatively independent public colleges to a regulator of institutional and systemic growth (Richardson et al. 1998).

Two primary types of statewide boards have developed: consolidated governing boards and coordinating boards (McGuinness 2003). Consolidated governing boards are policy-making boards with authority over whole state college and university systems. Some governing boards encompass multiple institution types such as the Board of Trustees of the Minnesota State Colleges and Universities, a system created by the legislature that merged 7 comprehensive state universities, 34 technical colleges and 21 community colleges under one board[4] (History and Background n.d.). Typically, such boards are responsible for setting a broad range of policies with regard to system planning, academic programmes and personnel, admissions standards and procedures and tuition. Thus, one board manages policy development and coordination across a number and variety of institutions. In states where individual campus or segmented system governing boards are in place, a statewide coordinating board manages higher education policy. Coordinating boards are generally not governing boards; their charge is to serve state interests by providing policy direction and planning for state systems and/or individual institutions, including the privates in the state. Some coordinating boards have fiscal authority over systems and institutions; some are primarily advisory and provide planning and policy analysis documents to the legislature and the institutions. Consolidated governing boards and coordinating boards represent the tension between values of institutional autonomy and decentralized governance on one hand and the needs for centralized planning and efficient use of state resources on the other. This is a tension that has largely not emerged at the federal level.

The oft-heralded example of state-level planning and governance occurred in 1960, when the president of the University of California,

---

[4] See 'History and Background' available at http://www.mnscu.edu/board/summary/1996/december-history.html

Clark Kerr, forged a multi-stakeholder negotiation into the Donahoe Higher Education Act, also known as the California Master Plan for Higher Education. The act established a segmented system of three sectors with specialized functions: research and teaching up through the doctoral level, undergraduate and masters level education, and lower division and vocational education. Eventually the plan included separate governing boards and a cross-sector coordinating board for the three segments and private institutions (Breneman and Lingenfelter 2012).

Extra-governmental structures also emerged in the post-war era in recognition of the growing state role in the development of higher education. In 1954, the State Higher Education Executive Officers Association (SHEEO) was founded by nine leaders of the 10 statewide boards then in existence (Thelin 2011). It is currently composed of leaders serving on statewide coordinating and governing boards in each of the 50 states as well as Puerto Rico and the District of Columbia with a mission to serve 'its members as an advocate for state policy leadership, as a liaison between states and federal government, as a vehicle for learning from and collaborating with peers, and as a source of information and analysis on educational and public policy issues' (SHEEOA 2012). State governors also discerned a stake in national dialogue and agenda-setting around elementary, secondary and postsecondary education policy and formally established the Education Commission of the States (ECS) in 1965 (ECS 2015). ECS is governor-driven, with the chairmanship held by a sitting governor for a term of two years. As extra-governmental organizations, SHEEO and ECS do not legislate state nor national policy; both establish policy initiatives, collect policy-relevant data, publish policy briefs and reports and facilitate cross-state and multi-stakeholder dialogue and collaboration. Current policy initiatives addressed by SHEEO and ECS include college-readiness standards, state higher education finance, student financial aid, state data systems, civic learning and engagement and standards and accountability.

HIGHER EDUCATION FINANCING

Higher education financing in the United States was, until the middle of the nineteenth century, almost entirely private—financed by tuition, by educational foundations or by private gifts. Indeed, many of the names of the earliest institutions, including Harvard, Yale, Cornell and Brown, are tied to generous benefactors. Public universities have traditionally been funded mostly by state and local governments and, to a much lesser extent, by tuition. The role of the federal government was limited to grants of federal lands to state (and to a few private) universities. These lands acted as endowments for the land-grant colleges and universities, providing them with regular revenues from leases and other business arrangements related to the use of the lands. As we have discussed, after World War II, the federal government greatly increased research funding and, with the GI Bill, provided a large amount of student aid to returning veterans. Both types of federal funding stimulated the rapid expansion of US higher education in the 1950s and beyond.

In the past 50 years, federal financing has remained focused on research funding for universities and student grants and loans. However, political shifts to the right after 1980 played into conservative anti-taxation movements at both the federal and state levels, making it increasingly difficult for states to increase state taxes to fund the rising costs of higher education. States began raising tuition in public institutions. In the flagship institutions in most states, tuition levels became very high by the early 2000s, although because of student funding opportunities, actual paid tuition was considerably lower than officially posted rates (see Figure 2.5). Private university tuition also rose rapidly (in real terms) during this period, but at a lower rate than tuition in public four-year universities (3.8% versus 4.5% annually). This trend greatly changed educational financing from public to private sources, and it created a gradually increasing role for the federal government because student enrolment expansion increasingly depended on the availability of federal student loans and grants.

The most extreme example of this was the growth of for-profit four-year higher education after 2000. These private for-profit institutions are heavily dependent on federal student loans for their students, and, for that reason, they are subject to federal scrutiny and accountability. The federal government is increasingly trying to use its power to audit universities—both private and public—in its role as an indirect lender to universities through student loans for paying tuition and other university student costs. Yet, beyond pursuing legal action against universities for the misuse of federal student loans, the

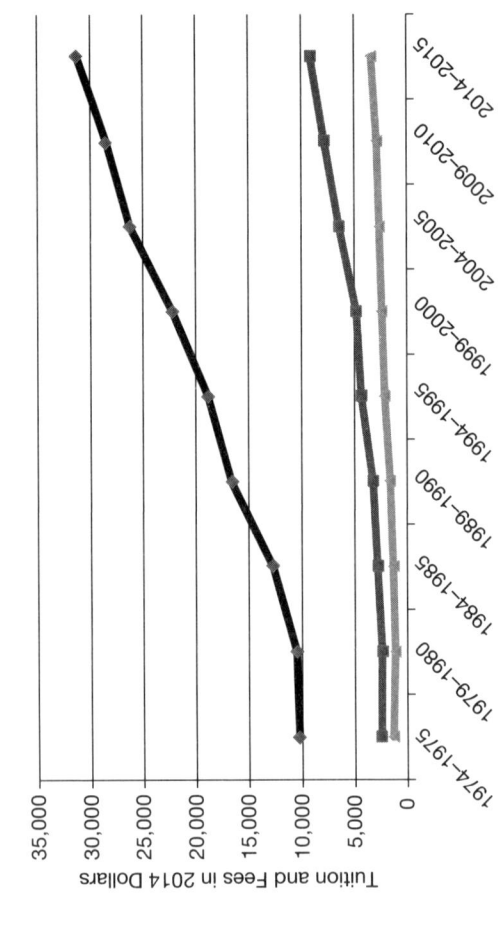

Figure 2.5 *Higher Education Tuition and Fees by Institutional Type, 1974–2014 (2014 Dollars)*

federal government has limited control of university policies. As we have noted, even credentialing is handled by agencies independent of the federal government.[5]

Structure of Higher Educational Financing, 1970–2010

The structure of educational financing varies considerably from state to state, as might be expected given the large variation in private/ public higher education enrolment. Before turning to that variation, we can analyse the broad changes in US higher educational financing that took place after the 1960s. One way to describe these changes is by the total current revenues going to public, private non-profit and private for-profit higher education institutions.

The current revenues of both public and private non-profit institutions increased rapidly in the period 1970–2010. These revenues are all estimated in 2010 dollars, so represent revenues adjusted for inflation (see Table 2.4). The private non-profit higher education sector's revenue increased somewhat more rapidly than the public sector and, once we include the private for-profit sector, the private higher education sector increased considerably more rapidly than the public. Total revenues increased much more in the 2000–2010 decade than in earlier decades, not only because of the enrolment growth of private non-profit institutions but also because of spending per student in all kinds of higher education institutions.

It is widely held that US higher education is being steadily 'privatized'. In popular thinking, privatization means that tuition is covering an increasing fraction of total revenues in higher education, replacing declining state contributions to public universities. Dan Hurley, vice-president of the American Association of State Colleges and

---

[5] The case of the University of Phoenix illustrates the problem. Phoenix is a major, largely online private for-profit university that caters to a diverse group of mainly undergraduate students. In 2008, Phoenix was the top recipient of student aid funds, at $2.5 billion, while at the same time being repeatedly fined by the US government for fraudulent student recruitment practices and fraudulent solicitation of student aid funds (Lauerman 2010a, 2010b). Yet, University of Phoenix has increased enrolment steadily since 2000 and now has the largest enrolment among US universities, with about 300 thousand students.

Table 2.4 *Current Revenues by Source and Institutional Type, 1970–2011 (2010 Dollars; %)*

	Year								
	1970	**1980**	**1985**	**1990**	**1995**	**2000**	**2005**	**2010**	**2011**
Public Higher Education									
Tuition & Fees	13.1	12.9	14.5	16.1	18.8	18.1	17	18.6	20.6
Federal Government	13.2	12.8	10.5	10.3	11.1	11.2	14.2	17.3	17.1
State Government	41.5	45.6	45	40.3	35.5	35.6	27.1	22.7	21.8
Local Government	5.4	3.8	3.6	3.7	4.1	4	3.4	3.2	3.3
Private Gifts/Grants*	2.3	2.5	3.2	3.8	4.1	5.1	5.1	5	5.3
Sales and Services	18	19.6	20	22.7	22.2	21.7	16.6	16.9	18.2
Total Revenue (2010 Dollars)	*87.1*	*114.3*	*131.8*	*158.4*	*176.7*	*223.7*	*275.6*	*323.8*	*327.2*
Private Non-profit Higher Education									
Tuition & Fees	36.8	36.6	38.6	40.4	43	38.1	29	29	38.9
Federal Government	13.7	18.8	16.5	15.4	13.8	16.3	12.9	11.7	14.9
State Government	1.7	1.9	1.9	2.3	1.9	1.4	1	0.8	1.2
Local Government	0.8	0.7	0.7	0.7	0.7	0.6	0.3	0.2	0.0
Private Gifts/Grants*	10.4	9.3	9.3	8.6	9.1	19.3	12.2	10.7	13.4
Sales and Services	23.8	23.3	23.4	22.9	21	19.3	15.2	15.6	21.1

						2000	2005	2010	2011
Total Revenue (2010 Dollars)	46.7	59.3	71.8	91.6	106.6	104.1	170.5	207.2	166.9
Private For-profit Higher Education									
Tuition and fees						86.1	87.5	89.1	89.3
Federal government						4.6	6.5	5.6	5.7
State government						1.7	0.5	0.6	0.4
Local government									
Private gifts/grants*						0.1	0	0.1	0
Sales and services						3.6	2.2	1.9	1.9
Total revenue (2010 dollars)						5.4	14.1	28.2	27.7
Total revenue: all types of higher education (2010 dollars)	133.8	173.6	203.5	250.0	283.4	333.2	460.2	559.2	521.9

Source: NCES, Digest of Educational Statistics, 1974 (Table 82; Table 141), 1990, 1999, 2005, 2012.
Note: *Does not include endowment income.

Universities, wrote in a Huffington Post article entitled, 'Stopping the Privatization of American Higher Education':

> The American public higher education finance system is broken. States' disinvestment in higher education in recent decades has driven tuition prices ever higher, placing us at the precipice of a college affordability crisis. The federal government's investment in student aid is substantial, yet the productivity of these dollars is not maximized to make college affordable for all students attending the nation's public colleges and universities. The end results are decreasing college affordability, increasing student debt, and a quickening state-to-student cost shift in who pays for a public college education. (Hurley 2014)

Hurley is correct that tuition is rising as a percentage of the revenues of public higher education (from 14.5% of total revenues in 1985 to 18.6% in 2010) and that the contribution of state and local governments to public colleges and universities is falling (from 48.6% of revenues in 1985 to 26% in 2010, see Table 2.5). However, another part of public financing—from the federal government—increased from 10.5 to 17.3 per cent in 1985–2010, and another part of 'private' funds, namely, the sales of services by public universities, including the services of university hospitals, decreased from 20 to 17 per cent in that same period. If we include the small increase in the percentage of public institution revenues coming from private gifts as a 'private' contribution, the total 'public' contribution was 59 per cent in 1985 and 43 per cent in 2010, a significant decrease, but the 'private' contribution in public higher education only rose from 38 to 41 per cent. The unaccounted 13 per cent came from increases in public institutions' investment income and revenues from other educational activities.

The larger question is whether tuition represents the privatization of American higher education any more than charging for services in university-run hospitals is considered privatization (Carnoy et al. 2014). One view is that tuition in public higher education represents families and students' fairly sharing in the costs of providing a good such as higher education that not only may benefit society with considerable externalities, called social returns, but surely also benefits individual students economically in the form of private returns. The contrary view, as expressed by Hurley, implies that charging tuition substantially alters the 'public' nature of public higher education.

Table 2.5 Public Higher Education, Revenue/Full-time Student Growth Rate and Percentage of Revenue from Various Sources, 1995 and 2011

State	Revenue/ FT Student Growth Rate (%/year) 1995–2011	% Revenue from Tuition 1995	% Revenue from Tuition 2011	% Revenue from Federal Funding 1995	% Revenue from Federal Funding 2011	% Revenue from State and Local Funding 1995	% Revenue from State and Local Funding 2011	% Revenue from Sales and Services 1995	% Revenue from Sales and Services 2011
Alabama	1.94	14.8	21.0	11.5	9.3	32.4	22.7	31.8	26.2
Alaska	3.38	13.7	12.6	13.4	6.4	52.2	45.1	6.0	4.1
Arizona	1.36	21.8	28.6	13.8	10.7	46.2	31.5	9.0	6.2
Arkansas	1.32	13.7	11.8	8.4	8.0	39.2	26.0	31.3	30.0
California	2.41	13.2	14.0	9.8	8.8	46.9	28.6	18.2	20.1
Colorado	2.39	27.5	31.2	18.7	17.3	29.3	12.2	13.1	17.7
Connecticut	1.89	20.8	19.0	6.9	5.6	41.2	31.8	23.6	18.0
Delaware	1.79	34.8	37.3	9.4	12.8	30.5	23.2	13.7	11.4
D.C.	3.94	12.1	16.2	6.5	8.3	71.8	47.6	0.6	0.2
Florida	1.11	17.0	19.7	9.6	10.2	54.1	37.4	9.2	7.3
Georgia	0.64	15.4	23.2	9.8	10.1	49.5	31.0	17.5	13.0
Hawaii	3.49	11.9	15.0	20.2	21.9	52.1	27.6	9.9	5.5

(Continued)

Table 2.5 (Continued)

State	Revenue/ FT Student Growth Rate (%/year) 1995–2011	% Revenue from Tuition		% Revenue from Federal Funding		% Revenue from State and Local Funding		% Revenue from Sales and Services	
		1995	2011	1995	2011	1995	2011	1995	2011
Idaho	1.38	17.4	25.2	12.2	9.4	47.2	29.7	11.5	9.5
Illinois	3.05	18.1	20.3	9.2	7.5	44.6	27.4	16.0	13.3
Indiana	0.57	24.8	32.4	8.6	9.2	36.5	25.5	17.9	11.0
Iowa	1.06	14.6	16.8	13.1	11.5	31.7	19.2	30.0	35.6
Kansas	1.13	17.4	22.8	8.7	11.1	42.6	34.4	20.3	9.3
Kentucky	1.81	17.1	18.5	6.9	8.5	40.0	23.9	21.1	26.9
Louisiana	0.98	19.3	19.8	7.1	8.3	38.3	34.7	19.4	15.7
Maine	1.06	23.9	23.5	9.2	7.3	42.8	35.2	12.7	10.0
Maryland	2.15	25.1	24.3	11.8	12.3	41.9	33.5	11.9	10.2
Massachusetts	2.54	29.5	25.5	9.1	8.8	43.5	27.7	11.2	9.2
Michigan	1.26	23.0	26.8	10.3	11.0	31.1	18.3	24.8	27.6
Minnesota	–0.05	17.4	25.0	10.4	10.2	35.8	28.6	22.9	11.8
Mississippi	1.72	14.8	13.7	10.8	9.6	43.8	29.3	23.9	24.2

Missouri	0.69	22.9	21.6	5.9	5.6	38.0	24.7	20.6	29.4
Montana	2.19	23.4	27.4	17.2	17.1	32.9	23.1	13.8	10.0
Nebraska	0.96	12.5	17.2	10.9	10.5	37.3	39.1	30.8	13.3
Nevada	0.33	16.6	24.6	11.2	10.4	51.0	39.1	8.9	6.7
New Hampshire	1.60	39.6	39.5	9.4	7.0	21.8	15.4	19.6	21.1
New Jersey	0.79	21.5	27.7	6.3	6.8	43.0	28.7	19.9	20.6
New Mexico	0.59	8.6	8.5	18.1	12.0	37.4	29.9	23.0	23.3
New York	1.52	23.3	15.4	7.5	5.1	45.0	38.8	17.7	21.6
North Carolina	1.68	11.5	15.0	11.7	8.0	50.1	38.0	18.1	13.9
North Dakota	2.38	20.6	24.7	17.1	14.7	32.5	30.3	15.4	10.1
Ohio	1.70	27.4	28.1	6.6	6.5	34.7	20.7	21.5	30.1
Oklahoma	3.14	16.4	19.1	14.9	6.7	45.1	30.7	15.7	13.0
Oregon	1.82	17.9	19.6	13.5	11.8	30.6	16.9	25.9	33.2
Pennsylvania	1.76	28.1	31.8	10.2	10.8	26.0	13.5	25.5	28.1
Rhode Island	1.67	32.5	33.8	12.4	11.2	36.0	23.0	13.5	13.2
South Carolina	0.08	18.7	32.1	9.1	10.2	35.2	21.9	30.0	9.8

(Continued)

Table 2.5 (Continued)

State	Revenue/ FT Student Growth Rate (%/year) 1995–2011	% Revenue from Tuition		% Revenue from Federal Funding		% Revenue from State and Local Funding		% Revenue from Sales and Services	
		1995	2011	1995	2011	1995	2011	1995	2011
South Dakota	2.13	24.3	26.8	12.9	15.6	41.5	25.3	10.1	8.3
Tennessee	0.68	15.8	23.1	8.2	7.7	42.9	29.4	23.1	7.0
Texas	2.72	15.1	15.4	10.2	6.9	47.6	28.2	9.7	10.5
Utah	2.93	13.2	13.4	12.6	8.6	31.5	16.3	25.8	29.2
Vermont	1.01	43.6	45.8	11.9	16.8	14.2	14.7	11.4	13.4
Virginia	1.38	21.6	25.0	8.4	9.2	26.0	17.9	35.6	25.4
Washington	1.85	17.8	21.0	16.3	16.8	35.1	22.1	20.2	21.1
West Virginia	2.23	24.2	26.9	9.9	7.6	47.1	32.0	11.5	11.5
Wisconsin	1.11	17.8	20.2	11.6	11.1	39.5	33.8	17.5	7.5
Wyoming	3.05	14.1	9.8	11.5	5.6	49.4	54.9	13.2	7.4

Source: NCES, *Digest of Educational Statistics*, 2015, Table 330.10.

What many analysts miss is that the main 'privatization' of the US higher education system is the gradual increase in the share of total enrolment and higher education revenues going to private institutions. Public institutions received 63.4 per cent of all higher education revenues in 1985, but, by 2010, it was only 58 per cent and falling steadily. Almost all of this decrease is due to the growth of private, for-profit institutions. By 2010, for-profits took in about 11 per cent of all revenues going to private institutions. At the same time, the public funding of private non-profit institutions has fallen, just as it has in the public institutions. Thus, private institutions are becoming more 'private', since they have less public money shaping their agenda, and because they are gradually becoming more driven by profits rather than some loftier ideal of public service. Figure 2.6 shows the decline in the share of public funding among types of higher education institutions.

Varying Financing Trends by State

These trends towards privatization and in the way states finance public higher education institutions vary greatly from state to state. We analysed the change in the private/public composition of higher education enrolment among states in the previous section (see Table 2.2). We now turn to changes in revenue composition in public institutions and focus specifically on a recent period, 1995–2011, when these trends were pronounced. Table 2.5 shows the great variation among states in the growth rate of real (in 2010 dollars) revenues per student and the percentage of revenue coming from tuition, federal funding, state and local funding and the sales of goods and services (including by university hospitals) by higher education institutions.

States producing large amounts of petroleum, such as Alaska, Louisiana, North Dakota, Oklahoma, Texas and Wyoming, generally had much greater than average increases in public higher education revenue per full-time student in this period. Louisiana is a notable exception. States with conservative legislatures also tended to be characterized by lower increases in revenue per student, although there seems to be little relation of the political party in control of the state legislature to the degree of reduction of the state and local fraction of total revenue. The fraction of revenues coming from federal funding

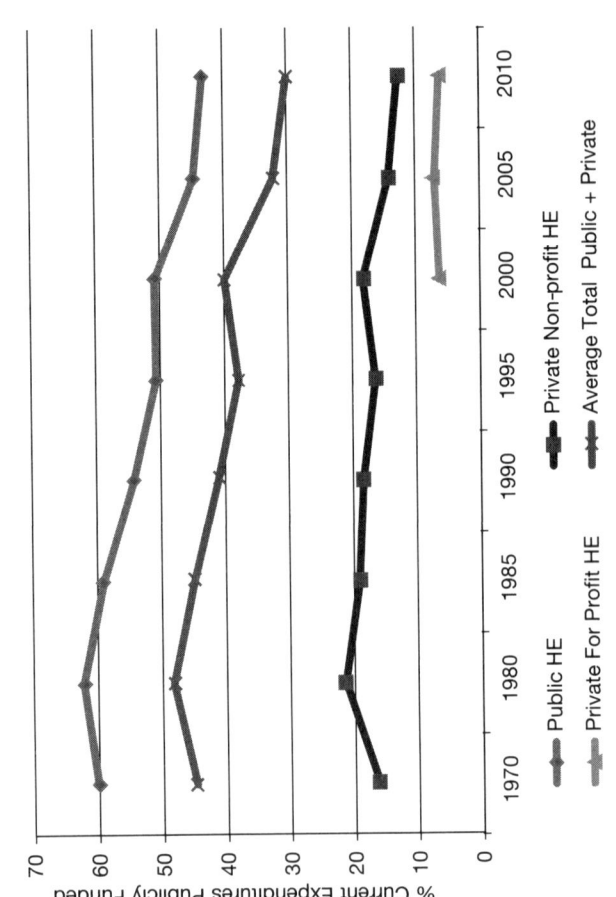

Figure 2.6 *Proportion of Current Higher Education Spending Publicly Funded, by Type of Institution, 1970–2010 (%)*
Source: National Center of Educational Statistics, *Digest of Educational Statistics*, various years, Tables 401, 405, 407 (2012).

Table 2.6 *Public Higher Education Ranking of States by Percentage of Revenue from Various Sources in 1995*

% Revenue from Tuition			% Revenue from Federal Govt.			% Revenue from State and Local Govt.		
State	1995	2011	State	1995	2011	State	1995	2011
Vermont	43.6	45.8	Hawaii	20.2	21.9	DC	71.8	47.6
New Hampshire	39.6	39.5	Colorado	18.7	17.3	Florida	54.1	37.4
Delaware	34.8	37.3	New Mexico	18.1	12.0	Alaska	52.2	45.1
Rhode Island	32.5	33.8	Montana	17.2	17.1	Hawaii	52.1	27.6
Massachusetts	29.5	25.5	North Dakota	17.1	14.7	Nevada	51.0	39.1
Pennsylvania	28.1	31.8	Washington	16.3	16.8	North Carolina	50.1	38.0
Colorado	27.5	31.2	Oklahoma	14.9	6.7	Georgia	49.5	31.0
Ohio	27.4	28.1	Arizona	13.8	10.7	Wyoming	49.4	54.9
Maryland	25.1	24.3	Oregon	13.5	11.8	Texas	47.6	28.2
Indiana	24.8	32.4	Alaska	13.4	6.4	Idaho	47.2	29.7
South Dakota	24.3	26.8	Iowa	13.1	11.5	West Virginia	47.1	32.0
West Virginia	24.2	26.9	South Dakota	12.9	15.6	California	46.9	28.6
Maine	23.9	23.5	Utah	12.6	8.6	Arizona	46.2	31.5
Montana	23.4	27.4	Rhode Island	12.4	11.2	Oklahoma	45.1	30.7
New York	23.3	15.4	Idaho	12.2	9.4	New York	45.0	38.8

(Continued)

Table 2.6 (Continued)

% Revenue from Tuition			% Revenue from Federal Govt.			% Revenue from State and Local Govt.		
State	1995	2011	State	1995	2011	State	1995	2011
Michigan	23.0	26.8	Vermont	11.9	16.8	Illinois	44.6	27.4
Missouri	22.9	21.6	Maryland	11.8	12.3	Mississippi	43.8	29.3
Arizona	21.8	28.6	North Carolina	11.7	8.0	Massachusetts	43.5	27.7
Virginia	21.6	25.0	Wisconsin	11.6	11.1	New Jersey	43.0	28.7
New Jersey	21.5	27.7	Alabama	11.5	9.3	Tennessee	42.9	29.4
Connecticut	20.8	19.0	Wyoming	11.5	5.6	Maine	42.8	35.2
North Dakota	20.6	24.7	Nevada	11.2	10.4	Kansas	42.6	34.4
Louisiana	19.3	19.8	Nebraska	10.9	10.5	Maryland	41.9	33.5
South Carolina	18.7	32.1	Mississippi	10.8	9.6	South Dakota	41.5	25.3
Illinois	18.1	20.3	Minnesota	10.4	10.2	Connecticut	41.2	31.8
Oregon	17.9	19.6	Michigan	10.3	11.0	Kentucky	40.0	23.9
Wisconsin	17.8	20.2	Texas	10.2	6.9	Wisconsin	39.5	33.8
Washington	17.8	21.0	Pennsylvania	10.2	10.8	Arkansas	39.2	26.0
Idaho	17.4	25.2	West Virginia	9.9	7.6	Louisiana	38.3	34.7
Kansas	17.4	22.8	Georgia	9.8	10.1	Missouri	38.0	24.7
Minnesota	17.4	25.0	California	9.8	8.8	New Mexico	37.4	29.9
Kentucky	17.1	18.5	Florida	9.6	10.2	Nebraska	37.3	39.1

State			State			State		
Florida	17.0	19.7	New Hampshire	9.4	7.0	Indiana	36.5	25.5
Nevada	16.6	24.6	Delaware	9.4	12.8	Rhode Island	36.0	23.0
Oklahoma	16.4	19.1	Maine	9.2	7.3	Minnesota	35.8	28.6
Tennessee	15.8	23.1	Illinois	9.2	7.5	South Carolina	35.2	21.9
Georgia	15.4	23.2	Massachusetts	9.1	8.8	Washington	35.1	22.1
Texas	15.1	15.4	South Carolina	9.1	10.2	Ohio	34.7	20.7
Alabama	14.8	21.0	Kansas	8.7	11.1	Montana	32.9	23.1
Mississippi	14.8	13.7	Indiana	8.6	9.2	North Dakota	32.5	30.3
Iowa	14.6	16.8	Virginia	8.4	9.2	Alabama	32.4	22.7
Wyoming	14.1	9.8	Arkansas	8.4	8.0	Iowa	31.7	19.2
Arkansas	13.7	11.8	Tennessee	8.2	7.7	Utah	31.5	16.3
Alaska	13.7	12.6	New York	7.5	5.1	Michigan	31.1	18.3
Utah	13.2	13.4	Louisiana	7.1	8.3	Oregon	30.6	16.9
California	13.2	14.0	Connecticut	6.9	5.6	Delaware	30.5	23.2
Nebraska	12.5	17.2	Kentucky	6.9	8.5	Colorado	29.3	12.2
D.C.	12.1	16.2	Ohio	6.6	6.5	Pennsylvania	26.0	13.5
Hawaii	11.9	15.0	D.C.	6.5	8.3	Virginia	26.0	17.9
North Carolina	11.5	15.0	New Jersey	6.3	6.8	New Hampshire	21.8	15.4
New Mexico	8.6	8.5	Missouri	5.9	5.6	Vermont	14.2	14.7

Source: NCES, Digest of Educational Statistics, 1999 and 2011.

also varies greatly from state to state—probably the single most important variable related to the intensity of federal funding is the percentage of students attending public four-year institutions since these are much more likely to get federal funding than two-year institutions.

One interesting relation is the fairly high (–0.4) negative correlation between the increase in the percentage of total revenue in public institutions coming from tuition and the rate of annual growth of revenue per student. This means that the greater the observed increase of revenues per student in this period, the smaller the increase in percentage of revenues derived from student tuition payments. Does that mean that the more public higher education institutions in a state came to rely over this period on tuition for its revenues, the smaller the annual increase in revenues per student? The opposite may also be true: the slower the increase in revenues per student in public institutions, the more the state had to rely on tuition to cover these increases.

Table 2.6 shows these changes from a different perspective. For each set of funding sources, we rank states by the percentage that source represented in the initial period (1995) for the state's higher education revenue stream. A few North-eastern states collect a relatively high fraction of revenues for public higher education from tuition, but the single best correlate of the proportion a state collects for public higher education from tuition is the percentage of higher education enrolment in two-year institutions. The higher that percentage, the lower the proportion of revenues the state collects from tuition ($\rho=-0.43$).

It is more difficult to explain why some states have a much higher proportion of federal spending, although if we studied the proportion of students attending the flagship state university or universities in each state, this might be an important factor. The flagship universities receive most of the federal funding for higher education in each state. In 2010, 57 per cent of federal funding to higher education went to 120 institutions (Snyder and Dillow 2013, Table 409). In 1995, 74 per cent have gone to 120 institutions (Snyder and Hoffman 2000, Table 341). If a public institution in a state receives a large amount of federal funding, such as, for example, the University of Washington in Seattle ($1.4 billion in 2010; $381 million in 1995), this has an enormous impact on the revenue stream for higher education in that state.

An interesting question is whether some states get more federal funding for higher education than other states because of closer relations between the federal government and some states than others. When we correlate the percentage of federal funding in university revenues across states in 1995 and 2011 (Table 2.6) with whether a state is dominated by Republicans (1) or Democrats (0) in those years, we found very low correlation coefficients both in 1995 ($\rho=0.14$) and 2011 ($\rho=-0.18$).[6] The political affiliation of the state (both in 1995 and in 2011, the federal House of Representatives was controlled by Republicans, but the Senate and the Presidency, by Democrats) had little if any influence on the proportion of federal funding to universities.

The drastic cuts in state and local participation in the funding of public institutions is a feature of the changes in higher education financing across states regardless of whether they had high percentages of state and local funding in 1995 or not. Only two states did not reduce the fraction of funding coming from state/local sources—Wyoming, starting at a very high level of state funding and an oil-rich state, and Vermont, where the state only got 14 per cent of its higher education funding from state and local sources even in 1995. Two other oil states—Alaska and Louisiana—also took small reductions in state funding in 1995–2011, and, a few other states, such as New York, saw relatively small decreases.

Although the federal government provides substantial resources to higher education via financial aid and research funding, the relationships and patterns evident in state funding suggest that local policy contexts are consequential for the development of state systems of higher education. Since rising tuition charged in both public and private institutions is a major political issue in the United States and a likely source of pressure on the US public higher education system to change its financing in the next decade, this variation in tuition increases in state public systems is important for our discussion of future trends in the next section of the chapter.

---

[6] The issue is somewhat complicated because some Southern states were still controlled by conservative Democrats in 1995, so could be considered 'blue states'. When we used state vote for President in 1996, the correlation coefficient was very low and negative ($\rho=-0.02$), meaning that public universities in Republican states got about the same proportion of their funding from the federal government.

HARBINGERS OF FUTURE FEDERAL INVOLVEMENT

The highly decentralized governance of American higher education has been the defining characteristic of its development since the founding of the Republic. Relative to most other countries in the world, American higher education enjoys strong state and institutional autonomy in its design and functioning. It is commonly viewed as a social institution, an institution serving society by providing 'a broader range of social functions that include such essential educational legacies as the cultivation of citizenship, the preservation of cultural heritage(s), and the formation of individual character and habits of mind' (Gumport 2000, 71). As we discussed earlier in this chapter, such institutional autonomy is reflected in the governance structures of public colleges and universities. Nevertheless, federal policy has been a continuous presence in its development, exemplified by policies, such as the Hatch Act, the Morrill Land-Grant Acts, the GI. Bill, the National Defense Act and the Higher Education Acts of 1965 and 1972. As Trow (1993) has noted, the broad effect of federal higher education policy has been to develop a competitive market in higher education characterized by relatively weak centralized authority and an absence of a strict regulatory approach. The federal role has been instrumental in the growth and development of the system but, as we have described, a rather light hand has allowed student and industrial demand as well as entrepreneurial-like institutional development to shape the system. In contrast, the state role has increased over time, particularly in the last 50 years, as the governance vacuum created by the weak federal role was filled by state government legislation, execution and coordination. Yet, we see signs of an evolving federal role, driven by a number of trends illustrated in this chapter. These trends raise possibilities for change in the traditionally decentralized higher education system, although history has illustrated reluctance of higher education institutions and states with regard to regulation and control.

Major Trends

We have discussed six major trends in US higher education:

- *Growing minority enrolments and stratification.* While racial/ethnic minority populations are fuelling rising enrolments, participation is highly stratified with the fastest growing group, Hispanics, clustered in public two-year institutions.

- *Growth of the for-profit sector.* Enrolments in for-profit private institutions are increasingly rapidly, particularly among four-year institutions, a sector that was relatively non-existent prior to the year 2000. Thus, although the public sector is also growing rapidly, the explosion of private for-profit (online) universities suggest a new trend towards increased privatization of higher education.

- *Rising costs in the face of continued high demand.* Demand for higher education remains high as the incomes of high school graduates continue to fall in real terms and the rate of return to higher education remains high. A confluence of increasing enrolments and rising spending per student has occurred amid declining state appropriations. On the other hand, the federal share of funding both public and private institutions is increasing. Despite this, the public share of higher education funding is steadily declining.

- *Increasing cost sharing in public institutions.* In addition to the rapid growth of private, for-profit institutions, public institutions are increasing private cost sharing through tuition to compensate for rising costs combined with a declining share of state public funding. In addition, even as scholarship grants for student financial aid are increasing, proportionally student financial aid is shifting towards loans and tax credits, representing yet another form of decreasing the direct public financing of higher education. With this shift, the federal government has been cast in the role of public banker for both public and private higher education, in effect greatly increasing private indebtedness and also increasing federal relative to state political responsibility for higher education expansion.

- *Internationalization of enrolment.* From a student perspective, American higher education is increasingly an international enterprise. Although the proportion of international students at undergraduate level has not increased despite rapid increases in the absolute number of undergraduate international students, the proportion of international graduate students continues to increase. More than one-third (36.6%) of MA graduates and almost 70 per cent of PhD graduates from United States in STEM fields are now international (NSF 2014, Appendix Tables 2–30 and 2–31), with a high proportion from China and India—27 per cent and 12 per cent of PhD graduates from those two countries in 1991–2011 (NSF 2014, Table 2–13).

- *Increasingly competitive global environment.* From another perspective, the explosion of higher education enrolment internationally in developing countries and the increasing proportion of the labour force with university degrees in developed countries is putting increased political pressure on US institutions to expand four-year college enrolment and particularly to improve its graduation rate. Politicians are casting the need for more labour with university degrees as crucial for US economic competitiveness.

Potential for Federal Involvement

Separately and in conjunction, these trends will demand federal attention. The nature of that attention, of course, depends in part on states' responses to the demands indicated by these trends. For instance, rising costs and privatization may reach a politically unstable point as many states begin to experience consequential decreases in access. If enough states are unable to remedy threats to access on their own, a federal solution may be initiated. The federal response, whether through student financial aid, state block grants or institutional aid, will be somewhat unprecedented. The government has historically acted to foster development and growth in the system, relatively unfettered by regulation. A heavier hand may be prescribed if the conditions dictate the creation of a safety net to prop up the system in the face of stagnation or worse, regression. Relative to its history, the federal government will be in a unique position under these conditions and, if acted upon, may signify a new approach to federal policy.

The for-profit sector presents a unique challenge to federal regulation of education. It is a relatively new institutional form, but it has already captured the attention of the federal government. In 2010, concern over the poor graduation, job placement and student loan default rates of for-profit institutions—who were then receiving revenues of over $32 billion in federal loan and grant aid—led to the development of so-called 'gainful employment' regulations by the Department of Education. These regulations set strict criteria aimed at the for-profit sector regarding eligibility to receive federal student aid. The regulations proposed the use of indicators such as students' loan repayment rates and debt-to-income ratios in high-stakes accountability fashion (the loss of federal funds). This relatively rare approach to policy-making may signal openness to a new era in federal higher education policy.

Rising costs and increased cost sharing further place the federal government in a position of great leverage. Almost 70 per cent of bachelor's degree graduates retain student loan debt, and the total amount of loan debt among all students hovers around $1.2 trillion (Denhart 2013). The vast majority of that debt is held by the federal government and produces a substantial net profit (negative subsidy) if students do not default. On the other hand, the sheer size of the debt also makes loan forgiveness a viable tool for economic stimulus. With increasing concern over rising student loan debt and relatedly, gainful employment, the government is in position to pursue further federal oversight and accountability measures. The federal government has yet to venture into high-stakes accountability policy in higher education, however, and given historical decentralization, may be unable to pursue such a path.

Nevertheless, high-stakes accountability approaches are not new in federal policy-making, as the current legislation for federal K-12 funding, 'No Child Left Behind' or NCLB requires districts to use student test scores to monitor school improvement and ultimately to restructure or close schools that are not meeting test score improvement standards. The current administration, in fact, has been seeking to tie all federal financial aid programmes to performance on a 'college scorecard', a rating system on affordability, student completion rates and the earnings of graduates. Public demand for accountability is reaching the tertiary education level. States that still fund a relatively high percentage of public higher education, such as Alaska, Nebraska, Nevada and Wyoming, clearly have much more leverage to impose accountability requirements on their universities and colleges than states where state funding represents only a small fraction of higher education revenues, such as Colorado, New Hampshire and Vermont. Part of the impetus for the accountability features of NCLB was the recognition of disparate educational outcomes by race in the K-12 sector. Continuing stratification and disparate outcomes by race at the tertiary level, particularly as racial minorities project to become the majority among school-age children in 2020, may also invite federal involvement.

Whether the pressure for greater accountability pushes states to begin to measure 'value added' in universities as well as to monitor graduation rates and use of funding or the federal government itself institutes testing in higher education, the growing gap between increasing costs per student in public higher education and the availability of public funding will continue to feed demands that public higher education institutions show that their cost increases are associated with increasing quality.

Finally, internationalization promises that the American higher education enterprise is no longer solely a domestic issue and certainly not one without an international audience observing its development and performance. In the current era of retrenchment of state funding, many American public universities are actively seeking international student enrolments paying higher out-of-state tuition as important additional revenue streams to their operating budgets. However, given their behaviour regarding out-of-state students more generally (Rizzo and Ehrenberg 2003), this is less likely in state 'flagship' universities, where the demand from international students for places is greatest but the political pressure from taxpayers in the state to restrict out-of-state enrolment is also the greatest. The growing popularity and legitimacy of international rankings, such as the Times Higher Education rankings in the United Kingdom and the Shanghai Ranking, are indicators of international attention to American higher education institutions that dominate the rankings. At the same time, the United States rank in tertiary educational attainment rates among young adults dropped from second among OECD countries in 2000 to 12th in 2012, a statistic that is widely quoted domestically as evidence of the diminishing performance of the American higher education system. Each of these examples suggests that domestic education policy will increasingly be considered in an international context, which may invite greater federal direction.

REFERENCES

Bennett, M. J. 1996. *When Dreams Came True: The GI Bill and the Making of Modern America*. McLean, VA: Brassey's.

Bloch, E. 1989. *Science and Technology in the Academic Enterprise: Status, Trends, and Issues*. Washington, DC: National Academy Press.

Breneman, D. W., and Lingenfelter, P. E. 2012. 'The California Master Plan: Influential Beyond State Borders?' In *Clark Kerr's World of Higher Education*

Reaches the 21st Century, edited by S. Rothblatt, 85–106. Rotterdam: Springer Netherlands.

Brint, S., and Karabel, J. 1989. *The Diverted Dream: Community Colleges and the Promise of Educational Opportunity in America, 1900–1985*. New York, NY: Oxford University Press. Available at http://eric.ed.gov/?id=ED309827

Carnegie Council on Policy Studies. 1976. *The States and Higher Education: A Proud Past and a Vital Future*. San Francisco: Jossey-Bass.

Carnoy, M. 1998. 'The Globalization of Innovation, Nationalist Competition, and the Internationalization of Scientific Training'. *Competition and Change* 3 (2): 237–262.

———. 2010. 'California's Impending College Graduate Crisis and What Needs to be Done About it (Policy Brief No. 10-2)'. *Policy Analysis for California Education*. Available at http://eric.ed.gov/?id=ED510163

———. 2014. 'The Globalization of Innovation and the Internationalization of Scientific Training in the Information Age: Implications for National Development'. Presented at the High Level Forum on University as Source of Innovation and Economic Development, Stanford Center at Peking University, Beijing, China.

Carnoy, M., Froumin, I., Loyalka, P. K., and Tilak, J. B. G. 2014. 'The Concept of Public Goods, the State, and Higher Education Finance: A View from the BRICs'. *Higher Education* 68 (3): 359–378.

Clotfelter, C. T. 1991. 'Financial Aid and Public Policy'. In *Economic Challenges in Higher Education*, 89–123. University of Chicago Press.

Cohen, A. M. 1998. *The Shaping of American Higher Education: Emergence and Growth of the Contemporary System*. New York: John Wiley & Sons.

Cooke, T., and Boyle, P. 2011. 'The Migration of High School Graduates to College'. *Educational Evaluation and Policy Analysis* 33 (2): 202–213.

Denhart, C. 7 August 2013. 'How the $1.2 Trillion College Debt Crisis is Crippling Students, Parents and the Economy'. Available at http://www.forbes.com/sites/specialfeatures/2013/08/07/how–the–college–debt–is–crippling–students–parents–and–the–economy/#6d1e04dc1a41

Education Commission of the States. 2015. *A Brief History of the Education Commission of the States*. Available at http://www.ecs.org/html/aboutECS/ECShistory.htm

Fleming, J. 1985. *Blacks in College. A Comparative Study of Students' Success in Black and in White Institutions*. San Francisco, CA: Jossey-Bass Inc., Publishers.

Gilbert, C. K., and Heller, D. E. 2013. 'Access, Equity, and Community Colleges: The Truman Commission and Federal Higher Education Policy from 1947 to 2011'. *The Journal of Higher Education* 84 (3): 417–443.

Gumport, P. J. 2000. 'Academic Restructuring: Organizational Change and Institutional Imperatives'. *Higher Education: The International Journal of Higher Education and Educational Planning* 39: 67–91.

———. 2011. 'Graduate Education and Research: Axes of Interdependence and Strain'. In *American Higher Education in the Twenty-first Century: Social, Political, and Economic Challenges,* 3rd edition, edited by P. G. Altbach, P. J. Gumport, and R. O. Berdahl, 398–426. Baltimore, MD: Johns Hopkins University Press.

Heller, D. E. 2002. 'Federal Funds for Higher Education'. In *Encyclopedia of Education.* Available at http://www.encyclopedia.com/doc/1G2-3403200241.html

Hoffman, C. M., Snyder, T. D., and Sonnenberg, B. 1996. *Historically Black Colleges and Universities, 1976 to 1994* (NCES Publication No. 96902). Washington, DC: US Department of Education.

Hurley, D. J. 2014. 'Stopping the Privatization of American Public Higher Education'. Available at http://social.huffingtonpost.com/daniel-j-hurley/stopping-the-privatizatio_b_4617230.html

Kerr, C. 1963. *The Uses of the University.* Cambridge, MA: Harvard University Press.

Lauerman, J. 2010a. 'For-profit Colleges Misled Students, Witnesses Say'. *Bloomberg.* Available at http://www.bloomberg.com/news/articles/2010-08-04/for-profit-colleges-boiler-room-recruiting-described-at-senate-hearing

———. 2010b. 'For-profit Colleges Charging More While Doing Less for Low-income Families'. *Bloomberg.* Available at http://www.bloomberg.com/news/articles/2010-12-31/for-profit-colleges-charging-more-while-doing-less-for-low-income-families

Mak, J., and Moncur, J. 2003. 'Interstate Migration of College Freshman'. *Annals of Regional Science* 37: 603–612.

McDonnell, L. M. 2005. 'No Child Left Behind and the Federal Role in Education: Evolution or revolution?' *Peabody Journal of Education* 80 (2): 19–38.

McGuinness, A. C. 2003. *Models of Postsecondary Education Coordination and Governance in the States.* Denver, CO: Education Commission of the States. Available at http://www.psu.edu/ufs/about_senate/committees/univ-gov/modelsofpostsecondarygovernance.pdf

Richardson, R. C., Bracco, K. R., Callan, P. M., and Finney, J. E. 1998. *Designing State Higher Education Systems for a New Century.* Phoenix, AZ: Oryx Press. Available at http://eric.ed.gov/?id=ED425679

Rizzo, M. J., and Ehrenberg, R. G. 2003. 'Resident and Non-resident Tuition and Enrollment at Flagship State Universities'. Working Paper No. 9516, National Bureau of Economic Research, Cambridge, MA. Retrieved from http://www.nber.org/papers/w9516

Schmidt, P. 2013. 'Supreme Court Puts off Big Legal Questions in Texas Affirmative-Action Case'. *The Chronicle of Higher Education* June 24. Available at http://chronicle.com.libweb.lib.utsa.edu/article/Supreme-Court-Puts-Off-Big/139991/

Snyder, T. D., and Dillow, S. A. 2013. *Digest of Education Statistics 2012.* National Center for Education Statistics. Available at https://nces.ed.gov/pubsearch/pubsinfo.asp?pubid=2014015

Snyder, T. D., and Hoffman, C. M. 2000. *Digest of Education Statistics 1999*. National Center for Education Statistics. Available at https://nces.ed.gov/pubsearch/pubsinfo.asp?pubid=2000031

———. 2003. *Digest of Education Statistics 2002*. National Center for Education Statistics. Available at https://nces.ed.gov/pubsearch/pubsinfo.asp?pubid=2003060

State Higher Education Executive Officers Association. 2012. About SHEEO. Available at http://www.sheeo.org/about

St. John, E. P. 2003. *Refinancing the College Dream: Access, Equal Opportunity, and Justice for Taxpayers*. Baltimore, MD: Johns Hopkins University Press.

Stefkovich, J. A., and Leas, T. 1994. 'A Legal History of Desegregation in Higher Education'. *The Journal of Negro Education* 63 (3): 406–420.

Thelin, J. R. 2011. *A History of American Higher Education*, 2nd edition. Baltimore, MD: Johns Hopkins University Press.

Thelin, J. R., and Gasman, M. 2010. 'Historical Overview of American Higher Education'. In *Student Services: A Handbook for the Profession*, 5th edition, edited by J. H. Schuh, S. R. Jones, and S. R. Harper, 3–23. San Francisco, CA: Jossey-Bass.

Trow, M. 1991. 'Origins and Development of Federalism in American Higher Education'. In *Higher Education in Federal Systems*, edited by D. Brown, P. Cazalis, and G. Jasmin, 69–94. Kingston, Ontario: Queens University, Institute of Intergovernmental Relation.

———. 1993. 'Federalism in American Higher Education'. In *Higher Learning in America, 1980–2000*, edited by A. Levine, 39–65. Baltimore, MD: Johns Hopkins University Press.

Chapter 3

Canada
Provincial Responsibility, Federal Influence and the Challenge of Coordination

Glen A. Jones and Christian Noumi

The analysis of higher education policy in Canada is inseparably linked to the realities of Canadian federalism and, in particular, the highly decentralized nature of higher education governance. Our objective in this chapter is to describe and analyse higher education in Canada by focusing attention on the divisions of responsibility between the federal and provincial governments that underscore this decentralized approach. We begin with a brief historical overview, followed by a more detailed analysis of governance, including issues of authority, policy, funding and student mobility.

HIGHER EDUCATION IN CANADA: AN OVERVIEW

The eastern territories of what would become Canada were colonized by two European powers. Given its quite small population, there was relatively little emphasis on higher education during the French colonial period, although the Séminaire de Québec, created in 1663, would come to be regarded as the first institution offering higher education in the region and would later evolve into Laval University (Harris 1976). With the Treaty of Paris in 1763, Britain obtained control of the French colonies in North America, although, in many ways, it was the American Revolution, and the movement north of tens of thousands of colonists loyal to the Crown following the defeat of the British armies, that provided the impetus for the emergence of the first institutions of higher education (Jones 1996, 2014). By the mid-nineteenth century, the remaining British colonies in North America could boast of a handful of colleges supported by colonial legislatures, and a somewhat larger number of denominational colleges supported by church organizations and tuition fees.

The Dominion of Canada was created in 1867 as a federation of colonies under the British North America Act. The constitutional arrangement divided responsibilities between two levels of government—a federal government, with responsibilities for major issues such as trade and defence, and provincial governments, with responsibilities for local issues such as education and hospitals. The creation of a national railroad provided a platform for the expansion of the western territories, and new provinces were created as other colonies joined the federation or new jurisdictions were carved out of the sparsely populated territories. The last province to join the federation was Newfoundland and Labrador in 1949. Canada currently has 10 provinces and 3 territories, and these jurisdictions vary dramatically in size and population, as illustrated in Table 3.1. Roughly 60 per cent of the Canadian population lives in only two provinces—Ontario and Quebec. The three northern territories, combined, represent roughly 35 per cent of the country in terms of landmass but have less than half of 1 per cent of the Canadian population.

Higher education in Canada received relatively little attention from governments until the twentieth century. The provincial governments had assumed responsibility for education under the constitutional arrangements, but their emphasis was on schooling, and higher education was composed of a small number of publicly supported universities and a larger number of private denominational colleges. Provincial government involvement in higher education was frequently limited to annual decisions on the level of grants that would be provided to the small number of publicly supported institutions. Four large western provinces had emerged following confederation and each decided to

Table 3.1 *Area, Population and Unemployment Rate of Canada's Provinces and Territories*

Province or Territory	Total Area (sq. km)[a]	% of Total Area	Canadian Population (1,000s)[b]	% of Canadian Population	Unemployment Rate % (2014)
Newfoundland and Labrador	405,212	4.06	526.7	1.5	11.4
Prince Edward Island	5,660	0.06	145.2	0.4	11.5
Nova Scotia	55,284	0.55	940.8	2.7	9
New Brunswick	72,908	0.73	756.1	2.2	10.4
Quebec	1,542,056	15.44	8,155.3	23.2	7.6
Ontario	1,076,395	10.78	13,538	38.5	7.5
Manitoba	647,797	6.49	1,265	3.6	5.4
Saskatchewan	651,036	6.52	1,108.3	3.2	4.0
Alberta	661,848	6.63	4,025.1	11.4	4.6
British Columbia	944,735	9.46	4582	13.0	6.6
Yukon Territory	482,443	4.83	36.7	0.1	4.3
Northwest Territory	1,346,106	13.48	43.5	0.1	7.1
Nunavut Territory	2,093,190	20.96	35.6	0.1	10.8
Canada	9,984,670	100	35,158.3	100	7.1

Sources: [a]Natural Resources Canada; [b]Statistics Canada (2013), CANSIM, Table 051–001, 2014 data.

create a single university that would serve the higher education needs of these new jurisdictions (Jones 1996).

It was World War II, and in particular the decision to provide higher education as a benefit to qualified veterans, that provided the impetus for the major expansion of the university sector and the emergence of higher education as a major area of public policy. The first phases of expansion were originally funded by the federal government, initially through the provision of veterans' benefits but later by agreeing to provide direct support to universities to sustain the continuing expansion of university places to meet increasing demands. While sympathetic to the goals of university expansion, the provinces of Quebec and Ontario were highly critical of federal involvement in an area of provincial responsibility. In response to these concerns, the federal government moved away from direct funding of universities and created a transfer mechanism that would provide funding to the provinces in support of higher education, a mechanism that was designed to support expansion while respecting provincial government authority and autonomy.

By the mid-1960s the provincial governments had assumed control of higher education policy and were moving towards the development of provincial systems through the relatively planned expansion of universities and university spaces, the creation of non-university postsecondary institutions to further expand access and serve the expanding technical and vocational needs of industry, and through the development of coordinating mechanisms, often advisory bodies that would provide governments with recommendations on policy, funding and regulation. The federal government contributed to university operating support through unconditional transfers to the provinces, but it also contributed directly to higher education through its support of university research, student financial assistance, the arts and a patchwork quilt of policy areas that intersected directly or indirectly with the work of universities.

By the early 1970s, the basic federal and provincial arrangements that continue to characterize higher education in Canada had emerged. Higher education policy was highly decentralized, with the provincial governments assuming the major role in the regulation and direct funding of institutions of higher education. Each province had expanded its university sector, but had also created new institutional types, commonly called colleges, that offered technical and vocational programmes (and, in some provinces, pre-university or university transfer programmes). The universities were largely autonomous and public in that they received the bulk of their funding from provincial operating grants. In the context of Canadian federalism, Canada's approach to higher education policy had become extremely decentralized, with the provinces playing the central role in terms of regulation, but with many of the most important decisions related to admissions, curriculum and strategic direction left in the hands of the individual universities. The system has high levels of access and, in comparative terms, high levels of government expenditure. Summary statistics on enrolment, expenditures and number of institutions by province are provided in Table 3.2.

THE GOVERNANCE OF HIGHER EDUCATION IN CANADA
Regulatory Aspects

Canada's approach to higher education policy is highly decentralized. There has been a long tradition of institutional autonomy, and provinces have generally left core academic decisions in the hands of individual institutions.

The regulatory role of the state in higher education

Universities are generally created as private, non-profit corporations with bicameral governance structures involving a governing board, often with a majority of members from outside the university, including government appointees and an academic senate, composed largely of faculty, students and academic administrators. The legislative Act creating the university also commonly delegates responsibility over the administrative affairs of the university to the board, including the appointment of a president,[1] and responsibility over academic matters

---

[1] Different terms, such as president, rector and principal, are used at different universities to denote the senior executive officer. While most university presidents are appointed by the board, usually on the recommendation of a search committee

Table 3.2 *Key Figures on Public Universities and Colleges in Canada*

	University Enrolment (2012)	College Enrolment (2012)	PSE Expenditures as % of GDP (2009)	Number of Public Universities	Number of Public Colleges	Universities in Shanghai 500 Ranking (2014)
Canada	1,263,747	727,983	2.8	76	126	22
Newfoundland and Labrador	18,417	9,774	2.6	1	3	0
Prince Edward Island	4,491	3,576	3.8	1	2	0
Nova Scotia	43,305	11,757	4	9	3	1
New Brunswick	23,250	8,382	3.1	7	3	0
Quebec	294,525	217,545	3	12	41	4
Ontario	495,906	287,289	2.8	20	25	9
Manitoba	44,769	16,212	2.5	6	5	1
Saskatchewan	33,276	20,103	2.5	3	11	1
Alberta	130,113	59,145	2.3	6	13	2
British Columbia	175,695	94,200	2.9	11	20	3

Source: Compiled by authors.

Note: Enrolment and expenditure data from Statistics Canada (2013).

to the senate (Jones 2002). These provincial acts of incorporation are usually unique to each institution, except in British Columbia and Alberta where universities operate under legislation that governs all universities, and each act specifies the unique governance structure of each institution.

Universities are relatively autonomous institutions created and regulated by the provinces. In addition to their role in creating universities, the regulatory role of the provincial governments has focused largely on issues of funding and accountability. Government operating grants and targeted funding mechanisms have become the foundation for the regulation and steering of the higher education system. Accountability mechanisms have largely focused on issues of funding and access. Generally speaking, the issue of quality has received quite modest attention within this regulatory environment, at least in comparison to many other nations, and most provinces assume that issues of quality and standards are best left in the hands of individual institutions or in the hands of the university sector as a collective (Weinrib and Jones 2014).

The role of provincial governments in the external governance of institutions

As we have already noted, the Canadian constitutional arrangement clearly assigns responsibility for education to the provinces and, while this is not uncommon in other federal systems, what is less common is the fact that the arrangement has largely limited the federal government's direct involvement in higher education as an explicit area of policy. There is no national minister, ministry or department of education for higher education and there is no national higher education policy. Higher education in Canada is best understood as the sum of 13 quite different and distinct provincial and territorial systems, each with its own, unique regulatory environment (Jones 1997).

The starting point, therefore, for understanding the external governance of higher education institutions in Canada is the recognition that

---

composed of board members, faculty, students and other constituencies, some rectors of Quebec universities are elected from within the university.

the locus of control over higher education policy rests with the regional (province/territory) government. Each province and territory has developed a higher education system designed to address the needs of the jurisdiction, and, while there are common, pan-Canadian themes, each provincial system is unique. There are important differences in terms of structure, institutional types, regulation, funding and fees (Fisher et al. 2014); these differences are reviewed in more detail here.

Since education and higher education are the responsibilities of the provinces and territories, the national body representing government in these policy areas is not the Government of Canada, but the Council of Ministers of Education, Canada (CMEC). The CMEC is an umbrella organization composed of the ministers of education and higher education from each jurisdiction. The CMEC secretariat works on behalf of the ministers to facilitate the exchange of information, and develop common frameworks and collaborative initiatives. In terms of higher education, the Council has developed national indicators and a degree qualifications framework, but its role as a policy or coordinating agency has been relatively weak. Annual changes in leadership and the rapid turnover of provincial ministers and deputy ministers have done little to further the cause of sustained pan-Canadian coordination, and there are relatively few pressures on the provinces to move to a more common policy approach. Differences in the size, population and financial circumstances of the provinces and their higher education systems also mean that the policy challenges of Prince Edward Island (PEI) are dramatically different in scope and scale than the challenges of Ontario or Quebec. As Table 2.2 shows, provinces such as PEI and Newfoundland have just a fraction of the number of institutions and enrolment of the more populous jurisdictions such as Ontario or Quebec. In that regard, policies on issues such as funding and governance do not have the same scope across all provinces. Nevertheless, the CMEC provides a forum for a national conversation among policy leaders, but its role in supporting pan-Canadian or provincial policy development is quite modest (Jones 1996; Weinrib and Jones 2014).

At the level of the provincial government, the governance of the higher education system is the responsibility of the government ministry assigned responsibility for the sector. In some provinces, this is a distinct ministry with responsibility for advanced or higher education, while in others the responsibility is combined with the governance and oversight of the school system (i.e., a ministry with responsibility for all levels of education). While all provinces at one point experimented with intermediary advisory agencies, these agencies have largely been abandoned in favour of direct relationships between government and the sector. In the three Maritime Provinces (New Brunswick, Nova Scotia and Prince Edward Island), a regional intermediary body, the Maritime Provinces Higher Education Commission, provides advice to the three provincial governments and coordinates some elements of these three provincial systems. Ontario has recently created the Higher Education Quality Council of Ontario, which has a research function and provides the provincial government with advice on policy issues. Some other provinces have created specific agencies to deal with particular policy issues, such as facilitating student mobility within the provincial system, but most policy and regulatory issues are dealt with through direct relationships between governments and institutions.

Quality assessment of higher education, as a policy issue, provides an interesting example of decentralization in Canadian higher education. While CMEC has developed a national degree qualifications framework, there is no national quality assessment mechanism or institutional accreditation system. None of the provinces operates university accreditation systems, and quality assessment mechanisms have tended to focus on the review of degree programmes, especially those offered by less-established universities. In the two largest and most populace provinces—Ontario and Quebec—quality assessment is the responsibility of the university sector itself; the provincial university umbrella organizations have created a quality assessment mechanism of periodic reviews that generally respects and reinforces the importance of university autonomy over academic standards. In the absence of a national university accrediting mechanism, membership in the national association of universities, Universities Canada (the new name, as of 2015, for the Association of Universities and Colleges of Canada), has become a *de facto* form of national recognition or accreditation within the sector (Weinrib and Jones 2014).

The role of federal government in the external governance of higher education institutions

The fact that the provincial governments play the central role in terms of higher education policy does not mean that the federal government has little influence or governing authority; it simply means that the federal government's role is defined in terms of 'other' policy areas that directly intersect with universities and have come to be viewed as legitimate under the federal arrangements. These policy areas include research and innovation, student financial assistance, education of Canada's First Nations populations and internationalization, among others.

The federal government has played the dominant role in terms of public funding for research and innovation since the creation of the National Research Council following World War I, and this role has expanded in the twenty-first century as the government seeks to support knowledge creation and the development of highly skilled human resources as a means to further social and economic development in the context of globalization. Government funding for research is particularly important in the Canadian context because the level of business investment in research and development is lower than in most OECD nations, and so government policies position universities as major components of the national research and innovation system, and encourage increasing interaction and research collaboration between universities and industry (Jones and Weinrib 2011).

Federal government involvement in research is largely through the funding of national research granting councils (which provide competitive grants based on peer review), funding research chairs programmes (the Canada Research Chairs programme and the Canada Excellence Research Chairs programme) that support the recruitment and retention of leading university researchers, and through support of the Canadian Foundation for Innovation, which provides funding for research infrastructure. The magnitude of federal investments in university research and development means that the government can influence the direction of university research initiatives and while most funding decisions continue to be based on peer-review, funding priorities are often linked to areas of research viewed as strategically important and have a direct or indirect steering effect on the sector (Fisher et al. 2006; Jones and Weinrib 2011). A number of the provinces have also created modest funding mechanisms to support university research and innovation, in some cases as a mechanism to leverage increasing federal government funding, or to provide start-up funding for local researchers so that they will have greater opportunities for success within national research competitions. Federal and provincial research funding agencies tend to be loosely coupled with little national or pan-Canadian coordination and, in some cases, quite different or competing priorities (Jones and Oleksiyenko 2011; Jones and Young 2004).

In the area of student financial assistance, the Government of Canada funds the Canada Student Loans Program (CSLP), a national mechanism for providing need-based student loans and supporting access to higher education. While the federal government controls and regulates this national programme, it is effectively administered by the provinces as a component of provincial student financial assistance policy. Using the CSLP as a foundation, each province has developed need- and merit-based financial assistance programmes that are built on top of the national programme. Other forms of student financial assistance can be found in both federal and provincial income tax systems, where tax credits are provided for tuition, family savings for education are incentivized, etc. (Fisher et al. 2006).

In other policy areas, the boundaries between federal and provincial areas of responsibility are complex and frequently overlapping. While the Government of Canada has responsibility for the education of a subset of Canada's Aboriginal populations as defined under the constitution and federal legislation, the fact that higher education is regulated by the provinces means that both levels of government need to be involved in any holistic discussion of addressing the issue of accessibility to universities for this diverse, under-represented population. In the area of internationalization, while the federal government has now adopted an international education strategy, it is commonly understood that international student recruitment and broader internationalization strategies require federal-provincial government coordination, especially since the federal government has responsibility for foreign affairs, including the issuing of visas and the operation of embassies, while the provinces have direct responsibility for higher education (Trilokekar and Jones 2013; Trilokekar, Jones and Shubert 2009).

The role of the federal government in the governance of higher education in Canada can be seen as complex and multifaceted. The provinces play the central role in the coordination and funding of higher education, and they have developed distinctive higher education system arrangements in order to address provincial needs. There is no explicit federal government role in higher education, especially in the university sector, but the government is directly involved in a wide range of policy areas that are extremely important to higher education, such as research and innovation, student financial assistance and international education. In some of these areas, there is overlap between federal and provincial policy initiatives and interests, a complex matrix of relationships and initiatives that are sometimes complementary and sometimes competing or disjointed (Jones and Young 2004).

Structural Aspects

As we have noted, each province has created its own higher education system, and, while there are common policy approaches, there are important structural differences between systems. In general terms, each provincial system is composed of at least two sectors: a university sector and a sector involving at least one type of non-university, post-secondary institution.

The university sector

While there are certainly important differences by institution, the university sector is regarded as relatively homogeneous and based on a common institutional form. Universities have both research and teaching functions, and most have some combination of undergraduate, professional and graduate programmes. They have considerable autonomy over academic decisions, and similar governance structures.[2] Until quite recently, there was no explicit stratification or hierarchy

---

[2] One notable exception is the University of Quebec, which was created as a provincial, multi-campus university system. Governance of this system involves

within the university sector, but there is now some differentiation in institutional categories within the university sectors of British Columbia (through the emergence of teaching-focused universities) and Alberta (under the Postsecondary Learning Act, which establishes a series of institutional categories within the provincial system; see Jones 2009) and the top 15 research intensive universities have formed U15 and taken steps to position themselves as a distinctive subcategory of universities. However, almost all Canadian universities belong to the same national umbrella association (Universities Canada) and each university accepts other Canadian undergraduate degree programmes as equivalent to their own; there has been no need for graduate or undergraduate admissions tests (Weinrib and Jones 2014).

The college sector

In contrast, the colleges sector (the 'other' sector within provincial systems) is composed of quite different institutional types. In the development of provincial systems in the 1960s and 1970s, the provinces made quite different decisions on the new forms of institutions that would be needed to address local needs. The Quebec college sector emerged as a component part of broad social and political reforms associated with the 'quiet revolution' that shifted the role of the Roman Catholic Church, dramatically increased access, especially for a historically underserved francophone population and involved major reforms of the entire educational system. Under these educational reforms, students graduated from the school system following grade 11 and then proceeded to a college where they could take a two-year pre-university programme of study (required for admission to a Quebec university) or enrol in a three-year technical/vocational programme. British Columbia and Alberta developed community colleges that more closely resembled the American model, with a mandate to provide university transfer programmes (with credits accepted by provincial university) as well as technical/vocational diploma programmes (frequently one or two years in length). Ontario created colleges that were designed to operate in parallel with the university sector. The Ontario Colleges of Applied

two levels: the central University of Quebec, which has some responsibility for steering and coordination, and increasingly autonomous component campuses.

Arts and Technology were not assigned a transfer function, and so they were viewed as offering an alternative pathway for students who might not enter university, or whose interests were in technical/vocational or trades programmes that were not associate with the university sector.

While this book focuses primarily on the university sector, it is important to note that the term 'higher education' is viewed as synonymous with postsecondary or tertiary education in the Canadian context, and so provincial systems of higher education are viewed as including the wide range of educational programmes offered by both the university and college sectors; this encompasses everything from doctoral and postdoctoral educational initiatives to short-cycle vocational programmes and trade apprenticeships.

The university and college sectors are usually subject to quite different levels of provincial government regulation and accountability. Generally speaking, universities have high levels of autonomy, including considerable discretion over academic matters. While there are major differences in the nature and governance of the college sector by province, these institutions are generally more heavily regulated and viewed more as instruments of public policy than the universities.

While universities and colleges are created by the provinces, both the sectors also have national umbrella associations—Universities Canada and Colleges and Institutes, Canada—and are actively engaged with the federal government. There is also a national umbrella association of university faculty associations and unions—the Canadian Association of University Teachers—and several national student organizations. These organizations actively lobby the federal government and are frequently engaged in federal/pan-Canadian discussions of higher education, research funding (including, most recently, funding for applied research in the college sector), student access and financial assistance and other issues. These organizations also play an important role in public discussions of higher education policy, for example, through publications such as *University Affairs* (published by Universities Canada) and the *CAUT Bulletin*.

Finally, it is important to note that while higher education in Canada is largely viewed as a public enterprise, there is a growing private sector of higher education (Li and Jones 2015). The expansion of higher education following World War II had largely emphasized access to publicly funded, secular institutions and private denominational institutions either affiliated with secular universities or became secular universities. Some provinces have approved the creation of private universities, and there are now approximately 19. Table 3.3 provides information on the number of private institutions by province.

Once again, different provinces have different policies on private institutions. All of Canada's private universities can be found in five provinces and each of these provinces has developed a mechanism for reviewing proposals for private universities or for allowing private universities to offer degree programmes. The vast majority of these private universities are small faith-based institutions, though they also include secular not-for-profit universities (e.g., Quest University in British Columbia) and secular for-profit institutions (e.g., Yorkville University in New Brunswick).

A vast majority of institutions classified as private colleges can be found in Quebec and are private religious CEGEPs, many of which receive public support but are classified as private because of their denominational affiliation. There is a large private career college sector, especially in the provinces of British Columbia, Alberta and Ontario. These are private vocational schools operating under provincial regulation, ranging in size from very small specialized schools offering programmes in hair styling or truck driving to larger, more comprehensive colleges that might offer a range of vocational or technical programmes. Other categories of private postsecondary institutions include language schools, theological schools and international institutions (foreign private institutions operating a satellite campus). Once again, these institutions are regulated by the provinces, and differences in provincial regulation (and of course the size of provincial markets) assist in explaining major differences in the number of institutions by category by province.

Financial Aspects

Under the Canadian federal arrangements, both levels of government have the ability to set levels of taxation—income tax, corporate tax, sales tax, etc.—and to make independent financial decisions. Both

Table 3.3 *Number of Private Postsecondary Institutions as of 2013, by Province*

Province	Universities[a]	Colleges[b]	Career Colleges[c]	Language Schools[d]	Theological Schools[e]	International Institutions[f]
British Columbia	4	8	317	55	16	4
Alberta	5	2	147	6	15	7
Saskatchewan	–	1	37	–	5	–
Manitoba	3	–	52	1	2	–
Ontario	2	5	601	47	17	5
Quebec	–	51	17	15	7	–
New Brunswick	5	–	59	–	2	–
Nova Scotia	–	–	44	5	–	–
Prince Edward Island	–	–	18	1	1	–
Newfoundland and Labrador	–	–	23	–	1	–
Total	**19**	**67**	**1,315**	**130**	**66**	**16**

Source: Li and Jones (2015, 13), compiled from Canadian Information Centre for International Credentials (CICIC).

Notes: [a]These institutions all have 'university' or 'university college' in their names.

[b]These are colleges, CEGEPs (Quebec), institutes, and polytechnics schools that offer degrees and/or diplomas.

[c]These are registered or licensed institutions for occupational and vocational training purposes.

[d]These schools offer second language programmes that meet the quality assurance standards of Languages Canada (LC), a voluntary association that accredits language training of Canada's two official languages, English and French.

[e]Some of these institutions offer both academic and theology degrees, and some offer only theology degrees, diploma, and certificate programmes.

[f]These are branch or satellite campuses of foreign private institutions that offer degree programmes in Canadian provinces.

levels of government provide funds to universities, either in the form of operating grants (provincial governments) or in support of research and other specific initiatives (federal government, provincial government and, in some cases, municipal government) as noted earlier. In addition, the federal and provincial governments provide financial support to eligible students in an integrated set of loans and bursaries programmes.

Fiscal arrangements

Canada has a very decentralized fiscal arrangement, which includes the ability of the federal government and of each province to set their tax rates. While some provinces have unified their provincial and federal taxes under a harmonized sale tax, other provinces collect their own provincial taxes. Overall provincial portions of sale and income taxes vary across the country (see Table 3.4), while fixed federal tax rates are applicable on top of provincial taxes (as of 2015 federal sales taxes amount to 5% and federal income taxes range from 15 to 33%).

In order for the provinces to meet their obligations in areas such as health, education and social assistance, the federal government provides financial support to the provinces via four main transfer programmes, which are expected to reach 17.3 per cent of provincial revenues in 2016 (Eisen, Lammam and Ren 2016): the Canada Health Transfer (CHT), the Canada Social Transfer (CST), Equalization and Territorial Formula Financing (TFF). Of all four programmes, funding for post-secondary education is specifically part of the CST. The share of the CST associated with postsecondary education is notionally 31 per cent, but this calculation has little policy importance since the funds are not targeted (the CST provides income to the province in block but since the transfer is non-conditional, there is no assumed relationship between revenue and expenses). In addition, provinces can potentially provide additional funds to their higher education systems through their own tax revenue as well as the Equalization programme, which is an unconditional transfer to enable have-not provinces to provide com-parable public services to their residents (Department of Finance 2015).

Even though universities receive their operating grants from their provincial governments, ultimately, the ability of provincial governments to fund their education systems is largely made possible by federal social

Table 3.4 *Provincial Income and Sales Taxes; Federal Transfers; FTE Student Funding and Provincial Operating Grants*

	Provincial Income Tax Rate in % (Lowest–Highest)	Provincial Sales Tax Rate (%)	Federal Transfers (Millions of Dollars)	FTE Student Funding (Dollars)	Provincial Operating Grants as % of Universities Income
Newfoundland and Labrador	7.7–15.3	8	693	19,142	79.3
Prince Edward Island	10–16	9	553	14,581	39.4
Nova Scotia	9–21	10	3,051	9,213	47
New Brunswick	10–26	8	2,658	10,119	55.4
Quebec	16–26	10	20,352	12,290	67.1
Ontario	5–13	8	20,437	8,233	42.3
Manitoba	11–17	8	3,432	11,818	64.9
Saskatchewan	11–15	5	1,486	15,088	60.1
Alberta	10–15	0	5,496	15,631	57.8
British Columbia	5–15	7	6,139	12,183	52.4

Source: CAUBO (2013), COU (2012), Department of Finance, Canada (2015).

transfers to the provinces. While the federal government briefly provided funds directly to institutions during the expansion of tertiary education after World War II, provinces quickly asserted their constitutional rights and the funds for tertiary education were eventually included in the package of social transfers to the provinces (Jones et al. 2014).

Student financial support

In Canada, students have access to a set of complex federal, provincial and jointly administered financial aid programmes. In essence, the need-based financial support provided to eligible students is the result of integrated loan and bursary programmes between the federal government's CSLP and the provinces. The CSLP provides 60 per cent of students' financial support and provincial governments take care of the remaining 40 per cent. Quebec is the only province that does not participate in the CSLP; instead, it administers its own programme through a special federal transfer payment (Maclaren 2014).

In 2011, the CSLP provided over $2 billion in loans to more than 400,000 students, representing 34 per cent of full-time students, and this percentage is projected to increase (Office of the Superintendent of Financial Institutions 2012). Attribution of financial assistance is decided at the provincial level, with each province having its own criteria for determining eligibility. As a consequence, the average amount a student receives will be determined by factors such as family income and pre-study income (Maclaren 2014). Moreover, provinces differ in the approach they use to offset the cost of tuition for student loan recipients. For instance, Ontario provides a 30 per cent off of tuition for student residents that meet certain family income requirements while in Nova Scotia, student can take advantage of loan forgiveness for the provincial portion of their loans.

In Canada, 53 per cent of adults have a postsecondary qualification, with all provinces well above the OECD average of 32 per cent (HEQCO 2013), though there are provincial variations in participation.

Universities are established as distinct, non-profit corporations with considerable autonomy over financial decisions. In the provinces of British Columbia and Alberta, universities are government reporting entities in that university finances are reported as components of government financial reports. In these provinces, the government closely monitors university finance and may limit the financial independence of universities by, for example, limiting the ability of the university to borrow funds since university borrowing may have an impact on the provincial government's credit rating. In other provinces, universities are regarded as financially independent from government, and, while there are clearly reporting and accountability requirements associated with receiving government grants, universities have the legal ability to make independent financial decisions, including buying and selling property, entering into contracts, borrowing money (or raising money by issuing bonds), etc. They are also free to generate revenue by selling goods and services, commercializing knowledge and investing. Universities are registered charities, and they have the ability to provide donors with tax receipts.

Two major sources of income for all Canadian universities are provincial government grants and tuition fees, both of which are largely controlled by provincial governments since the provinces usually regulate the level of fees for domestic students. Since each province determines the level of financial support that will be provided to each university, and there are major differences in tuition policy by province, the share of total university revenue associated with these two sources of income varies by province and by institution. For example, in Newfoundland and Labrador, which has the lowest tuition fees in Canada (see Table 3.4), tuition represented only 13.1 per cent of university operating revenue in 2012, compared to 48 per cent of operating revenue, on average, in Ontario universities (CAUT 2014).

For Canada, provincial grants and transfers represented approximately 42 per cent of total university revenue in 2011–2012, although again there were considerable variations by province. Provincial grants represent, on average, 66 per cent of total university income in Newfoundland, 46 per cent in Alberta, and 33 per cent in Ontario (CAUT 2014, 5). There are important differences by province in the ratio of total funding for tertiary education and provincial GDP (Table 3.2), ranging from 2.3 per cent in Alberta, Canada's richest province, to 4 per cent in Nova Scotia, one of Canada's poorest provinces.

University revenue from the federal government is primarily associated with research funding. There are three major granting councils—the Social Sciences and Humanities Research Council of Canada (SSHRC), the Natural Sciences and Engineering Research Council (NSERC), and the Canadian Institutes of Health Research (CIHR). Transfers from these three councils represented, on average, approximately 6 per cent of university revenue in 2011–2012. Transfers from all federal government agencies and departments (including granting councils) represented about 11 per cent of total university revenues in 2011–2012. Since much of this funding is competitive, there are major differences in the magnitude of federal government grants and contracts by institution.

In addition to grants from provincial and federal governments, other major sources of income for Canadian universities (2011–2012) include grants and contracts with non-government (including businesses and non-profit) organizations, approximately 6 per cent of total revenues, the sale of goods and services, which represented 8 per cent of total revenues, donations (3.7%) and investments (including revenue from endowments, representing approximately 1.6% of university revenues).

University faculty salaries are relatively high when compared to public universities in many other jurisdictions. Salaries are set at the institutional level, often through collective bargaining with faculty unions. There are differences in salary levels by institution, and regional variations in salaries, related in part to regional differences in living costs (Jones and Weinrib 2012).

INTRA-CANADIAN EDUCATIONAL MIGRATION/MOBILITY

Educational migration within Canada includes out-of-province (OOP), transfer and mobile students. Heath (2012) defines transfer students as those who started their programme at another institution, move to a new institution and receive some credits for courses already completed. Mobile students, who also have a university experience, do not receive credits for past courses, often because their second enrolment is in a completely different programme.[3]

---

[3] Analysing educational migration in Canada is challenging, in part because of inconsistencies in the categorization of students and in part because of the limited

Existing data, although limited, show that the extent of student mobility is modest. As already noted, the quality of higher education is viewed as being relatively even across provinces. For instance, all regions of the country have institutions on the Maclean's university rankings (one of the main university rankings in Canada). Institutions from seven provinces are represented in the top 15 doctoral medical universities in Canada, while six provinces have institutions in the top 15 comprehensive universities ranking. The lack of clear institutional hierarchies or stratification means that the vast majority of students choose to attend a university close to the home of their parents. In addition, in the majority of provinces, university-bound students can study most of the traditional programmes (e.g., medicine, dentistry, law and engineering) without leaving their home province. There are few exceptions, such as the Maritime region, where the faculty of medicine at Dalhousie University, with two campuses in Nova Scotia and New Brunswick, serves three provinces through affiliations with various health institutions in the region.

In 2013, approximately 10 per cent of all university undergraduates study outside their home province (Maioni 2014). This percentage is slightly above the proportion of international students, which represent 8 per cent at Canadian postsecondary institutions (CBIE 2015). In 2012, at Ontario universities, 11 per cent of first year undergraduates were international students, but only 5 per cent were OOP students (COU-CUDO 2014); and, in 2013, British Columbia universities enrolled 16 per cent international students but only 10 per cent OOP students. Some of the strongest universities in the country do not attract significant number of students from other provinces. In the fall 2013, the University of Toronto, the University of Alberta and the University of British Columbia respectively enrolled only 7 per cent, 9 per cent and 13 per cent of undergraduates from other provinces.

---

availability of data. Statistics Canada discontinued the collection of pan-Canadian data on student mobility in 2009. A number of provinces (e.g., Ontario, the Maritime provinces and, to some extent, British Columbia) keep track of what they call 'OOP' students, defined as first year undergraduates, who have not yet attended a postsecondary institution and who resided outside of their province of study in the previous year.

The general pattern of educational migration appears to be influenced by geography and cultural–linguistic factors. While provinces such as Alberta and Saskatchewan have been able to attract workers from across the country and beyond, the favourable job market has not turned out to be a pull to significantly attract OOP students. The region where educational migration is more common is Atlantic Canada, where provinces are relatively small in size and closer to each other than the rest of the country. Educational migration also appears to follow the linguistic line. It mostly happens between Anglophone provinces, because they share the same language and have similar higher education structures. 'Quebec's higher education system is significantly different from other provinces' (Heath 2012, 22).

Overall, Atlantic Canada—Newfoundland and Labrador, New Brunswick, Nova Scotia and Prince Edward Island—appears to be the region where students are more likely to leave their province for study. This is partly a function of supply: In last ten years, there has been a 16 per cent decline in home students from within the Atlantic region (MPHEC 2015), and regional institutions are advertising in Ontario (Charbonneau 2015). The highest rates of OOP students are found in small to medium size institutions renowned for their undergraduate-focused liberal arts education: Bishop's, Mount Allison, Dalhousie (Millar and Ajadi 2013; MPHEC 2008, 2014). The highest proportions of first time students who decide to study outside of their home provinces can be found in Nova Scotia and Newfoundland. In 2012, the province with the highest proportion of 'OOP' students enrolled in their universities was Nova Scotia at 32 per cent, although the province has one of the highest average tuition fees and is the least affordable province for middle-income students (Macdonald and Shaker 2012). In addition to drawing students from neighbouring provinces, Nova Scotia universities also attract students from further away. Of all OOP students in Nova Scotia, 47 per cent were from Ontario (MPHEC 2012). At Dalhousie University, the largest institution in the province, only 30 per cent of students are from Nova Scotia, while 56 per cent were from other provinces and 14 per cent international (MPHEC 2013).

It is a different story in the neighbouring province of Newfoundland and Labrador, largely as a consequence of the province having the lowest tuition in the country and being the most affordable place to study. Between 1999 and 2009, the number of students from Nova Scotia increased by 1,079 per cent (Kirby et al. 2011). During the same period, average tuition increased by 7.7 per cent in Nova Scotia, but dropped in Newfoundland by 37.4 per cent (Kirby et al. 2011). The tuition differential with Nova Scotia amounts to $3,000 in favour of Newfoundland. More recently, the province has seen a substantial increase in students from other provinces. At Memorial University, the only university, the latest figures show that 18 per cent of students were other provinces, mostly originating from Nova Scotia (34%) and Ontario (25%; Memorial University 2014).

There is a mixture of regulatory and financial incentives and disincentives affecting mobility. There are instances of caps on the number of OOP students, and many provincial governments have preferential bursary and tuition arrangements for resident students. On the other hand, many provincial financial aid programmes are portable, in the majority of provinces, OOP students are not charged differential tuition, and there are instances of subsidized loans. In Newfoundland, with the lowest tuition rate in the country, all domestic students pay the same rate regardless of their province of origin. Many provincial governments have implemented financial incentives to encourage graduate retention and attract new graduates from other provinces, such as grants or tax credit for graduates staying in the province of their university or establishing in the province (Shaker, Macdonald and Wodrich 2013). Saskatchewan Graduates Retention Program offers up to a maximum of CN$20,000 in tuition refunds to any graduate wishing to establish in the province. New Brunswick has a similar measure for graduates from anywhere in the world.

There are no formal and specific guidelines for transfer and credit recognition between provinces, and, in the absence of a federal department in charge of higher education, the CMEC has been a modest voice advocating for more student mobility. Its contribution of CMEC has been limited to regularly published declarations encouraging mobility, mostly focused on improving and expanding transfer mechanisms. A statement of principles issued by Ministers of Education in 2009 recognized the need to improve credit transfer, but barely mentioned interprovincial transfer (CMEC 2009). For a number of years now, the Pan-Canadian Consortium on Admissions and Transfers have organized

Table 3.5 *Average Tuition, Postsecondary Education Attainment, Average Bachelor Degree Graduate Salary, Educational Migration, International Students, by Province*

	Average Undergraduate Tuition (Dollars)	PSE Attainment 25–64 Years Old	Average Expected Annual Bachelor Graduate Salary CN$	OOP Students as % of All Students	Distribution of Canada's International Students (%)
Canada	5,313	53	53,000	10	100
Newfoundland and Labrador	2,649	40	65,000	18	0.6
Prince Edward Island	5,258	52	47,000	–	0.3
Nova Scotia	5,722	52	47,000	32	2.8
New Brunswick	5,728	48	49,400	–	1.2
Quebec[a]	2,520	50	50,000	7	14.2
Ontario[b]	6,815	59	53,900	5	43.0
Manitoba	3,638	46	57,000	–	2.3
Saskatchewan	5,734	41	59,800	–	1.4
Alberta	5,663	47	64,000	–	5.3
British Columbia	4,919	51	49,000	10	28.9

Sources: Data compiled from Statistics Canada (2013), Institutions' websites and the Canadian Bureau of International Education.
Notes: [a]2005 Data.
[b]2012 Data.

annual meetings to bring together representatives from provincial governments, universities, colleges and postsecondary associations to facilitate the implementation of policies and practices that support student mobility within and across provinces (ACCC 2011).

CONCLUSION

Under Canada's federal arrangements, the primary responsibility for higher education is assumed by the provincial and territorial governments. Each province has developed its system of education (primary and secondary) and higher education. Despite these differences, a relatively common model of the university emerged across the country, and the homogeneity of the sector has meant that there is no formal hierarchy or institutional stratification, although this is changing as a function of the emergence of new institutional arrangements in some provinces—especially Alberta and British Columbia—and the growing importance of international rankings, which reinforce differences between institutions in terms of research activity. The assumption that universities have relatively common standards is one of the reasons why there is relatively little student mobility, at least, at the undergraduate level, across the country with the exception of the smaller eastern provinces. Given the size of the country and the high costs of transportation, most students decide to enrol in a university that is close to the family home.

These provincial systems are further decentralized by the reality that Canadian universities continue to have a relatively high level of autonomy, especially over decisions about academic programmes, programme standards, the admission of students, faculty and staff employment, internal financial decisions and institutional direction. Even quality assurance, now a major mechanism for steering universities in many jurisdictions, has been largely left in the hands of institutional institutions or in the hands of the leadership of the university sector (Weinrib and Jones 2014).

Given their responsibility for higher education, the provincial governments have used their independent authority to develop distinctive higher education systems to address the needs of their jurisdiction. There are major differences in the role of non-university postsecondary institutions, funding arrangements, accountability mechanisms and tuition fee policies. All of the provinces have relatively high levels of access to postsecondary education, but there are variations, and given the size of some provinces, regional differences within provinces.

While the Government of Canada has a quite limited formal constitutional role in higher education, the federal government has staked out policy territory in a number of important areas, including research and innovation, student financial assistance, the education of Canada's aboriginal populations and internationalization. The federal government has become by far the largest fund provider of university research in Canada, and federal research initiatives clearly have an impact on the research activities of Canadian universities.

Perhaps the greatest and most obvious disadvantage of the division of responsibilities that have emerged between the two levels of government is the tremendous challenge of national policy coordination. The provincial governments value their independence and have fiercely protected their constitutional role in postsecondary education and resisted federal interference. While the CMEC provides a forum for information sharing, there has been little interest in developing pan-Canadian policy initiatives or a national strategy. The absence of strong mechanisms for federal-provincial coordination mean that federal and provincial initiatives in areas of common interest, such as research policy, may be disconnected and in some cases, involve quite different if not conflicting priorities. This lack of coordination has been recognized as important challenge for international education since initiatives related to international student recruitment much involve both levels of government. Given the historic absence of policy coordination, it is the universities themselves that have largely played the central role in determining internationalization strategies and recruiting international students.

On the other hand, there are clear advantages associated with Canada's decentralized approach to higher education policy. Given important regional differences in culture, language and industry, decentralization represents a logical approach to developing higher education systems that address these regional needs. From a pan-Canadian perspective, decentralization also allows for provincial policy experimentation; provinces can develop policy initiatives that are designed to address local needs, but they can also observe and learn from policy experiments in other provinces. Policy borrowing is not uncommon. One could also argue that decentralization has also had a moderating influence on reform; the absence of national policy has also prevented large-scale national reforms, and provinces may be reluctant to undertake reforms that might be poorly received by other jurisdictions. The end result, after all, is a collection of different but high access provincial systems of higher education that provide a quality of education that is well-respected by other jurisdiction, and includes a number of internationally recognized research universities.

REFERENCES

ACCC. 2011. *Transferability and Postsecondary Pathways: The Role of Canadian Colleges and Institutes*. Ottawa, Ontario: ACCC.

AUCC. 2011. *Trends in Higher Education, Vol. 1: Enrolment*. Ottawa: AUCC.

BC Headset. 2014. 'British Columbia Higher Education Accountability Dataset'. Available at http://bcheadset.com

CAUBO. 2013. 'Financial Information of Universities and Colleges 2012/2013'. The Canadian Association of University Business Officers. Ottawa, Ontario.

CAUT. 2014. *Almanac, 2014–15*. Ottawa: Canadian Association of University Teachers.

CBIE. 2015. 'Facts and Figures'. Available at http://www.cbie.ca/about-ie/facts-and-figures.

Charbonneau, L. 27 February 2015. 'Atlantic Canada Sends a Signal on Enrolment'. *University Affairs*. Available at http://www.universityaffairs.ca/opinion/margin-notes/atlantic-canada-sends-a-signal-on-enrolment/

CMEC. 2009. 'CMEC Ministerial Statement on Credit Transfer in Canada'. Available at http://www.cmec.ca/Publications/Lists/Publications/Attachments/216/ministerial-statement-credit-transfer-2009.pdf

COU. 2012. *Interprovincial Comparison of University Revenue*. Council of Ontario Universities. Available at http://cou.on.ca/papers/interprovincial-comparison-of-university-revenue

COU-CUDO. 2014. *University Works: 2014 Employment Report*. Available at http://cou.on.ca/publications/reports

Department of Finance, Canada. 2015. 'Federal Support to Provinces and Territories'. Available at http://www.fin.gc.ca/access/fedprov-eng.asp

Eisen, B., Lammam, C., and Ren, F. 2016. *Are the Provinces Really Short-changed by Federal Transfers?* Vancouver: The Fraser Institute.

Fisher, D., Rubenson, K., Bernatchez, J., Clift, R., Jones, G., Lee, J., MacIvor, M., Meredith, J., Shanahan, T., and Trottier, C. 2006. *Canadian Federal Policy and Postsecondary Education*. Vancouver, BC: CHET, UBC.

Fisher, D., Rubenson, K., Shanahan, T., and Trottier, C., eds. 2014. *The Development of Postsecondary Education Systems in Canada: A Comparison Between British Columbia, Ontario and Quebec*. Montreal: McGill-Queen's University Press.

Harris, R. 1976. *A History of Higher Education in Canada: 1663–1960*. Toronto: University of Toronto Press.

Heath, N. 2012. 'Student Mobility in Canada: Across Canadian Jurisdictions. 2007/08–2009/10'. *Nicholas Heath Consulting Services Inc*. Available at http://www1.uwindsor.ca/pccat/system/files/PCCAT_mainreport_final-EN%20Full%20Document%20with%20logos.pdf

HEQCO. 2013. 'Ontario Postsecondary Education System Performance'. The Higher Education Quality Council of Ontario. Toronto, Ontario.

Jones, G. A. 1996. 'Governments, Governance, and Canadian Universities'. In *Higher Education: Handbook of Theory and Research*, Vol. XI, edited by J. C. Smart, 337–371. New York, NY: Agathon Press.

———. ed. 1997. *Higher Education in Canada: Different Systems, Different Perspectives*. New York, NY: Garland.

———. 2002. 'The Structure of University Governance in Canada: A Policy Network Approach'. In *Governing Higher Education: National Perspectives on Institutional Governance*, edited by Alberto, Amaral, Glen A. Jones, and Berit Karseth, 213–234. Dordrecht, The Netherlands: Kluwer Academic Publishers.

———. 2009. 'Sectors, Institutional Types, and the Challenges of Shifting Categories: A Canadian Commentary'. *Higher Education Quarterly* 63 (4): 371–383.

———. 2014. 'An Introduction to Higher Education in Canada'. In *Higher Education Across Nations*, Vol. 1, edited by J. M. Joshi and S. Paivandi, 1–38. Delhi: B. R. Publishing Corporation.

Jones, G. A., Gopaul, B., Weinrib, J., Metcalfe, A. S., Fisher, D., Gingras, Y., and Rubenson, K. 2014. 'Teaching, Research and the Canadian Professoriate'. In *Teaching and Research in Contemporary Higher Education: Systems, Activities and Rewards,* edited by A. Arimoto, W. K. Cummings, J. C. Shin, and U. Teichler, 335–356. Dordrecht, The Netherlands: Springer.

Jones, G. A., and Oleksiyenko, A. 2011. 'The Internationalization of Canadian University Research: A Global Higher Education Matrix Analysis of Multi-level Governance'. *Higher Education* 61 (1): 41–57.

Jones, G. A., and Weinrib, J. 2011. 'Globalization and Higher Education in Canada'. In *Handbook on Globalization and Higher Education*, edited by Roger King, Simon Marginson, and Rajani Naidoo, 222–240. Cheltenham, UK: Edward Elgar Publishing.

———. 2012. 'The Organization of Academic Work and the Remuneration of Faculty at Canadian Universities'. In *Paying the Professoriate: A Global Comparison of Compensation and Contracts*, edited by P. Altbach, L. Reisberg, M. Yukevich, G. Androushchak, and I. F. Pacheco, 83–93. New York, NY: Routledge.

Jones, G. A., and Young, S. 2004. 'Madly Off in All Directions: Higher Education, Marketization, and Canadian Federalism'. In *Markets and Higher Education: Rhetoric or Reality?*, edited by P. Teixeira, B. B. Jongbloed, D. Dill, and A. Amaral, 185–205. Dordrecht, The Netherlands: Kluwer Academic Publishers.

Kirby, D., Greene, M., Bourgeois, M., and Sharpe, D. 2011. 'Migrating Eastward: Maritime Student Migration to Newfoundland'. Available at http://files.eric.ed.gov/fulltext/ED521707.pdf

Li, S. X., and Jones, G. A. 2015. 'The "Invisible" Sector: Private Higher Education in Canada'. In *Private Higher Education Across Nations*, edited by J. M. Joshi and Saeed Paivandi, 1–33. Delhi: B. R. Publishing Corporation.

Macdonald, D., and Shaker, E. 2012. *Eduflation and the High Cost of Learning*. Ottawa, Canada: Canadian Centre for Policy Alternatives. Available at http://www.policyalternatives.ca/sites/default/files/uploads/publications/National%20 Office/2012/09/Eduflation%20and%20High%20Cost%20Learning.pdf

Maclaren, J. 2014. *It's Complicated: An Interprovincial Comparison of Student Financial Aid*. Ottawa, Canada: Canadian Centre for Policy Alternatives.

Maioni, A. 26 May 2014. 'See the World: But See Canada Too'. *The Globe and Mail*. Available at http://www.theglobeandmail.com

Memorial University. 2014. 'Vital Signs and Financials'. Available at http://www.mun.ca/presidentsreport/2013/vital-signs.php

Millar, E., and Ajadi, T. 22 October 2013. 'Help Choosing a University in the Atlantic'. *The Globe and Mail*. Available at http://www.theglo-beandmail.com/news/national/education/canadian-university-report/help-choosing-a-university-in-the-atlantic/article14980149/?page=all

MPHEC. 2008. 'Surveying the Enrolment Landscape: Update of Selected Tables and Figures'. Available at http://www.mphec.ca/resources/TrendsSurveyingUpdten.pdf

———. 2014. 'Trends Maritime Higher Education'. *Annual Digest* 11 (1). Available at http://www.mphec.ca/media/63021/TrendsV11N1_2014.pdf

———. 2015. *Maritime University Enrolment Weakening*. Available at http://www.mphec.ca/media/89995/media_release_digest_enrolment_2013-2014.pdf

Office of the Superintendent of Financial Institutions. 2012. *Actuarial Report on the Canada Student Loans Program 2011*. Available at http://www.osfi-bsif.gc.ca/eng/oca-bac/ar-ra/cslp-pcpe/Pages/CSLP_2011.aspx#toc-iib

ONCAT. 15 October 2014. *Provincial Councils on Credit Transfer to Sign Memorandum of Understanding to Enhance Student Mobility in Canada*. Available at http://www.oncat.ca/index_en.php?page=news_1410

Shaker, E., Macdonald, D., and Wodrich, N. 2013. *Degree of Uncertainty: Navigating the Changing Terrain of University Finance*. Ottawa, Canada: Canadian Centre for Policy Alternatives.

Statistics Canada. 2013. *National Graduate Survey, 2009*. Ottawa, Ontario: Statistics Canada.

Trilokekar, R. D., and Jones, G. A. 2013. 'Finally, An Internationalization Strategy for Canada'. *International Higher Education* 71 (Spring): 18–19. Available at https://htmldbprod.bc.edu/pls/htmldb/f?p=2290:4:0::NO:RP,4:P0_CONTENT_ID:119714

Trilokekar, R. D., Jones, G. A., and Shubert, A. eds. 2009. *Canada's Universities Go Global*. Toronto: James Lorimer and Company.

Weinrib, J., and Jones, G. A. 2014. 'Largely a Matter of Degrees: Quality Assurance and Canadian Universities'. *Policy and Society* 33 (3): 225–236.

Chapter 4

Australia
Benefits and Limits of the Centralized Approach

Simon Marginson

INTRODUCTION
The Federation and Higher Education

Australia is a federation of seven states based on geographic territories carved out by British colonization after 1788. In 1901, it became a self-governing dominion of the British Empire with nationhood status. The federal constitution was negotiated between the colonies in 1890–1900 when states' rights were paramount. Since 1901, Australia has gained fuller sovereignty in relation to the United Kingdom but the constitutional framework of federation has changed a little. In the founding constitution, all matters were subject to state jurisdiction unless an exception was made, for example, the role of national government in defence and foreign trade. In legal terms, education was, and in large part still is, a state rather than national government responsibility.

This would suggest that as in fellow federated British settler state Canada, the country often most similar to Australia, the higher education system is likely to be engaged in complex federal/state relationships and issues of double jurisdiction. Perhaps surprisingly, this is not so. Consistent with the evolution of the Australian polity in other spheres—notably in economic management and especially in taxing power—in the last 60 years in higher education, the national government has become overwhelmingly dominant in each of policy, funding and regulation. Higher education is more unitary than in federal systems elsewhere. That is the main story. However, as will be discussed, there are exceptions and caveats. The states retain their foundational legal and political identities in Australia. They remain the seat of much of service provision and, in constitutional terms, cannot be permanently excluded from higher education.

Although Australia has exhibited remarkable stability in governance and society in the modern period, the nature of the federation has altered. The state-dominated constitutional framework of 1901 has proven obsolete in the face of the nation-building agendas of a modernising state; in this case, a British-heritage settler state located off the south-eastern edge of Asia. It has proven very difficult to shift the legal structure of the constitution, and the political economy, including higher education provision, has evolved alongside and partly separated from the legal structure.

Since 1901, there has been a drift of power to the federal/national ('Commonwealth') government, associated with changes in the expectations, scale and machinery of government; industrial and social modernization; and changes in Australia's place in the world. The process of centralization was quickened during the national emergency in World War II, when Japanese troops occupied New Guinea immediately North of Australia, and was consolidated in four years of post-war reconstruction policy after 1945 (Macintyre 2015). The decisive moment, and the continuing condition of the growth of national power, was the national government's monopoly over income taxation in 1942. The partial shift in the national/state balance of functions and powers has been manifest more in the realpolitik and the power of money than in the formal legal framework but also supported by accumulated High Court decisions and by a handful of constitutional amendments, although only some of the successive referendum proposals to expand the powers of the national government have won electoral support. Australian federalism, and within it, higher education, have been shaped at the intersection of heterogeneous systems of law and political economy, sometimes in synergy and sometimes in tension. Although the law started with foundational advantages, it came to be led by political economy. Yet law can still set limits.

The result is a federal system with more than one possible outcome in the social sectors. Some state functions have become national while others, with similar legal status, have not. Schooling and technical–vocational education remain primarily state responsibilities, as do health, hospitals and housing, but not social welfare payments and student benefits. Degree-level higher education, and research, moved from the states to the national sphere because while the legal basis for national intervention in higher education was weak, from the 1950s the universities, and later other degree-granting institutions, became a matter of national political priority.

The taxing power was and is the key. The states did not have the fiscal capacity to develop and modernize higher education on the scale required. The national government exercises control over higher education through its fiscal supremacy within the federation, its funding power in higher education and the capacity to set conditions attached to funding. The Australian higher education system is organized in a manner closer to the unitary English (as distinct from federal British) system than higher education in the federated United States, where both state governments and independent private institutions play a leading role.

One outcome of national supremacy in Australian higher education has been homogeneity. In student enrolments, funding and research, higher education is dominated by the 37 largely public universities in the 'Unified National System', a term dating from the system overhaul of 1988–1993 (Croucher et al. 2013). These institutions are all comprehensive in disciplinary terms. All offer places at International Standard Classification of Education (ISCED) (UNESCO, 2018) Level 6 and above, and at least some doctoral places. Following further reforms in 2009–2014, the private sector, with 8 per cent of enrolled students of ISCED Level 6 and above (Australian Department of Education 2015), is also accredited, financed and regulated at national level.

Because Australia remains a federation, as noted, there are exceptions (and larger potential exceptions) to this picture of blanket national control in higher education. First, while the states are bypassed and partly suppressed, the legal framework contains the potential for a future challenge to national authority and/or a voluntary transfer of functions and powers back to the states. In an age in which devolved models of federation are gaining ground in parts of the world, facilitated by evolving communications systems, these possibilities are real.

Second, because universities continue to be governed by state-based Acts of Parliament and are important players in state and regional economies, the states sometimes intervene in various areas. Their limited taxing powers preclude the large-scale funding of student places, but this does not block the potential for selective investments in research. In the recent past, some states facilitated new private universities. The states also retain a formal responsibility for university governance, and they affect higher education through the regulation of land use, transport, municipal services, regional development, policing and public safety, and their capacity to affect the relationship between schools and universities, for example, in student selection.

Third, the states play the main governmental role in Vocational Education and Training (VET), a large post-school sector with 13.5 per cent of its enrolments at tertiary level. VET sits on the fault line between national and state government, resulting in inconsistent, unstable structures and funding, and gaps and dysfunctions in relations between VET and universities. VET exemplifies problems of coordination and heterogeneity of provision largely absent in the nationally run Australian higher education system, although part of higher education in some other federal nations. However, only a handful of VET students are in degree-length programmes.

This chapter is focused on the national system of higher education and principally the public universities. These institutions enrol more than two thirds of all ISCED 5 and 6 students and 99.5 per cent at ISCED 6. In terms of resources, their proportion of full-time students, student learning hours and degree completions, the designated public research universities constitute not just the elite layer of the tertiary system in Australia, as in many countries, but most of the mass tertiary education as well. Australia stands out in the extent to which the economic and social role of tertiary and higher education has become concentrated in designated national research universities. Whereas the United States divides tertiary students between two-year and four-year programmes, Australia follows the British pattern, concentrating students at three-year degree level, and sub-tertiary level, and like the

United Kingdom locating most degree level provision in research universities. Again, as in the British jurisdiction, there is a sharp variation between designated research institutions in the intensity of research. The last few universities on the public schedule have few funded research projects (Australian Department of Education 2015). The private sector plays a minor role in research. On the whole, however, the research role is spread more evenly in Australia than in the United Kingdom. The middle layer of universities has significant weight.

Australia has no research universities in the world top 30 for research performance, but there are 23 institutions in the Shanghai Academic Ranking of World Universities top 500, all but two positioned in the top 400, servicing a population of 24.1 million people (2016), one top 500 university for every million people. This compares with 135 top 500 universities in the United States with 323.1 million people, and 38 in the United Kingdom with 65.6 million (ARWU 2017; World Bank 2017). Australia's relatively broad spread of research university capacity and reputation is an outcome of the consistent application since the 1960s of homogenizing national system templates, despite the strong policy adherence to market competition, which normally differentiates capacity over time (in relation to North America, see Davies and Zarifa 2012). The outcome in Australia is also described less kindly as a bland 'vanilla' system of higher education in which mission diversity has been largely ironed out (Marginson and Marshman 2013, 73).

Contents of the Chapter

Following the introduction, the second section expands on Australia, the Australian States and Territories, and higher education. The third and fourth sections trace the evolution of Australian federalism and the national government's role in higher education, exploring the constitutional position and the legal, policy and financial aspects of national funding and regulation, and reflect on the homogenous character of the national system. The fifth section looks at exceptions to national control of higher education—the episodic role of the states in governance, regulation and fostering activity, especially research. The sixth section explores the intersection between Australian federalism in higher education and globalization, internationalization and the world-class university (WCU) movement. The conclusion, the seventh section, summarizes the implications of federalism for core aspects of system design such as homogeneity/heterogeneity; privatization, marketization, competition; and university autonomy and accountability. It also reflects on possible future developments.

THE NATION AND HIGHER EDUCATION
History, Geography, Economy and Demography

The nation Australia occupies an island continent in the Southwest of the Pacific, located off the South-eastern end of Asia, with an area of 7.7 million square kilometres, not much smaller than the United States. The inner part of the continent is arid and the population, sparse relative to land area, is concentrated in a small number of cities on the Pacific, Southeast and Southwest coasts. Sydney, Melbourne and Brisbane house half the nation between them. Distance is a significant factor in service provision, especially in Queensland and Western Australia. Most tertiary education outside the major cities is by remote delivery or in small VET institutions.

Australia has a stable polity and affluent economy dominated by commodities and services. In 2014, Gross Domestic Product (GDP) per head in current USD was $43,902 in Purchasing Power Parity (PPP) terms, just behind Canada, compared to $54,630 in the United States. GDP in 2014 was $1,454 billion, 12th on the list, between Canada and South Korea (World Bank 2017). Total taxation revenue as a proportion of GDP was 27 per cent in 2013–2014. As a percentage of GDP, national government taxation revenue was 22 per cent, state government 4 per cent and local government 1 per cent, although part of national taxation is distributed to state/territory and local governments to help them to finance their services. National unemployment was at 5.9 per cent in October 2015, with an adult labour force participation rate of 65 per cent (ABS 2015).

Australia is shaped by the combination of its British settler history and Asia-located geography and economy. Its increasingly mixed demography reflects this dual character. Australia is a large commodity exporter, mostly to China, South Korea and Japan. Educational services are the third largest export after coal and iron ore with four-fifths of incoming students from Asia, especially China. India and China are two of the three largest sources of migrants. Successive waves of migration have also fostered subpopulations from Southern and Eastern Europe, Turkey and Lebanon, and Vietnam. Migration from the United Kingdom and Ireland continues to be significant.

Australia retains the British monarch as the nominal head of state, and its flag includes the imperial British ensign. Although Australia has been fully independent in foreign policy since World War II and there is no longer imperial preference in trade or migration, it continues to be patterned by British norms in government and policy, business, the professions, higher education and science—while also influenced by the United States, like all English-speaking nations. The need to define and sustain Australia as a British-heritage nation on the edge of Asia, and then to manage an increasingly hybrid nation on the Europe/Asia border of identity, has advanced the role of national government within the federation. The need to develop Australia's vast hinterland—initially to strengthen settler-state territorial claims, later to open up the resource industries, and to bring equality of opportunity to all parts of the country—has also exceeded the capacity of individual state governments, strengthening the national authority.

The Australian States and Territories

Table 4.1 lists 2014 populations in the seven states, and the two territories directly subject to national legislation. Each state and territory has its own elected parliament and administration, while also subject to the national parliament and government in many areas. On the whole, Australia is more notable for national homogeneity than for state-based cultural variability. However, there is a significant demographic and cultural difference between the cosmopolitan cities that attract most migrants from Asia and continental Europe—principally, Melbourne, Sydney and Canberra—and the other cities and the countryside, more traditionally Anglo-Australian in demography and culture.

The states have varied industry configurations. Western Australia, Queensland and, to a lesser extent, South Australia and New South Wales are resource rich and lifted when commodity prices are high; New South Wales and Queensland are strongest in agriculture.

Table 4.1 *Australian States and Territories: Land, History and 2014 Population and Economy*

State/Territory (Capital)	Population (Millions)	Land Area (Mil sq. km)	Population Density (per sq. km)	Gross Product ($ mil AU)	Income per Head ($ AU)	Governance History
New South Wales (Sydney)	7.439	0.800	9.29	506,918	49,026	British colony 1788, self-governing 1854
Victoria (Melbourne)	5.769	0.277	25.37	355,580	41,938	British colony 1834/5, self-governing 1855
Queensland (Brisbane)	4.676	1.731	2.70	300,270	43,673	British colony 1824, self-governing 1859
Western Australia (Perth)	2.536	2.530	1.00	276,312	51,469	British colony 1829, self-governing 1890
South Australia (Adelaide)	1.675	0.983	1.70	98,539	43,729	British colony 1834, self-governing 1855
Tasmania (Hobart)	0.513	0.068	7.51	25,419	40,493	British colony 1804, self-governing 1855
Australian Capital Territory (Canberra)	0.383	0.002	167.94	34,866	79,999	Territory of national government since 1901
Northern Territory (Darwin)	0.242	1.349	0.18	22,450	53,740	Territory of national government, part statehood
AUSTRALIA	23.236	13.589	1.71	1,620,355	46,440	National sovereignty as federation of colonies 1901

Source: Compiled by the author from Australian Bureau of Statistics data.

Table 4.2 *Australian States and Territories: Post-school Education, 2014*

State/Territory	Population (Millions)	Higher Education Students	Students per 1,000 Population	VET Students Approx.	Higher Education Institutions Public	Higher Education Institutions Private	Higher Education Students (%) Public	Higher Education Students (%) Private
New South Wales	7.439	420,957	56.6	1,131,400	10	40	89.3	10.7
Victoria	5.769	365,154	63.3	1,052,400	8	28	93.9	6.1
Queensland	4.676	239,040	51.1	881,600	7	9	93.7	6.3
Western Australia	2.536	142,168	56.1	372,400	4	10	89.8	10.2
South Australia	1.675	92,903	55.5	242,200	3	13	89.8	10.2
Tasmania	0.513	29,316	57.1	62,900	1	1	99.7	0.3
Australian Capital Territory	0.383	39,400	102.9	76,800	2	1	99.8	0.2
Northern Territory	0.242	11,575	47.8	50,500	1	0	100.0	0
Other	–	32,717	–	38,100	1	1	90.5	9.5
AUSTRALIA	23.236	1,373,230	59.1	3,908,000	37	103	92.0	8.0

Source: Compiled by the author from Australian Bureau of Statistics data; DET (2015) and NCVER (2015).

Notes: VET = Vocational Education and Training. VET students include those in secondary education-level programmes. Only 0.2 per cent of VET students are at ISCED Level 6 and 13.5 per cent at two-year diploma level, i.e., ISCED Level 5, with the others sub-tertiary. 'Other' includes students enrolled in multi-state institutions in higher education and overseas/other in VET. Income per head = Gross household disposable income per capita. Gross product and household income data for June 2015, current Australian prices. On 4 December 2015, AUD 1.00 = USD 0.7317.

Manufacturing, which is concentrated in Victoria, struggles: wages are relatively high, and Australia enjoys design and productivity advantages in a narrow range of sectors. The most populous states, New South Wales and Victoria, have strong services, including higher education. Queensland's universities have gained ground in the last two decades. Canberra, dominated by the presence of the national government, is a services city led by professional employment with high average earnings. Tasmania has pockets of boutique high value agriculture and like most states, a strong tourist industry, but is the poorest state in income per head with a narrow range of job opportunities. These differences, the demographics—high migration states have lower average incomes, which affects Victoria—and scale factors, are associated with episodic variations between the states in average incomes and unemployment. In October 2015, the unemployment rate ranged from 7.5 per cent in South Australia to 4.5 per cent in the Northern Territory (ABS 2015).

Political economic differences between the states have diminished since federation in 1901. The two largest states in area, Queensland and Western Australia, then much less urbanized and developed than New South Wales and Victoria, were brought up to the national average in service provision through fiscal equalization policies in the distribution of national taxation revenues. They also benefited from mineral and energy resources, especially Western Australia, which on a per capita basis is now wealthier than all but the two territories. The urban precincts and service profiles of all state capital cities are now broadly similar. However, the indigenous population, largely concentrated in Western Australia, Queensland and the Northern Territory, is well below the norm in income per head, professional employment rates, health indicators and educational attainment. The provision of access for indigenous students has become a significant national policy responsibility of higher education institutions in those states/territories.

Higher Education

Expenditure on tertiary education at 1.8 per cent of GDP is above the OECD average of 1.6 per cent. Public source spending at 0.7 per cent of GDP is well below the OECD average of 1.1 per cent, while Australia's 1.1 per cent private source spending is high (OECD 2017,

187). Private investment in higher education and VET mostly consists of student tuition payments, including international student fees. Domestic student obligations to repay through the income contingent loans scheme are recorded as private spending.

Participation in Australian upper secondary and higher education is at OECD average levels. The high first time tertiary education graduation rate (76%) is boosted by Australia's large international student population. Without international students, the level drops to 45 per cent, near the OECD average of 44 per cent (OECD 2017, 74). The proportion of graduates in social sciences, business and law is 10 per cent higher than the OECD average, while the proportion graduating in engineering at 8 per cent is just over half the OECD average of 14 per cent (p. 72). Participation rates improve with age. Among the 15–19 years old age group, 92 per cent of Australians are enrolled in all education and training compared to the OECD average of 85 per cent. At later ages, the Australian participation rate is well above the average (OECD 2017, 254). However, many mature age students have previously enrolled in higher education.

Because the Australian states initially developed public services separately from each other, there are inherited differences in the structures of schooling, the transition to university, VET and recent state regulation in higher education. The effects of these historical differences will be discussed further. Table 4.3 shows that, in 2011, the proportion of non-indigenous 20- to 24-year-olds who completed year 12 of schooling, the main gateway to higher education, especially high demand universities, varied from 60.8 per cent in Tasmania to 85.4 per cent in the Australian Capital Territory, with indigenous school completion much lower (ABS 2015). However, after 60 years of national policy designed to provide equal opportunity between states/territories, the density of higher education students in each state/territory has converged on the national average of 59.1 students per 1,000 people (Table 4.2). Participation is lowest for rural families, especially indigenous families in the Northern Territory, boosted by international students in Melbourne in Victoria, and lifted well above the national average in Canberra by mobile students from other states and territories, and work-related enrolment by national public servants.

Table 4.3 *Rates of Completion of Schooling, 20–24 Years Old, States and Territories, 2011*

State/Territory	Proportion of Indigenous 20–24 Years Old Who Had Completed Year 12 (%)	Proportion of Non-indigenous 20–24 Years Old Who Had Completed Year 12 (%)
New South Wales	36.7	74.0
Victoria	41.8	77.9
Queensland	48.1	75.4
Western Australia	34.0	70.5
South Australia	29.0	70.8
Tasmania	36.4	60.8
Northern Territory	17.8	64.9
Australian Capital Territory	56.6	85.4
AUSTRALIA	37.1	74.6

Source: ABS (2015).

Public Universities

As Table 4.2 shows, there were 1,620,355 students in Australian higher education in 2014, including 1,373,230 (92%) in the 37 research universities on the main public schedule, all government-sector institutions except the multi-state Australian Catholic University which is legally private but regulated like a public university. Australian universities are large in size by international standards. In 2014, 19 institutions had more than 30,000 students, and five had over 50,000, four of them research-intensive universities. One reason was the 347,560 fee-paying international students, 25.3 per cent of all students. International education supplied 18 per cent of university income (Australian Department of Education 2015) and in 2014–2015 generated $12.5 billion AU in exports, including the travel and living costs of students and their families (ABS 2015). Australia enrolled 6 per cent of the world's foreign students in 2013 (OECD 2015, 356).

Australian universities are similar to British universities in their disciplinary groupings, organizational cultures, academic career structures, modes of governance and university–state relations. The higher education system is less hierarchical than that of the United Kingdom, with no equivalent of Oxford and Cambridge, but the top 20 per cent of universities in the 'Group of Eight' receive 70 per cent of research funding (Australian Department of Education 2015). This group includes five universities founded in the colonial period or just after— Sydney, Melbourne, Adelaide, Queensland and Western Australia. The Australian National University (ANU) in Canberra and the second universities in Melbourne and Sydney, Monash and New South Wales were created 15 years after World War II. The University of Melbourne, with an ARWU (Academic Ranking of World Universities) ranking of 39, is seen as Australia's strongest research university. Queensland is at 55, Monash 78, Sydney 83, Western Australia 91, ANU 97 and New South Wales and Adelaide are in the top 150 (ARWU 2017).

Private Higher Education and VET

As Table 4.2 shows, the private sector commands 8 per cent of students in 103 institutions, most of them small and many offering low-cost business education. Enrolments have grown since 1996 when the sector gained access to government managed income contingent tuition loans. It was facilitated also by permissive state government policies on the licensing and accreditation of new colleges (the national government has now taken control of accreditation). However, the demand for private education is constrained by the workings of positional competition. The ground is occupied by stable public universities and the private sector lacks prestige. Only two private institutions have been designated as 'universities', a title which in Australia requires a threshold level of research activity—Bond University and University of Notre Dame. These are the largest private institutions but each has less than 4,500 students.

Table 4.2 also shows that in 2014, 3.9 million Australians were in VET programmes, although almost nine in ten were sub-tertiary. VET is subject to national regulation and coordination and from time to time national governments consider taking control and regulating it in parallel with higher education, though some states and industry interests resist this notion. However, only 8,600 VET students, 0.2 per cent, are in ISCED Level 6 degree or graduate diploma programmes.

AUSTRALIAN FEDERALISM

Australian federalism has been described as a 'pragmatic federalism' that has evolved in adaptive fashion (Hollander and Patapan 2007). Federalism is not highly theorized in Australia, but when the High Court is called on to interpret the 1901 constitution, intergovernmental relations are open to shifting norms and subtle twists. There is much scope for interpretation and strategic responses to need (and prejudice). The constitution is silent on some points, ambiguous on others and often out of kilter with expectations and practices. National policy and funding in higher education have evolved as much despite the constitution and outside it, as they have developed within it and consistent with it. Given the obsolescence of the 1901 state-dominated constitution, plus the difficulty of changing it, it was inevitable that once higher education became seen as a matter of national priority, that it would be shaped more by politics and economics than by the legal framework in which it was formally embedded. Yet the state-oriented legal structure continues and remains a potential influence.

World War II and Vertical Fiscal Imbalance

In the founding constitution, the states retained authority over economic policy and social programmes, except for matters involving international transactions or relations between the states. Under the first exception, the national government controlled the revenues from customs duties. Under the second business, activities across more than one state came under national authority. With the advent of World War I, the national government introduced estate duties in 1914 and its own income tax in 1915; and, by the end of the war in 1918, it was raising almost twice as much in income tax as the states. However, for the most part the states were still able to finance their own responsibilities, although at varying levels of taxation (Twomey 2014, 14–15).

All changed in World War II. The national government again needed to increase income tax. Under the constitution, it was unable to discriminate between states, and, rather than undertaking a complex adjustment of states taxes, the national and state governments agreed to a national monopoly of fixed rate income tax, provided Canberra passed part of the revenue back for state purposes. At first, the tax monopoly was conceived as a temporary expedient to finance the war, but it was reasserted after the war and survived challenge in the High Court in 1942 and 1957.

The states tried various expedients to improve their independent financial position but mostly failed. In 1997, the Higher Court struck down state taxes on petrol, liquor and tobacco (Twomey 2014, 17). This led to the introduction of a uniform system of indirect taxation, the GST (Goods and Services Tax), whereby the national government again took the whole revenue and passed part of it to the states. In the outcome, the states were left little better off than before in net fiscal terms (p. 18). The national government now collects about 85 per cent of all taxation in Australia, and national grants to the states constitute about 45 per cent of state revenues (p. 19), underlining the high level of state dependence on the national government.

Australian federalism is affected by both 'horizontal fiscal imbalance' and 'vertical fiscal imbalance' (Burton, Dollery and Wallis 2016; Mathews 1981; Twomey 2014). Horizontal imbalance occurs when the same level of taxation revenue cannot ensure a common standard of service in every state because of diseconomies of scale in states with smaller population (e.g., Tasmania) or the high cost of servicing large thinly populated hinterlands, for example, in relation to transport, communications, schools and hospitals in Western Australia and Queensland. Classically, horizontal imbalance was dealt with by distributing taxation revenues to the states on the basis of a differential formula that recognized variations in per capita costs, so as to enable the states to maintain a common standard. As noted, differential distribution has created a relatively uniform pattern between the states in facilities, services and hence in lifestyles. In recent years, the need for financial differentiation in favour of the less populated states has been reduced by the high level of mining-related revenues flowing to Western Australia and Queensland.

Vertical fiscal imbalance is more difficult to address. It occurs when there is lack of fit between the intergovernmental distribution of revenues and the distribution of responsibilities. In Australia, financial power has enabled national government to expand its scope and effectiveness without a clear limit, although there has always been potential for that expansion of national power to face legal challenge on the grounds that it breaches the constitution.

Some academic experts in constitutional law and political science are critical of the national accumulation of powers (Twomey 2014). Others see it as the right response to the circumstances in which Australia finds itself (Groenewegen 1979), or a pragmatic inevitability, or have argued that vertical fiscal imbalance is inevitable in federal systems (Dollery 2002, 29). To the extent that the strengthening of national government beyond the limits of the founding constitutional framework has been seen as driven by nation-building requirements, including the needs to secure the landmass and modernize the economy, the Australian elite has tolerated it. In politics, this tendency has been especially supported by the Australian Labor Party, which was in power during the crucial centralizing periods in each world war. After World War I, the legal authority with the power to interpret the constitution and determine the character and limits of government, the High Court, also facilitated a gradual shift in the balance of power from states to national. In the 1920 Engineers case, the Court affirmed the capacity of national government to make laws about matters that crossed state boundaries. In 1927 and again in 1942, the Court undermined the doctrine that the states had a 'reserve' power in which state authority was exclusive and the national government could have no authority. In this manner, the Court conferred on itself a greater freedom to expand the scope for national legislation (Birch 1975, 61–64).

However, Australia is a limited liberal state in the Anglo-American tradition. Anti-statism is endemic to political life and a core characteristic of the conservative side of politics. Often the growth of national power in specific areas has been resisted, and the population is habitually wary of changing the constitution to permanently enlarge national authority. Moves to abolish the states have never had more than large minority support on a temporary basis. In World War II, the states conceded to Canberra not only taxing power but also functions in other areas, including economic management, labour-power allocation, industry development, infrastructure, housing and communications. At a time when expanded government was legitimated by Roosevelt's New Deal in the United States and the Beveridge plan for the welfare state in Britain, there was much support in Australia for government-driven post-war reconstruction accompanied by a permanent shift of powers to the national level. In 1944, the wartime government proposed a combined referendum to expand the national authority over employment, prices, monopolies, national health and family allowances and Indigenous Australians. Education was not included. The proposals were defeated in all but two states (Macintyre 2015, 253–270). In 1946, the same government tried again, with a more limited set of propositions. Only one referendum was passed, granting the government power to make payments for social services, including 'benefits to students' (pp. 385–386). This later facilitated the growth of the national role in higher education.

Section 96 and Regulatory Federalism

Hence after World War II, the growth of national power was largely reliant on fiscal weight and became increasingly tenuous in legal terms. Under section 96 of the constitution, the national government could attach conditions to the grants it made to the states, providing the states agreed to those conditions. Because the states were dependent on national taxation revenues as primary income, they had little choice but to accept Section 96 grants, although they retained some scope to negotiate over terms. Section 96 grants became the main medium through which Canberra influenced state provision in education, hospitals, urban development and other sectors within state authority. The national government used Section 96 to expand its policy influence, and later control, in higher education and schooling. Tied grants grew especially during two periods of Australian Labor Party government 1972–1975 and 1983–1996, partly replacing the general revenue funds over which the states had full control (Dollery 2002, 36).

In the programme of neoliberal reform that began with floating the Australian dollar in 1983 (Kelly 1992), the national government used its financial capacity to shape state activity to implement a new era of federalism which has been described as 'regulatory federalism'. National government regulated the states on a standardized basis through contract and consent, requiring the states in turn to regulate themselves according to New Public Management precepts such as competition, performance regimes and output budgeting. The archetypal policy was the intergovernmental agreement on National Competition Policy which obliged the states to adopt a common template for microeconomic reform, including contestable open markets in many service areas, including VET. The states resembled 'regulated agencies operating, with varying degrees of collaboration or friction, within Commonwealth-dominated clusters of regulatory regimes' (Parkin and Anderson 2007, 1, 6). This paralleled the two stage forms of regulation in the higher education sector, whereby the national government used incentives, conditions, targets and rules to manage the universities on a nationally consistent basis, requiring university executive managers to regulate their academic units in the same manner.

Regulatory federalism continues. Currently there are active intergovernmental agreements in relation to schooling, national skills and workforce development. Neoliberalism is well fitted to maximizing the national government's position within the constitutional framework. Despite its power over taxation, following the failure of the 1944 referendum on expanded powers, national government has been large in ambition but limited in formal scope. It has been unable to rely on hierarchical forms of control to the extent possible in the comprehensive states. It has been dependant on negotiation underpinned by financial logic, rule setting and networked structures based on incentives—elements endemic to neoliberal forms of government. No doubt, because of a long familiarity with such mechanisms, national government has been especially effective in using the indirect forms of control in the neoliberal toolkit to further advance national power. Parkin and Anderson (2007) conclude that 'National Competition Policy-compliant reforms have reduced the scope for discretionary action by States'. Further, 'by agreeing to collaborative national regimes subject to new structures of cross-governmental supervision and compliance, the states are ceding (vertically to a higher level in the federal system) some of their own capacity for autonomous action' (Parkin and Anderson 2007, 7–8). In 2012, an OECD report on neoliberal reforms in 13 countries, including the United Kingdom, Canada and most of the Western Europe, stated that in the 1990s Australia went further than any other country 'in the implementation of New Public Management reforms' (OECD 2012, 11).

Yet the states have to agree to the arrangement, this takes time, and negotiated consent in nominally horizontal systems is never guaranteed. Section 96 grants limit the federal government where the states do not agree. National commonality in Australia can be difficult to enforce. This has led the national government to explore legal mechanisms by which it might intervene without constraint via conditions attached to direct funding. Section 51 of the constitution gives the national government power to make laws on matters the subject of executive decisions, while Section 81 allows it to make appropriations for 'the purposes of the Commonwealth'. The government has interpreted this to mean that if it can raise ('appropriate') money for a purpose, it can spend the money on that purpose and then make laws in relation to it. Over the years, High Court judges have had conflicting opinions on this, but the national government has expanded its use of direct funding in the neoliberal period, enabling it to operate increasingly outside Section 96's requirement for state government consent and administration (Twomey 2014, 26).

After the switch to a Liberal–National Coalition government in 1996, education became 'replete with examples' of direct funding of institutions and programmes driven by national policy (Parkin and Anderson 2007, 11). Commitment to direct funding was maintained by the Australian Labor Party government of 2007–2013. The national government has played an especially significant role in fostering private schooling and higher education and has increasingly done this via direct funding. It has shifted from Section 96 grants to direct funding of higher education with little political resistance from the states, and without a legal challenge. Yet the legality has never been certain.

FEDERALISM AND HIGHER EDUCATION

'It is characteristic of the growth of Commonwealth involvement in education that the fields which received its earliest attentions were those that were most remote from the direct administrative controls of the states', note Polesel and Teese (1998, 6). The universities were ripe for cultivation as a national sector. They were underfunded, neglected and little understood by the states; and national government, located remotely in Canberra, was less of a direct threat to the autonomy of their affairs. Once it secured a monopoly control over revenues from income taxation, Canberra also had the means to make a difference. Generally, after World War II, the universities welcomed the national government's growing role. It was to be 40 years before government as benefactor began to be displaced in university minds by government as regulator.

Beginnings

The national government's wartime control over labour generated early initiatives in training and universities. Students in medicine, dentistry, engineering, veterinary science, agriculture and some natural science courses were classified in 'reserved occupations' and exempt from military conscription, and received free tuition and living allowances. In 1942, the Universities Commission was established to administer the scheme (Birch 1975, 39; Macintyre 2015, 213–215).

There was enthusiasm in government for an expanded national role in education but the legal structure retarded progress. However, the Universities Commission was made permanent in 1945. In 1946, the ANU was established in Canberra with a mandate to develop research and doctoral education (Macintyre 2015, 215–218), the 'benefits to students' clause passed at referendum; and in 1949, in the final act of the wartime-established national department of post-war reconstruction, a new Commonwealth Scholarship scheme was created (p. 459).

National Government Takes Over

In 1950, the newly elected Liberal–National Coalition government established a committee to make recommendations on the needs of the universities, although legislation to establish the first round of the States Grants (Universities) Bill was delayed for 15 months as the states negotiated over the conditions attached to the grants. The Bill obliged them to provide matching funds to ensure that the national grants would augment total university resources. This formula, used through the

1950s and 1960s (Gallagher 1982, 49–50), eventually made the growth of universities and of national funding too expensive for the states, so that they welcomed the full national takeover of funding. The 1960s and early 1970s were years of acute financial crisis at state level (Marginson 1997). Perhaps the states conceded more readily to national power over the universities because they had 'little interest in the policy area' (Parkin and Anderson 2007, 10). The growing cost of universities and research undermined their capacity to fund the much larger government school systems, which unlike universities were seen as core business.

A major committee of inquiry in 1957 led to the Australian Universities Commission (AUC), which functioned as a 'buffer' between Canberra and the universities, while marginalizing the states. Eventually the triple character of the AUC—autonomous expert body trusted by the universities, policy adviser to government, arm of government administration—proved difficult to sustain (Gallagher 1982). A further commission of inquiry in 1963–1965 extended the national role in sub-university technical and advanced education. Between 1960 and 1975, there was great growth in funding through Section 96 grants to the states, in institutions and students, and in university research (Marginson 1997). The national government assumed full financial and policy responsibility for higher education when the Whitlam Government of 1972–1975 extended full funding to the remaining colleges of advanced education and state teachers' colleges. This provided the government with an unambiguous capacity to structure provision so as to converge participation rates across the states/territories, while establishing an adequate research-intensive university infrastructure. The second objective was accomplished everywhere by the early 1980s, except in the northern territory where it took another two decades.

When it could the national treasury department baulked at the cost, but there was no opposition from state treasuries. Yet the states maintained the idea that it was 'their' universities and colleges the national government was funding (Gallagher 1982, 63, 98) and retained coordinating bodies for higher education, with a varying intensity of regulation, after 1975. In the next three decades, these bodies gradually faded in importance and disappeared. The New South Wales Higher Education Board played a larger, longer role than its equivalents elsewhere.

The 'Unified National System' and After

In a thoroughgoing system reform in 1987–1992, the then national minister John Dawkins dramatically recast the Australian higher education system from the centre in neoliberal terms, using a mix of grants, incentives, rules, deregulation and new kinds of regulation (Dawkins 1987, 1988). This completed the process of national takeover, largely extinguishing state role in higher education policy and the coordination of institutions, without altogether extinguishing the role of the states in regulation, which derived from their residual role under the Constitution.

The driver of reform was the assumption that an expanded and modernized higher education system was essential to Australia's global economic competitiveness (Smith and Wood 1991, 95–98). Higher education policy was explicitly defined as a branch of economic policy, albeit one committed also to social equity. Dawkins consolidated the national takeover of all higher education—he was less successful taking over VET—and remade the mixed group of nationally funded institutions on the public schedule as a singular 'Unified National System'. This consisted exclusively of one type of institution, government designated universities. The minister shaped a complex set of mergers and institutional upgrades to achieve this homogenizing objective. Dawkins' reforms rested on the national government's established policy and funding supremacy. They would have been unimaginable in the context of a situation of genuinely mixed state/national authority, but the states had been marginalized in the preceding period. In the Dawkins reforms, their only real role was to assist in implementing the mergers agenda.

Reform was facilitated by an overarching emphasis on the growth of participation and new conditions for funding that eliminated small institutions. The government set out to expand enrolments by 60 per cent, partly financing this by a new system of tuition loans repayable on an income contingent basis through taxation, the Higher Education Contribution Scheme. Growth smoothed the way for new public management corporate reforms that transformed institutions into more business-like and entrepreneurial institutions, raising part of their own incomes, led by a strategic executive (Marginson and Considine 2000). At the same time, a commercial market in international education was established. Government grants per student were reduced by 8 per cent (Burke 1988) and the main sources of revenues for institutional development were the rapid growth of domestic students, enabling economies of scale and international recruitment. The price of domestic student places was fixed, and after 1995 cost indexation was discounted, but universities could set international student fees at their own chosen level. International education enrolments grew by 14 per cent per annum in the two decades after 1988 (Marginson 2007).

The reform rhetoric emphasized deregulation, corporate autonomy and diverse responses to diverse markets. Dawkins stated that institutional mission was a matter for the university to determine and that not all designated universities had to conduct research (Dawkins 1987, 27–28, 35). However, the subsequent evolution of national system management based on rules, formulae and incentives, together with the pressures of competition in a unitary system—all institutions needed status in the global market for international students and later, a global university ranking when these began in 2003—brought about a remarkable degree of standardization. All public universities adopted an explicit research mission. The newly upgraded universities moved to strengthen research capacity by upgrading staff to PhD level, designating staff positions as 'teaching and research', drawing surplus from commercial research to appoint researchers and building doctoral enrolments. A requirement that a designated 'university' must conduct research and doctoral education in at least three fields was formally agreed by all governments and sector organizations in 2000 (Australian Government 2014).

The forms of the Dawkins Unified National System have continued largely unchanged since 1992, although the level of tuition payable by income contingent student loans has risen. The publicly regulated Australian system described in Table 4.4 is a unitary sector in which all but Melbourne College of Divinity University, and Bachelor Institute, are comprehensive teaching and research universities. All are self-accrediting with degree awarding powers. All receive federal funding for teaching places, research projects and infrastructure. All recruit fee-paying cross-border students. All enrol as many students as they wish. On average, student contributions via income contingent tuition loans

Table 4.4 *Homogeneity and Stratification in Australian Higher Education, 2012–2014*

Institution (Bold Indicates Shanghai ARWU Top 500, 2015. Grey = Group of Eight Univ.)	Research Block Grant Allocation 2014 $ Million	Total Income for All Purposes 2012 $ Million	Research Income % of All Income 2012 %	Competitive Academic Research Grants 2012 $ Million	Total Published Research Outputs[a] 2012	Papers in Top 10% by Citation 2009–2012	International Student % of All Income 2012 %	Total Student Load 2012 EFT	ATAR[b] B. Bus./Equival. 2014
U Melbourne	189.2	1,807.8	20.8	207.5	4,741.2	1,198	18.3	38,243	93.0
U Sydney	179.5	1,736.5	18.8	192.1	5,118.2	1,056	16.3	40,916	95.0
U Queensland	163.2	1,582.7	23.3	180.3	4,194.8	1,089	16.9	37,022	96.3
U New South W.	156.2	1,479.2	22.4	148.1	4,918.1	852	19.9	37,245	85.8
Monash U	141.3	1,620.1	19.0	157.5	3,851.8	890	19.7	49,626	82.6
Australian NU	98.9	994.9	21.8	101.2	3,049.4	582	9.9	14,368	80.7
U West'n Aust.	90.4	916.2	22.9	100.6	2,367.6	443	10.4	20,387	80.0
U Adelaide	84.1	789.7	22.9	96.2	2,010.3	430	16.8	20,086	70.7
Queensland UT	44.6	873.1	9.9	25.8	1,911.6	179	14.8	32,627	67.7
U Tasmania	41.5	530.5	17.9	34.6	1,115.9	146	8.6	17,108	65.0

(Continued)

Table 4.4 (*Continued*)

Institution (Bold Indicates Shanghai ARWU Top 500, 2015. Grey = Group of Eight Univ.)	Research Block Grant Allocation 2014 $ Million	Total Income for All Purposes 2012 $ Million	Research Income % of All Income 2012 %	Competitive Academic Research Grants 2012 $ Million	Total Published Research Outputs[a] 2012	Papers in Top 10% by Citation 2009–2012	International Student % of All Income 2012 %	Total Student Load 2012 EFT	ATAR[b] B. Bus./ Equival. 2014
U Newcastle	40.5	646.2	14.3	40.5	1,312.3	229	10.4	24,515	60.3
Curtin UT	38.0	792.4	8.0	20.4	1,487.7	190	22.8	32,813	70.0
Griffith U	37.3	804.4	8.2	27.4	1,900.9	184	17.4	31,221	68.5
Macquarie U	34.0	721.5	6.1	27.7	1,679.5	193	29.2	28,538	81.0
U Wollongong	33.5	498.3	11.1	29.4	1,373.9	201	18.3	22,038	72.0
U South Aust.	32.0	544.9	11.0	18.9	1,461.0	149	16.0	23,624	70.3
Royal Melb. ITU	30.2	836.7	5.9	13.6	1,386.7	114	28.5	41,458	70.1
Flinders U	27.4	394.4	14.4	20.2	953.2	119	9.8	14,619	70.6
La Trobe U	27.0	597.4	8.4	15.9	1,067.7	116	16.3	26,158	55.0
Deakin U	25.5	759.1	6.1	18.0	1,368.7	170	18.1	30,579	61.9
UT Sydney	25.2	640.3	8.5	16.4	1,322.1	146	22.8	25,777	90.0

James Cook U	21.7	417.6	10.1	21.3	892.6	181	10.2	15,230	n.a.
Murdoch U	19.4	373.2	6.8	9.6	532.3	n.a.	13.2	15,739	70.0
U West Sydney	16.9	627.1	3.4	12.5	1,152.1	104	9.2	30,179	65.0
Swinburne UT	16.7	516.0	4.3	11.8	811.7	n.a.	20.4	19,213	60.0
U New England	14.6	295.5	9.6	9.3	592.4	n.a.	4.8	11,181	72.6
Charles Darw. U	14.1	255.8	15.4	17.3	222.5	n.a.	4.9	5,135	60.0
Victoria U	11.3	467.0	3.0	3.0	630.6	n.a.	11.3	19,101	45.3
Edith Cowan U	10.7	375.3	4.1	3.0	509.7	n.a.	15.2	17,652	55.0
Charles Sturt U	9.1	444.7	2.6	6.1	643.5	n.a.	8.8	21,804	65.0
U Canberra	8.4	226.2	7.6	3.4	480.1	n.a.	16.8	11,187	66.0
South'n Cross U	8.2	194.2	6.7	4.0	349.1	n.a.	8.0	9,487	65.0
U Southern Q'ld	7.2	268.6	3.3	2.5	501.0	n.a.	11.9	13,950	59.9
Central Q'ld U	5.4	250.9	3.1	1.6	365.6	n.a.	29.3	11,726	61.4
Aust. Catholic U	5.3	320.2	2.6	1.4	434.6	n.a.	11.2	17,887	58.7
Federation U^c	3.8	266.7	1.3	0.8	220.8	n.a.	22.5	9,219	50.0
U Sunshine Coas.	3.2	159.1	4.4	2.3	191.3	n.a.	7.2	6,564	50.3
Bond U	3.0	n.a.	n.a.	1.3	280.2	n.a.	n.a.	6,126	n.a.

(Continued)

Table 4.4 *(Continued)*

Institution (Bold Indicates Shanghai ARWU Top 500, 2015. Grey = Group of Eight Univ.)	Research Block Grant Allocation 2014 $ Million	Total Income for All Purposes 2012 $ Million	Research Income % of All Income 2012 %	Competitive Academic Research Grants 2012 $ Million	Total Published Research Outputs[a] 2012	Papers in Top 10% by Citation 2009-2012	International Student % of All Income 2012 %	Total Student Load 2012 EFT	ATAR[b] B. Bus./ Equival. 2014
MCD U Divinity	1.6	n.a.	n.a.	0	73.8	n.a.	n.a.	700	n.a.
U Notre D. WA	1.1	142.0	0.6	0.1	96.9	n.a.	2.8	8138	80.0
Bachelor I[d]	0.4	43.1	1.9	0.03	9.0	n.a.	0	19	n.a.
Total	1,721.9	25,210.0	13.5	1,603.6	57,582.6	n.a.	16.4	844,240	—

Sources: Australian DE (2014a, 2014b); Leiden University (2014); Student Empowerment (2014). AUD 1.00 = USD 0.7317 (4 December 2015).

Notes: [a]Based on a formula whereby single authored book = 5.0, single authored journal article, chapter, refereed conference paper each = 1.0.
[b]*ATAR* is percentile expression of required minimum student achievement to enter Bachelor of Business or equivalent. ATARs are estimated by a private company. Consistent with published data for NSW (UAC 2014) but data for other states/territories may not be as reliable. These figures differ from published data on 'first cut-off' student offers as second and subsequent offers are made at lower scores.
[c]*Federation* University is a merger of former University of Ballarat and Churchill Campus of Monash University.
[d]Most higher education enrolments of Bachelor Institute of Indigenous Tertiary Education absorbed into Charles Darwin University from 2012.

cover almost half of the costs of domestic student places. Instead of competition fostering a diversity of sub-markets and specialist products, as in markets for retail cultural goods, in the Unified National System supply side competition and growth incentives, regulated on the basis of common policy, funding and accountability requirements, have fostered large generalist institutions that jostle for broad market coverage of aggregated demand pools in each state capital, in the manner of free-to-air commercial television. Mission statements and strategic plans are near uniform. All are global research universities providing global competences and employability, all are socially engaged, all are student-centred, etc.

The mission is homogeneous but the universities are differentiated by resources and status. The national system is modelled as a market of competing universities. All compete for first-degree students, fee-paying international students, international students, scholarship-bearing doctoral students, research monies from public and private sources, and in provision of consultancy and commercial services. All compete informally but continually for social status in Australia and global prestige abroad. In these competitions, historical advantages, in prestige, inherited resources and the path-dependent behaviour of elite families and of academics are continually reproduced, enabling the older universities in the Group of Eight (mid-grey in Table 4.4) to maintain the strongest position. If anything, the gap to other universities has increased.

In singular higher education systems as in Australia and the United Kingdom, without formal subsectors, classifications or mission-based tiers, competition fosters uniformity. This is not just because brand capital (and social reproduction) demand stability and predictability. It is easier for governments to administer homogeneity than difference, and the game logic of competition itself drives sameness. If an initiative fails, innovating university leaders risk losing ground vis-à-vis their competitors. It is safer and more intuitive to imitate each other, to follow common and predictable paths. Then if all institutions fail, one does not lose competitive position. Whereas policy intervention in higher education can secure either diversity or homogeneity, depending on the policies, competition fosters homogeneity, unless firm steps are taken to factor in diverse missions, or an individual university is strong and bold enough to break out of the mould.

The Dawkins reforms also accelerated a transition to direct national funding of institutions, bypassing the states and Section 96. In November 1991, a Special Premiers' Conference of national and state governments formalized the national government's responsibility for the public funding of higher education and agreed it was responsible for 'determining national priorities and accountability of institutions'. At that stage, the states continued to control the use of the term 'university' and were 'to ensure that institutions met reporting obligations, financial management and accounting standards for public authorities'. The conference also agreed that 'commonwealth funds provided directly to higher education institutions would no longer be regarded as payments to the states/territories had been done previously'. The universities, rather than the states, were now directly accountable for public funds (DEST 2005b, 6).

Within the Unified National System, there is continuing scope for the national government to multiply its interventions, despite its model of universities as self-making corporations. It can attach conditions to grants so as to establish common rules, and negotiate case-by-case with individual universities. In the recent past, it has set tuition charges and scholarship schemes, course profiles, enrolments by field and level of study, new teaching programmes, and conditions for recruiting international students. Over the last 60 years, it has incrementally expanded standardized data and reporting requirements. It has also multiplied its performance-based instruments for shaping academic practices. All universities work to maximize their research grading in the Excellent Research for Australia (ERA) audit, lift their student and graduate satisfaction rates as measured in annual surveys, and increase their rate of graduate employment.

The national government has repeatedly floated its intention to achieve more total control. Craven (2006, 3) describes the desired outcome as 'a national higher education regime', including 'a national higher education authority' and 'over-arching higher education legislation'.

In 2005, the then minister, Brendan Nelson, pointed to 'variation between the States and Territories in terms of the legal, regulatory and accountability requirements on universities within their jurisdictions', and 'a lack of consistency in application' of certain 'agreed national requirements', which, he said, could 'constrain the capacity' of the sector 'to meet the requirements of a competitive global environment' (DEST 2005a, 4). He called for greater consistency in the regulations governing institutions' use of land, power to invest and operations outside their foundational jurisdiction, and in the restructuring of governing bodies to improve capacity in commercial matters—all areas within state prerogative. Nelson also argued that variations between states and territories in recognition and accreditation could be 'costly for providers seeking to operate in more than one state and territory and confusing for customers'. Interstate differences in regulatory requirements were not associated with variations in institutional mission, social access, research capacity and performance or recruitment of foreign students. Rather, dealing with eight separate jurisdictions added to the national government's transaction costs and time delays. The Minister suggested that a more uniform approach could be achieved by referral of state and territory governmental powers to the national government, enabling the national government to 'take over' the establishment legislation of universities (p. 5); by the adoption of common legislation in all jurisdictions; the 'establishment of universities as trusts'; or 'selective testing of the Commonwealth's constitutional corporations power' (p. 2).

National Accreditation Regime

In 2008, a national government review proposed the creation of a new national regulatory framework for accrediting both public and private tertiary institutions (Bradley 2008, xx–xxi). The need for national consistency was agreed across both state and national jurisdictions.

This led to the creation of the Tertiary Education Quality and Standards Agency (TEQSA) in 2011,[1] responsible for registration, course accreditation and standards setting for all institutions. This removed an important area of state discretion, furthering the evolution of a national approach with a single regime determining market entry and the definition of the product in higher education. TEQSA did not include VET as originally proposed. A separate national regulator was established for the registration and accreditation of all VET institutions.

---

[1] For further information about TEQSA, see http://www.teqsa.gov.au

The High Court, the Corporations' Power and the 'Nationhood' Power

In the Workplace Relations case of 2006, the High Court appeared to take a large step in the direction of stronger national power within the federation. It found the national government's power over corporations in Section 51 of the constitution was not limited to the 'trading' aspect of corporations but potentially extended to all of their activities. The Court stated that the starting point for interpreting the corporation's power should be the specific words about that power in the constitution, not the implications for the role of the states as intended in the constitution, and the federal/state balance. It argued that a state's power over industrial matters was not essential for it to govern effectively. This suggested the national government might have jurisdiction over all aspects of the operation of those higher education institutions that were legally incorporated as corporations engaged in trade. This included all public universities, which provided commercial international education and maintained commercial companies in research and other areas.

Initially the national government claimed the High Court decision as a decisive step towards a single national legal regime in higher education, matching the single national financial regime already achieved. The national government stated that it would ask the states to formally refer their legal powers over financial management of universities to the national level of government, in order 'to reduce red tape'. The national government threatened to intervene directly, using the corporations power, if the states refused. However, there was doubt about whether the trading and corporate aspects of public universities were sufficient to bring them under the newly defined corporations power, given their public duties and their intrinsic character as institutions of education and knowledge as noted previously by the High Court.

At the time of writing, the extent of the corporations power in higher education remained untested. However, the pathway suggested by the 2006 decision remained a possible strategic opening for national government and may prove important in higher education in the future—not least because the full application of the corporations power in the sector would complete the tendency set in train by the Dawkins reforms, the refashioning of higher education as an economic sector with an economic logic, as a national and global business in place of its foundational character as a servant of state, the public interest and local community.

Aside from the potential of the corporations power under Section 51 of the constitution, and the 'benefits to students' clause, which appears to support grants for student scholarships or loans rather than for universities themselves, the national government has three possible vehicles whereby it can allocate funds to higher education institutions and set conditions governing those funds. The first vehicle, Section 96 grants, is clear-cut in constitutional terms but relies on a form of cooperative federalism whereby national government works through the states. As noted, the government believes that it has a second vehicle under Sections 51 and 81, enabling it to make appropriations and laws directly without recourse to the states, even in matters such as education outside its constitutional authority. The third vehicle, which like the second vehicle is asserted by Canberra but has been subject to various and conflicting interpretations on the Higher Court, is the use of a combination of Sections 51 and 61 to enable the government to 'engage in enterprises and activities peculiarly adapted to the government of a nation and which cannot otherwise be carried on for the benefit of the nation'. This is known as the 'nationhood' power.

High Court decisions in 2012 and 2014 placed the second and third vehicles for national funding in doubt and suggested that the possibility that the long drift in favour of national power might be reversed, with implications for higher education. In 2012, the court found unanimously that Section 81 was not sufficient to support the expenditure of monies appropriated under it, suggesting that another constitutional or legislative power was required to spend the money. The Court left open the possibility that the nationhood power could be invoked to support expenditures previously supported under Section 81, but the Chief Justice found that the nationhood power 'cannot be invoked to set aside the distribution of powers between Commonwealth and States', and two other judges noted the 'limited powers' of the national government (Twomey 2014, 20, 30). The national government ignored the implications of these statements and universities, and private education continued to operate through direct expenditures rather than Section 96. However, in 2014 in the Williams Case, the High Court emphasized that the potential of the nationhood power was limited, and it could not be applied coercively, relying on implied 'federal considerations' in its interpretation of national power, in notable contrast with views that had been expressed in the 2006 Work Relations case. The High Court was concerned that national spending in fields within the competence of the states had the capacity to 'diminish the authority of the states in their fields of operation'. Several judges emphasized their concern about the use of direct expenditures in place of Section 96 grants to the states (Twomey 2014, 34–40).

These findings place in jeopardy the national government's direct funding of higher education and its administrative control through conditions attached to its grants to universities. They suggest the government might be forced to return to Section 96 grants in higher education, allowing the states to intervene in the conditions of funding and possibly fostering a greater diversity of approach over time. However, at the time of writing, the national government's regime of direct grants and administrative conditions had not been challenged in the High Court.

RESIDUAL POTENTIAL OF THE STATES

In a country note on Australian education in 1997, the OECD remarked that 'although the universities are established under State legislation.... The university sector is generally perceived in national terms, and we heard no views expressed that the States should play a bigger role in their operations' (OECD 1997, 24). This is no longer wholly correct, even if it was wholly correct in 1997. Although the national government has thoroughly eclipsed the states in practice, the potential of the states remains large and from time to time becomes apparent.

Governance and Audit

Although the national government makes payments directly to institutions, the states can intervene in relation to financial management standards. They can also audit university activities in any area. For example, in the mid-1990s, the Western Australian Auditor General issued a report on the compliance of university staff with regulations governing consultancy activities and private professional practice. Subsequently, the Victorian Auditor-General released a report on international education which uncovered significant flaws in welfare provision and suggested the universities' commitment to the rapid commercial growth of full fee international student places had compromised their other institutional objectives.

The states are most active in relation to institutional governance. They control the University Acts and must be engaged when a university wants to change its Act. They shape the structure of governing councils of universities—while mindful of national policy on smaller, more business-capable councils—and often name the government and community representatives on councils. This confers on them indirect authority in the selection of vice-chancellors and other leaders.

Regional Development

All universities depend on municipal and state government authorities for cooperation in relation to land use, buildings and planning regulation. Some universities play a more proactive and responsive role in state and regional development, especially those in regional Queensland. Universities are important in the local economies of provincial cities, in collaboration with civic authorities and industry, often as the primary employer.

South Australia has built a globally focused education precinct in Adelaide by encouraging entry of foreign institutions. These include Carnegie Mellon University and Torrens University, part of the Laureate group. University College London has now withdrawn. It has become apparent that the international mini hub in Adelaide is entirely subsidy dependent. The inward flow of fee-paying international students is stronger in four other states.

The States and Research

Since the establishment of the Unified National System in 1987–1992, the largest financial role taken by the states has been in research and development. In 1998, Queensland announced a 'Smart State' strategy focused in building the state-based research sector. Between 1998 and 2012, its spending on research and development doubled, and the number of scientists in Queensland more than doubled (Wheeler

2012). State funding was joined to major donations from the US-based foundation Atlantic philanthropies and matching national government funds. The emphases have been on clinical medicine, bioscience and pharmaceutics and associated life sciences, with an emphasis on fostering commercialization of results (Nickless 2006). The University of Queensland established an applied bioscience precinct with academic laboratories and commercial companies facing each other and recruited leading researchers from Melbourne and Sydney. These developments helped its continuing rise in the Shanghai ARWU top 100. The Queensland University of Technology has also lifted its research capacity and global position. The state has played a key role not just in planning and funding but also in bringing the parties together, facilitating common facilities and managing the regulatory framework.

No other state governments have been as active as Queensland in research, but Victoria has funded a cross-university synchrotron facility shared by physical scientists and consistently funded medical research. Since the early 1990s, the proportion of university funding sourced to the combined state governments has crept from 2 to 4 per cent, but this is only one-tenth of the level of national government funding. State fiscal capacity remains highly constrained.

Vocational Education and Training

VET operates at the upper secondary, postsecondary non-tertiary and tertiary levels of education, but as noted, only 13.5 per cent of VET students are at tertiary level, nearly all in programmes at ISCED Level 5, diplomas of two-year full-time equivalent. VET's ISCED Level 6 programmes are mostly provided in cooperation with universities. Although VET is not formally designated as 'higher education', its existence alongside higher education means that Australia has a binary tertiary system, although it is rarely described as such.

The Dawkins ministry attempted a concerted national approach to VET, including the creation or reworking of national training standards, in collaboration with unions and employers, in all industries; the fostering of a competitive national training market that encouraged entry by new private providers; the direct national funding of VET alongside state grants; and steps to more closely articulate VET and higher education, for example, through a combined Australian Qualifications Framework and conventions governing student mobility and credit transfer. The possibility of a complete national takeover of VET was floated in the early 1990s. National training standards were established, but Dawkins was unable to influence state policy sufficiently through the funding power to ground a national approach in the other areas. The universities were slow to offer credit to VET graduates, and the Qualifications Framework emphasized competition between higher education and VET at the two-year diploma level. Many employers wanted to keep VET close at hand and saw the state jurisdiction as more amenable.

In the late 1990s, the intergovernmental agreement governing shared funding collapsed. Federal grants were switched from direct funding to tied grants to the states (CGC 2007, 3). Since then, VET has been severely under-funded compared to higher education (Ross 2010). In some public VET institutions, full-time permanent staff has been largely emptied out.

A large number of small private providers have entered VET, but the public sector remains much the largest provider. In the first half of 2015, students enrolled in 1828 training provider institutions, of which 54 were public Technical and Further Education (TAFE) colleges, 14 other public providers and 1,445 private providers. TAFE and other public institutions were 3 per cent of the training providers in VET but enrolled 63 per cent of VET students (NCVER 2015). However, there is variation between the states. In Victoria, which pioneered the development of a regulated training market, 45 per cent of the 2015 enrolments were in the private sector. The proportion was higher in Queensland (48%) and also above one-third in South Australia and Tasmania, but only 6 per cent in New South Wales, where 89 per cent of all government-funded students were in public sector institutions (NCVER 2015). In New South Wales, but not in Victoria, TAFE has retained the structure of a single centrally administered state system.

GLOBALIZATION, INTERNATIONALIZATION AND WCUS

As noted in the introduction to the chapter, Australian universities have made a success of the more global era post 1990. They are strong relative to population size in the number of ARWU top 500 universities and their share of cross-border students.

World-class Universities

The number of ARWU top 500 universities increased from 14 universities in 2004, with two in the top 100, to 23 universities in 2017 and six in the top 100. Most universities have risen, although ANU has declined. Melbourne, Queensland and Monash have made notable advances. Although its reliance on Nobel indicators is questionable,[2] the ARWU is a bona fide measure of research performance and the improved performance of Australian universities has lifted their reputation in the global student market. Australian universities have lifted their ARWU position without special research funding for the leading universities, unlike China, South Korea or Germany. Instead, government has relied on New Public Management reform to strengthen the strategic capacity of executive leaders and performance cultures in research. Australian universities have subsidized research from income for teaching and learned to manage the rankings indicators effectively. In the case of the ARWU, that means recruiting more high citation researchers, publishing in *Science* and *Nature*, and ensuring that all faculty publications are included in publication, counts with an institutional designation. (Whether these strategies augment creativity as breakthrough ideas is a different question; see Murphy 2015.)

Where the Australian model has faltered has been in the failure to achieve a top 30 university, unlike the United States, United Kingdom, Switzerland and Canada. The Unified National System template depends on an enforced scarcity of public funds, so that even the top research universities pump international students above 10,000, so as to draw resources for research from their tuition fees. This is a somewhat precarious platform for research, and it contributes to neglect of doctoral student scholarships. International PhDs are seen as another source of fees. Relatively, few top international doctoral students go to Australia.

---

[2] Performance in the Times Higher and QS rankings can be ignored. These lack objectivity and validity (Marginson 2014).

Global Student Market

Universities with strong global rankings have a sizeable individual advantage in attracting international students. The performance of these universities also feeds into the value of the common national template fostered by the Dawkins reforms. A 2005 ministerial discussion paper on 're-aligning Commonwealth and State responsibilities' argued that Australia needed 'a sector with a wide diversity of institutions with the flexibility to pursue their own distinct missions and develop innovative responses to opportunities that arise'. The nationally standardized system worked against that outcome. But the same paragraph specified a more relevant objective: 'We need a nationally consistent, well defined "brand" to support our engagement with the international marketplace for higher education' (DEST 2005a). The Unified National System is that brand. Brand Australia functions as a singular claim to quality. This especially benefitted the research-weaker universities outside global rankings, while providing a platform on which the strong universities can erect their specific claims to status and recruit successfully.

The part-commercialization of the Australian universities in the early 1990s enabled them to build comparative advantage in marketing, recruitment and international student servicing at a time when global student mobility was gathering pace. International students tend to concentrate in global cities, which, in Australia, primarily mean Melbourne, Sydney, Brisbane, the smaller but cosmopolitan national capital in Canberra, and Perth in Western Australia, geographically close to Southeast Asia. Enrolment levels of onshore and offshore international students vary substantially between universities. Two of them—RMIT University and Monash University in Melbourne—have over 20,000 international students. There is greater diversity in the international strategies of universities in Australia than in other aspects of their mission. This diversity includes bricks-and-mortar offshore campuses, offshore franchising and twinning, distance and online education in various forms, and national variations in the student intake. Nevertheless, all states/territories have a significant presence in international education (see Table 4.5).

Problems related to federalism have arisen in international education, due to a combination of national domination, state neglect and lack of state/national cohesion. The national government regulates provider

Table 4.5 Export Income from International Education 2014–2015, and International Student Enrolments in Higher Education 2014, by State/Territory

State/Territory	Export Income from International Education (All Education Sectors) 2014–2015 AU$ Million	Onshore International Students in Higher Education 2014	Onshore International Students in Higher Education as a Proportion of All Onshore Students 2014 %
New South Wales	6,722	79,192	19.49
Victoria	5,615	81,937	25.24
Queensland	2,708	47,192	20.16
Western Australia	1,345	19,183	15.43
South Australia	1,127	16,399	18.81
Tasmania	164	3,220	11.60
Northern Territory	55	1,804	15.59
Australian Capital Terr.	436	9,699	24.95
Multi-state	–	2,947	9.05
AUSTRALIA	18,775	243,617	20.31

Source: Australian Department of Education (2014, 2015).

Note: In 2014–2015, the higher education sector alone generated $12.5 billion in export income, which was 68.6 per cent of all export revenues. The total includes tuition fees and the living and transport expenses of international students and their families into and in Australia.

institutions and visa policy, while state and municipal authorities play the main role in student housing, welfare, policing and safety and urban planning of facilities. When in 2008–2010 there was a crisis of student safety in Victoria, which particularly affected Indian students, the state government denied the problem rather than addressing it. This played into negative publicity in India (Marginson et al. 2010) and the collapse of demand from South Asia in 2010–2012. Firmer national standards of care could have prevented this.

CONCLUSIONS
A System Stuck

The Australian story of federation and higher education is atypical. In some chapters in this book, national/regional differentiation is associated with problems of coordination and forms of heterogeneity that compromises policy objectives. Federation seems to interrupt an incomplete process of modernization and development. In other chapters, regional differences, possibly accompanied by a structured diversity of institutional type and mission, is seen as an asset within a larger system. This is a later stage of modernization in which decentralization is more clearly positive. Australia belongs to neither camp. It has completed the early modernization stage without embarking on the later stage of decentralization and more nuanced provision. Despite the national/state fault line running through the polity, Australia has achieved a full coherent national integration of tertiary education, except for two-year programmes in VET. It is a considerable achievement. But where to from here? The logic of reform points towards evermore fine-grained accountability and closer control. Having hailed national centralization amid 1970s capacity building, the universities now find that centralized control is less enabling when it takes the form of neoliberal austerity, more from less and from the ever-faster turnover of competition, rather than additional funding and the freedoms it brings. Canadian universities, funded by province as well as nation, have more generous financing and a healthier decentralized university autonomy.

In a more global era, federalism is one means of combining worldwide access and connectivity with smaller society and local agency (Twomey and Withers 2007, 19). In this vision of federalism, nations and supra-national bodies become switching stations for managing the shifts between different scales, registers and communities. Australian federalism is in another place. It is still bounded by the nation and its interest, and it has not moved as far from its legal foundations as first appears. The older process of nation-building between fragmented communities is still playing out. It is difficult for well-realized nations to let go and find the way to embrace the rich but complex benefits of decentralization. Consider Spain and the Catalans, for example.

What Does Australia Tell Us About Federalism and Higher Education?

The markedly centralizing federalism in Australian higher education, generating outcomes different from those in the most other countries in these chapters, allows scholars to assess the developmental dynamics of a federal system positioned at one extreme of the spectrum.

In Australia, close national system management has enabled homogeneity of institutional type, whether measured by mission, size, scope, fields and levels of study or inner culture. If the states had remained funders as in Canada, and the universities served two governments, there would be greater variety today. There is diversity of mission and size, through the private sector. It remains to be seen whether the shift to one national regulator across both sectors leads to homogenization in the private sector and/or between sectors or an overall pluralization. The former seems more likely, and, regardless, the large public universities are unlikely to change quickly.

At the same time, centralized control has enabled an advanced level of system design. The competitive Unified National System and national funding regime together constitute a well-developed government-run quasi market. Executive leaders are animated by drives for status, revenues and global impact. There are established product formats in research and proxy forms in relation to education, such as student satisfaction measures and graduate employment rates. The international student market sharpens commercial skills. This crisp clear policy outcome would not have evolved in a regime of mixed jurisdictions. Correspondingly, the downsides of markets are more fully apparent: inhibited cooperation between faculty and between institutions, hyper-accountability and a frenetic performance regime probably inimical to deeper creativity, student engagement strategies not cognitive learning strategies, scarce resources squandered on the costs of corporate competition and, in some universities, weak faculty disciplinary identities. In addition, in Australia, there is now diminished attention to public goods in higher education, as distinct from the private benefits for individual graduates. The normative shift from public to private goods was facilitated by the practical removal of universities from the state sphere, where public goods were more concrete and localized than they are in the national sphere.

The quasi market has also run up against its limits. Large-scale neoliberal privatization has not happened. It is impossible to turn public universities with inherited social functions into a large vibrant private sector in a contestable market, and, despite market ideology, these lumbering public beasts have blocked the challenge of the new commercial players. The Unified National System consists of semi-commercialized public universities with little real potential for market entry. New private sector institutions are growing, fed by subsidy, but remain marginal. They have low resources, small size, narrow programme profiles, no research and crucially, little status.

Overall, the Australian case illustrates the effects of one kind of centralization. Singular government control perhaps facilitates neoliberal homogeneity or at least has made it possible. Still, this is not the sum of all possible centralizations. For example, a chief casualty of the national approach is the more freewheeling kind of institutional autonomy and academic practices free of regulated objectives and modes of work. Yet it is possible to imagine a different kind of national regime that encourages organizational creativity rather than conformity and isomorphism, and leaves faculty alone to develop ideas. Arguably, also, this outcome could be more readily achieved in a mixed state/national regime than in today's centralized system.

The Future

Australian federalism shifted from an early period of *separated federalism* in which the states had the main role and the national government performed demarcated functions in international and intra-national relations (Gallagher 1982, 24) to *cooperative federalism* in which the national government pursued its objective through state governments— overlapping with *coercive fiscal federalism* whereby the states were prodded into line by national government control of revenues—to *regulative federalism* whereby the states were harnessed as vehicles of neoliberal forms of government. The OECD describes the evolution of Australian federalism as follows:

> While Commonwealth government activism in many areas has been seen in terms of creeping centralism by some observers, it responds to the twin realities of a changing economic and social environment and a Constitution that, while remaining largely unaltered for over a century, has seen attempts by the Commonwealth to extend its reach largely being validated, or enabled, by decisions of the constitutional court. (OECD 2012, 60)

Yet, evolving judicial interpretations of national and state power can move in either direction. Despite the intergovernmental architecture for facilitating negotiations and commonality of view, the situation is unstable. 'Increasing involvement of the Commonwealth government in policy areas previously managed wholly or largely by the states has caused increased tensions between the Commonwealth and the states' (OECD 2012, 60–61). On one hand, direct grants for higher education and research are open to legal challenge. The High Court has made clear its desire to rein in a freewheeling notion of the scope of the national government. On the other, the pervasive use of special purpose grants to the states under Section 96 has 'the effect of turning every state government function into a concurrent function', implying 'substantial reductions in economic efficiency' (OECD 2012, 61). There are many possibilities. It is even conceivable that higher education could fragment between a quasi-independent national/global universities and other institutions that are more specifically tied to the states—paralleling system design in, say, China or the United States—though at this time there is no sign of system differentiation.

An open set of possibilities calls up normative as well as empirical judgment. In the period from World War II onward in Australia, the national government was more imaginative in its perspective, more advanced in expertise and less corrupted by routine or by private interest than were the states. If modernization and capacity building are seen as the primary objectives, the drift to national control in higher education was beneficial overall, at least, from 1942 to 1992. Since then the 'vanilla' downside of national uniformity has become more apparent, and national government has often used its fiscal control to hold down or privatize funding rather than increase it. It is also less clear that the old state/national gap in expertise still exists.

The European Union suggests the benefits of a decentralized approach premised on unity in diversity, in which common systems enable productive internal and external relations rather than operating as means of homogenizing activity. The network is standardized, not the nodes, which are expected to make use of their agency freedom. Recent High Court decisions in Australia foreshadow the possibility of a reassertion of state constitutional power. In higher education, this could enable a more decentralized approach, with a larger autonomy and creativity in the states and/or the institutions themselves. On a good day, this could lead to a broader pluralization of university mission, for example, through the fostering of specialist strengths, with a lesser number of universities committed to the mega-large fully comprehensive model.

This alone would not break the single model of high science multiversity, reinforced as it is by global ranking. Australian policy is not the only mimetic force. Moreover, a federalism based on unity in diversity requires a more sophisticated (and higher risk) approach than Australia has so far devised. Both sides of Australian politics remain committed to a linear expansion of national executive power. The most likely next change in tertiary education is still a national takeover of VET, not the partial decentralization of the university system. In the case of VET, where there is still modernization to be done, stage one centralization, it would be appropriate.

REFERENCES

Academic Ranking of World Universities (ARWU). 2017. *2017 Academic Ranking of World Universities*. Shanghai Jiao Tong University. Available at http://www.shanghairanking.com

Australian Bureau of Statistics (ABS). 2015. 'Statistical Series, Various'. Available at www.abs.gov.au

Australian Department of Education. 2014. 'Selected Higher Education Statistics'. Available at http://education.gov.au/higher-education-statistics

————. 2015. 'Research Infrastructure Block Grants'. Available at https://education.gov.au/research-infrastructure-block-grants

————. 2015. 'Export Income to Australia from International Education Activity in 2014–15'. Available at https://internationaleducation.gov.au/research/Research-Snapshots/Documents/Export%20Income%20FY2014-5.pdf

Australian Government. 2014. 'National Protocols for Higher Education'. Available at http://www.industry.gov.au/highereducation/StudentSupport/NationalProtocolsForHigherEducationApprovalProcesses/Pages/default.aspx

Birch, I. 1975. *Constitutional Responsibility for Education in Australia*. Canberra: Australian National University Press.

Bradley, D. 2008. *Review of Higher Education: Final Report*. Canberra: Australian Government.

Burke, G. 1988. 'How Large Are the Cuts in Operating Grants per Student?' *Australian Universities Review* 31 (2): 42–43.

Burton, T., Dollery, B., and Wallis, J. 2016. 'A Century of Vertical Fiscal Imbalance in Australian Federalism'. *History of Economics Review* 36: 26–43.

Commonwealth Grants Commission (CGC). 2007. *Trends in Commonwealth State Financial Relations: A Grants Commission Perspective*. Background Paper. Canberra: GCA.

Craven, G. 2006. 'Commonwealth Power over Higher Education: Implications and Realities'. *Public Policy* 1 (1): 1–13.

Croucher, G., Marginson, S., Norton, A., and Wells, J. 2013. *The Dawkins Revolution: 25 Years on*. Melbourne: Melbourne University Publishing.

Davies, S., and Zarifa, D. 2012. 'The Stratification of Universities: Structural Inequality in Canada and the United States'. *Research in Social Stratification and Mobility* 30 (2): 143–158.

Dawkins, J. 1987. *Higher Education: A Policy Discussion Paper*. Canberra: Australian Government Publishing Service.

————. 1988. *Higher Education: A Policy Statement*. Canberra: Australian Government Publishing Service.

Department of Education, Science and Training (DEST). 2005a. *Building Better Foundations for Higher Education in Australia: A Discussion About Realigning Commonwealth-state Responsibilities*. Canberra: DEST.

————. 2005b. *Rationalising Responsibility for Higher Education in Australia*. Canberra: DEST.

Dollery, B. 2002. 'A century of vertical fiscal imbalance in Australian federalism'. *History of Economics Review* 36 (1): 26–43. [Page numbers cited in text are from mimeo version]

Gallagher, A. 1982. *Coordinating Australian University Development: A Study of the Australian Universities Commission*. Brisbane: University of Queensland Press.

Groenewegen, P. 1979. 'Federalism'. In *From Whitlam to Fraser*, edited by A. Patience and B. Head, 50–69. Melbourne: Oxford University Press.

Hollander, R., and Patapan, H. 2007. 'Pragmatic Federalism: Australian Federalism from Hawke to Howard'. *Australian Journal of Public Administration* 66 (3): 280–297. [Page numbers cited in text are from mimeo version]

Kelly, P. 1992. *The End of Certainty: The Story of the 1980s*. Sydney: Allen and Unwin.

Leiden University. 2014. *The Leiden Ranking 2014*. Centre for Science and Technology Studies. Available at http://www.leidenranking.com/ranking/2014

Macintyre, S. 2015. *Australia's Boldest Experiment: War and Reconstruction in the 1940s*. Sydney: NewSouth Publishing.

Marginson, S. 1997. *Educating Australia: Government, Economy and Citizen since 1960*. Cambridge: Cambridge University Press.

———. 2007. 'Global Position and Position-taking: The Case of Australia'. *Journal of Studies in International Education* 11 (1): 5–32.

———. 2014. 'University Rankings and Social Science'. *European Journal of Education* 49 (1): 45–59.

Marginson, S., and Considine, M. 2000. *The Enterprise University: Power, Governance and Reinvention in Australia*. Cambridge: Cambridge University Press.

Marginson, S., and Marshman, I. 2013. 'System and Structure'. In *The Dawkins Revolution: 25 Years on*, edited by G. Croucher, S. Marginson, A. Norton, and J. Wells, 56–74. Melbourne: Melbourne University Publishing.

Marginson, S., Nyland, C., Sawir, E., and Forbes-Mewett, H. 2010. *International Student Security*. Cambridge: Cambridge University Press.

Mathews, R. 1981. 'The Development of Australian Fiscal Federalism'. In Advisory Commission on Intergovernmental Relations (ACIR) (ed.), *Studies in Comparative Federalism—Australia*, 1–26. Washington, DC: ACIR.

Murphy, P. 2015. *Universities and Innovation Economies: The Creative Wasteland of Post-industrial Society*. Farnham: Ashgate.

National Centre for Vocational Education Research (NCVER). 2015. *Government-funded Students and Courses: January to June 2015*. Adelaide: NCVER.

Nickless, R. 2006. 'All Jokes Aside, Money Talks for the "Smart State"'. *The Australian Financial Review*, 5 June.

Organization for Economic Cooperation and Development (OECD). 1997. *The Transition from Initial Education to Working life. Country Note: Australia*. Paris: OECD.

———. 2012. *Value for Money in Government: Australia 2012*. Paris: OECD.

———. 2015. *Education at a Glance, 2015*. Paris: OECD.

———. 2017. *Education at a Glance, 2017*. Paris: OECD.

Parkin, A., and Anderson, G. 2007. 'The Howard Government, Regulatory Federalism and the Transformation of Commonwealth-state relations'. *Australian Journal of Political Science* 42 (2): 295–314. [Page numbers cited in text are from mimeo version]

Polesel, J., and Teese, R. 1998. 'The "Colleges": Growth and Diversity in the Non-university Tertiary Sector. Evaluations and Investigations Program, 97/20, Higher Education Division, Department of Employment, Education, Training and Youth Affairs (DEETYA). Canberra: DEETYA.

Ross, J. 2010. 'Howard Starved TAFE Worse Than Unis: Productivity Commission'. *Campus Review*, 22 February.

Smith, R., and Wood, F. 1991. 'Higher Education in Federal Systems: Australia'. In *Higher Education in Federal Systems. Proceedings of an International Colloquium held at Queens's University, May 1991*, edited by D. Brown, P. Cazalis, and G. Jasmin, 95–123. Kingston, Ontario, Canada: Queen's University.

Student Empowerment. 2014. 'Course Entry Requirements: ATAR University Scores'. Available at http://australianuniversities.co/atar-course-entry-requirements.html

Twomey, A. 2014. 'Federal-State Financial Relations and the Constitutional Limits on Spending Public Money'. Report No. 4, 2014 Constitutional Reform Unit, Sydney Law School, Sydney: University of Sydney.

Twomey, A., and Withers, G. 2007. *Federalist Paper 1: Australia's Federal Future.* A report for the Council for the Australian Federation.

United Nations Educational, Social and Cultural Organization (UNESCO). 2018. International Standard Classification of Education, ISCED 2011. Available at http://uis.unesco.org/sites/default/files/documents/international-standard-classification-of-education-isced-2011-en.pdf

Universities Admissions Centre (UAC), New South Wales. 2014. ATAR information. Available at http://www.uac.edu.au/atar/ (accessed 1 December 2014).

Wheeler, D. 2012. 'An Australian "Smart State" Serves up Lessons for a Knowledge Economy'. *The Chronicle of Higher Education*, 15 April.

World Bank. 2017. *Data and Indicators.* Available at https://data.worldbank.org/indicator/SP.POP.TOTL?view=chart

Chapter 5

Germany
Continuous Intergovernmental Negotiations

Ulrich Teichler

INTRODUCTION: THE OVERALL SETTING

Government Between Cultural Diversity and Homogeneity of Living Conditions

The Federal Republic of Germany was founded in 1949 as a successor state to the German *Reich* of the pre-war time and as a merger of the post-war Western German–British, French and US occupation zones. In 1990, the German Democratic Republic, previously the post-war Soviet occupation zone, ceased to exist and became part of the Federal Republic of Germany.

The constitution (*Grundgesetz*) of 1949 makes provision for a Federal system, whereby some rights are granted solely to the Federal authorities, others jointly to the *Bund* and the *Länder* (the functional equivalent of provinces in Canada, states in the United States, *Kantone* in Switzerland, etc.), and finally others solely to the *Länder*, or local communities in the framework of the *Länder* authorities. There are two parliaments on the national level—the *Bundestag*, elected by the German population with voting rights, and the *Bundesrat*, a second chamber with between three and five government representatives of each *Land* (11 *Länder* in 1949 and 16 since 1990). If legal power rests on the national level, both chambers vote initially but the *Bundestag* has the final say. If the legal power rests on both *Bund* and *Länder* level, a law needs to be agreed by both the chambers. If the legal power rests on the *Länder* level, the parliament of each *Land* can decide separately. The heads of the governments of the *Länder* meet regularly in the *Ministerpräsidentenkonferenz*, and they can make joint decisions for the purpose of national coordination. For example, the decision in 1968 to establish *Fachhochschulen* as a second type of higher education institutions alongside universities was made that way. In such cases, the parliaments of all *Länder* have to subsequently approve the decision.

Germany, however, has been a loose or somewhat federated system for more than 1,000 years except for the short period of the *Nazi* regime. After World War II, a centralized political system was seen as vulnerable to power misuse. The option for a Federal system, which was formally legalized in 1949, did not imply a preference for a completely decentralized system. Two ways of managing this were envisaged and implemented—either as so-called 'joint tasks' of authorities on national and *Länder* level or through coordination between the *Länder*. While the former are spelled out in the constitution, the latter is left open to respective initiatives and agreements.

The German constitution names principles according to which the powers should be allocated. On the one hand, the power of the *Länder* of supervising the education system rests on the principle of 'cultural diversity'. On the other hand, Article 72.3 of the constitution calls for preserving 'homogeneous living conditions' (*Einheitlichkeit der Lebensverhältnisse*) in all parts of the country. In addition, international relations in education (e.g., German schools abroad, support of academic mobility, development aid in the area of education, etc.) are seen as Federal government responsibilities for foreign affairs (like international diplomatic ties and the military). Coordination and funding of such activities might be the task of the Federal Ministry in charge of foreign affairs, or economic cooperation, or education and science.

Higher education in the Federal Republic of Germany is understood as rooted primarily in the principle of 'cultural diversity'. As a consequence, the individual *Länder* are in charge of establishing, supervising and funding higher education institutions. However, higher education is seen as highly important for the 'homogeneity of living conditions' and therefore in need of coordination and possibly joint action in at least some respects (cf. Teichler 1992; as regards the legal setting, see Heilbronner and Geis 2012; Reich 2012; Thieme 2004). Germany is among the federal systems in which national power and nationwide coordination plays a relatively strong role (cf. Cortés and Teichler 2010).

Thus, federalism in higher education in the Federal Republic of Germany faces a 'fundamental dilemma' (Peisert and Framhein 1978)—not only the constitution but also public expectations call for ways of reconciling these two principles. The views of the various actors tend to be controversial, and the interpretations as regards the needs of coordination have changed over time. The constitution was frequently revised between 1969 and 2014 (in each case, a majority in both the *Bundestag* and the *Bundesrat* was required) in order to redefine what is included in the joint tasks of higher education and research.

The Structure of the Chapter

The aim of this chapter is to provide an account of the interrelationships between the national (Federal) and the regional (*Länder*) level in the higher education system of Germany (see Braband 2004; Heidenheimer 1994; Heilbronner and Geis 2012; Onestini 2002; Peisert and Framhein 1997; Teichler 1992, 2006; Webler 1990). It begins with an overview of the higher education system and its basic characteristics. Subsequently, developments of the Federal–*Länder* relationships as regards higher education will be shown from the early years after World War II until 2014. Finally, funding and national–regional interactions are addressed, notably with respect to homogeneity versus variety in higher education, and to the consequences beyond higher education.

THE HIGHER EDUCATION SYSTEM IN GERMANY

A General Overview

Most descriptions of higher education underscore the two-type institutional pattern.

- The majority of new entrant students are enrolled at universities—institutions that award doctoral degrees and emphasize both teaching and research. Long study programmes led traditionally, and still in part lead today, to a *Diplom, Magister* or a state examination in selected fields—all considered equivalent to a master degree in Anglo-American countries. Most professors have an identical teaching load based on the expectation that they spend about the same amount of time on teaching and research.

- In the wake of expanding student numbers, *Fachhochschulen* were established around 1970 as a second institutional type. They differ from universities in their more applied curricula, in that the teaching load of professors is more than twice as high as for university professors, in not being expected to train junior academics and award doctoral degrees, and in doing applied not basic research, on a moderate scale (Enders 2010; Klumpp and Teichler 2008). Initially, study programmes often comprised three years of learning in classes and one-year internships. The *Diplom* awarded tended to be viewed internationally as between bachelor and master level. To increase international comparability and visibility, since about 1990 the study programmes have been officially called four-year programmes. The institutions began at that time to translate their name into English as 'universities of applied sciences'.

- Various overviews of German higher education present a longer list of institutional types. *Kunsthochschulen* (colleges of art and music) are characterized by specific selection procedures, a strong emphasis in teaching and learning on practical performance and only awarding doctoral degrees in select scientifically oriented programmes, such as art history.

Traditionally, four years of elementary schooling and nine years at a *Gymnasium* led to the *Abitur* which in principle entitles those who passed this demanding final examination to enrol in any field and any university. Even when admission restrictions (*Numerus clausus*) grew in some fields and institutions in the 1960s, admission regulations ensured university entry at least after a waiting period (see Teichler 1985). The entry qualification for *Fachhochschulen* (*FHs*) is based on 12 years of schooling. Over the years, the entry routes to higher education

diversified, to include even enrolment following upon successful vocational training subsequent to compulsory schooling.

In the wake of the so-called Bologna Process in Europe since 1999,
both universities and universities of applied sciences transformed their
study programmes into (often three-year) bachelor programmes and
(often two-year) master programmes. The right to award doctoral
degrees remained confined to universities.

The total number of institutions of higher education in the Federal
Republic of Germany was initially about 100 and 126 in 1960. It
doubled with the establishment of *FHs* and remained about 250 in
the 1970s and 1980s. The increase to 350 in the year 2000 was predominantly due to German unification (see Kehm 2006). In the winter
semester 2012–2013, there were 399 institutions of higher education
in Germany, including 93 public universities, 52 public art and music
colleges and 105 public *Fachhochschulen*. In addition, the number of
church-related institutions on university level, for the study of theology,
was 14 and the number of church-related *FHs*, for example, active in
the area of social work, was 19. Finally, there were 21 private universities and 92 private *FHs* (Autorengruppe Bildungsberichterstattung
2014, 120). The total number of students was about 2.6 million, with
over 1.6 million enrolled at universities.

Institutional size varies substantially. Public universities with a broad
disciplinary range tend to have more than 30,000 students. About
half of all university students are enrolled in the 25 largest institutions. *FHs* offer a smaller range of fields of study and have on average
less than quarter as many students as universities. Private universities
are normally very small and specialize in a few fields. The size of the
various sectors can be illustrated by the proportion of new entrant
students—92.7 per cent in the public sector, 1.1 per cent in the church
sector and 6.2 per cent in the private sector. As regards institutional
types, 60.4 per cent of the new entrants were at university-type institutions, 1.3 per cent at art and music colleges and 38.4 per cent at
Fachhochschulen (Autorengruppe Bildungsberichterstattung 2014, 120).

The entry rate to higher education in the Federal Republic of
Germany was below 5 per cent in the early post-war period. It increased

from about 15 per cent in 1970 to 20 per cent in 1980 and 30 per cent in 1990. It was again 30 per cent in 2000, now including regions that previously belonged to the German Democratic Republic, which had long had lower entry rates than the West. In 2010, the national entry rate reached 42 per cent, still only about two-thirds as high as the average of OECD countries (see OECD 2012). More recently, the entry rate leaped quickly forward to 50 per cent (see Teichler 2014).

NATIONAL CHARACTERISTICS

Such a quantitative-structural overview on national systems of higher education is often viewed as indispensable basic information. In order to grasp why policy discourses vary substantially between countries despite apparently similar quantitative patterns, it is necessary to take into consideration national characteristics of higher education which reflect the 'philosophy' of the system; its links to society; and other features that cannot be described in simple data presentations. As regards Germany, it seems appropriate to point out four characteristics—the emphasis on Humboldtian principles, the flat prestige hierarchy among universities, the strong professional emphasis and, last but not the least, the strong role of government. The final characteristic is essential in order to understand the discourse about the federal system.

Legacy of the Humboldtian Principles

The University of Heidelberg (1386) was the first university in Germany. Several others followed within about a century. Yet most analysts consider the incorporation of the 'idea of the university' into the University of Berlin, founded in 1810, as its most important feature and as the start of the modern university (see Germany. Sekretariat 2002, 2013; Huber 1983; Kehm 1999, 2006; Kehm and Teichler 1992; Krais and Naumann 1991; Oehler 1989, 2000; Teichler 1986, 1990, 2014; Turner 2001; cf. also Rüegg 2011). Humboldt had developed three key principles for the University in communication with various scholars—'unity of teaching and learning' (*Einheit von Forschung und Lehre*), 'solitude and freedom' (*Einsamkeit und Freiheit*) and the 'community of those teaching and learning' (*Gemeinschaft der Lehrenden und*

Lernenden). Accordingly, all university professors should undertake research, teaching should be largely based on research, and teaching should elicit creative feedback to research.

This basic concept had a strong impact on internal governance. It gave enormous power to 'professors' over the growing number of junior academic staff. The latter were dependent on professors up to the point of passing their *Habilitation* and eventually getting a 'call' to become a professor. 'Self-administration' by university professors was the key feature of university governance until the 1960s. Even now, surveys show that more university professors in Germany than in other countries believe they have a say in core academic issues (see Teichler 2011). In contrast, rectors and deans had predominantly symbolic power, and the task of synthesizing the will of the professors. This does not mean that research was expected to be a monopoly of the universities. A substantial proportion of publicly funded research in Germany is located in institutes outside the universities. Neither does a powerful professoriate imply a weak role for government. Traditionally, governments of the individual *Länder* influence higher education access and admissions and play an important role in professorial appointments by making the final choice from a list of three candidates presented by the university. Occasionally, government may not accept any of the three.

Flat Prestige Hierarchy Among Universities

The second characteristic of German higher education is a very *flat hierarchy of quality and reputation among universities*. The bearer of quality traditionally was assumed to be not the institution or department but the individual professor (and possibly other staff of the '*Lehrstuhl*' or chair), who could raise his or her reputation and income by being approached by another institution and being willing to move. Both the high value placed on inter-institutional mobility and the greater trust in external than internal review of professors are linked to the rule that the first promotion to a professor position and remuneration cannot occur at the university where the candidate was active immediately prior (*Hausberufungsverbot*). In addition, students are free to move between universities at any time. The mobility of both academics and students are viewed as simultaneously indicating the strength and contributing to the strength of the system.

The emphasis placed on equivalent quality among universities was traditionally reflected in governmental funding of universities, based on the number of students in each discipline. It was also reinforced by state agencies' recruiting of new graduates on the basis of grades awarded, without differentiating among universities. However, moderate quality differences do exist. University professors at the 10 universities receiving the most awards from the major public research funds granting agency, the *Deutsche Forschungsgemeinschaft* (DFG), raise about twice as much as average (see Teichler 2014, 147–171).

A Strong Professional Emphasis

The third salient characteristic of German higher education is a *relatively close link between field of study and future occupation*. Upon completion of secondary education, most students see the choice of field of study as a choice of occupation. This is exemplified by those disciplines that lead directly to public sector employment or into occupations directly supervised by the public sector, such as medicine, law, teacher training and social work. Until recently, all (and most of them still do) terminate in a state examination rather than a university degree.

The combination of a track system of secondary education and the expectation of a close link between field of study and employment are frequently named as the major reason that enrolment in higher education in the Federal Republic lagged behind the rest of the Western Europe in the twentieth century. Certainly, from about 1970 to the mid-1990s, the concern prevailed in German higher education policy that high rates of graduates would cause serious problems, initially often characterized as *akademisches Proletariat* and subsequently as *Verdrängungswettbewerb* (displacement competition) and *Überqualifizierung* (over-education).

This professional emphasis in higher education as well as the widespread pride in Germany of the quality of vocational training with a strong element of apprenticeships contributed to the fact that the enrolment rate in higher education remained below the average of economically advanced countries from the early post-war years until about 2010. However, many experts perceive a gradual process of reconsideration in Germany as regards the links between study and career in the wake of rapid growth of enrolment and dynamic changes in the world of work.

The Strong Role of Government

A fourth characteristic of the German university system is *the strong influence of the state on higher education*. More than 90 per cent of students are enrolled at public institutions. These institutions until recently were state-subordinated agencies (*nachgeordnete Behörden*), with most professors as civil servants. Students, as a rule, do not pay tuition fees. The governments of the individual *Länder* supervise the higher education institutions, among them the few universities of the Federal government (for the military and for training some civil services) located in their respective territory, as well as the private higher education institutions. Traditionally, the *Länder* governments approved study programmes, but, recently, most *Länder* governments discontinued this practice in favour of accreditation schemes. The *Länder* fund public institutions of higher education. This funding is expected to cover the educational provisions, a baseline of research and all facilities. The supervision and funding of higher education through the individual *Länder*, however, is embedded into various mechanisms of nationwide coordination and support—either through joint inter-*Länder* or joint Federal–*Länder* mechanisms, which are further explained here.

Since 2000, discourse on the funding needs of higher education and the roles of the Federal and *Länder* governments have been strongly influenced by the very large increase in the number of students. This is not viewed as temporary. According to various predictions, the absolute number of new entrants in 2025 is expected to remain more or less unchanged, as a result of a further increase of the entry rate and some demographic decline, and the number of students is expected to increase slightly (Germany. Statistische Ämter des Bundes und der Länder 2013).

THE HISTORY OF NATIONAL-REGIONAL RELATIONSHIPS IN HIGHER EDUCATION

In higher education in the Federal Republic of Germany, the national–regional relationship is important. An overview book on higher education, widely distributed by the Federal ministry in charge of higher education (its name changed over the years), classifies the historical development of higher education from 1945 until the 1970s, according to changes in the national–regional relationship (Peisert and Framhein 1997). That history is divided into three periods—'Decentralized Reconstruction' (1945–1956), 'System-wide Initiatives' (1957–1969) and 'Cooperative Federalism' (beginning in 1969). Subsequently, other typologies of the national–regional relationship have appeared, and these are also discussed in the next sections.

Decentralized Reconstruction, 1945–1956

During the early post-war period, Federal responsibilities were confined to a few legislative measures, to financial support for scientific research and to funding activities of cultural relations with other countries. Already in 1948, before the foundation of the Federal Republic of Germany, a decision was made to establish the Permanent Conference of the Ministers of Culture, later of the Ministers of Education and Cultural Affairs (*Ständige Konferenz der Kultusminister der Länder in der Bundesrepublik Deutschland—KMK*). After initially serving as a forum of communication, from the mid-1950s, this body was responsible for setting guidelines for minimum conformity in the education system. If an issue was viewed as necessarily similar across the whole country and if *Länder* agreed unanimously, the *KMK* could prepare the respective inter-*Länder* contract. Each *Land* was bound to implement such a decision, after it was made legally binding by the parliament or government of the *Land* had issued an order.

During this period, some organizations were created on the Federal level, notably the West German Rectors' Conference (*Westdeutsche Rektorenkonferenz—WRK*), which served as a voice of the higher education institutions, the German Academic Exchange Service (*Deutscher Academic Exchange Service—DAAD*), the largest organization for the

distribution of public funds for international mobility and cooperation between higher education institutions, and the German Research
Association (*Deutsche Forschungsgemeinschaft*), a body officially self-
governed by the community of German scholars, which received more
than half of its funds from each of the Federal government and the
governments of the *Länder*. The *DFG* supported upon application individual research projects and research networks, primarily at universities.

Various national coordination practices not explicitly addressing
higher education also affected the sector. Employment conditions
and salaries at public higher education institutions were largely determined by national regulations for civil servants as well as for other staff
employed in the public sector.

System-wide Initiatives, 1957–1969

During the second period, beginning in the mid-1950s, the German
Federal government became a visible actor in higher education and
research. It established a Federal ministry specifically for this domain,
created regular funding arrangements between the Federal government
and the *Länder* governments, and established a major advisory organ
with the involvement of both governmental levels.

In 1955, it also established the *Bundesministerium für Atomfragen*
(Federal Ministry of Nuclear Issues), broadened by 1962 into the
Bundesministerium für wissenschaftliche Forschung (Federal Ministry of
Scientific Research). With the widening of federal coordination functions in education, notably higher education, two respective Federal
Ministries existed from 1969 onward for more than two decades—
the *Bundesministerium für Bildung und Wissenschaft* (Federal Ministry
of Education and Science) and the *Bundesministerium für Forschung
und Technologie* (Federal Ministry of Research and Technology). In
1994, the two ministries were merged into the *Bundesministerium
für Bildung, Wissenschaft, Forschung und Technologie*, in 1998 renamed
the *Bundesministerium für Bildung und Forschung* (Federal Ministry of
Education and Research; see Weingart and Taubert 2006, 11).

Since 1956, there has been a coordinated system of research cost
sharing between the Federal government and the *Länder* governments.

Initially, the Federal government assumed more than half of the expenditures of the *DFG* and the research projects in higher education it promoted, and half the expenditures of the *Max-Planck-Gesellschaft* (Max Planck Society), an association for coordinating public institutes for basic research. Later, 90 per cent of the *Fraunhofer-Gesellschaft*, an association in charge of the coordination of public institutes for applied research, and a varying proportion of other research institutes, went under the umbrella of the *Wissensgemeinschaft Gottfried Wilhelm Leibniz*. Moreover, the Federal government funded 90 per cent of the costs of public large-scale research institutes founded or extended since the 1950s (i.e., in nuclear research and cancer research) and eventually coordinated by the *Helmholtz-Gemeinschaft Deutscher Forschungszentren* (see Hohn 2010). Award decisions on financial support for large-scale research and development projects in science and technology rested in the majority of cases within the ministry in charge of education and research, with the rest handled by other Federal ministries (see Stucke 2010).

In 1955, the Federal government and the *Länder* governments agreed to establish and to share the costs of a system of student aid (grants and loans), initially called *Honnefer Modell* for some years and subsequently *BAFöG*, the abbreviation of the respective Federal law enacted in 1969, that is, *Bundes-Ausbildungs-Förderungsgesetz* (Federal Law for the Support of Training). Most of the time, the Federal government covered 65 per cent of the costs of this need-based scholarship system, which varied in its magnitude over the years between one-tenth and one-quarter of the living and study costs of German students (see Schäferbarthold 1999). Concurrently, the legal and financial situation of the so-called *Deutsche Studentenwerke* was consolidated, a nationwide association running the publicly supported dormitories, dining halls and other student services at German institutions as well as managing the student aid system (see Von Mutius 1996).

Finally, the *Wissenschaftsrat*, the *WR* (translated either as Science Council or as Council of the Sciences and Humanities, the latter in order to underscore that the term *Wissenschaft* and the function of the council covers all disciplines), was established in 1957 as the first central agency in the area of higher education and science in which the Federal government and the governments of the *Länder* worked together on a regular basis. The *WR* initially was composed by a Science Commission of 16 scholars and an Administrative Commission with 11 votes by representatives of the Federal government and one vote of each of the initial 11 *Länder* at that time. Both commissions could take initiatives for higher education policy, for example, recommendations for long-term developments or proposals for funding and evaluation, and they voted provisionally, with a two-thirds majority required. Final recommendations and other decisions are made by the general assemblies of both commissions, again requiring a two-thirds majority. The recommendations are not binding, but they have had great impact on quantitative, structural and resource planning over the years and have often influenced the general public discourse on long-term higher education policies.

Cooperative Federalism (Beginning in 1969)

Two developments paved the way for the third period, characterized by a switch from a predominantly decentralized to a cooperative setting (see Peisert and Framhein 1978). First, in the wake of a rapid expansion of higher education and research, the Federal government was called upon to increase substantially the financial support for the sector. Second, subsequent to the student unrest of the late 1960s, concepts of appropriate higher education reforms became so diverse that the 'homogeneity of living conditions' as regards higher education was viewed as at risk.

In 1969, there was an amendment to the constitution of the Federal Republic of Germany to include facilities and construction in higher education as among the *Gemeinschaftsaufgaben* (common tasks). The new Higher Education Construction Act envisaged that the Federal government and the government of the respective *Land* for each provide 50 per cent funding for the construction of university buildings. Both the *WR* and the new (Federal–*Länder*) Planning Committee for Construction in Higher Education became major agencies of higher education planning. Practically, all establishments of new universities and extensions of existing universities had to pass through this complex coordination process. Parliaments of the respective *Land* could overrule such decisions and establish or expand public higher education on their own, but did not do so because they would forego the 50 per cent Federal subsidy.

The Federal and the *Länder* governments signed an agreement in 1970 to form a joint agency for educational planning—*Bund-Länder-Kommission für Bildungsplanung und Forschungsförderung* (*BLK*). The purpose of the *BLK* was to reach agreements on financial and quantitative long-term planning for all educational sectors.

Finally, agreement was reached on developing framework legislation which would determine which matters were regulated uniformly nationwide by individual *Länder* legislation and which were determined by the specific regulations of each *Land*. Preparations for such a Framework Act for Higher Education began in 1970.

Dynamics of Reform and Legislation (Early and Mid-1970s)

In another overview book on higher education in Germany (Kehm 1999), Peisert and Framhein (1997), switched the periodization to a different logic. They moved from primary emphasis on the links between the two levels of government to actual developments in the system of 'cooperative federalism'.

The potential of joint activities of the Federal government and the *Länder* governments, enabled by the constitutional change of 1969, was soon weakened by controversy about the direction of reform. Hopes of an emergent consensus on key issues faded by 1972, when no agreement could be reached about the first *Bildungsgesamtplan*, the General Plan for Education expected to serve as a framework for long-term quantitative-structural planning. The *BLK* never became a body of detailed planning, amid divergent views between the Federal government, various *Länder* governments and various political parties concerning the desirability of educational expansion and the affordability of educational expenditures. However, the *BLK* played a role in promoting innovations within higher education institutions. For example, curricular innovations through the *Modellversuchsprogramm* (model experiment programme) were funded half each by the Federal government and the government of the respective *Land*.

The enactment of a *Hochschulrahmengesetz* (*HRG*; Framework Act for Higher Education) was postponed repeatedly during more than five years of debate about admission to higher education, the new configuration of institutional types, the power of the university management and the representation of others than professors in the responsible bodies within institutions of higher education. Another central agency became a major player amid these controversies. The *Bundesverfassungsgericht* (Federal Constitutional Court) was frequently called upon to examine whether certain components of higher education legislation were compatible with the principles laid down in the constitution. The court made two principal decisions that enforced compromises in the preparation of the Framework Act. First, it concluded in 1972 that there is a constitutional right of persons having passed the *Abitur* to study at a university in any field of study at universities. Therefore, modes of admission in *Numerus clausus* fields have to be established so that even secondary school leavers with low school grades or low marks in entry tests have some chance of being enrolled. Second, a 1973 ruling found that constitutionally ensured academic freedom implies that in intra-university committees in charge of key academic matters, at least 51 per cent of the votes have to be reserved to professors.

The Post-experimental Truce (1977-Late 1980s)

After the enactment of the *HRG* in 1976 (see Germany. Bundesministerium für Bildung und Wissenschaft 1978a), hopes faded that new mechanisms of coordination between the national and *Länder* levels would facilitate the growth of the system, support reforms in higher education and safeguard the desired homogeneity of the system. In 1978, the Federal government published a report pointing at various problems in higher education as well as the difficulties of reaching minimum agreement. It called for stronger federal powers to ensure the generally desired minimum homogeneity of living conditions (Germany. Bundesminister für Bildung und Wissenschaft 1978b; cf. Teichler 1981; Oehler and Teichler 1984).

The *Länder*, however, joined in reducing the influence of the Federal government. Notably, the *KMK* claimed the coordination of the new Study Reform Commissions called for by the *HRG*. The *HRG*'s objective had been to ensure a degree of similarity of curricula within individual disciplines, and across disciplines, amid diverse reform concepts. When these commissions began in 1978, the governments of the *Länder*, the rectors' conference and academics were strongly represented, but the Federal government had only an advisory role (on curricular coordination in Germany, see Mc-Daniel, Gauye and Guin 1989).

At this time, higher education institutions were being expected to increase their number of students without a corresponding increase in resources. The Federal government was no longer prepared to strongly support the expansion of higher education. In the 1980s, the number of students rose by about 50 per cent, while the overall public expenditures for higher education did not increase more than the inflation rate. Later, in the period that followed, the absolute number of students did not fall because demographic decline was outweighed by an increased enrolment in the age cohort (see Kehm and Teichler 1992).

The Federal government and the *WR* began advocating greater diversity in the higher education system. Widespread protests against higher education reforms in the 1970s and the call for a greater diversity led to a substantial revision of the *HRG* in 1985, which now set fewer requirements for homogeneous higher education legislation of the *Länder* (see Gieseke 1987; Pritchard 1986; Teichler 1991). But the general mood against federal involvement was so strong on the part of the *Länder* that some of them even refused legislative revisions according to this more flexible framework (Schimank and Lange 2006, 324).

Unification and Renewal in Higher Education and Research in the East (Early 1990s)

The process of German unification, beginning with the fall of the Berlin Wall in November 1989 and legalized when the Eastern territories opted to become *Länder* of the Federal Republic in October 1990, led to a strengthening of governmental collaboration on Federal and state level. In the summer of 1990, the *WR* took over the major policy coordination role in the transformation of higher education and research in the *Neue Länder*. From 1990 to 1992, it issued recommendations that became the reform blueprint, mostly adaptations to the situation in the West. The higher education system in the German Democratic Republic had been centrally coordinated; the enrolment rate had been relatively low, and a generous number of academic staff positions had led to a relatively low student–staff ratio. The role of research at universities had been limited in a system that largely restricted research to academies of science. There was no institutional type similar to *Fachhochschulen* (see Möhle 1992).

In the wake of the transformation process after unification, about one-third of the positions for academic and non-academic staff were eliminated. Most public research institutes outside higher education were either closed or integrated into universities. *FHs* were established. Most of the regulatory system in the eastern *Länder* was fitted to that prevailing in the West. Enormous financial resources were provided for the transformation and renewal. Major tax transfers to the East were needed for the new *Länder* governments to fund higher education. In addition, a substantial *Hochschulerneuerungsprogramm—HEP* (Higher Education Renewal Programme) was set up for the period 1991–1996, funded by the Federal government and by the governments of the new *Länder* at the ratio of 75:25 (see Kehm 1999, 20–23; Peisert and Framhein 1997, 18–30; cf. also Mayntz 1994).

New Reform Paradigms and the Official Re-decentralization of Higher Education (From the Mid-1990s Through the Early Years of the Twenty-first Century)

After the 'tour de force' of German unification (Kehm 1999, 22), there was increased interest in pursuing higher education reforms similar to those discussed or implemented in various other economically advanced countries since the 1980s. This became a period when the Federal government—as in the period between the late 1960s and the mid-1970s—tried to achieve a stronger influence in shaping the development of higher education (see Pasternack 2011a).

At the same time, debates about the strengths and weaknesses of Federal–*Länder* cooperation and coordination in higher education were energized by the decision of the Federal and the *Länder* governments to realign Federal–*Länder* relations across all policy sectors, to reduce overlap and joint tasks. This resulted in a constitutional revision in 2006, which signalled almost the end of an active role of Federal government in higher education policy (Pasternack 2011b).

The first major area of higher education reform was governance and administration (see Bogumil and Burgi 2013; Hüfner 2003; Kehm and Lanzendorf 2006; Mayer and Ziegele 2009). Various components of detailed governmental supervision were revoked, the power of the university management was strengthened, stakeholder involvement was realized through the establishment of *Hochschulräte* (boards; see Lange 2010), more elements of evaluation became mandatory, and a system of accreditation of study programmes was established. The *HRG* was revised in 1998—most regulations on university governance and administration were abolished, freeing the *Länder* to opt for individual approaches (see Sandberger 2011).

In this framework of reforms, an accreditation system was established in Germany in 1999 on a provisional basis and in 2003 on a permanent basis. This aimed to replace the traditional system of approval of individual study programmes by the government of respective *Land* with a mandatory accreditation system, whereby individual *Länder* could keep a system of approval primarily on the basis of the results of accreditation. This new system enabled the stronger influence of academia as well as a greater diversity of study programmes, while preserving a degree of similarity and opportunities for inter-institutional student mobility. In the *Akkreditierungsrat* (Accreditation Council), established by the cooperating *Länder*, representatives of the *Länder* governments, the rectors of higher education institutions and academics, students and the employment system were expected to set guidelines for programme accreditation as well as accredit and supervise the activities of the individual accreditation agencies, which the institutions could invite to accredit their individual study programmes (see Erichsen 2006; Kehm 2007; Röbbeke 2010; Schade 2004; Suchanek et al. 2012). Not all the individual *Länder* accepted this accreditation system. After some years, a system of institutional accreditation (*System-Akkreditierung*) was established alongside, which, according to some observers' and actors' views, was likely to substitute programme accreditation in the long run. In addition, changes were made in academic careers and the remuneration of academics (see Kehm 2006; Konsortium Bildungsbericht Wissenschaftlicher Nachwuchs 2013; Teichler and Bracht 2006).

In 2003, the *Bundestag* established a committee expected to reduce the joint and overlapping functions of the Federal and the *Länder* governments in all policy areas. In 2006, the so-called *Föderalismusreform* was legally enacted. In the domain of higher education, the 'joint tasks' of educational planning, framework legislation regarding the tasks and structures of higher education, regulations regarding civil servants working in higher education and the funding of construction in higher education were all discontinued. The reform of the Federated system has made higher education one of the few policy areas where individual *Länder* are solely in charge.

Surprisingly, the Framework Act for Higher Education was not abolished. Various political efforts were made to abolish it, but not consistently pursued. Yet, it seems appropriate that a former senior official of the Federal Ministry of Education and Research published an 'obituary' a few years later (Gieseke 2012) because various *Länder* began to change their legislation without any concern about the still existing formal national legal framework. The *HRG* was not abolished, but it was more or less phased out.

A closer view, however, suggests that the restriction of the tasks and functions of the Federal government were not as substantial as widespread interpretations in 2006 signalled (see Pasternack 2011c). First, the promotion of research outside higher education remained a joint task within the constitution. Second, continuous involvement of the Federal government in a reduced range of programmes concerning research and teaching in higher education was constitutionally safeguarded as joint task (*Förderung von Vorhaben der Wissenschaft und Forschung*). Third, the Federal government kept the right to enact legislation regarding admission to higher education, degrees, student aid and fixed term contracting of academic staff as well as the rights and duties of civil servants employed in the higher education system. Fourth, the joint task of educational planning was substituted by that of cooperation in examining the performance of education in international comparison and the associated reporting and recommendations. The *BLK* was discontinued, and instead Federal and *Länder* governments established the *Gemeinsame Wissenschaftskonferenz*—GWK (see Pasternack 2011a).

Increasing Diversity, Joint Major Strategic Programmes and Eventual Reestablishment of Federal Powers (2006-2014)

The major constitutional reform of the relationships between the Federal and *Länder* levels as well as the gradual erosion of the role of the Framework Act for Higher Education reinforced the process of a growing diversity between the *Länder* in regulatory systems of higher education. This process had already started with the revisions of the *HRG* in 1998. Now, most actors do not know the extent to which regulations in their respective *Land* differ from those in other *Länder*. A multitude of studies has been published which aim at providing comparative overviews on the situation in the 16 *Länder*, for example, regarding enrolment rates (Autorengruppe Bildungsberichterstattung 2014), global versus item-wise funding of higher education institutions, modes of indicator-based funding, modes of contracts between governments and individual higher education institutions, professors' teaching loads, the introduction of bachelor and master programmes compared to the preservation of traditional programmes, salaries, provisions for sabbaticals (Pasternack 2011c), composition and tasks of university boards (Hüther 2010), categories of academic staff and criteria for the appointment of professors (Konsortium Bundesbericht Wissenschaftlicher Nachwuchs 2013). These differences between the *Länder* might be viewed as substantial, if the ideal of 'homogeneity of living conditions' is taken as the criterion, but are small in comparison to differences between member countries of the European Union.

The *Länder* did not enlarge the domains of inter-*Länder* coordination in response to their increased constitutional powers. But they continued to coordinate in areas in which they had been active in the past. For example, the *Länder* took care jointly of the process of establishing qualification frameworks for higher education curricula, in the wake of corresponding moves in the Bologna Process or European Union. They also repeatedly changed the regulatory framework of accreditation, and agreed in 2009 on widening access to higher education for persons without traditional secondary education credentials. Finally, they reorganized in 2010 the national coordination system for admission in *Numerus clausus* fields (see Germany Sekretariat 2013).

Surprisingly, the legislative changes from 1998 to 2006, aimed at weakening the role of national coordination in general and the role of the Federal government in system coordination, did not reduce the overall involvement of the Federal government in higher education policy. The Federal contribution to overall higher education and research expenditures increased after 1998 and again strikingly after 2006—federal expenditures for higher education doubled from 2006 to 2014, and their share among all public expenditures for higher education rose from over 10 per cent to 18 per cent. Moreover, after 2000, the Federal government was more active in higher education reform policy than in the 1980s/1990s. For some years, reform discourses were intertwined with controversies about the appropriate power of the Federal and *Länder* level. But, ironically, after the legal issue was formally resolved in 2006 in favour of an increased power of the *Länder*, the Federal government became more influential through a range of new or extended financial support programmes, several of which explicitly required major reforms in higher education.

Federal financial involvement in research projects, the funding of research institutes outside higher education and the support for need-based student aid continued without major changes but the funds increased. The increased Federal role became visible in four major support programmes—three new and one continuing the previous schemes of research promotion. They altogether comprised almost 2 billion euro in annual federal fund, and they were intended to have a major impact on the character and the quality of higher education and research.

First, the *Pakt für Forschung und Innovation*, decided by the heads of the Federal and the *Länder* governments in 2005, ensured a continuation of joint funding of research projects through the *DFG* and public research institutes outside higher education, whereby the total funding by the Federal government clearly exceeds total funding by the *Länder*.

Second, there was the *Exzellenzinitiative*. In 2004, the Federal Ministry of Education and Research suggested special support for research and institutional development in a limited number of universities to raise their quality and status in the international rankings of world-class universities. The initial fancy terms of 'brains up!' and *Elite-Universitäten* gave way to the *Exzellenzinitiative*, adopted by the heads of the Federal and the *Länder* governments in 2005. The funds provided were not completely concentrated as initially intended on supporting a few institutions, but rather split into three programme lines: (a) *Graduiertenschulen*, (b) *Exzellenzcluster* (large networks of cooperation between universities and eventually research institutes and industry) and (c) *Zukunftskonzepte* of a few excellent universities (future concepts; see Bloch et al. 2008; Horn-Bostel 2008; Kehm 2013; Leibfried 2010). While the former two were not substantially different from previously existing *DFG* promotion schemes, and were managed by the *DFG*, the 'future concepts' envisaged support of up to about €100 million over five years each for 10 universities successful in the competition aimed at innovative strategic research thrusts and quality enhancement of research. The Federal government covers 75 per cent of the costs of the *Exzellenzinitiative*, while the *WR* plays a key role in managing the assessment of applications. A first tranche of nine universities were awarded support from the year 2007 to 2012; the majority were again among the 10 winners of the competition from 2012 to 2017. A decision was made in 2014 to extend this support programme beyond 2017, but there is a widespread discussion about desirable changes in its character.

Third, the Federal and *Länder* governments agreed in 2007 to provide funds in the framework of the 'Hochschulpakt 2020' for covering substantial parts of the costs incurred by the increase in student numbers. New entrant students increased by 44 per cent between 2005 and 2012, and a further increase was predicted. The Federal government made available more than €1 billion annually on average to subsidize each new entrant student at €13,000, on the condition that the respective *Land* also provides the university with €13,000 (see Germany. Gemeinsame Wissenschaftskonferenz 2014).

Fourth, the *Federal and Länder* governments agreed in 2010 to support the quality of teaching provisions in the framework of the

'*Qualitätspakt Lehre*' from 2011 to 2020. Institutions of higher educa-tion could apply for funds to improve the employment conditions of academic staff, to train academics for teaching functions and to improve teaching through other means.

Moreover, the Federal government either took a leading role or cooperated with the *Länder* in other programmes. These included support for the establishment of junior professor positions, a *Professorinnenprogramm* to contribute to gender equality in academia, scholarships for gifted students (*Begabtenförderung*), support for the doctoral study of foreigners (*International Promovieren in Deutschland*) and for undertaking educational research (*Rahmenprogramm zur Förderung empirischer Bildungsforschung*) and in this framework research on higher education (see Konsortium Bundesbericht Wissenschaftlicher Nachwuchs 2013, 118–120).

Finally, the Federal government established new student aid schemes. Already in 2001, it established a student loan system (*Bildungskreditprogramm*) additional to the combined need-based grant and loan system *BAFöG*. This loan ensures moderate interest rates as well as possible postponement of repayment in hardship cases. In 2010, the Federal government initiated a scholarship programme called *Deutschland-Stipendium*. In this framework, the government covered half of the scholarship, if a university succeeded raised the other half from employers, foundations or private persons. In 2014, the Federal government agreed to take over 100 per cent of the public subsidies for the need-based grant and loan system *BAFöG*, thus freeing the *Länder* from the previous share of 35 per cent; this arrangement was made under the assumption that the *Länder* would use this money for covering the basic costs of public higher education institutions.

Thus, while the right of the central level of government and parlia-ments to directly specify the governance and the structure of higher education was substantially reduced in this period, the involvement of the Federal government in funding higher education and its indirect influence in shaping governance and structure increased in the first part of the twenty-first century. The Federal role as regards the quantity and quality of study was extended. Last but not the least, a paradigmatic shift occurred—the Federal government lost influence in standardizing the higher education system as part of the 'homogeneity of living conditions' and instead became a driver for diversity.

A Renewed Federal Role in Coordinating Higher Education (Since 2014)?

The role of the Federal government in funding reform activities in higher education has been so strong in recent years that it became increasingly seen as contradicting the constitutional provisions of 2006, which set the clear dominance of the *Länder*. Eventually, not only the Federal government and major organizations acting on nationwide level, such as the *HRK* (the umbrella organization of the institutions of higher education in Germany), but also the *Länder* governments came to the conclusion that the German constitution had to be changed again to legitimate a stronger role of the Federal level.

In December 2014, the German Grundgesetz was modified again. The respective sections now say:

> The Federation and the *Länder* can cooperate on the basis of agreements in cases of supra-regional relevance in the support of *Wissenschaft*, research and teaching. Agreements focusing on higher education need the approval of all *Länder*. This does not apply to agreements about construction and large facilities in the area of research. (Germany. Bundesgesetzblatt 2014)

It remains to be seen whether this renewed constitutional change is just a post-hoc confirmation of what has happened anyway after the constitutional change of 2006 or whether this will lead to a further strengthening of the Federal role.

FEDERAL FUNDING: SHARE OF OVERALL FUNDING AND REGIONAL DIFFERENCES IN EXPENDITURES

The Increasing Share of Federal Funding

As stated, the *Länder* level is the prime level for running, supervising and funding public institutions of higher education in Germany. The

Federal level plays a supplementary funding role, with most of its funding activities embedded in joint Federal–*Länder* actions and schemes, in which the Federal government might cover between half and nine-tenths of the costs.

Many international comparisons provide figures about the funding of research. This usually includes total expenditures of the higher education system or estimated shares of higher education expenditures for research purposes, expenditures on public research institutions and research and development expenditures by industry. Germany tends to be viewed as a country that spends a higher proportion of its GDP on research and development than the average for economically advanced countries. Most figures reported for Germany in the first decade of the twenty-first century were around 2.5 per cent, with some increase over time and no reversal, as in some countries, during and after the crisis around 2008. Over the years, only about 30 per cent of research expenditures in Germany were borne by public sources, about half each by the Federal government and the *Länder* governments. Although some funds cross sectors, the map of institutions spending these funds is similar. Almost 20 per cent is spent by the mostly public higher education institutions, somewhat more than 10 per cent by public research institutions or governmental agencies, and almost 70 per cent by the private economy (see Hinze 2010).

Public expenditures on higher education increased from €17.2 billion in 2000 to €18.4 billion in 2005, €22.5 billion in 2010 and are expected to reach €28.1 billion in 2014. This increase of 64 per cent in 14 years was more than twice as high as the inflation rate. The funds contributed by Federal sources increased from €1.9 billion to €5.0 billion, while the *Länder* sources grew from €15.3 billion to €23.1 billion, that is, 51 per cent. The proportion of Federal funds among all public funds provided to higher education in Germany was 12 per cent in 2000 and 11 per cent in 2005, and increased thereafter to 18 per cent in 2014 (Germany. Statistisches Bundesamt 2014)—during the period when the constitutional reform had weakened the position of the Federal government in higher education and strengthened the position of the *Länder* governments.

Two scholars recently undertook a detailed secondary analysis of higher education expenditures in Germany from 2000 to 2010 (Dohmen and Krempkow 2014). Their data differ slightly from those presented by the Federal Statistical Office—the latter include some supplementary financial provisions—but come to similar interpretations. They conclude that

- The proportion of costs covered by the *Länder* declined from 86 per cent to 65 per cent, while those covered by Federal funds increased from 9 per cent to 18 per cent, between 2000 and 2010.
- The estimated teaching-related expenditures of the German higher education system increased from €11.6 billion in 2000 to €15.9 billion in 2010. This increase of 37 per cent constitute a reduction in absolute expenditures per student, as the number of students rose by more than 40 per cent: When inflation is taken into consideration, there was a real reduction of more than one quarter.
- The *Länder* increased teaching-related expenditures from €10.2 billion in 2000 to €13.7 billion in 2010, almost 35 per cent. Federal support for teaching-related expenditures increased from less than €0.5 billion to more than €0.8 billion, by 71 per cent, and private means grew from €0.9 billion to €1.3 billion, that is, 44 per cent. The Federal share increased from 4.2 per cent to 5.3 per cent.
- Estimated research-related expenditures in German higher education increased from €8.4 billion in 2000 to €13.4 billion in 2010, 52 per cent in 10 years. This is a much higher increase than the overall inflation rate. While the *Länder* funding declined from about 70 per cent to less than 60 per cent, the Federal sources grew from about 15 per cent to almost one quarter.

The *Länder* were the prime funders of higher education in Germany in 2000 and continue to be so today. But the increase of the Federal share to the current proportion of 18 per cent, from between 9 per cent and 12 per cent in the previous period, is by no means negligible.

Yet, if it is assumed that academic staff increased in accordance with student numbers and the real research costs per academic staff were constant, a higher increase of public research expenditures would have been needed. Thus, the substantial increase of Federal funds did not compensate for the decline in per student expenditures by the *Länder* for teaching purposes and did not contribute to an increase of expenditures in accordance with student growth.

The overall financial sources of higher education in Germany include also support of research from private sources, income for medical services and tuition fees at private institutions. Moderate tuition fees were charged at public universities for a few years in some German *Länder* and thereafter abolished. Altogether, the income of universities in terms of research grants more than tripled over the recent two decades. The share of public research grants continued to be higher than that of private research grants (Bode 2015; Hinze 2010; Teichler 2008).

Differences in Financing Levels Among *Länder*

Germany remains a country in which the 'homogeneity of living conditions' is high on the agenda. Economic, social and cultural conditions are more balanced across regions than in most other countries. There is some pride in the fact that income disparities between regions are relatively limited, cultural life is relatively dispersed across the country and there are many regions of economic strength. The transfer of some tax income from the relatively rich *Länder* to the relatively poor *Länder* and various funding activities of the Federal government, including those for higher education, are viewed as valuable measures to keep disparities between regions in limits while enjoying their different cultural accents. In this framework, it is widely deplored that the East German *Länder* have not yet socially and economically caught up with the West in spite of enormous subsidies over more than two decades since German unification.

The available data, however, suggest the funding of higher education, and higher education provision, vary by *Länder* by a non-negligible amount. Individual *Länder* spent on average 6.5 per cent of their public budget on higher education and research between 1998 and 2008. This ratio ranged from over 10 per cent in Berlin (10.4%) and Sachsen (10.2%) to less than 6 per cent in Nordrhein-Westfalen (5.9%), Hessen (5.6%), Rheinland-Pfalz (5.4%) and Schleswig-Holstein

(5.3%) and even 4.1 per cent in Brandenburg—the *Land* surrounding Berlin (Pasternack 2011b, 341).

Participation in education also varies. For example, the proportion of school dropouts qualified to study at universities or at least at *Fachhochschulen* (*allgemeine Hochschulreife* and *Fachhochschulreife*, both including qualifications acquired through vocational education and training paths) averaged 57.3 per cent in Germany in 2012. It was higher than 70 per cent in Baden-Württemberg (78.8%), Bremen (73.5%), Berlin (72.4%) and Brandenburg (70.4%), but lower than 45 per cent in Sachsen (43.2%), Schleswig-Holstein (41.7%), Mecklenburg-Vorpommern (39.3%) and Sachsen-Anhalt (37.3%; Autorengruppe Bildungsberichterstattung 2014, 274). The most recent statistics suggest that the proportion of those entitled to enrol who actually took up study at higher education institutions varied between the *Länder* from 66 per cent to 81 per cent (Autorengruppe Bildungsberichterstattung 2014, 296). About one-third of students began studying in a *Land* different from that of their prior schooling. The new entrant rate to higher education (including foreigners and those with non-traditional entry qualifications) averaged 51.4 per cent in 2012. As many students prefer to study in large cities, the entry rate was very high in the three *Länder* comprised by just city (*Stadtstaaten*)—87.5 per cent in Bremen, 81.1 per cent in Berlin, and 79.5 per cent in Hamburg. But it also varied in the other *Länder*, from 60.1 per cent in Sachsen, 56.2 per cent in Hessen, 55.7 per cent in Thüringen and 55.1 per cent in Nordrhein-Westfalen to 30.0 per cent in Schleswig-Holstein and 36.4 per cent in Niedersachsen—the latter two *Länder* close to the *Stadtstaaten* Hamburg and Bremen (see Autorengruppe Bildungsberichterstattung 2014, Table F 2).

The total student–teacher ratio in German universities was 16.6:1 in 2012. It ranged from 8.1:1 in Mecklenburg-Vorpommern to 25.3:1 in Thüringen. At Fachhochschulen, the average ratio was 21.6:1, ranging from 11.6:1 in Baden-Württemberg to 37.1:1 in Bremen and 37.4:1 in Sachsen-Anhalt (Germany. Gemeinsame Wissenschaftskonferenz 2014, Table 11).

Until the early years of the twenty-first century, salary scales for university professors as well as for other staff in the public sector were more or less uniform for all German *Länder*. Recently, the principle was discontinued. The Federal Statistical Office calculates the average running expenditures per student (thereby excluding expenditures for medicine and health sciences) as €6,300 for the whole Germany. This figure ranged from €7,800 in Niedersachsen and €7,500 in each of Hamburg and Thüringen to €5,400 in Nordrhein-Westfalen and Rheinland-Pfalz and only €5,200 in Brandenburg (Germany. Statistisches Bundesamt 2014).

In order to assess these differences, one has to take into consideration the pattern of living, studying and being mobile across types of localities and regions. In Germany, students and academics have some preference for metropolitan areas and for other large cities. This holds true, even though there are various smaller towns well known for their university, where the life of the town is strongly shaped by academia, such as Tübingen, Marburg and Göttingen. The same applies for various small towns where universities or *FHs* have been established in recent decades. Large cities have relatively high new entrant rates from youth already residing there before they enrol as well as a clear surplus of inward mobility over outward mobility. After graduation, many graduates move outwards, but the large cities still keep a higher share of higher education-trained young persons in the labour force. They are the winners of the mobility pattern, due to their above-average provision of study places (see Flöther 2012; OECD 2010).

Some of the differences between the German *Länder* in enrolments and funding in higher education can be explained by their different situation in respect of metropolitan area. The three *Länder* composed by a city—Berlin, Hamburg and Bremen—naturally have relatively high enrolment rates and high overall higher education expenditures per capita, while *Länder* with a relatively small population, located outside but in the vicinity of major metropolitan areas, such as Brandenburg and Schleswig-Holstein, tend to have relatively low rates.

Hence a distinction based on city size and population density, as often analysed by human geographers, might be more revealing. A study undertaken in 2011, which employs six types of regions ranging from big cities to rural areas, notes only very small differences between regions in the ratio between qualified secondary school dropouts and study opportunities, ranging from 0.82:1 to 0.96:1. However, the share of persons with a higher education degree among the population in the 25–34 years age group ranged from 19 per cent in rural areas to 33 per cent in major cities (Schoof et al. 2011, 23). Obviously, there are differences, but these can be viewed in international comparison terms as relatively low and as a relative success of policies aimed at striving for a relatively high degree of 'homogeneity of living conditions'.

Similarly, research activities and opportunities for contacts between research and local industry are most pronounced in metropolitan areas and some other locations with a concentration of higher education and research resources. There are noteworthy differences, and higher education and research institutions are often called on to be more active in seeking contacts with small and medium size enterprises, even when enterprises are not located close to these institutions (see Dunkel, Teichler and Schneijderberg 2009; Kosmützky and Kretek 2012). Overall, however, relatively, public research provisions in Germany are widely distributed across regions.

CONCLUSION: THE IMPACT OF THE MIXED CENTRAL DE-CENTRALIZED SYSTEM IN GERMANY

There have been continuous, lively and controversial debates in Germany about the extent of the degree of centralization and de-centralization, the respective powers of the *Länder* and Federal governments, as well as whether the interaction or non-interaction between the actors on the centralized and the de-centralized levels had been beneficial or detrimental for higher education in Germany. There is no way of 'proving' one point of view or another. Yet, it is possible to summarize the discourse in Germany about the actual experience over the years.

First, Germans view as assets the relatively similar quantity of study opportunities and research activities, the similar quality of higher education, which facilitates inter-institutional mobility of students and academics and the similar quantity of provision of highly qualified labour across Germany. Analysts also agree that this would not have been achieved or maintained if there had not been a mechanism of coordination across the whole country and if there had not been mechanisms of financial transfers and subsidies from the Federal government.

Second, the nationwide coordination of higher education was achieved in Germany predominantly through inter-*Länder* or Federal–*Länder* mechanisms. Inter-*Länder* mechanisms seem to have played a major role in access and administration, curricula, accreditation, structure of study programmes and degrees. Inter-*Länder* coordination requires a consensus of all *Länder*. Federal–*Länder* coordination seems to be a better option if reform of higher education is at stake and full consensus about the directions of reforms could not be expected. Under those conditions, a majority decision was possible in Federal–*Länder* coordination activities, for example, through negotiations influenced by the political party or parties in the majority position at Federal level as well in some *Länder*. Federal–*Länder* cooperation has facilitated such reforms, but, as some reforms remained controversial over the years or were regretted years later by a majority of actors, this strength of Federal–*Länder* coordination was not always viewed as an advantage.

Third, Germans have viewed Federal–*Länder* coordination as indispensable when a substantial increase of public expenditures was necessary, that is, in periods of substantial increase of numbers of students, when research in Germany needed to be strengthened, and under the specific conditions of German unification in the 1990s. The German practice of 'joint' tasks and activities of the Federal and *Länder* governments assured that improved financial conditions were linked to higher education reforms with majority support, instead of the Federal 'power of the purse' possibly conflicting with the majority of *Länder* approaches. Analysts considered Federal–*Länder* coordination often as complicated and at times slow and cautious in making 'courageous' reforms. Yet, it might have been more successful than the alternatives of either non-involvement of the Federal level or involvement of the Federal level as a separate player.

Fourth, it is most difficult to assess whether the German system has been successful in striking a reasonable balance between the constitutional principles of 'homogeneity of living conditions', which calls for inter-*Länder* coordination and the involvement of the Federal level and 'cultural variety', which justifies the power of the *Länder* to run, supervise and predominantly fund higher education institutions. For many years, there was more concern about the former than about the latter principle. In addition, it is not clear whether German institutions of higher education within a relatively homogeneous overall system serve cultural diversity and the needs of different regions and localities in a better way than, for example, in countries such as the Netherlands, where overall homogeneity is just as highly valued as in Germany, but where the institutions are run, supervised and funded by the national government.

Fifth, the impact of the German mix of centralization and decentralization cannot be assessed properly without taking into account a paradigm shift in the extent to which a relatively homogeneous higher education system is seen as desirable. Beginning in the mid-1990s, but more forcefully in the first decade of the twenty-first century, the traditionally high value placed on a relatively homogeneous higher education system weakened somewhat. Greater system variation was put on the agenda in two respects.

On one hand, the move towards strengthening the power of individual universities, and notably the power of the university leadership and management, was accompanied by the notion that the regulation of a broad range of organizational matters could be left to individual *Länder*. As a consequence, the respective regulations were taken out of the Framework Act for Higher Education in 1998. The *Länder* opted for varied solutions in law and other regulations, for example, with regard to the power of presidents and rectors, the composition and tasks of committees within higher education institutions, the composition and role of university boards, junior staff positions, staff remuneration and other areas (see Hüther 2010; Kehm and Lanzendorf 2006; Konsortium Bundesbericht Wissenschaftlicher Nachwuchs 2013; Stifterverband 2004). Some experts consider the differences emerging between the *Länder* as substantial, for example, Hüther (2010, 332) argues that the *Länder* have 'excessively' used their new 'organizational freedom'. Other experts consider the cross-*Länder* range of options not so wide when compared to the internationally visible variety of options.

One interesting case suggests abolishing coordination does not necessarily lead to increased variation. When the Federal government and some *Länder* agreed to assure tuition-free study at German higher education institutions by inserting a paragraph in the Framework Act for Higher Education, *Länder*, in favour of tuition fees, challenged the legitimacy of the legal provision, and the Federal Constitutional Court decided that individual *Länder* were free to introduce tuition fees or not. Some *Länder* introduced tuition fees for initial study programmes and others did not. After a few years, however, the former abolished fees, moving back to a homogeneous situation (see Hüther and Krücken 2014) but in response to public opinion, not to nationwide regulation.

On the other hand, the Excellence Initiative initiated by the Federal government in 2004 is often seen as a departure from the mandate of 'homogeneity of living conditions' towards the promotion of a hierarchy in university quality and reputation. Ironically, while the withdrawal of Federal involvement was seen as promoting greater variation in organizational matters, in the case of the Excellence Initiative the Federal government was seen to promote variation of quality and reputation between institutions. It remains to be seen whether the Excellence Initiative really will have a strong impact in terms of a more diverse higher education system. The political reactions, however, appropriately reflected by subsequent statements of the Science Council (see Wissenschaftsrat 2010, 2013) suggest that there is widespread concern about how to strike a balance between both having a small number of more globally visible universities, and reinforcing a variety of programmes, strengthen the roles of other universities, and making sure that the quality of teaching and learning is not sacrificed while research quality is enhanced.

The constitutional reform in 2006 aimed at marginalizing the participation of the Federal government in the coordination of the higher education system. Actually, however, the Federal government has argued increasingly that the development of human potentials and of research and innovation should be so high on the agenda in the twenty-first century as to be one of the few policy sectors where growing public expenditures are in place. In contrast, the *Länder*, although principally supporting such arguments as appropriate for a 'knowledge society', did not consider themselves able to increase expenditures substantially on higher education and research. As a consequence, Federal–*Länder* coordination activities grew in contrast to the mandate of the constitutional reform. As noted, this paradox was resolved by revising the

Germany constitution again in 2014, in favour of substantial 'joint tasks' of the Federal and *Länder* governments.

Overall, the mix of responsibilities and joint actions in the higher education system are not smooth, consistent, efficient and successful. But it is also not a stifled system where traditions dominate, or where the political views of one current government easily determine everything. There is room for initiatives and impulses, filtered in a complex process of decision-making.

REFERENCES

Autorengruppe Bildungsberichterstattung, ed. 2014. *Bildung in Deutschland 2014*. Bielefeld: W. Bertelsmann.

Bloch, R., Keller, A., Lottmann, A., and Wüurmann, C. eds. 2008. *Making Excellence: Grundlagen, Praxis und Konsequenzen der Exzellenzinitiative*. Bielefeld: W. Bertelsmann.

Bode, C. 2015. 'Annotated Charts on Germany's Higher Education and Research System'. In Universities in Germany, edited by C. Bode, C. Habbich, T. Kalthöfer, D. Rüland, and A. Schlüter, 327–362. München: Prestel.

Bogumil, J., and Burgi, M. 2013. *Modernisierung der Universitäten: Umsetzungsstand und Wirkungen neuer Steuerungsinstrumente*. Berlin: Edition Sigma.

Braband, G. 2004. Federalism and Higher Education Policy: A Comparative Study of Canada and Germany. PhD Thesis: Queen's University Belfast, Faculty of Legal, Social and Education Sciences, Belfast.

Cortés, M. A. M., and Teichler, U. 2010. 'Higher Education in Federal Systems'. In *International Encyclopedia of Education*, edited by P. Petersen, E. Baker, and B. McGaw, 603–608. Oxford: Elsevier.

Dohmen, D., and Krempkow, R. 2014. *Die Entwicklung der Hochschulfinanzierung – von 2000 bis 2025*. Berlin: Konrad-Adenauer-Stiftung.

Dunkel, T., Teichler, U., and Schneijderberg, C. 2009. 'GOODUEP: National Report Germany'. INCHER-Kassel, Kassel (mimeo).

Enders, J. 2010. 'Hochschulen und Fachhochschulen'. In *Handbuch Wissenschaftspolitik*, edited by D. Simon, A. Knie, and S. HornBostel, 443–456. Wiesbaden: VS Verlag für Sozialwissenschaften.

Erichsen, H.-U. 2006. 'Grundlagen, Zielsetzungen, gegenwärtiger Stand und Zukunft des Akkreditierungswesens in Deutschland'. In *Handbuch Qualität in Studium und Lehre*, edited by W. Benz, J. Kohler, and K. Landfried, 1–28. Berlin: Raabe.

Flöther, C. 2012. 'Regionale Mobilität von Hochschulabsolvent (inn) en – Ergebnisse von Absolventenstudien'. In *Funktionswandel der Universitäten: Differenzierung, Relevanzsteigerung, Internationalisierung*, edited by B. M. Kehm,

H. Schomburg, and U. Teichler, 126–140. Frankfurt and New York, NY: Campus Verlag.

Germany. Bundesgesetzblatt. 2014. *Gesetz zur Änderung des Grundgesetzes* (Artikel 91b): Vom 23. Dezember 2014. *Bundesgesetzblatt Jahrgang 2014*. Teil I Nr. 64.

Germany. Bundesminister für Bildung und Wissenschaft. 1978a. *Framework Act for Higher Education*. Bonn: BMBW.

———. 1978b. *Strukturprobleme des Bildungssystems im Bundesstaat*. Bonn: BMBW.

Germany. Gemeinsame Wissenschaftskonferenz. 2014. *Hochschulpakt 2014: Bericht zur Um-setzung im Jahr 2014*. Bonn: GWK.

Germany. Sekretariat der Ständigen Konferenz der Kultusminister der Länder in der Bundesrepublik Deutschland, ed. 2002. *Das Bildungswesen in der Bundesrepublik Deutschland 2001*. Bonn: KMK.

Germany. Sekretariat der Ständigen Konferenz der Kultusminister der Länder in der Bundesrepublik Deutschland, ed. 2013. *Das Bildungswesen in der Bundesrepublik Deutschland 2011/2012*. Bonn: KMK.

Germany. Statistische Ämter des Bundes und der Länder. 2013. *Bildungsvorausberechnung: Vorausberechnung der Bildungsteilnehmerinnen und Bildungsteilnehmer, des Personal- und Finanzbedarfs bis 2025*. Wiesbaden: Statistisches Bundesamt.

Germany. Statistisches Bundesamt. 2014. *Bildungs-Finanzbericht 2014*. Wiesbaden: Statistisches Bundesamt.

Gieseke, L. 1987. *Into the Future by Tradition: Higher Education in the Federal Republic of Germany*. Bonn: Inter Nationes.

———. 2012. 'Nachruf auf das Hochschulrahmengesetz'. *Wissenschaftsrecht* 45 (1): 3–12.

Heidenheimer, A. J. 1994. 'Universitäten im politischen Rahmen: Ein Vergleich der Hochschulsysteme Deutschlands, Japans, der Schweiz und der USA'. *Aus Politik und Zeitgeschichte* B 25: 23–33.

Heilbronner, K., and Geis, M.-E., eds. 2012. *Hochschulrecht in Bund und Ländern: Kommentar*, 40th edition. Heidelberg: C. F. Müller.

Hinze, S. 2010. 'Forschungsförderunge in Deutschland'. In *Handbuch Wissenschaftspolitik*, edited by D. Simon, A. Knie, and S. Horn-bostel, 162–175. Wiesbaden: VS Verlag für Sozialwissenschaften.

Hohn, H.-W. 2010. 'Außeruniversitäre Forschungseinrichtungen'. In *Handbuch Wissenschaftspolitik*, edited by D. Simon, A. Knie, and S. Horn-Bostel, 457–477. Wiesbaden: VS Verlag für Sozialwissenschaften.

Horn-Bostel, S. 2008. 'Exzellenz und Differenzierung'. In *Hochschule im Wandel: Die Universität als Forschungsgegenstand*, edited by B. M. Kehm, 145–154. Frankfurt and New York, NY: Campus Verlag.

Huber, L., ed. 1983. *Ausbildung und Sozialisation in der Hochschule*, Vol. 10. Stuttgart: Klett-Cotta (Enzyklopädie Erziehungswissenschaft).

Hüfner, K. 2003. 'Governance and Funding of Higher Education in Germany'. *Higher Education in Europe* 28 (2): 145–163.

Hüther, O. 2010. *Von der Kollegialität zur Hierarchie? Eine Analyse von New Managerialism in den Landeshochschulgesetzen.* Wiesbaden: VS Verlag für Sozialwissenschaften.

Hüther, O., and Krücken, G. 2014. 'The Rise and Fall of Student Fees in a Federal Higher Education System: The Case of Germany'. In *Students, Markets and Social Justice: Higher Education Fee and Student Support Policies in Western Europe and Beyond,* edited by H. Ertl and C. Dupuy, 85–110. Oxford: Symposium Books.

Kehm, B. M. 1999. *Higher Education in Germany: Developments, Problems and Perspectives.* Wittenberg and Bucharest: Institute for Higher Education Research and UNESCO-CEPES.

———. 2006. 'Germany'. In *International Handbook of Higher Education. Part 2: Regions and Countries,* edited by J. J. F. Forest and P. G. Altbach, 729–745. Dordrecht: Springer.

———. 2007. 'The Evaluative State and Higher Education Policy in Germany'. In *Towards a Cartography of Higher Education Policy Change,* edited by J. Enders, and F. Van Vught, 139–148. Enschede: University of Twente, CHEPS.

———. 2013. 'To Be or Not to Be: The Impact of the Excellence Initiative on the German System of Higher Education'. In *Institutionalization of World-class University in Global Competition,* edited by J. C. Shin and B. M. Kehm, 81–97. Dordrecht: Springer.

Kehm, B. M., and Lanzendorf, U. 2006. 'Germany: 16 Länder Approaches to Reform'. In *Reforming University Governance: Changing Conditions for Research in Four European Countries,* edited by B. M. Kehm and U. Lanzendorf, 135–185. Bonn: Lemmens.

Kehm, B., and Teichler, U. 1992. 'Germany, Federal Republic of'. In *The Encyclopedia of Higher Education,* edited by B. R. Clark and G. Neave, 240–260. Oxford: Pergamon Press.

Klumpp, M., and Teichler, U. 2008. 'German Fachhochschulen: Towards the End of a Success Story'. In *Non-university Higher Education in Europe,* edited by J. S. Taylor, J. Brites Ferreira, M. de Lourdes Machado, and R. Santiago, 99–122. Dordrecht: Springer.

Konsortium Bildungsbericht Wissenschaftlicher Nachwuchs, ed. 2013. *Bildungsbericht Wissenschaftlicher Nachwuchs.* Bielefeld: W. Bertelsmann.

Kosmützky, A., and Kretek, P. 2012. *Forschung an Hochschulen: Literaturstudie.* Berlin: Expertenkommission Forschung und Innovation (Studien zum deutschen Innovationssystem, No. 17).

Krais, B., and Naumann, J. 1991. 'Higher Education in the Federal Republic of Germany'. In *International Higher Education: An Encyclopaedia,* edited by P. G. Altbach, 685–709. New York, NY: Garland.

Lange, S. 2010. 'Hochschulräte'. In *Handbuch Wissenschaftspolitik,* edited by D. Simon, A. Knie, and S. Horn-Bostel, 347–360. Wiesbaden: VS Verlag für Sozialwissenschaften.

Leibfried, S., ed. 2010. *Die Exzellenzinitiative: Zwischenbilanz und Perspektiven.* Frankfurt and New York, NY: Campus Verlag.

Mayer, P., and Ziegele, F. 2009. 'Competition, Autonomy and New Thinking: Transformation of Higher Education in Federal Germany'. *Higher Education Management and Policy* 21 (2): 1–20.

Mayntz, R., ed. 1994. *Aufbruch und Reform von oben: Ostdeutsche Universitäten im Transformationsprozess.* Frankfurt and New York, NY: Campus Verlag.

Mc-Daniel, O., Gauye, P., and Guin, J. 1989. 'Government and Curriculum Innovation in the Federal Republic of Germany'. In *Governmental Strategies and Innovation in Higher Education*, edited by F. A. van Vught, 125–142. London: J. Kingsley.

Möhle, H. 1992. 'German Democratic Republic'. In *The Encyclopedia of Higher Education*, edited by B. R. Clark and G. Neave, 231–240. Oxford: Pergamon Press.

OECD. 2010. *Higher Education in Regional and City Development: Berlin, Germany.* Paris: OECD.

———. 2012. *Education at a Glance: OECD Education Indicators 2012.* Paris: OECD.

Oehler, C. 1989. *Hochschulentwicklung in der Bundesrepublik Deutschland seit 1945.* Frankfurt and New York, NY: Campus Verlag.

———. 2000. *Staatliche Hochschulplanung in Deutschland.* Neuwied: Luchterhand.

Oehler, C., and Teichler, U. 1984. 'Changing Approaches to Planning in Higher Education in the Federal Republic of Germany'. *Higher Education in Europe* 9 (1): 13–20.

Onestini, C. 2002. *Federalism and Länder Autonomy: The Higher Education Policy Network in the Federal Republic of Germany.* New York and London: Routledge Falmer.

Pasternack, P. 2011a. 'Die föderale Kompetenzordnung im deutschen Hochschulwesen: Entwicklung und Status'. In *Hochschulen nach der Föderalismusreform*, edited by P. Pasternack, 21–60. Leipzig: Akademische Verlagsanstalt.

———. 2011b. 'Fazit: Traditionelle Differenzen und neue Ähnlichkeiten. Trends nach der Föderalismusreform'. In *Hochschulen nach der Föderalismusreform*, edited by P. Pasternack, 340–353. Leipzig: Akademische Verlagsanstalt.

———., ed. 2011c. *Hochschulen nach der Föderalismusreform.* Leipzig: Akademische Verlagsanstalt.

Peisert, H., and Framhein, G. 1978. *Systems of Higher Education: Federal Republic of Germany.* New York: International Council for Educational Development.

———. 1997. *Higher Education in Germany*, 3rd edition. Bonn: Federal Ministry of Education, Science, Research and Technology.

Pritchard, R. M. O. 1986. 'The Third Amendment to the Higher Education Law of the Federal Republic of Germany'. *Higher Education* 15 (6): 587–607.

Reich, A. 2012. *Hochschulrahmengesetz mit Wissenschaftszeitvertragsgesetz: Kommentar*, 11th edition. Bad Honnef: Bock.

Röbbeke, M. 2010. 'Akkreditierung'. In *Handbuch Wissenschaftspolitik*, edited by D. Simon, A. Knie, and S. Horn-Bostel, 334–346. Wiesbaden: VS Verlag für Sozialwissenschaften.

Rüegg, W., ed. 2011. *A History of the University in Europe*, Vol. 4: *Universities Since 1945*. Cambridge: Cambridge University Press.

Sandberger, G. 2011. 'Die Neuordnung der Leitungsorganisation der Hochschulen durch die Hochschul¬rechtsnovellen der Länder'. *Wissenschaftsrecht* 44 (2): 118–155.

Schimank, U., and Lange, S. 2006. 'Hochschulpolitik in der Bund-Länder-Konkurrenz'. In *Das Wissensministerium*, edited by P. Weingart and N. C. Taubert, 311–346. Weilerswist: Velbrück Wissenschaft.

Schade, A. 2004. 'Shift of Paradigm in Quality Assurance in Germany: More Autonomy But Multiple Quality Assessment'. In *Accreditation and Evaluation in the European Higher Education Area*, edited by S. Schwarz and D. Westerheijden, 175–196. Dordrecht: Kluwer Academic Publishers.

Schaeferbarthold, D. 1999. 'The Financing and Costs of Studies in Germany'. *European Journal of Education* 34 (1): 69–74.

Schoof, U., Blinn, M., Schleiter, A., Ribbe, E., and Wiek, J. 2011. *Deutscher Lernatlas: Ergebnisbericht 2011*. Gütersloh: Verlag Bertelsmann Stiftung.

Stifterverband Für Die Deutsche Wisssenschaft. ed. 2004. *Eine (un)endliche Geschichte? Beiträge für Föderalismusdiskussion*. Essen: Stifterverband.

Stucke, A. 2010. 'Staatliche Akteure in der Wissenschaftspolitik'. In *Handbuch Wissenschaftspolitik*, edited by D. Simon, A. Knie, and S. Horn-Bostel, 363–376. Wiesbaden: VS Verlag für Sozialwissenschaften.

Suchanek, J. Pietzonka, M., Künzel, R. H. F., and Futterer, T. 2012. 'The Impact of Accreditation on the Reform of Study Programmes in Germany'. *Higher Education Management and Policy* 24 (1): 2–24.

Teichler, U. 1981. 'Higher Education for the 1980s: The Case of West Germany'. In *Higher Education for the 1980s: Challenges and Responses*, 140–151. Hiroshima: Research Institute for Higher Education (RIHE), Hiroshima University 1980.

———. 1985. 'The Federal Republic of Germany'. In *The School and the University: An International Perspective*, edited by B. R. Clark, 45–76. Berkeley, CA: University of California Press.

———. 1986. Higher Education in the Federal Republic of Germany: Developments and Recent Issues. Kassel: Wissenschaftliches Zentrum für Berufsund Hochschulforschung der Gesamthochschule Kassel (Werkstattberichte, No. 16). 93–106, Federal Systems of Higher Education – the Case of the Federal Republic of Germany.

———. ed. 1990. *Das Hochschulwesen in der Bundesrepublik Deutschland*. Weinheim: Deutscher Studien Verlag.

———. 1991. 'The Federal Republic of Germany'. In *Prometheus Bound: The Changing Relationship Between Government and Higher Education in Western Europe,* edited by G. Neave and F. van Vught, 29–49. Oxford: Pergamon Press.

Teichler, U. 1992. 'Higher Education in Federal Systems: Germany'. In *Higher Education in Federal Systems*, edited by D. Brown, P. Cazalis, and G. Jasmin, 141–168. Kingston: Queen's University, Institute of Intergovernmental Relations.

——. 2006. 'Hochschulsystem – Studium – Arbeitsmarkt: Die lehrund studienbezogene Hochschulpolitik des Bundesministeriums'. In *Das Wissensministerium*, edited by P. Weingart and N. C. Taubert, 347–377. Weilerswist: Velbrück Wissenschaft.

——. 2008. 'Where Shall the Money Come from? Publicly versus Privately Financed Higher Education'. In *Beyond 2010: Priorities and Challenges for Higher Education in the Next Decade*, edited by M. Kelo, 65–95. Bonn: Lemmens.

——. 2011. 'Germany: How Changing Governance and Management Affects the Views and Work of the Academic Profession'. In *Changing Governance and Management in Higher Education: The Perspectives of the Academy*, edited by W. Locke, W. K. Cummings, and D. Fisher, 223–241. Dordrecht: Springer.

——. 2014. *Hochschulsysteme und quantitativ-strukturelle Hochschulpolitik: Differenzierung, Bologna-Prozess, Exzellenzinitiative und die Folgen.* Münster: Waxmann.

Teichler, U., and Bracht, O. 2006. 'The Academic Profession in Germany'. In *Reports of Changing Academic Profession Project Workshop on Quality, Relevance, and Governance in the Changing Academia: International Perspectives*, 129–150. COE Publication Series, No. 20, Research Institute for Higher Education, Hiroshima University, Hiroshima (RIHE).

Thieme, W. 2004. *Deutsches Hochschulrecht: Das Recht der wissenschaftlichen, künstlerischen, Gesamtund Fachhochschulen in der Bundesrepublik Deutschland*, 3rd edition. Köln: Heymann.

Turner, G. 2001. *Hochschule zwischen Vorstellung und Wirklichkeit: Zur Geschichte der Hochschulreform im letzten Drittel des 20 Jahrhunderts.* Berlin: Duncker & Humblot.

Von Mutius, A. 1996. 'Studentenwerke'. In *Handbuch des Wissenschaftsrechts*, Vol. 1, 2nd edition, edited by C. Flämig, et al., 601–630. Berlin: Springer.

Webler, W. D. 1990. 'Externe Einflüsse auf die Hochschulen'. In *Das Hochschulwesen in der Bundesrepublik Deutschland*, edited by C. Flämig, O. Kimminich, H. Krüger, E.-J. Meusel, H.-H. Rupp, D. Scheven, et al., 65–100. Weinheim: Deutscher Studien Verlag 1990.

Weingart, P., and Taubert, N. C. 2006. 'Das Bundesministerium für Bildung und Forschung'. In *Das Wissensministerium: Ein halbes Jahrhundert Forschungs- und Bildungspolitik in Deutschland*, edited by P. Weingart and N. C. Taubert, 11–29. Weilerswist: Velbrück Wissenschaft.

Wissenschaftsrat. 2010. *10 Thesen zur Hochschulpolitik.* Köln: WR.

——. 2013. *Perspektiven des deutschen Wissenschaftssystems.* Köln: WR.

Chapter 6

Brazil
Problematics of the Tripartite Federal Framework

Robert Evan Verhine and Lys M. V. Dantas

INTRODUCTION

In July of 2014, the President of the Federal Republic of Brazil signed into law the National Education Plan, establishing objectives, goals and strategies designed to guide public policy in the field of education over the next 10 years. The National Plan took three years to be approved by Congress, in part because of the inclusion of a controversial proposal to create a National Education System in two years. The measure was strongly supported by educators, politicians and government officials who believe that Brazil's three overlapping public school systems, administered separately and simultaneously by federal, state and municipal governments, are prejudicial to public education as whole. Others, however, considered the measure to be an affront to the distribution of powers and responsibilities inherent to federalism and safeguarded in the Brazilian Constitution. As a compromise, a National Education System is mentioned in the final version of the document, but the wording makes it clear that the new system would not replace, but merely increase the existing coordination between the three systems (Brasil 2014a).

In the eyes of most people, the introduction of a national system of education would only have a positive impact on the sub-tertiary level of education, where the absence of adequate overall coordination is clearly evident. Few thought of the National Plan as relevant for higher education, primarily because it was believed that on this level the competing systems offered valuable complementarities. However, this chapter argues that the tripartite federal framework has had negative implications for higher education as well, generating costly redundancies and perpetuating socioeconomic and geographic inequalities with respect to both access and quality. These and related tendencies, associated with federalism in Brazil, are discussed in subsequent sections, illustrating why the creation of a national system that pertains to all instructional levels would prove to be highly beneficial for the development of higher education in the country.

The nature of Brazil's federal model, its effect on higher education and the lessons that the Brazilian experience provides for the improvement of higher education in 'federal type' systems represent the key issues addressed by the present chapter. The remainder of the text is composed of four sections. The first provides an overview of the Brazilian context and federal structure. Then, the nature of higher education in Brazil is summarized, considering the background, current situation, regulatory and legal issues, economic aspects and tendencies pertaining to research, internationalization and excellence. The final two sections provide an analysis of the impact and implications of Brazil's federal structure for higher education and a review of the major findings, conclusions and recommendations produced by this study.

OVERVIEW OF THE BRAZILIAN CONTEXT AND FEDERALISM

Brazil is a large country, the fifth largest in the world in both population and land area, and its GDP is currently ranked as the seventh in the world.[1] Upon gaining independence from Portugal in 1822, the country adopted a constitutional monarchy that implemented a unitary form of governance. The imperial regime was characterized by severe

---

[1] Brazil's GDP in 2014 was ranked as seventh in the world in terms of both nominal and purchasing power parity (PPP) measures (see World Bank 2015b).

centralization despite (and because of) major regional disparities and territorial fragmentation. The monarchy was overthrown in 1889 and the military government that replaced it established, via a new Constitution ratified in 1891, a federal system of governance which was, at least ostensibly, presidential and democratic in nature. Brazil has maintained its federal framework ever since, but with varying degrees of centralization and decentralization over time (Costa 2010).

Between 1891 and 1930, decentralization prevailed. The so-called First Republic was toppled in 1930, and the regime that replaced it adopted a centralized approach, culminating in the establishment of a dictatorship in 1937. Democracy was restored in 1946 and a new Constitution successfully advanced the notion of relative parity between the states and the federal government. A movement to the left in the early 1960s precipitated a military takeover, resulting in the imposition of strong centralization. A democratic resurgence in the mid-1980s led to the Federal Constitution of 1988, which, for the first time, recognized municipalities as federal entities, with independent powers and responsibilities that had formerly been vested in the states (Brasil 1988). Thus, differently from many federal systems, Brazil's model of governance is tripartite in structure, encompassing federal, state and municipal spheres (Araújo 2013; Arretche 2004; Oliveira and Ganzeli 2013).

Brazil is composed of 26 states and a federal district. The states are divided into 5,561 municipalities. Both states and municipalities have autonomous administrations, collect their own taxes and receive a share of the taxes collected at higher (federal and/or state) levels. In all three spheres, the executive and legislative branches are organized independently, but the judiciary is restricted to federal and state levels. Brazil has been said to have a 'cooperative' form of federalism. Indeed, in the 1988 Constitution, the notion of intergovernmental cooperation and collaboration is mentioned multiple times, and numerous mechanisms are provided to facilitate mutual policy formulation and implementation. However, major power is reserved for the federal government. The federal government assumes centrality with respect to national coordination and financial assistance, as it has been given exclusive responsibility for establishing national norms and for raising funds via the imposition of an income tax (Cury 2008). Thus, states in Brazil have relatively less power than their counterparts in many federal-type countries, such as Germany and the United States (Abrúcio 2010). At the same time, most municipalities are relatively weak from economic and political standpoints, remaining highly dependent on the state and federal spheres for financial support and policy leadership.

Brazil is notably homogeneous in terms of language and national identity, but it is marked by grave disparities in socioeconomic development across its states, which are informally organized according to five major regions, known as the North, Northeast, Southeast, South and Centre-west. Wealth, population and political power tend to be concentrated in the Southeast, which includes the states of São Paulo, Rio de Janeiro and Minas Gerais. Comprising only 10.9 per cent of the land area, the Southeast represents 42.1 per cent of the population and 55.2 per cent of the GDP. In contrast, the North, where the Amazon basin is located, contains 45.3 per cent of Brazil's land area, but it has only 8.3 per cent of its population and 5.6 per cent of its wealth (IBGE 2010a). Poverty levels are most acute, however, in the Northeast, where a tropical coastline still suffers the negative consequences of the slave-based economy that prevailed until late in the nineteenth century and a semiarid interior is plagued by severe droughts. The Centre-west region is the most diverse from an economic standpoint, since it includes the Federal District (where the capital city, Brasília, is located), the wealthiest federal unit in the country, and a vast hinterland composed of farm and grazing lands, extensive swamps and dense rain forests (IBGE 2014).

Between-region disparities are noteworthy. Per capita income for the Southeast and Centre-west regions is nearly four times that of the Northeast region. However, as mentioned, economic figures pertaining to the Centre-west are somewhat misleading due to the impact of the Federal District, which has a per capita income which is nearly twice that of São Paulo, the country's richest state. In turn, the per capita income of São Paulo exceeds that of the country's poorest state (Piauí) by a factor of four (IBGE 2010b). Acute regional differences are also evident with respect to higher education, as will be seen in the following section.

HIGHER EDUCATION
Background

The 1988 Constitution states that education is a public good. When offered by government, whatever the sphere, it constitutes a public service (Brasil 1988). Thus, the federal government is responsible for education in terms of establishing norms and directives for the entire nation. Such dictates must be complied with by all federal entities. With respect to sub-tertiary education, in Brazil Basic Education, the 1988 Constitution and the 1996 National Education Law attribute to the federal government, the states, the Federal District and the municipalities the responsibility for managing public education in the country through three systems—federal, state and municipal—(Brasil 1988, 1996). Although dictated by a common set of rules and regulations, each system is responsible for maintaining its own institutions, managing its own funds, and implementing its own mechanisms for obtaining financial resources.[2]

After many years of neglect, pre-tertiary education in Brazil remains weak, especially by international standards.[3] Education indicators vary significantly between the five regions, in correspondence with differences in wealth. In 2012, for example, upper secondary net enrolment rates varied from 40 per cent in the North and Northeast to 62.5 per cent in the Southeast (average for Brazil = 54%). Similarly, higher education net enrolment was 11 per cent in the North and Northeast and 20 per cent in the South (average for Brazil = 15%). Indicators also differ among public and private pre-tertiary education sectors, with the former primarily serving lower class populations and the latter catering to a large proportion of the country's middle and upper class segments.

---

[2] For descriptive information in English about Brazil's public education systems, see, for example, Preal and Lemann Foundation (2009).

[3] Results from the Program for International Student Assessment (PISA) reveal that, of the 65 countries that participated in the 2012 study, Brazil placed 58th in Mathematics, 56th in Reading and 59th in Science (OECD 2015).

The decentralization that characterizes basic education is not historically relevant to the tertiary level.[4] Starting in 1920, with the founding of Brazil's first university in Rio de Janeiro, a succession of national regimes sought to require all higher education institutions to conform to the model of organization and governance pioneered in the national capital (Cunha 1980). From the outset, many key elements were institutionalized, such as the tradition of top-down, federal control of universities that were created and maintained as dependencies of the Ministry of Education.[5] The system expanded markedly and, by 1964, it included 37 universities, 564 colleges and nearly 150,000 students. During this period, the federal government continued to play a dominant role, federalizing and integrating disparate state, municipal and private institutions into a unified network (Sampaio, Balbachevsky and Peñaliza 1998).

In the mid-1960s, the military regime sought to integrate higher education into a modernization process and, at the same time, to diffuse and control campus-based political activity. Beginning in 1966, the government issued a variety of decrees that brought about major changes in the higher education system. Departments rather than colleges were designated as the fundamental administrative unit, and every university was required to promote not just teaching but also research and extension. Complementary legislation requiring university professors to hold graduate degrees led to the creation and rapid expansion of graduate programmes throughout Brazil, at both master and doctoral levels (Cunha 1988).

In the years thereafter, the number of federal university students grew, but the number of those at private institutions increased much more rapidly. As a result, the private/public enrolment ratio shifted

---

[4] A detailed history of higher education in Brazil is provided by the trilogy produced by Cunha (1980, 1983, 1988). Summaries in English can be found in Levy (1986), Verhine (1991) and Balbachevsky and Schwartzman (2011).

[5] Other elements included the organization of universities as an assemblage of semi-autonomous faculties linked by a weak central administrative apparatus and an almost exclusive focus on the preparation of professionals, minimizing the importance assigned to both general education and scientific research (Plank and Verhine 2002).

decisively during a 10-year period, with the share of all students enrolled in private institutions rising from 40 per cent in 1964 to 60 per cent in 1974. Most of the growth in private sector enrolments was concentrated in low quality, single purpose colleges whose students, in great part, had failed to gain admittance to higher quality, more prestigious and user-free public institutions (Levy 1986). It was during this period that states began to invest their own resources into the creation of institutions of higher education to meet burgeoning demand. The number of state universities grew from nine in 1980 to 31 by 1996. In contrast, the number of federal universities increased only slightly during the period, from 34 to 39. Meanwhile, a small number of municipalities created higher education institutions, often focusing on the training of local schoolteachers. By 1996, six municipal universities had been established, mostly concentrated in a single Brazilian state— Santa Catarina—located in the South Region (Sampaio et al. 1998).

The 1988 Constitution determined that all recognized public institutions must be free of charge, democratically governed and staffed by professionals competitively selected (Article 206).[6] The Constitution also mandated that universities are to be guaranteed 'didactic, scientific, administrative and financial autonomy' and that they must promote teaching, research and extension in an integrated fashion (Article 207). It clarified that education via private initiative is permitted, but that the private sector must adhere to national norms and be subjected to the processes of authorization and evaluation conducted by the federal government (Article 209). Moreover, research and extension activities at both public and private institutions are permitted to receive public resources (Article 213), and a national plan must be formulated to develop the different levels of education in an integrated fashion (Article 214; Brasil 1988).

---

[6] The 1988 Constitution was the seventh to be promulgated in Brazil, and, as those that came earlier, it reflected the political milieu in which it was adopted. Whereas the previous Constitution, approved in 1967, supported military centralism, the 1988 Constitution strongly emphasized democratic principles and administrative decentralization. Thus, with respect to higher education, it provided a framework for the adoption of participatory governance and institutional autonomy.

The National Education Law, approved in 1996, determined that the Federal Government should exercise a redistributive and supplemental role, providing technical and financial assistance to states and municipalities and promoting, through mutual inter-sphere collaboration, the evaluation of higher education (Brasil 1996). The Law also clarified responsibilities and established structures for the functioning, financing and regulation of higher education, as will be detailed in subsequent sections.

Current Situation

Brazil's system of higher education is a complex, nationwide network composed of approximately 2,400 institutions distributed within both public and private domains. Public institutions can be divided according to the responsible governmental sphere, and private establishments can be classified as confessional, community, philanthropic, private non-profit and private for-profit. In addition to classification by legal status, higher education institutions in Brazil are officially categorized in accordance with academic structure into four organizational types— universities, university centres, colleges and technological institutions— as illustrated by Figure 6.1.

By definition, a university must offer a plurality of disciplines, promote institutionalized academic output (e.g., publications, social interventions, etc.), have at least one-third of its faculty with a graduate degree, and employ at least one-third of its professors full-time. University centres are also comprehensive, but designed to have a teaching rather than research focus. Mostly private, they are legally defined in a loose manner as institutions exhibiting academic excellence. Both universities and university centres are guaranteed some academic autonomy. Those in the public domain can select faculty and students (but not determine the number of faculty and student slots), authorize the opening of new undergraduate programmes of study (but these must be subsequently approved through external evaluation and regulation) and establish their own research agendas (Brasil 1996). Colleges, on the other hand, often have a single purpose, such as business administration or pedagogy, and are afforded little academic

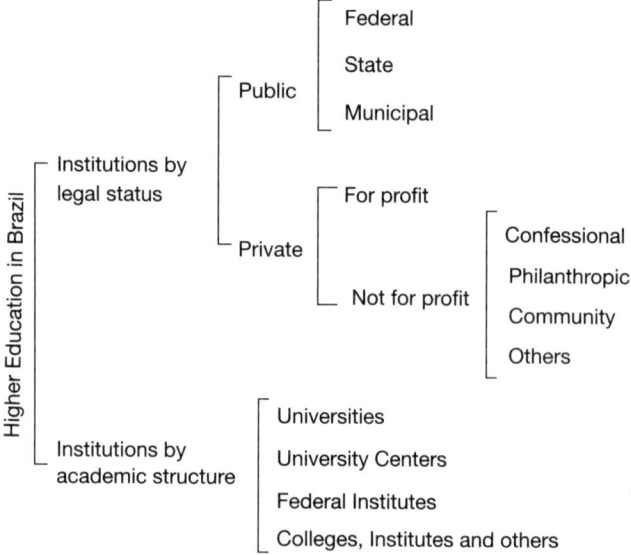

Figure 6.1 *Structure of Higher Education in Brazil*
Source: Authors.

autonomy. The fourth group is composed of federal technological institutes, which offer three-year vocational programmes and approximate Type B establishments, as defined by the Organization for Economic Co-operation and Development (OECD).[7] However, they also have key characteristics associated with Type A entities, including the fact that students who successfully conclude their studies can compete for slots on the graduate level (Brasil 2008).

A look at national statistics, resulting from data collected via an annual, countrywide census, reveals that Brazil's institutions of higher education currently enrol about 7.5 million students, representing

---

[7] Tertiary Type A institutions largely offer theory-based programmes of a duration of at least three years that are designed to provide sufficient qualifications for entry to advanced research programmes and professions with high skill requirements. Tertiary Type B institutions, in contrast, typically provide programmes with a minimum duration of two-years that focus on practical, technical or occupational skills for direct entry into the labour market (OECD 2014, 25).

around 3.5 per cent of the country's population.[8] Overall higher education is dominated by the private sector, with over 85 per cent of the institutions and about 73 per cent of all higher education enrolees. Of those enrolled in the public sector, which is composed of 300 institutions and 2.1 million students, 53 per cent are in federal establishments, 30 per cent are in state entities and 17 per cent study in municipal units. As for universities, there are 195 of them. Within the public sphere, the dominant force is the federal government, which through the Ministry of Education operates 63 universities, distributed so that at least one university is located in every state of the union. State universities are currently 37 in number and exist in 21 of the 26 Brazilian states. Municipal institutions are relatively insignificant in number and appear to be headed towards extinction. The private universities include 17 religious institutions and half a dozen of other high prestige establishments, but most of the private institutions of higher education are low-cost, low quality and non-university in nature, with approximately half of them operated for profit.[9] The distribution of higher education institutions by type and region is shown in Table 6.1. As with population and income, most tertiary level offerings are in the Southeast, with the Northeast (primarily because of population) and the South (primarily because of wealth) vying for a distant second place.

---

[8] Unless otherwise specified, statistics pertaining to higher education institutions, enrolments and professors have been gleaned from the National Higher Education Census, produced annually by the Ministry of Education (Brasil 2013).

[9] The characteristics of private higher education in Brazil, including issues related to student profiles, academic quality and the growth and implications of the for-profit sector, have been widely discussed in the literature (see Barreyro 2008; Nunes 2012; Oliveira 2009; Sampaio 2011; Secca and Leal 2009). The estimate of the relative number of for-profit institutions is based in Reis et al. (2014), since the category is not treated separately by the National Higher Education Census Reports. It should be noted that for-profit institutions of higher education range from small, family-run affairs to institutions that are operated by mega-international companies that raise money on global markets through publicly traded stock. In 2009, the 15 largest private education companies in Brazil represented 27 per cent of the total market, with yearly profit rates above 21 per cent, helping to make the country's private education sector the 10th largest component of the Brazilian economy (*The Economist* 2014).

Table 6.1 *Higher Education Institutions by Type and Region for Brazil, 2014*

Region	Total	Universities		University Centre		Colleges		Technological Institutes	
		Public	Private	Public	Private	Public	Private	Public	Private
Brazil	2,368	111	84	11	136	136	1,850	40	0
Centre-west	239	9	5	1	13	5	201	5	0
Northeast	452	32	7	0	12	24	366	11	0
North	149	15	2	1	7	2	115	7	0
Southeast	1,126	28	50	5	84	102	846	11	0
South	402	27	20	4	20	3	322	6	0

Source: INEP (2014).

A key characteristic of higher education in Brazil is its extraordinary growth in recent years. The number of programme offerings has increased tenfold since 1984, from 3,800 to 6,200 in 1995, to 16,500 in 2003, and doubled again to 32,000 in 2013. Whereas most of the growth in the last decades of the twentieth century was concentrated in the private sector—private sector programmes increased from 56 per cent in 1995 to a high of 72 per cent in 2007—the public sector has made a major contribution to overall expansion in recent years.[10] This growth is closely related to a federal university reform initiative, known as REUNI, which was implemented by the Ministry of Education in 2007. This initiative sought to double federal higher education enrolment by 2014.[11] Meanwhile, the private sector has also tended to expand,[12] but not as dominantly as before, even though it has benefitted from two initiatives financed by the federal government. One involves greatly expanding the Fund for Student Financing (FIES), which enables students at private institutions to borrow money under favourable conditions to pay for tuition and other expenses.[13] The

---

[10] Between 2003 and 2013, higher education enrolments increased 76 per cent, rising 73 per cent for new entrants and 79 per cent for undergraduate completers. They increased 95 per cent in both federal and private establishments, but only 30 per cent at state institutions and 50 per cent at those provided by municipalities. With respect to the number of institutions, public establishments increased 55 per cent, whereas the number of private ones rose 27 per cent (Brasil 2013).

[11] The term REUNI refers to the Program for the Restructuring and Expansion of Federal Universities. Through it, federal universities were offered additional financing if they agreed to meet goals pertaining to completion rates (90%) and student–professor ratio (18:1) within a five-year period. They were also expected to provide night courses and to create new campuses away from major urban centres (see Gomes 2008).

[12] It has been estimated that since 2004, about one-half of the student places made available yearly through the private sector have gone unfulfilled. Data suggest that students apply in large numbers to private institutions, but only a fraction of those admitted actually attend, since they prefer to study at a tuition-free public institution (Carnoy et al. 2013).

[13] In 2014, FIES loans benefited more than 500,000 students enrolled in private institutions. In addition to funds provided by MEC, FIES is supported by government bonds and contributions from a national lottery. Unlike similar programmes found in many countries, the FIES loan is given directly to the institution at which the student is enrolled. To participate, students must obtain a passing grade on the national test for secondary school students (ENEM—Exame Nacional do Ensino

other, referred to as the University for All Programs (ProUni), waives federal taxes for private institutions that provide full tuition grants to at least 10 per cent of their student bodies.[14] Taken together, these two programmes serve about a third of the private sector student body and represent a key incentive for the transformation of non-profit entities into for-profit establishments (Máximo 2013).[15]

In spite of rapid expansion, however, net higher education enrolment rates remain low by international standards, rising from 11.0 per cent in 2003 to just 16.5 per cent in 2013.[16] Moreover, enrolments are segmented according to economic, racial and geographic lines. The net enrolment rate for students in the top income quartile is 40 per cent, compared to a figure of 5 per cent for those in the bottom income quartile. Likewise, whereas the net enrolment rate is 24 per cent for white higher education students, it is only about 10 per cent for their non-white counterparts. Between-group disparity is also evident when comparing urban net enrolment of 18 per cent and rural at 6 per cent.

Médio [National Secundary Education Exam]) and the institutions need to be approved by the Ministry of Education's national evaluation system of higher education (SINAES— Sistema Nacional de Avaliação da Educação Superior [National System for the Evaluation of Higher Education]). In 2015, the FIES interest rate was increased from 3.4 per cent to 6.5 per cent (FIES 2016).

[14] ProUni is a federal programme that offers tax exemptions to private universities in exchange for full or partial scholarships to low-income students. It was created in 2005 and has since benefitted over 1.4 million students. In order to qualify for a full exemption from four different types of taxes, private higher education institutions must offer scholarships equivalent to 8.5 per cent of their annual revenue. Priority must be given to full scholarships, with a required ratio of at least one scholarship student to every 22 paying students. If full scholarship students do not meet the 8.5 per cent requirement, private institutions are allowed to complement their count with half scholarships until the threshold is met (ProUni 2016).

[15] Federal programmes designed for the private higher education sector are highly controversial in Brazil. For some, they represent an undesirable transfer of public money to private interests. To others, they constitute a practical, low cost mechanism for providing higher education opportunities to students of low socioeconomic standing. See Pedrosa et al. (2014) and Sampaio (2011).

[16] The National Education Plan, approved in 2014, establishes the goal of doubling the higher education net enrolment rate by 2024 to 33 per cent (Brasil 2014a). The goal, which derives from the current OECD average, is considered by some observers to be overly ambitious (Lima and Ramos 2013).

Undergraduate students enrolled in the country's 2,400 higher education institutions are distributed among 32,000 courses of study.[17] Slightly over half (56%) study in bachelor programmes, whereas the remainder participate in either licenciatura (teacher training) courses (25%) or technological offerings (19%).[18] Courses of study at the undergraduate level are predominantly professional in nature and vary from three to six years in length. They also vary with respect to the socioeconomic level of their students, in accordance with differentials in programme prestige.[19] As indicated in Table 6.2, the distribution of enrolment according to programme type by region follows the demographic and economic patterns discussed in the second section, with about 50 per cent of all entering students and approximately 60 per cent of those studying in technological fields residing in the industrialized Southeast.

Since the early 2000s, institutions have been permitted to offer undergraduate programmes via distance learning, a modality that encompasses about 16 per cent of undergraduate students. Most of these online distance programmes are either licenciatura (47%) or technological (34%) in nature. Distance education is overwhelmingly a private sector phenomenon, as private institutions account for 86 per cent of all distance education enrolees (Brasil 2013).

---

[17] Student characteristics of interest include the facts that 45 per cent of those enrolled are 25 years of age or older, 57 per cent are women, 68 per cent work 40 hours or more per week and 60 per cent study at night. Of course, the more elite the university, the more likely that students are young, do not work and study during the day. The predominance of women, however, is evident across all types and categories of higher education, with the exception of the technological institutes, where males outnumber females (Nunes 2012).

[18] Technological courses include a diverse array of vocational offerings, typically lasting three years. Both federal technological institutes and specialized private establishments provide these types of courses.

[19] Acute socioeconomic differences among students across professional fields of study are revealed by findings from a national student questionnaire applied annually. For example, in the field of medicine, students are disproportionally white (74%), in the top income bracket (44%) and private secondary school graduates (89%). The corresponding figures for students in the field of pedagogy are 46 per cent, 5 per cent and 19 per cent, respectively (Ristoff 2014).

Table 6.2 *Number of Students Entering in Undergraduate Programmes by Programme Type and Region, 2013*

Regions	Total	Number of Entering Students			
		Bachelor	Licenciatura	Technological	Unspecified
Brazil	2,227,545	1,584,909	301,264	327,697	13,675
North	135,416	88,470	30,958	14,529	1,459
Northeast	425,104	303,120	71,486	49,690	808
Southeast	1,109,126	781,955	126,194	192,720	8,257
South	331,619	246,390	41,143	42,509	1,577
Centre-west	226,280	164,974	31,483	28,249	1,574

Source: INEP (2013).

Although most students study at the undergraduate level (97%), there are about 200,000 students enrolled at the graduate level, with those working to complete the academic doctorate (PhD) representing about one-third of that total.[20] In contrast to undergraduate enrolment, graduate enrolment is concentrated in public institutions (81%), with federal and state universities responsible for 57 per cent and 24 per cent of the total, respectively. The relative predominance of federal university graduate programmes is evident via other indicators as well, such as the percentage of students (57%), the percentage of professors (59%) and the percentage of federal student scholarships awarded (66%). In terms of regional distribution, graduate level offerings are in accordance with population and wealth differentials, with the Southeast and South responsible for 58 per cent and 24 per cent of all programmes, respectively. However, if only very top tier programmes are considered, the regional disparities are much more acute, as the Southeast (82%) and the South (17%) account for all but one of the 116 programmes situated in the uppermost rung of the national evaluation rating scale (CAPES 2016).[21]

There are more than 300,000 tertiary level professors in the country, with a little over half in the private sector. Over 60 per cent of those who work at public institutions are employed by federal universities. About one-third of all higher education professors hold a doctorate, and another 40 per cent have obtained the master's degree.[22] The percentage of those professors with a doctorate is much higher at public

---

[20] The number of graduate programmes has increased steadily since the early 1970s, at a rate of about 5 per cent per annum, and now there are about four thousand master and two thousand doctoral programmes in operation, spread across the spectrum of academic fields (for details, consult CAPES 2016).

[21] As discussed in the section of the chapter dealing with regulation and legal issues, all graduate programmes are evaluated by an agency linked to the Ministry of Education (see Footnote 16) every three years and are given a grade ranging from 1 to 7. Top tier programmes (those receiving a grade of 7) comprise only about 3 per cent of the overall total (CAPES 2016).

[22] Although national law requires all professors of higher education to have graduate training, there are still 9,000 professors who have just an undergraduate degree (2.5% of total professors). Many of these professors, however, are high-level professionals, such as medical doctors and lawyers (medicine and law are undergraduate programmes in Brazil; Brasil 2013).

institutions (54%) than at private establishments (18%). At public institutions, most professors (81%) are full time, with the percentage surpassing 90 per cent for the federal institutions. The corresponding figures are 75 per cent for state institutions, 30 per cent for municipal entities and 25 per cent for the private sector. Not surprisingly, the percentage of professors holding a PhD varies not only by type of institution but also according to region, distributed similarly as other indicators. Although there is some relation between regional distribution of highly qualified professors and consequent PhD output, the latter is much more concentrated than the former—in 2013, 62 per cent of doctorates were conferred in the Southeast region (Todos pela Educação 2015).

Within public universities, major power rests with the Rector, the institution's chief administrator. For federal universities, the rector is chosen by the president of Brazil from a list of three names submitted by the institution after confirmation by the vote of a representative electoral college. The situation is similar with respect to state universities, except that it is the governor who selects the rectors from lists developed through participatory processes at the institutional level. In the case of the Pontifical Catholic Universities, the list of candidates is submitted to the church authority who acts as the university's chancellor. At non-denominational private institutions, key decisions are usually made by a board of directors and implemented by two top executives, with a chief executive officer (CEO) handling administrative matters and a rector responsible for academic issues (Plank and Verhine 2002).

Regulatory and Legal Issues

For the purposes of higher education regulation, national legislation establishes two systems—the Federal System, comprised of all federal and private institutions, and the State System, made up of all state and municipal higher education establishments (Brasil 1996). Thus, whereas federalism in Brazil is tripartite, it is only bipartite with respect to the regulation of higher education. This determination emanates from two considerations. First, the formulators of the 1996 National Education Law strongly advocated decentralizing lower levels of education to the municipal level and did not want to divert municipal attention to the tertiary level. Second, since they understood all education to be a public good and were concerned about private sector quality control, they sought to ensure that private tertiary education establishments were closely monitored by public authorities.

For both federal and state systems, regulation is the responsibility of a board of education (National Board/State Board) and the designated administrative unit (Ministry of Education/Secretariat of Education). The concept of regulating higher education via collegial boards has existed in Brazil since the early twentieth century, and the relative power of such boards has tended to ebb and flow in accordance with tendencies of federal centralization and decentralization (Nunes 2012). The National Board of Education, in its current form, was established by law in 1995, and it is composed of 24 members, equally divided between two chambers, one for basic education and the other for higher education. The members are selected by the President of Brazil, in accordance with names submitted by representative associations active in the field of education. Among other attributes, the National Board is responsible for establishing curricular directives for under-graduate programmes and for the periodic accreditation (*credenciamento*) of all federal and private institutions of higher learning. It also gives official recognition (*reconhecimento*), at periodic intervals, to graduate programmes (Brasil 1995). The National Board of Education was originally responsible for authorizing and recognizing undergraduate programmes as well, but, in the early 2000s, this responsibility was transferred to a secretariat within the Ministry of Education.

The law that created the National Board of Education also specified that its regulatory decisions must be based on evaluation results supplied by the Ministry of Education. That same year, the Ministry established a nationwide higher education evaluation procedure based on a written test to be applied to students in their final year of undergraduate study. A year after implementing the exam, the Ministry introduced a process for the external evaluation of courses and institutions using commissions composed of members of the academic community (Verhine, Dantas and Soares 2006).

A new evaluation approach was introduced by federal law in 2004, which led to the creation of the National System of Higher Education

Evaluation (SINAES; Brasil 2004). The notion of a nationwide standardized exam was maintained, but its centrality was reduced, since it now was just one of three interrelated components designed to evaluate student performance (via the exam), undergraduate courses (via visits by commissions composed of academic peers) and higher education institutions (also via visits by peer commissions).[23] SINAES is coordinated by a commission known as CONAES, composed of 13 members representing both the federal government and the academic community, whereas responsibility for implementation has been attributed to INEP, an agency linked to the Ministry of Education that specializes in educational evaluation.[24] Early on, CONAES and INEP made some adjustments in the original SINAES model. The most important of these involved the evaluation of undergraduate courses of study, since visiting over 30,000 programmes at regular intervals was deemed-to-be impossible. Thus, in 2008, an indicator was developed, based on information gleaned from the national exam, the accompanying student questionnaire, and the national higher education census, encompassing variables pertaining to student performance, professor degree level, the terms of professor employment and the quality (according to student opinion) of the programme's pedagogical organization and physical infrastructure. Only programmes receiving a negative result for this indicator were to be visited, thereby making the operationalization of SINAES viable (Verhine 2010).

If a higher education institution or programme receives an 'unsatisfactory' evaluation from the visiting commission, it must sign a 'protocol of commitment' with the Ministry of Education, agreeing to a set of goals and responsibilities to be accomplished within a set period of time. Should the Ministry, through a process of systematic supervision, determine that the terms of the protocol have not been achieved, it can apply one or more possible penalties, ranging from

---

[23] Detailed information concerning the history, philosophy and organization of SINAES is provided in Brasil (2009). For an overview in English, see Pedrosa, Amaral and Knobel (2013).

[24] CONAES and INEP are widely used acronyms for the Comissão Nacional de Avaliação da Educação Superior and the Instituto Nacional de Estudos e Pesquisas Anísio Teixeira, respectively.

suspending new admissions to cancelling altogether the programme's or institution's right to function (Pedrosa, Amaral and Knobel 2013).

Meanwhile, as of 1961, in accordance with national legislation, states began installing their own boards of education, with members appointed by state governors. The structure and functioning of the state boards mirror the national board, with 24 members, two chambers and a direct link to the state secretariat of education. The boards accredit, supervise and evaluate state and municipal higher education institutions and formally recognize undergraduate programmes of study. Unlike in the federal system, there is no evidence any state boards have transferred their prerogatives in the regulation of programmes to the corresponding administrative authority. To make their regulatory decisions, states tend to rely on visits by commissions composed of recognized academics. However, whereas the visits conducted within the SINAES framework are highly structured, the visits undertaken at the state level are often unstructured, resulting in a report with no predetermined format. Since all state institutions now participate in the nationwide exam process, the state boards often use the exam's results and related indicators produced by the federal government to make their regulatory decisions.

The private sector is also evaluated and regulated by the federal system of education using the same structure that is applied to the federal institutions. This has led to complaints by private sector representatives of unfair treatment. They contend, for example, that the national exam discriminates against their institutions, since most private establishments cater to low-income students who suffer testing difficulties which are independent from the quality of their programme of study. They also allege that visiting commissions, comprised of members of an academic community dominated by the public sector, often express bias against the private institutions in their evaluation reports. Thus, the private sector has struggled to overturn (or at least significantly alter) the SINAES law ever since its passage, but, so far, it has not been successful in this endeavour.

Whereas SINAES focuses on the evaluation of higher education institutions and undergraduate programmes, offerings at the master and doctoral levels are evaluated separately, through a national system established in 1980.[25] Originally designed to guide the distribution of federally funded student scholarships, the system has evolved over time so that today every graduate programme in the country is evaluated at pre-established periodic intervals with respect to five academic dimensions—proposal, faculty, student body, intellectual output and societal contribution. As a result, each programme is graded on a scale that ranges from one to seven. To be accredited, programmes must be attributed a grade of at least three. To receive a grade of '6' and '7', a programme is required to meet international standards of academic excellence. Importantly, the higher the grade, the greater the federal funding allotted to the programme. This creates incentives for programme improvement, but since lower quality programmes tend to receive less funding, it is difficult for them to improve in relationship to those programmes at the top of the scale. Thus, regional inequalities are often fortified, as higher quality programmes getting the most money tend to be concentrated in the country's most prosperous regions (Verhine 2008).

Economic Aspects

The public sector in Brazil is financed by a large array of taxes, fees and contributions which vary according to federal sphere and are explicitly defined in the Constitution of 1988.[26] About two-thirds of the tax receipts available to the federal government for expenditures on education are derived from a federal income tax, although monies

---

[25] Whereas the evaluation of higher education institutions and graduate programmes is conducted by INEP, the evaluation of graduate programmes is administered by another agency linked to the Ministry of Education, known as CAPES (Coordenação de Aperfeiçoamento de Pessoal de Ensino Superior).

[26] Article 145 of the Constitution of 1988 distinguishes between taxes (*impostos*), fees (*taxas*) and contributions (*contribuições*), determining that taxes are raised from the general population for discretionary use, fees represent charges for specific public services (such as lights and water) and contributions provide funds raised for pre-established purposes (such as social security, industrial training, basic education and health care). All told, the Constitution institutes six federal taxes (Article 153), three state taxes (Article 155) and three municipal taxes (156). In addition, there currently exist a total of 34 different fees and 31 different contributions (Portal Tributário 2016).

are also obtained via taxes on imports, exports, industrial products and financial operations. About a fifth of such receipts are required by the Constitution to be transferred to the state and municipal governments, according to population size. In poor states and municipalities, these transfers represent a significant portion of their total receipts, but, in almost all states, the most important source of income is a value-added merchandise tax which benefits, for the most part, the state where products are produced rather than the state where they are ultimately purchased.[27] Thus, whereas the federal government, through transfers and spending based on national priorities, tends to serve a redistribution function, the tax structure on the state level serves to reinforce regional wealth differences. One finds, therefore, that despite federal support which is designed to be equitable, the governments of rich states in the Southeast and South regions benefit from per capita tax receipts that are at least twice as much as those garnered by the governments of the poor states situated in the country's other three regions.[28]

The federal government is required to spend 18 per cent of its tax receipts (minus transfers) on education, and, since lower levels of schooling are mostly financed by states and municipalities, the Ministry of Education can allocate about 70 per cent of its total spending to its higher education system. As a result, almost 20 per cent of all public spending in Brazil currently goes to higher education, although public higher education comprises only about 4 per cent of total public school enrolments.[29] At the state and municipal levels, the corresponding constitutional requirement is 25 per cent of all tax receipts (plus transfers), but most (at least 20%) of these funds must go to basic education. Many states ostensibly provide a set percentage of state tax revenues (usually 5%) for higher education, but the percentage is often not adhered

---

[27] On average, the merchandise tax and federal transfers constitute about 80 per cent and 10 per cent of state tax receipts, respectively. In very poor states, such as Piauí and Maranhão, the merchandise tax and the federal transfers contribute about equally to the state budget (FNDE/SIOPE 2014).

[28] Statistics pertaining to tax receipts were calculated by the authors from data available at FNDE/SIOPE (2014).

[29] Percentages were calculated by the authors based on data available in Todos pela Educação (2015).

to in practice. The state of São Paulo is unique in this respect, since it guarantees, through automatic monthly transfers, a predetermined percentage of the state merchandize tax to each of its three universities (combined percentage = 9.57%).

Individual economic payoffs for tertiary-level education in Brazil have been high,[30] and this has motivated demand for more spending on higher education, which currently accounts for about 1 per cent of the country's GDP and approximates 4 per cent of its public spending. Brazil's higher education expenditure is very high in relation to primary level spending (ratio of 3:1). Higher education spending in Brazil rose 210 per cent between 2005 and 2012, far above the OECD average of 121 per cent (OECD 2015). However, during the same period, national income and higher education enrolments increased at similar rates, meaning that expenditures per student and as a percentage of the GDP have remained remarkably stable over the past decade (Barbosa and Veloso 2015).

The current expenditure per public higher education student in Brazil is about US$10,500. Although the amount is higher than that found in many countries that belong to the so-called developed world, it is considerably below the OECD average of approximately US$15,000 per student (OECD 2015). Estimates suggest that annual per student expenditures are roughly US$13,000 for federal universities, but only about US$8,500 for state establishments and US$5,200 for municipal entities. The inclusion of expenditures made by the huge private sector, with its many low cost offerings, results in an overall expenditure per student figure for Brazil of about US$6,000 annually.[31]

---

[30] Carnoy and associates calculated the private rate of return to higher education in Brazil to be 24.6 per cent in 2008 (Carnoy et al. 2013, Table 3.5). Barbosa and Veloso (2015) came to a similar conclusion, estimating the private premium for completing higher education to be 25.6 per cent in 2012. Both sources indicate that private rates, although high, have fallen in recent years, having hovered around 30 per cent during the 1990s and early 2000s.

[31] Estimates pertain to 2014 and were made by authors from student data available at INEP (2014), financial data found at FNDE/SCIOPE (2014) and an exchange rate of R$2.45 to US$1.00. In 2015, expenditure values in dollars fell significantly due to a major devaluation of the R$.

In sharp contrast, the country's premier university, the University of São Paulo, spent over US$25,000 per student in 2013.[32]

Despite a constitutional dictate to the contrary, financial autonomy at public institutions is severely limited. The federal government is required to provide, as part of its regular budget, the resources necessary to sustain the institutions of higher education that are under its direct control. Federal institutions obtain 88 per cent of their funding from federal government (Amaral 2008). However, the federal government restricts institutional financial independence by earmarking funds within specific categories, making it virtually impossible to transfer money from one category to another, and by requiring resources not utilized by the end of the fiscal year to be returned to the Ministry of Education.

States adopt similar procedures with respect to their higher education, with the exception of the state of São Paulo, which utilizes a block grant approach. State governments provide 87 per cent of the financing received by state institutions. On the other hand, resources used by municipal and private institutions are primarily derived from user fees. Municipal institutions are allowed to charge students despite constitutionally protected rights to free public education because a constitutional article enables institutions of higher education that were fee-based prior to the 1988 Constitution to remain so. Thus, they get 80 per cent of their resources from tuition fees, just slightly lower than the 88 per cent coming from fees in private institutions.

The budgetary allotment for federal institutions use to be based on historical precedent, political influence and direct negotiations, but distributions since the late 1990s have been made in accordance with enrolment size and a series of productivity indicators related to institutional efficiency and quality (Amaral 2009). Since more than 80 per cent of federal funding for higher education goes to pay salaries (including pensions), it is this factor, rigorously controlled by civil service legislation, that actually determines funding levels. Productivity indicators are also used by state systems, although the interference of other factors, especially those of a political nature, tends to be greater (Sampaio et al.

---

[32] Estimate pertains to 2013 and was made by the authors based on data available at http://www.transparencia.usp.br/?page_id=18

1998). Since salary scales are uniform within the federal system and student body size is the most important criteria used in distributing other federal resources, the variation between institutions of per student federal allocations is somewhat mitigated. Even so, substantial differences exist because of significant variations with respect to special funding for research and graduate study and income received from university services. Such differences tend to follow regional wealth differentiations, largely because of the greater availability in the most developed portions of the country of highly qualified scholars who can effectively compete for additional funds that are distributed according to merit.

Whereas federal public spending on higher education has increased in recent years, states have not followed the suit, as financial restrictions aggravated by a recent economic downturn and pressures to give priority to basic education have checked enthusiasm for state-level higher education spending. It is likely that federal expansion has also helped to curtail state growth, as states have tended to always view their systems as complementary and supplemental to the federal system. Moreover, relative to federal institutions, state universities are characterized by large interstate disparities. These disparities reflect not only differential wealth and state tax receipts but also differences in priority emanating from factors such as the degree of federal university coverage and the nature of competing social demands (Table 6.3).

Professors' salaries are strongly influenced in the public sector by government/labour union negotiations and by the widely accepted principle of intra-system salary isonomy, whereby all members of a given class or category of employment receive the same salaries. Although the concept of isonomy is a familiar feature of civil service employment, its extension to university faculties creates problems within public higher education systems. For example, faculty members at the same level with the same formal qualifications (degrees, years of service) receive the same remuneration, without regard to performance or productivity criteria, reducing incentives to increase academic output (Plank and Verhine 2002). Among state universities, salaries tend to be uniform within each state, but they vary significantly between states in accordance with the relative distribution of wealth. Interstate salary differentials explain a significant portion of the interstate spending variations depicted in Table 6.3.

Table 6.3 *Annual Expenditure per State University Student by Region for Brazil, 2014 (in US$)*

Region	Annual Expenditure per State University Student			
	No. of Students	Avg. Exp. ($)	High State Exp. ($)	Low State Exp. ($)
Brazil	615,849	8,530	14,993	2,187
North	50,870	4,242	5,495	3,363
Northeast	195,705	4,881	6,631	2,187
Southeast	244,912	12,062	14,993	5,033
South	87,332	9,312	11,062	4,968
Centre-west	40,030	7,867	11,498	3,215

Sources: Calculations by the authors from data from INEP (2014) and FNDE/SIOPE (2014).

It is likely that several factors will slow the growth rate of investment in higher education in Brazil over time. First, reduced fertility rates will eventually have impact on higher education, although current low net enrolment rates still leave room for continued expansion. Second, both private and social rates of return (which include public spending per student) for higher education are falling due to a combination of higher costs and a greater relative supply of college graduates. Although private rates remain high, at about 25 per cent, the social rate of return has dropped to less than 10 per cent. Pressures could increase to redistribute public funds not only between educational levels but also between education and competing social investment sectors (Barbosa and Veloso 2015). A third constraining factor pertains to the persistence of high levels of federal expenditure in relation to government receipts. Between 1991 and 2014, income increased (in real terms) by 103 per cent, but corresponding tax receipts rose by 184 per cent, causing public sector tributes to grow from 25 per cent to 35 per cent of the GDP. The imbalance between public receipts and expenditures became especially acute after 2010, with the annual growth in expenditures significantly outpacing the annual growth in receipts (5.4% versus 1.5%). Many respected economists argue that the existing fiscal situation requires major reductions in public expenditure. Although spending on higher education has not increased as fast as that of social services in general, it will undoubtedly be impacted negatively as austerity measures are implemented (Almeida Jr., Lisboa and Pessoa 2015).

Research, Internationalization and Excellence Initiatives

The Brazilian University was traditionally a teaching institution focused on preparing students for professional careers. Serious research was conducted by specialized institutes supported by public funds. The creation of graduate programmes after 1970 altered this arrangement and now graduate-level faculty members represent the primary source of knowledge production. By linking graduate programme funding from the federal government to the scientific contribution of faculty members, the federal government has created research incentives that do not exist for those who teach exclusively at the undergraduate level. Because of these incentives, scientific output in Brazil tripled between 1998 and 2012, and the country is currently ranked by the Web of Science as the world's 14th most productive country in terms of publications in indexed journals (Web of Science 2016).[33] However, Brazil is ranked 22nd with respect to the impact of its output (H Index) and is 47th with regards to the annual registration of patents. Whereas Brazil produces 2.4 per cent of the world's publications, it accounts for only 0.2 per cent of total worldwide patents (FAPESP 2010). Innovation tends to be restricted by two factors: (a) most of the country's researchers work in higher education rather than in private enterprise and (b) much of the technology developed by private enterprise occurs in the context of research centres maintained by multinational firms located outside of Brazil.

According to the World Bank (2015a), Brazil spends about 1.1 per cent of its gross national product on research and development—below

---

[33] Despite rapid growth in scientific output subsequent to the mid-1990s, the tempo dropped off after 2010, causing Brazil to fall from 13th to 14th place between 2012 and 2014 in terms of number of indexed publications. The country is currently ranked as number 17th with respect to cites per paper, suggesting that scientific impact lags behind scientific output (Web of Science 2016).

many other countries.[34] Since a great part of the country's research is conducted within graduate programmes, the distribution of research output by state and type of institution closely mirrors the national distribution of high quality doctoral offerings. Statistics for the period 2002–2006 reveal that 74.5 per cent of the country's total indexed publications are produced in the Southeast, as compared to 19 per cent for the South, 12 per cent for the Northeast, 5 per cent for the Centre-west, and 3 per cent for the North. Remarkably, about 50 per cent of the county's scientific output is produced by only three universities, all sponsored by the state of São Paulo (FAPESP 2010).

Well over half of the funding for science, technology and innovation derives from public coffers. The most important public sources include both the National Research Council (CNPq), which is part of Brazil's Ministry of Science, Technology and Innovation, and state-based foundations for research funding. Of the country's 27 states (including the Federal District), 22 states currently have a scientific funding foundation in operation. Overall, the state foundations provide about US$1 billion annually, an amount equivalent to that distributed on the federal level by CNPq (FAPESP 2010).

Although Brazil's investment in research and development relative to GDP is similar to the OECD average, the country lags far behind with respect to other indicators of scientific output. For example, the percentage of researchers per inhabitant and per labour market participant is far below that of the countries which make up North America, Western Europe and East Asia (OECD 2014). A mere 5 per cent of the researchers in Brazil are foreign born, and scientific output continues to be highly endogenous, as only about 10 per cent

---

[34] According to Brazil's Ministry of Science and Technology, Brazil invests 1.74 per cent of its GDP on science, technology and innovation, with this percentage distributed among the federal government (0.60%), state governments (0.31%), and the private sector (0.83%; Brasil 2014b). The OECD (2014), on the other hand, paints a much more negative picture, indicating that R&D spending is only a fraction of 1 per cent of the GDP and that R&D expenditure per student, at US$762, is far below the OECD average of US$4,405 (see OECD 2014, 216). The optimistic percentage of GDP reported by the Ministry of Science and Technology is also below the OECD average of 2.37 per cent (OECD 2015).

of Brazil's international publications involve an author from another country (Mugnaini, Digiappietri and Mena-Chalco 2014).[35] Only about 0.5 per cent of all higher education students and less than 3 per cent of those who study at graduate level are not Brazilian citizens. In contrast, as an average 8 per cent of tertiary-level students in OECD countries and 19 per cent of those who study at top-ranked institutions can be classified as foreigners (OECD 2014).

Several historical factors contribute to the insularity of Brazil's higher education, including the belief that the country's limited number of tertiary-level slots should be reserved for nationals, the tendency on the part of the academic community to be distrustful of foreign models and interventions, and the fact that the Portuguese language is not widely utilized within international scientific circles (Lima and Contel 2011). In recent years, however, Brazil's national government has made a concerted effort to promote university internationalization through the wide scale provision of scholarships and other benefits both to Brazilian students who want to study abroad and to foreign students who wish to study in Brazil. The most important initiative in this respect is the Science without Borders programme, implemented in 2011 with the goal of sending 100,000 students to study abroad over a four-year period. As of 2015, US$3 billion had been allocated to the programme, and, according to governmental sources, the key targets had been reached.[36]

Yet, unlike many countries, Brazil has not attempted to implement government-sponsored national excellence initiatives that focus on specific institutions. The official viewpoint in recent years has been to favour the expansion of higher education opportunities for the Brazilian population over the development of a small number of universities of worldwide stature. The goal, therefore, is to assure minimum standards of quality for all higher education institutions rather than to maximize

---

[35] That the 10 per cent figure for Brazil is low by international standards is indicated by the fact that for Argentina. Mexico and Chile, the corresponding value exceeds 30 per cent (Mugnaine et al. 2014).

[36] For more information about Brazil's Science without Borders programme, consult *The Economist* (2012) and also www.cienciasemfronteiras.gov.br or www.laspau.harvard.edu

the quality for a few of them. According to the Academic Ranking of World Universities (ARWU 2016), six Brazilian universities place within the top 500, three state (all located in São Paulo) and three federal (situated in three of the country's richest states). Together, these universities provide a third of the doctoral programmes in the country and consequently benefit disproportionately from federal funds for graduate study and research. They are also supported by the country's wealthiest state foundations for research funding and thus can sustain and improve their status as high quality institutions. Thus, despite its focus on minimum standards, the federal government appears to foster disparities between regions and systems through research and graduate study policies.

IMPLICATIONS AND IMPACTS OF FEDERAL RELATIONSHIPS IN HIGHER EDUCATION IN BRAZIL

The analysis presented in this section highlights and interprets information presented above regarding the relationship between federalism and higher education in Brazil. The following discussion addresses interrelated themes, denoted as homogeneity/heterogeneity, accessibility, autonomy/accountability and academic mobility/regional development.

Homogeneity/Heterogeneity

Higher education in Brazil has been historically dominated by a unitary, homogeneous model that gives priority to public research universities. However, Brazilian higher education is today heterogeneous, differentiated by spheres of government (federal, state and municipal), sector of the economy (public versus private), academic focus (research versus teaching) and level of prestige (elite versus mass). The private sector is further diversified in accordance with religious, non-profit and for-profit institutions. Even if differences between public institutions run by different governmental spheres tend to be relatively small, state institutions are more differentiated than federal ones in terms of quality and prestige. In most states, the major research university is federal. The state institutions tend to serve a complementary function, providing higher education opportunities to those unable to compete effectively for the limited federal slots, both because of academic performance limitations and because of geographic barriers resulting from the concentration of federal universities in major urban areas. Municipal institutions also serve populations in outlying areas, but they are few in number, operate in only a few states and are in the process of being transformed into private establishments, as most municipalities are severely strapped for funds and are constitutionally required to give priority to the provision of preschool and primary education.

The diversity and responsiveness of higher education in the country is guaranteed through its huge private sector, which provides significant variety in terms of institutional type, organization, size, curricular options and delivery mechanisms. Private institutions, especially those for profit, have been aggressive in responding to changing labour market demands, offering courses related to new occupations or occupations which did not previously require a college education (Sampaio 2011). Their non-traditional approach is reflected by their nationwide dominance in the fields of distance education and technical study. Their dynamic nature is also suggested by the fact that the most rapid growth in private sector enrolments has, in recent years, occurred outside of capital cities and the country's most developed regions (Brasil 2013).[37]

Two conclusions therefore emerge from the Brazilian experience. First, federalism itself does not necessarily lead to higher education diversity, especially when uniform legal arrangements and regulatory processes are implemented on a national level. Second, higher education diversity does not necessarily break down social, economic and geographic divisions. In Brazil, diversity both within and between public and private higher education sectors tends to be accompanied by quality differentials that mirror interclass and interregional disparities. Thus, higher education within a federal setting may promote, rather than reduce, existing inequalities.[38]

---

[37] Growth patterns and the diversity of course offerings and student characteristics with respect to the private higher education sector have been dealt with in detail by Barreyro (2008), Sampaio (2011), and Secca and Leal (2009), among others.

[38] That higher education diversity may do more to reinforce rather than reduce social inequalities has been observed by a number of scholars, such as

Accessibility

Accessibility relates to both coverage and equity. With respect to coverage, federal universities, which for many years were virtually the only universities to exist outside of São Paulo, were high public cost, low private cost institutions with student access available to only a select few. This scenario provoked high rates of return for those obtaining a university credential, and, along with the increasing number of students completing the secondary level, promoted the rapid expansion of higher education from the 1970s onward. In terms of student access, Brazil has counted on complementary contributions from both the public (federal and state) and private (for-profit and non-profit) sectors. It is unlikely that any one system alone could have produced similar results. Federalism in Brazil has served to increase both the number of higher education providers and the quantity of available financial resources. It has also enabled a large variety of constituents (national and local, elite and non-elite) to exert social and political pressures favourable to the expansion of tertiary-level coverage.

On the other hand, the growth of higher education is not sufficient nor entirely positive. Despite rapid expansion, tertiary-level education in Brazil is still characterized by very low levels of coverage. In recent years, state and municipal higher education expansion has tended to stagnate, as most subnational governments are hampered both by limited resources and by the constitutional requirement that they give priority to the lower levels of schooling. Meanwhile, the private sector is showing signs of market saturation due to overexpansion, and it is increasingly dependent on tax exemptions and student loans dispensed by the federal government.[39] Moreover, some indicators suggest rapid

---

Dias Sobrinho (2010) and Neves, Raizer and Fachinetto (2007). These and other authors argue that measures to produce equity through education must focus on the basic education level.

[39] The overexpansion of private higher education is discussed in Carnoy et al. (2013) and Sampaio (2011). It is illustrated statistically by the fact that whereas there are, on average, 15.7 candidates per opening in the public universities, there are only 1.7 candidates per opening at private institutions (Brasil 2013). Also, as indicated in Footnote 3, about one-half of annual private sector student places go unfulfilled. This saturation, however, has not seriously hurt much of the private

expansion has jeopardized the overall quality of higher education, as class size and professor teaching loads have tended to increase in the public sector (Pedrosa et al. 2014), and institutions in the private sector often try to reduce costs in order to increase profits and other forms of income surplus (Carnoy et al. 2013).

Regarding the issue of equity, the selective nature of both higher education admission and secondary school instruction (most high standard secondary schools are private and only about half of the relevant age cohort completes the upper-secondary level) contribute to the fact that higher education accessibility is disproportionately restricted to students from middle- to high-income families and who are ethnically white. The socioeconomic bias is especially evident at the most prestigious universities (Nunes 2012) and in high-status fields of study, such as medicine, engineering and law (Ristoff 2014).

To deal with the problem, Brazil's federal and state systems of higher education have progressively adopted affirmative action measures since the early 2000s (Daflon, Feres Junior and Campos 2013). The first initiatives were undertaken on the state level, in states where the Afro-Brazilian population is both large and well organized. In these instances, therefore, the susceptibility of state legislatures and institutions to local pressures helps account for early subnational leadership in the adoption of equity measures. Several federal universities quickly followed suit, establishing quota systems that, though varying from one institution to another, reserved a set percentage of slots for non-white and/or economically disadvantaged students.

Meanwhile, on the state level, policy variations were evident. Some states, for example, rejected the quota approach and implemented a procedure whereby bonus points were added to entry test scores to make public school and minority students more competitive. By 2010, most public universities, both federal and state, had adopted policies of affirmative action. In 2012, a national law was passed and subsequently upheld by Brazil's Supreme Court that made the quota

---

sector, as public support through FEIS and ProUni and market consolidation have helped maintain high profits for many institutions, especially the largest ones (see Footnote 10).

system mandatory at all federal institutions. The law requires that, at federal institutions, 50 per cent of the vacancies be filled by public school graduates, with sub-quotas for blacks and native populations determined in accordance with their proportion in the population of the state where the institution of higher education is located. Although Brazil's affirmative action experience is relatively recent, studies suggest that its impact has been positive. Students who enter through the quota system tend to be highly motivated and do well academically, except in subjects requiring maths, a field characterized throughout the country by severe instructional deficiencies on lower schooling levels (Matos et al. 2013; Peixoto et al. 2013; Velloso 2009). At the same time, the federal government has promoted affirmative action within the private higher education sector through ProUni, a programme that gives federal tax exemptions to institutions that provide scholarships to poor students. All in all, it is apparent that higher education accessibility and equity in Brazil have benefitted from complementary actions involving different governmental spheres.

Autonomy and Accountability

As with other aspects of Brazil's network of higher education, the degree of institutional autonomy is based more on type of institution and legal status than on governmental sphere and geographic region. Universities and university centres are guaranteed academic autonomy with respect to course offerings, research agendas, staff hiring and student admission. However, they remain dependent on government financing. Budgets, salaries, admission openings and professor slots are externally controlled. Nevertheless, public institutions are also characterized by a high degree of faculty autonomy and by collegial arrangements for academic decision-making. Their professors have near absolute job security and their work is very loosely monitored. According to some observers, this situation represents a reaction to the military repression of the 1960s and 1970s, and it has led to cronyism, lax evaluation criteria and an absence of academic rigor (Durham 2005; Plank and Verhine 2002).

The autonomy enjoyed by the faculty at public institutions varies somewhat in accordance with governmental sphere. A recent survey suggests that state governments are more involved than the federal government in decisions regarding staff appointments, faculty promotion and teaching load. Thus, at the regional level, the interests of external stakeholders are more evident, although the faculty is still seen as dominant, especially with respect to the internal selection of institutional authorities (Balbachevsky and Schwartzman 2011). Although the chief institutional authority at public institutions wields considerable influence, his or her power is curtailed by a host of internal and external factors, including the need to run for re-election after four years in office, the influence of powerful faculty and non-faculty labour unions, the demands made by external governmental auditors, and the personnel restrictions imposed by civil service legislation. Local politicians have an impact as well, especially at the subnational level. Their influence is particularly evident with respect to the location of new campuses, as they lobby within legislatures and administrative policy-making sectors to serve constituent interests. As a result, campus locations of federal and state higher education institutions often overlap, generating redundancy and inefficiency within the higher education network as a whole (Fialho 2012).[40]

Most private institutions, in contrast, are run like businesses. Authority is hierarchical, with major power given to administrative leaders and little academic autonomy allotted to faculty members. A small number of elite private universities serve 'niche markets' which require them to invest in high quality professors in order to attract fee-paying students. They offer their professors a modicum of academic autonomy, although not nearly that given by public entities (Balbachevsky and Schwartzman 2011).

As for system wide and institutional accountability, Brazil has implemented elaborate evaluative and regulatory mechanisms designed to ensure minimum standards of higher education quality. Despite similarities in the approaches adopted by national and state spheres, accountability policies have provoked tensions between the

---

[40] For example, the State University of Rio Grande do Norte (UERN) and the Federal University of the Semi-Arid Region (UFERSA) offer similar courses of study and have campuses that are located adjacent to one another, in the city of Mossoró. Many similar cases can be found throughout the country.

two regulatory systems. The national government is legally responsible for evaluating student achievement and institutions at the tertiary level, in collaboration with the states. Thus, those responsible for creating SINAES felt confident that the new evaluation system would be a 'national' system since state governments had agreed to cooperate. In the case of SINAES, however, the state boards of education were negatively disposed because they believed that residents of their state, who were familiar with local realities, should be permitted to participate as members of the commissions responsible for the external visits.

Federal authorities attempted to convince state-level educators to see the value of receiving an outside evaluation, but their efforts to do so were undermined by a major flaw in the legislation. Although purportedly a law about evaluation, it contained an article dealing directly with regulation. This article, as already noted, required that programmes and institutions receiving an unsatisfactory evaluation must submit to supervision and possible penalties to be administered by the Ministry of Education. Whereas few doubted that the federal government could lead these evaluation efforts, the notion that it could also override the regulatory responsibility of the states with respect to their own systems of education was widely believed to be contrary to the nation's federal framework. In subsequent negotiations, an accord was reached whereby no effort would be made by the states to nullify the law and, in return, no state would be required to participate in the SINAES system. To this day, no state institution of higher education participates in all components of the national evaluation system. Whereas they all voluntarily accept application of the national exam, in part because of the high cost of developing a comparable instrument, none of them has been willing to let the commissions mounted by the Ministry of Education conduct external visits. Thus, the national system is not national. States continue not only to regulate but also to evaluate their own tertiary-level programmes and institutions. By so doing, they undermine efforts to establish and maintain comparable levels of quality among the country's institutions of higher education. Hence, in terms of higher education accountability, federalism has unexpectedly generated negative consequences.

Academic Mobility and Regional Development

The relationship of higher education to national versus regional/local concerns is complex in Brazil because almost all institutions, including those in the federal system, are focused on their respective states and localities. The names of the federal universities reflect this fact, as they all emphasize that the institution is 'of' a specific state, city or sub-state region. The great majority of the students and most of the professors at these institutions are products of the local context. Data collected by the Ministry of Education reveal that over 80 per cent of all students did their upper secondary study in the city in which their higher education institution is located. Only 12 per cent came to study from another city within the state, 5 per cent from another state and less than 0.5 per cent from another country.[41] The Ministry of Education recently installed a computer-based system that permits students to apply to multiple universities, based on the results of a single, national test administered to secondary-level graduates. The electronic system serves to distribute students nationwide to both federal and state institution. It has probably generated some geographic mobility on the part of students and helped to integrate institutions belonging to the country's two systems of higher education, but its impact has been limited because of the local loyalties and the limited finances of entry-candidates and their families. The vast majority of tertiary-level students continue to live at home and approximately 60 per cent work while attending classes at night.

Tertiary-level professors also exhibit low levels of interstate and interregional mobility. A significant proportion of faculty members were students at the institution where they now teach. This lack of mobility is particularly detrimental to the poorest regions of the country, such as the North and the Northeast, since it is difficult for them to attract faculty members from the more prosperous regions, where doctoral degree holders are relatively plentiful. Both state and federal governments have attempted to create special incentives to attract professors to poorer areas, but efforts to do so have met with little

---

[41] These percentages were determined by the authors of this chapter based on data provided by Ministério da Educação (Ministry of Education) (MEC) from the ENADE 2012 student questionnaire.

success, in part because the salary levels of faculty members cannot be manipulated due to the 'isonomy' principle.

Comparative regional indicators suggest that the pattern of growth during the great expansion in higher education after 1995 made some progress in breaking down regional disparities in access, but it continues to be concentrated in the Southeast and its national distribution closely corresponds to levels of regional income (Table 6.4).

Indeed, since institutional quality is distributed in a similar manner, the expansion of higher education may be strengthening (and legitimizing) geographic inequality.[42] It is likely that higher education's most important contribution to regional development has been made through its spread, within each state, to previously remote areas. Both state and national governments have recently created new institutions and campuses for existing establishments outside of major urban zones, thereby geographically expanding not only study opportunities but also

Table 6.4 Growth of Total Number (Public Plus Private) of Higher Education Institutions by Region, 1998–2013

Region	1998		2013	
	N	%	N	%
Brazil	973	100.00	2.391	100
North	40	4.11	146	6.11
Northeast	124	12.74	446	18.65
Southeast	570	58.58	1.145	47.89
South	131	13.46	413	17.27
Centre-west	108	11.10	241	10.08

Source: INEP (2013).

---

[42] Analyses conducted by the authors using data provided by INEP serve to illustrate the relationship between regional development and university quality in Brazil. The General Course Index (IGC), a measure of the mean evaluation grade of all courses offered by the higher education institution, was, on average, 26.3 per cent higher in the South and Southeast regions than in the North region.

instruments (jobs, knowledge, etc.) for the generation of wealth. The private sector has also contributed, as many private institutions operate (especially via distance education) in places where no public higher education institution has ventured.

One would expect this geographic widening of higher education opportunities in the country to be accompanied by the promotion of regional and local development. But the relevant research in Brazil offers results that are mixed and inconclusive about the relationship between higher education and regional development. Among studies that suggest positive effects for higher education are those indicating university contributions to local/regional income (Caldarelli, Camara and Perdigão 2015) and to the development of community leadership (Costa and Miranda 2011). Results from other investigations, though, are less optimistic. A study by Lopes (2012), for example, shows that the regional university of study is only a small component of the overall production process and that it has done little to affect local socioeconomic indicators other than to increase inequalities between the host municipality and those that surround it. Ferreira and Leopoldi (2013) present findings that are equally discouraging, revealing that the investigated university makes only minor contributions to the local community because of its rigid bureaucracy and inward-looking orientation. It is clear, therefore, that more research is needed on these relationships.

CONCLUSIONS AND FINAL CONSIDERATIONS

Federalism in Brazil is based on a tripartite structure in which national, state and municipal governments are given distinct independent powers and responsibilities. Spheres are expected to work in a collaborative fashion in accordance with overall coordination provided by national legislation and by the federal government. Thus, whereas formally collaborative, the federal system in Brazil is also hierarchical: the national government assumes leadership due to its broad powers of taxation, its influence on overarching legal matters and its supremacy in formulating policies on a national scale. Federal domination is particularly evident in the field of higher education. The federal university is usually the most prestigious higher education institution in any given state, and, historically, it has provided an organizational and academic model typically adhered to by non-federal institutions of higher learning.

This tendency, however, should not obfuscate the current complexity of higher education in Brazil. The public sector includes institutions provided by federal, state and municipal governments, while the private sector, which is responsible for a great majority of higher education enrolments and establishments, offers a wide diversity of universities, university centres and single purpose colleges, of both high and mainly low quality. This scenario is somewhat simplified since all tertiary-level institutions are regulated through two national systems. The 'federal system' is under the auspices of the national government and includes all federal and private institutions. The 'state system' is really a collection of systems, each under the jurisdiction of a given state and responsible for state and municipal higher education entities. That the private sector is regulated by the federal government is important, because it reflects the viewpoint in the country that all education is a public good and indicates the need to include the sector in efforts to understand relations between higher education and federalism in Brazil.

Higher education in Brazil has benefited from a variety of inter-sphere complementarities. States and a few municipalities have been crucial for expanding funding for higher education and for extending tertiary instruction beyond major urban centres. Local political pressures in conjunction with statewide policies have led to the creation of multi-campus configurations that have assumedly contributed to the development of previously remote areas. The private sector has also played a role, especially through its use of distance education and its contribution to the differentiation of institutional structures, course offerings and learning environments.

Yet, federalism in Brazil has also affected higher education in a negative fashion. It has produced overlaps and redundancies, especially regarding campus locations and courses of study. It has also generated inter-sphere tensions, particularly with respect to the utilization of public funds and evaluation of higher education. This is unfortunate, as one of the greatest problems facing higher education in Brazil is its uneven quality. Federalism has aggravated the variation in quality. States and municipal institutions are often of inferior quality because of limited funding due to regional and local poverty and because subnational governments are constitutionally obligated to give priority to lower schooling levels. The limited expansion of public universities, fuelled by an emphasis on expensive research institutions, has opened the door to profit-seeking private establishments. These private undertakings are often more concerned with cutting costs than with improving quality. Special federal funding for cutting-edge research, for top-level graduate programmes and for university internationalization efforts has been disproportionately distributed to the nation's best institutions, usually located in its most affluent regions, thereby fortifying disparities in inter-regional and inter-institutional quality. Further, the lack of a national evaluation system, due to inter-sphere rivalries, means that minimal higher education standards cannot be guaranteed on a nationwide basis.

The key question, therefore, is how to remedy the negative aspects of federalism while preserving the positive ones. As noted in the chapter's introduction, Brazil's new National Education Plan calls for the creation of a national system of education to coordinate the educational initiatives of the different governmental spheres. Those advocating for a national system have tended to focus on its importance for basic education (pre-school, primary and secondary), but our analysis suggests that it is also crucial to the improvement of higher education. Such a system requires national directives, an overall coordinating body and the legal mandate to enforce inter-sphere collaboration with respect to matters relating to evaluation, core curriculum and campus location. The system should be financed by a national fund made up of a pre-established percentage of federal, state and local taxes to be utilized to ensure minimum levels of quality among all public institutions in the country. Brazil already has experience with such a fund for basic education. The federal contribution to the fund would have to be greater, in both absolute and relative terms, than that made by the subnational units since the latter are principally responsible for the development of lower schooling levels.

Some will suggest that the recommended system, if adopted, would undermine state and local autonomy. But possibilities of implementation exist, especially if the system's coordinating body is truly representative and it leads to a more equitable distribution of public monies. This type of system is also possible if it appears conducive to the genuine improvement of higher education, something highly valued in the context of Brazilian society.

REFERENCES

Abrúcio, F. L. 2010. 'A dinâmica federativa da educação brasileira: diagnóstico e propostas de aperfeiçoamento'. In *Educação e federalismo no Brasil: combater as desigualdades, garantir a diversidade*, edited by R. P. Oliveira and W. Santana, 39–70. Brasília: UNESCO.

Almeida, M., Jr, Lisboa, M. B., and Pessoa, S. 2015. 'O ajuste inevitável ou o país que ficou velho antes de se tornar desenvolvido'. *Folha de São Paulo*, 19 July.

Amaral, N. C. 2008. 'O financiamento das universidades brasileiras e as assimetrias regionais: um estudo sobre o custo do aluno'. In *Educação superior no Brasil e diversidade regional*, edited by V. L. Chaves and J. R. Silva, Jr., 127–152. Belém: Editora Universitária da UFPA.

———. 2009. 'Expansão-Avaliação-Financiamento: tensões e desafios da vinculação na educação superior brasileira'. In *Reformas da educação superior: cenários passados e contradições do presente*, edited by D. Mancebo, J. R. Silva, Jr., J. F. Oliveira and A. M. Catani, 113–146. São Paulo, Xamã.

Araújo, G. C. 2013. 'Federalismo e políticas educacionais no Brasil: equalização e a atuação do empresariado como projetos em disputa para a regulamentação do regime de colaboração'. *Educação e Sociedade* 34 (124): 787–802.

Arretche, M. 2004. 'Federalismo e políticas sociais no Brasil. Problemas de coordenação e autonomia'. *São Paulo em Perspectiva* 18 (2): 17–26.

ARWU. 2016. 'Academic Ranking of World Universities'. Available at http://www.shanghairanking.com/

Balbachevsky, E., and Schwartzman, S. 2011. 'Brazil: diverse experience in institutional governance in the public and private sectors'. In *Changing Governance and Management in Higher Education: the Perspectives of Academy*, edited by W. Locke, W. Cummings, and D. Fisher, 35–56. Dordrecht: Springer.

Barbosa, F. H., and Veloso, F. 2015. 'Costs and Economic Benefits of Education'. In *Education in South America*, edited by S. Schwartzman, 155–178. London: Bloomsbury.

Barreyro, G. B. 2008. *Mapa do ensino superior privado*. Brasília, DF: MEC/INEP, 2008.

Brasil. 1988. *Constituição da República Federativa do Brasil de 1988, promulgada em 5 de outubro de 1988*. Brasília: Diário Oficial da União.

———. 1995. *Lei N° 9.131, de 24 de novembro de 1995. Altera dispositivos da Lei n° 4.024, de 20 de dezembro de 1961, e dá outras providências*. Brasília: Diário Oficial da União.

———. 1996. *Lei N° 9.394, de 20 de dezembro de 1996. Lei de Diretrizes e Bases da Educação Nacional. Dispõe sobre a reforma do sistema educacional brasileiro*. Brasília: Diário Oficial da União.

Brasil. 2004. *Lei N°. 10.861, de 14 de abril de 2004. Institui o Sistema Nacional de Avaliação da Educação Superior e dá outras providências.* Brasília: Diário Oficial da União.

――――. 2008. *Lei N° 11.892, de 29 de dezembro de 2008. Lei dos institutos federais.* Brasília: Diário Oficial da União.

――――. 2009. *Ministério da Educação. Instituto Nacional de Estudos e Pesquisas Educacionais. SINAES: da concepção à regulação*, 5th edition. Brasília: INEP.

――――. 2013. *Ministério da Educação. Instituto Nacional de Estudos e Pesquisas Educacionais. Censo da Educação Superior 2012.* Brasília: INEP.

――――. 2014a. *Lei no 13.005, de 25 de junho de 2014. Plano Nacional da Educação. Aprova o Plano Nacional da Educação – PNE e dá outras providências.* Brasília: Diário Oficial da União.

――――. 2014b. 'Ministério da Ciência e Tecnologia. Brasil: Dispêndio nacional em ciência e tecnologia (C&T), em valores correntes, em relação ao total de C&T e ao produto interno bruto (PIB), por setor institucional, 2000–2012'. Available at http://www.mct.gov.br/index.php/content/view/29140/Brasil_Dispendio_nacional_em_ciencia_e_tecnologia_C_T_sup_1_sup__em_valores_correntes_em_relacao_ao_total_de_C_T_e_ao_produto_interno_bruto_PIB_por_setor_institucional.html

Caldarelli, C. E., Camara, M. R. G., and Perdigão, C. 2015. 'Instituições de ensino superior e desenvolvimento econômico: o caso das universidades estaduais paraenses'. *Planejamento e políticas públicas*, 44: 85–112.

CAPES. 2016. 'GEOCAPES – Sistema de Informações Georreferenciadas'. Available at http://geocapes.capes.gov.br/geocapes2/

Carnoy, M., Loyalka, P., Dobryakova, M., Dossani, R., Froumin, I., and Kuhns, K. 2013. *University Expansion in a Changing Global Economy: Triumph of the BRICs?* Stanford, CA: Stanford University Press.

Costa, P. L. S., and Miranda, M. R. F. A. 2011. Educação Superior e desenvolvimento no Estado da Bahia: um estudo sobre as universidades estaduais baianas. Anais do I Circuito de Debates Acadêmicos. Salvador: IPEA, pp. 1–25.

Costa, V. M. F. 2010. 'Federalismo e relações intergovernamentais: implicações para a reforma da educação no Brasil'. *Educação e Sociedade* 31 (112): 729–748.

Cury, C. R. J. 2008. 'Sistema Nacional de Educação: desafio para uma educação igualitária e federativa'. *Educação e Sociedade* 29 (105): 1187–1209.

Cunha, L. A. 1980. *A universidade temporã.* Rio de Janeiro: Civilização Brasileira.

――――. 1983. *A universidade crítica.* Rio de Janeiro: Francisco Alves.

――――. 1988. *A universidade reformada.* Rio de Janeiro: Francisco Alves.

Daflon, V. T., Feres Jr. J., & Campos, L. A. 2013. 'Race-based Affirmative Actions in Brazilian Public Higher Education: An Analytical Overview'. *Cadernos de Pesquisa* 43 (148): 302–327.

Dias Sobrinho, J. 2010. 'Democratização, qualidade e crise da educação superior: faces da exclusão e limites da inclusão'. *Educação & Sociedade* 31 (113): 1223–1245.

Durham, E. 2005. 'Educação superior pública e privada'. In *Os desafios da educação no Brasil*, edited by C. Brock, and S. Schwartzman, 197–224. Rio de Janeiro: Nova Fronteira.

FAPESP. 2010. *Indicadores de Ciência, Tecnologia e Inovação em São Paulo 2010*. São Paulo: Fundação de Apoio à Pesquisa do Estado de São Paulo.

Ferreira, A., and Leopoldi, M. A. 2013. 'A contribuição da universidade pública para a inovação e o desenvolvimento regional: a percepção de gestores e pesquisadores'. *Revista GUAL* 6 (1): 60–82. doi: http://dx.doi.org/10.5007/1983-4535.2013v6n1p60.

Fialho, N. H. 2012. 'Universidades estaduais no Brasil: pauta para a construção de um sistema nacional articulado de educação'. *Revista da FAEEBA* 21 (38): 81–93.

FIES. 2016. 'Programa de Financiamento Estudantil'. Available at http://sisfies-portal.mec.gov.br/index.html

FNDE/SIOPE. 2014. 'Sistema de informações sobre orçamentos públicos em educação – SIOPE'. Available at https://www.fnde.gov.br/siope/

Gomes, A. M. 2008. 'As reformas politicas a educação superior no Brasil: avanços e recuos'. In *Reformas e políticas: educação superior e pós-graduação no Brasil*, edited by D. Mancebo, J. R. Silva, Jr, and J. F. Oliveira, 23–51. Campinas: Alínea.

IBGE. 2010a. 'Censo Demográfico 2010. Rio de Janeiro: IBGE'. Available at www.ibge.gov.br/home/estatistica/populacao/censo2010/

———. 2010b. 'Contas regionais do Brasil. Contas Nacionais 2010, n 38'. Available at ftp://ftp.ibge.gov.br/Contas_Regionais/2010/contasregionais2010.pdf

———. 2014. *Perfil dos Estados Brasileiros 2013. Pesquisa de informações básicas estaduais*. Rio de Janeiro: IBGE.

INEP. 2013. 'Sinopse estatística da educação superior 2013'. Available at http://portal.inep.gov.br/superior-censosuperior-sinopse

———. 2014. 'Sinopse estatística da educação superior. Graduação. Censo da Educação Superior 2014'. Available at http://portal.inep.gov.br/superior-censosuperior-sinopse

Levy, D. 1986. *Higher Education and the State in Latin America: Private Challenges to Public Dominance*. Chicago, IL: University of Chicago Press.

Lima, F. J., and Ramos, M. N. 2013. 'Os desafios da educação superior para a próxima década. Observatório do PNE'. Available at http://www.observatoriodopne.org.br/metas-pne/12-ensino-superior/analises/os-desafios-da-educacao-superior-para-a-proxima-decada

Lima, M. L., and Contel, F. B. 2011. *Internacionalização da educação superior: nações ativas, nações passiveis e a geopolítica de conhecimento*. São Paulo: Alameda.

Lopes, R. P. M. 2012. 'Universidade, externalidades e desempenho regional: as dimensões sócio-economicas da expansão do ensino superior em Vitória da Conquista'. PhD Dissertation, Universitat de Barcelona, Barcelona, Spain.

Máximo, M. L. 2013. 'Fies e ProUni já respondem por 31% de matrículas de universidades privadas'. Available at http://www.andifes.org.br/fies-e-prouni-ja-respondem-por-31-de-matriculas-de-universidades-privadas/

Matos, W. R. De; Macedo, K. A. S. De & Mattos, I. G. de. 2013. '10 anos de ações afirmativas na UNEB: desempenho comparativo entre cotistas e não cotistas de 2003 a 2009'. *Revista da ABPN* 5 (11): 83–99.

Mugnaini, R., Digiappietri, L. A., and Mena-Chalco, R. 2104. 'Comunicação científica no Brasil (1998–2012): indexação, crescimento, fluxo e dispersão'. *Transformação* 26 (3): 239–252.

Neves, C. E. B., Raizer, L., and Fachinetto, R. F. 2007. 'Acesso, expansão e equidade no ensino superior: novos desafios para a política educacional brasileira'. *Sociologias*, 9 (17): 124–157.

Nunes, E. O. 2012. *Educação superior no Brasil: estudos, debates, controvérsias.* Rio de Janeiro: Garamond.

OECD. 2014. *Education at a glance – OECD indicators.* Paris: OECD Publishers.

————. 2015. *Education at a glance – OECD indicators.* Paris: OECD Publishers.

Oliveira, R. O. 2009. 'A transformação da educação em mercadoria no Brasil'. *Educação e Sociedade* 30 (108): 739–760.

Oliveira, C., and Ganzeli, P. 2013. 'Relações intergovernamentais em educação: fundos, convênios, consórcios públicos e arranjos de desenvolvimento da educação'. *Educação e Sociedade* 34 (125): 1031–1047.

Pedrosa, R. H., Amaral, E., and Knobel, M. 2013. 'Assessing Higher Education Learning Outcomes in Brazil'. *Higher Education Management and Policy* 24 (2): 55–71.

Pedrosa, R. H. L., Simões, T. P., Carneiro, A. M., Andrade, C. Y., Sampaio, H., and Knobel, M. 2014. 'Access to Higher Education in Brazil'. *Widening Participation and Lifelong Learning* 16 (1): 5–33.

Peixoto, A. L. A., Ribeiro, E. M. B. A, Bastos, A. V. B., and Ramalho, M. C. K. 2013. 'Cotas e desempenho acadêmico na UFBA: um estudo a partir dos coeficientes de rendimento'. *Anais do XIII Coloquio Internacional sobre Gestão Universitária nas Américas.* 1–15. Available at https://repositorio.ufsc.br/handle/123456789/114822

Plank, D. N., and Verhine, R. E. 2002. 'Flight from Freedom: Resistance to Institutional Autonomy in Brazil's Federal Universities'. In *Higher Education in the Developing World: Changing Contexts and Institutional Responses*, edited by D. W. Chapman and A. E. Austin, 69–92. Westport, CT: Greenwood Press.

Portal Tributário. 2016. 'Tributes'. Available at www.portaltributario.com.br/tributos.htm

Preal & Lemann Foundation. 2009. *Overcoming Inertia? A Report Card on Education in Brazil.* São Paulo: Preal\Lemann Foundation.

ProUni. 2016. 'Programa Universidade para Todos'. Available at http://siteprouni.mec.gov.br/

Reis, J. A. F., Martins, R. R. R., Gaio, J., and Lohmann, L. M. 2014. 'Estrutura da educação superior brasileira: um diagnóstico estratégico societário'. *REBRAE–Revista Brasileira de Estratégia* 7 (1): 88–99.

Ristoff, D. 2014. 'O novo perfil do campus brasileiro: uma análise socioeconômico do estudante de graduação'. *Avaliação* 19 (3): 743–757.

Sampaio, H. 2011. 'O setor privado de ensino superior no Brasil: continuidades e transformações'. *Revista Ensino Superior Unicamp* 4: 28–43.

Sampaio, H., Balbachevsky, E., and Peñaliza V. 1998. Universidades estaduais no Brasil – características Institucionais. São Paulo: Núcleo de Pesquisas sobre Ensino Superior, Universidade de São Paulo.

Secca, R. X., and Leal, R. M. 2009. 'Análise do setor de ensino privado no Brasil'. *BNDES Setorial* 30: 103–156.

The *Economist*. 2012. 'Education in Brazil. Studying the world. A Huge Scholarship Programme Could Boost Economic Growth'. Available at http://www.economist.com/node/21550306

———. 2014. 'Higher Education: Creative Destruction'. Available at http://www.economist.com/news/leaders/21605906-cost-crisis-changing-labour-markets-and-new-technology-will-turn-old-institution-its

Todos pela Educação. 2015. *Anuário brasileiro da educação básica*. Moderna. Available at http://www.todospelaeducacao.org.br//arquivos/biblioteca/anuario_edu-cacao_2015.pdf

Velloso, J. 2009. 'Cotistas e não-cotistas: rendimento de alunos na Universidade de Brasília'. *Cadernos de Pesquisa* 39 (137): 621–644.

Verhine, R. E. 1991. 'Brazil'. In *International Higher Education: An Encyclopaedia*, Vol. 2, edited by P. G. Altbach, 885–898. New York, NY: Garland Publishing.

———. 2008. 'Avaliação da CAPES: subsídios para a reformulação do modelo'. In *Reformas e Políticas: Educação Superior e Pós-graduação no Brasil*, edited by D. Machado, J. R. Silva, Jr, and J. F. Oliveira, 165–188. Campinas: Alínea.

———. 2010. 'O novo alfabeto do SINAES: reflexões sobre o IDD, CPC e IGC'. In *Convergências e tensões no campo da formação e do trabalho docente*, edited by A. Dalben, L. Diniz and L. Santos, 632–650. Belo Horizonte: Autêntica.

Verhine, R. E., Dantas, L. M. V., and Soares, J. F. 2006. 'Do Provão ao ENADE: uma análise comparativa dos exames nacionais utilizados no ensino superior brasileiro, Ensaio'. *Avaliação e Políticas Públicas em Educação* 14 (52): 291–310.

Web of Science. 2016. 'InCites – Essential Science Indicators'. Available at https://esi.incites.thomsonreuters.com/IndicatorsAction.action?SID=A1-FTv20ECk-8v14WhqHcRJExxnbIe3Ytx2Fyr4-18x2dRctcSRAy57bsoix2BefrHXe-Ax3Dx3DQx2FQxxxxAn2B8dx2Fx2FXV2uz1x2Bdwx3Dx3D-YwBaX6hN-5JZpnPCj2lZNMAx3Dx3D-jywguyb6iMRLFJm7wHskHQx3Dx3D&SrcApp=IC2LS&Init=Yes

World Bank. 2015a. 'Data, GDP Ranking, Gross Domestic Product 2014'. Available at http://data.worldbank.org/data-catalog/GDP-ranking-table

———. 2015b. 'Research and Development Expenditure (% of GDP)'. Available at http://data.worldbank.org/indicator/GB.XPD.RSDV.GD.ZS

Chapter 7

India
The Unfulfilled Need for Cooperative Federalism

Jandhyala B. G. Tilak*

INTRODUCTION

India has one of the largest higher education systems in the world, with some 33 million students. The British established the first modern university in the nineteenth century in India during their colonial rule.[1] They introduced a small number of public colleges to train Indian civil servants, engineers and other professionals needed for the colonial administration. They did so using a version of the British higher education model that includes lead universities, owned and operated by provincial governments, certified and regulated affiliated institutions (colleges) that provided the actual education, and were operated almost as independent entities. The provincial governments prescribed policies that the universities implemented through setting standards, but the provincial governments provided no funding for or operational control over its affiliated private colleges.

* The author is grateful to Isak Froumin for his keen interest in the author's work and for discussions at the early stage of the study, A. Mathew for valuable inputs and comments and Martin Carnoy for reading earlier drafts and effecting substantial improvements in the paper.

[1] The first three universities, University of Bombay, University of Calcutta and the University of Madras, were established in 1857. During ancient period, however, India had some of the best universities in the world, namely Nalanda, Takshashila (Taxila) and Vikramaditya.

[The British colonial administration] replicated the University of London 'federal university' system in which the university is an affiliating body for local colleges, and reports to its local government. The universities' role was to support the goals of its constituent colleges by designing curricula, holding examinations and awarding degrees. (Carnoy and Dossani 2013, 4)

As we shall show, this model, where universities operate mainly as a governance system, and relatively less as knowledge generating and disseminating or teaching bodies, has heavily influenced Indian higher education system until the present day.

In the later colonial period, provincial governments began to invest in relatively high-quality higher education, *albeit* on a limited scale. They created state universities with which the colleges were affiliated. Again, this sets an important precedent: Provincial governments would take the lead in expanding the higher education system—a policy trend that continues to today.

Once India became independent from British rule in 1947, it became a federal state, with the union government at the central level and constituent states (provinces) and union territories (local provinces administered by the union government due to special characteristics) at the subnational or local level. As in other federal systems, the Constitution of independent India gave constituent member states considerable control over all education, including higher education. This reflected the state of affairs under British rule in which provinces were effectively in charge of university expansion and regulating their affiliated colleges.

There is a considerable literature on various aspects of India's higher education system (Altbach 2012; Kumar 1975; Tilak 2008, 2010a, 2018; etc.). In this chapter, we focus on the impact that the special nature of Indian federalism has had on shaping of the higher education system and its expansion. We shall argue that despite the legal provisions made to give states control over educational expansion, the same Constitution gave asymmetric power to India's union government to regulate higher education and to shape its expansion. In the next section, we describe the complex nature of the Indian federal system as outlined in the Constitution. In the following section, we analyse union–state relations in education more generally, and, in the third section, we describe the higher education system, including its rapid expansion over the last 30 years. In the fourth section, we discuss the trends in financing higher education within the context of the Indian federal system, and the last section presents a short summary of the chapter along with a few concluding observations.

THE INDIAN 'FEDERAL' SYSTEM
Overall Picture

The Indian federal system is more complex than federal systems in the United States, Canada and Australia. The Indian system does not possess all the features of a typical federation. For example, the Constitution of India does not use the term 'federal'. Nevertheless, the Constitution provides for a structure of governance which is essentially federal in nature. India is a 'unitary state with federal features rather than a federal State with subsidiary unitary features' (Wheare 1953, 20). In fact, India is 'neither purely federal nor purely unitary, but is a combination of both. It is a union or composite state of a novel type. It enshrines the principles that, in spite of federation, the national interest ought to be paramount' (Basu 1965, 55). Some have argued that India is a 'quasi-federal' system because the Constitution accords so little autonomy in practice to the states (Hardgrave and Kochanek 1986, 44; Nair and Jain 2000).

The Constitution of India provides for separate governments at the level of the centre and the states with separate legislative, executive and judicial wings of governance. It also spells out in detail the legislative, administrative and financial relations between the union government and the states and demarcates their jurisdictions, powers and functions. This is done in three separate 'lists'—List I is the Union List; List II is the State List; and List III is the Concurrent List. List I includes all those subjects which fall in the exclusive jurisdiction of the national Parliament. List II consists of all the subjects under exclusive jurisdiction of the state Legislatures and List III, called the Concurrent List, consists of subjects that can be legislated by both the national parliament and the state legislatures.[2]

---

[2] The classification of education under three lists in the Constitution is similar to the provisions made in the Government of India Act 1919 under British rule,

A crucial feature of the Concurrent list is that in the event of conflicts between state and central law, the latter always prevails (Hardgrave and Kochanek 1986, 146). Thus, the Concurrent list includes items on which both the union government and the state government can enact legislation. The interpretation is that so long as there is no conflict between the two levels of legislation, both co-exist, but if there is a conflict, the union government's legislation prevails over the other. The Article 254 (1) of the Constitution states:

> If any provision of a law made by the Legislature of a State is repugnant to any provision of a law made by Parliament which Parliament is competent to enact, or to any provision of an existing law with respect to one of the matters enumerated in the Concurrent List, then, … the law made by Parliament, whether passed before or after the law made by the Legislature of such State, or, as the case may be, the existing law, shall prevail and the law made by the Legislature of the State shall, to the extent of the repugnancy, be void.

Constitutionally, then, the union government and states have been envisaged as organically linked structures working together on cooperative principles. States are coordinate structures of the federal system rather than subordinate entities of the federal government. Union–state relations are premised on the principle of cooperative federalism.

However, within this basic framework of federalism, the Constitution gives overriding powers to the union government. States must exercise their executive power in compliance with the laws made

---

according to which the subject of education was 'partly all India, partly reserved, partly transferred with limitations, and partly transferred without limitations' and those made in the Government of India Act 1935 that improved the anomalous position 'considerably' by making a few areas of education federal subjects and retaining major areas of education as state subjects (Naik and Nurullah 1945, 365). In reality, the union government obtained 'a larger authority over education' than under the 1919 and 1935 Acts of Government of (British) India (Rao 1972, 179). In the British period, education, including university education, was moved back and forth between the federal and provincial governments. In some cases, powers were granted to provinces and, at other times, power over education was centralized in the federal government, later again transferred to the provinces, and so on. See Tilak (1989) and Carnoy and Dossani (2013).

by the union government and must not impede the executive power of the union within the states. The power of any state legislature to legislate on matters enumerated in the State List has been made subject to the power of the national Parliament to legislate on matters enumerated in the Union and Concurrent Lists, and entries in the State List must be interpreted accordingly. Article 246 of the Constitution also states that 'Parliament has power to make laws with respect to any matter for any part of the territory of India not included in a State not withstanding that such matter is a matter enumerated in the State List'. Given these overriding powers of the union government, the federation has often been described as a 'quasi-federation', 'semi-federation', 'pragmatic federation', or a 'federation with strong unitary features'.

The overall system of financial devolution by the union government to the states follows from this. The union government until very recently transferred federally collected tax revenues to the states through two main organizations: the Planning Commission, which is a non-statutory body,[3] and the Finance Commission, a statutory body. These two channels exist in addition to the union government's channel to make discrete transfers directly to the states. The Planning Commission's grants were essentially development ('plan') grants; they were negotiated transfers and were specific or tied to specific programmes/projects/schemes,[4] while the Finance Commission makes grants for maintenance (or 'non-plan') purposes. They are lump sum and untied. States also receive non-plan grants from the Finance Commission as a matter of right, rather than of grace or through negotiations.

There are five types of taxes that come under the purview of the Finance Commission for devolution. They are (a) taxes levied and collected by the union government that are not shared with the states (e.g., customs duties corporate taxes); (b) taxes levied and collected by the union government that are *necessarily* shared with the states, based on certain formulae (e.g., the income tax); (c) taxes levied and collected by the union government that *may* be shared with the states (e.g., excise taxes on tobacco); (d) taxes levied and collected by the union

---

[3] See Footnote 9.

[4] The Planning Commission was also vested with the power to approve plans of the states, irrespective of funding by the Planning Commission.

government that are wholly transferable to the states (e.g., estate duties, taxes on sales and taxes on purchases of newspapers); and (e) taxes levied by the union government, but collected and used by the states (e.g., excise taxes on medicine and toiletries).

Besides sharing these tax revenues, the Finance Commission provides grants and loans to the states. Additional grants and loans are needed because, as in all federal systems, not all states have the same revenue raising capacity; the union government assumes the role of 'equalizing' national economic and social development and/or of promoting regional balanced development. In India, as in all federal systems, the mechanisms of revenue sharing, the principles and criteria[5] adopted and the amounts distributed have often been subject of discussion and discontent between the union government and the states.[6]

Centre–State Relations in Education[7]

Influenced by the general model adopted in the United States and the Hartog Committee recommendation in 1929 in British India, the framers of the Indian Constitution of independent India took a fundamental decision to treat education as a state subject and to vest the residuary powers in education in the states by specifying the powers reserved for the union government. Entry 11 of List II of the Seventh Schedule to the Constitution lays down that 'education including universities, subject to the provisions of Entries 63, 64, 65 and 66 of List I and Entry 25 of List III should be a state subject'.

Nevertheless, the Constitution also delegated considerable educational responsibilities to the union government. The entry nos. 62, 63,

---

[5] The criteria are largely based on population, area, requirements for maintenance of assets, income distance and fiscal gap in the budgets of the states.

[6] The available data on union–state shares in finances relating to any sector or all sectors combined refer to the post-devolution of funds by the Finance Commission, as data on pre-devolution expenditures are hard to get. Thus, the figures for state expenditure in any sector are inclusive of transfers made by the union government through the Finance Commission.

[7] On earlier writings on centre–state relations in education in India, see Naik (1963), Rao (1972), Baker (1976) and Tilak (1989).

64, 65 and 66 in the Union List of the Seventh Schedule provide exclusive jurisdictional competence to the union government in specified areas, such as certain museums 'of national importance', 'central' universities, such as University of Delhi, and other universities and institutions of technical and professional education declared by Parliament to be of national importance, and agencies that determine standards for institutions of higher education and of scientific research. In addition, Entry 20 of the Concurrent List relating to economic and social planning empowers the union government to take a proactive role in giving direction to education in the desired areas (MHRD 2016a,b).

Thus, the Constitution defines education as predominantly a state subject, but certain major functions are included in the Union List and a few aspects in the Concurrent List. The rest, such as school education as a whole and others, were listed in the state list, making all education virtually a responsibility of the state. The role of the union government is limited to playing an enabling role in terms of extending to the states cooperation and support of various kinds, including financial resources.

Although school education is a state subject, the Constitution made an exception in the case of elementary education. Because of the perceived relationship between the provision of universal free and compulsory education and the successful working of a democracy, the Constitution decided to include elementary education as a Directive Principle of State policy under Part IV by stating that 'The State shall endeavour to provide within a period of ten years from the commencement of this Constitution, for free and compulsory education for all children until they complete the age of 14 years' (Article 45),[8] where the 'state' in this case includes the union government, state governments and local bodies.

---

[8] In 2002, the Constitution was amended to make elementary education a fundamental right (Article 21A), following which, in 2009, the national Parliament passed the Right to Free and Compulsory Education Act, covering elementary education. But, for a few limited options made available to the states in implementing its various provisions, the Act is rather uniformly applicable to all states and union territories.

Similarly, the Constitution makes it an obligatory responsibility of the union government to promote the educational interests of the weaker sections of the population: 'The State shall promote with special care the educational and economic interests of the weaker sections of the people, and, in particular, of the Scheduled Castes and the Scheduled Tribes, and shall protect them from social injustice and all forms of exploitation' (Article 46). This Article in the Constitution makes it a responsibility of the union government to bring about equalization of educational opportunities in all parts of the country and, to that end, to give special assistance to the populous states and to disadvantaged (less developed) states.

These major 'exceptions' of assuring provision of free and compulsory education (Article 45), equalization of educational opportunities between different geographical areas or different sections of society (Article 46) and safeguarding the cultural interests of the minority and provision of adequate facilities to receive at least primary education in their own mother tongue (Article 350A) give considerable power to the union government in educational provision even as the Constitution formally assigns jurisdiction to the state over the education system.

Further, the union government considered that higher education required national planning and development; so the Constitution accords the union government the power to coordinate and determine standards in universities and scientific, technical or research institutions (Entry 66 of List I). Because of factors such as the high costs of university education and costs of scientific research, the difficulty of getting high quality teaching personnel and the importance of international collaborations to do the research and to train students in technical fields, scientific research, technical education and the higher types of professional and vocational education jurisdiction over these aspects of higher education were also assigned to the union government (Entries 64 and 65 of List I).

Finally, a very powerful means of control by the union government was created when 'economic and social planning' was made a concurrent responsibility (Entry 20 of List III). This has an indirect but significant bearing upon the union government's role in education. It implies that the union government has a constitutional responsibility for economic and social development of the nation. Given that economic and social development is intimately related to several sectors including, specifically education, the union government is given a major responsibility for educational policies.

Actual policy issues and plans relating to national development plan are discussed and approved in the National Development Council, an interstate council set up in 1952 through an executive order as a non-statutory body, consisting of the all states (chief ministers) and union territories along with the Prime Minister, the union cabinet ministers and members of the Planning Commission,[9] which serves as an important platform for consultations between the states and the union government. Besides the National Development Council, specifically in education, the Central Advisory Board of Education (CABE) forms a similar policy-making body. Originally set up in 1920 in British India after education was made a provincial and transferred subject in the Government of India Act, 1919, the CABE, consisting of representatives of all states and the union government, besides education experts, is the highest advisory body to facilitate interactions between the union and state governments, to advise them in the field of education, and to enable them to come to a consensus.

In practice, there are three ways in which the union government makes specific interventions in education. These are as follows:

- *The central sector* in education, consisting of, for example, central universities, central schools (in school education), the National Council of Educational Research and Training, Regional Colleges (Institutes) of Education, other central institutions, such as the Central Board of Secondary Education (CBSE),[10] the National

---

[9] The Planning Commission was replaced by a new body, called NITI Aayog—National Institution for Transforming India—in 2015. It is widely felt that the National Development Council will also stand automatically abolished (see Mehra 2016).

[10] The CBSE works like a regulating body in secondary education, providing recognition and affiliation to secondary schools, prescribing curriculum and syllabus, conducts national examinations at the end of secondary and higher secondary levels of education etc. While all central schools—those established by the union government—are affiliated to the CBSE, states also have their own state boards of

Institute of Open Schooling, the University Grants Commission (UGC), the Indian Council of Social Science Research, the Indian Council of Historical Research, the Indian Council Philosophical Research, the national professorship and national scholarships, all under the exclusive jurisdiction of the union government. The responsibility of financing, planning, implementation and every aspect of these institutions and programmes lies with the union government.

- *The centrally sponsored sector*, including items/areas where the union government assumes responsibility of planning/development/design and funding, and the state government is responsible for execution or implementation, areas for which the states do not necessarily accept responsibility on their own. The union government persuades the states to accept responsibility for their implementation and they are normally 100 per cent funded by the union government. Examples include promotion of Sanskrit, Hindi in non-Hindi speaking states and promotion of students' tours and excursions.
- *The centrally assisted sector*, including programmes in which the union government is actively interested, but which are embodied in state plans and for which financing responsibilities are shared by the union and the state government in varying proportions (e.g., enrolment of handicapped students in the integrated schools).

Over the years, the distinction between centrally sponsored schemes and centrally assisted schemes disappeared, and these schemes are referred to as centrally sponsored schemes. The very purpose of centrally sponsored schemes is to utilize the financial resources of the union government and the administrative machinery available in the states (Chaturvedi 2011, 63), specifically in the case of those activities that the union government considers important for the country, serving different national goals such as national integration, uniformity and national level standards. Wide interstate variations that would result in

---

secondary/higher secondary education to which all government schools in the state are affiliated. Private schools in the states have an option to get affiliated to either the state board or the central board. Generally, the CBSE syllabus is found to be of high quality and standards, and hence a good number of high quality private schools opt for affiliation with the CBSE instead of with a state board.

such activities, if not attended by the union government, are regarded as undesirable.

However, over the years, these central schemes formed an area of tension in the union–state relations. The states' resistance and resentment was mainly due the large number of central schemes, many of high cost, designed by the union government mainly in areas enumerated in state/concurrent list of the Constitution, but requiring implementation by the states. These schemes are criticized as reducing state autonomy and not allowing much regional flexibility. Further, they required matching funding, therefore straining state budgets and forcing states to redirect funds from state-initiated programmes.

HIGHER EDUCATION
Size and Structure

Independent India inherited from the colonial past a higher education system that was limited to a minuscule percentage of the college age population—indeed, the entire Indian education system had a narrow base of students. During the colonial period, from 1857 to 1947, barely 20 universities were set up. There were less than 500 colleges in 1947 when the country became independent, with a student population much below 200 thousand. During the last seven decades, India has made impressive progress in terms of expansion of higher education. Today, the Indian higher education system is the second largest in the world with 799 universities, nearly 40,000 colleges and 34 million regular students, who form 24.3 per cent of the 18–23 years age group population (gross enrolment) of the country. The higher education system employed approximately 1.5 million teachers in 2015–2016.

The system is also highly complex. There is a wide variety of higher education institutions including conventional universities, colleges and special categories of university equivalent institutions. The main categories of university and university-level institutions are central universities, state universities, deemed-to-be universities, national institutions of importance and other university-level institutions. A central university is a university established or incorporated by an Act of the union government. The union government provides

Table 7.1 *Growth of Higher Education in India*

Year	Universities	Colleges	Enrolment (million)
1857–1858	3	27	250*
1947–1948	20	496	0.2
1950–1951	28	578	0.2
1990–1991	184	6,627	4.4
2000–2001	254	10,152	8.6
2014–2015	757	38,056	29.4
2015–2016	799	39,071	34.6

Source: Education in India, All-India Survey of Higher Education and UGC *Annual Report* (various years).
Note: * Actual number.

grants to the UGC and establishes central universities and institutions of national importance in the country. A state university is a university established or incorporated by a state Act. A private university is established through a state/central Act by a sponsoring body, that is, a society registered under the Societies Registration Act of 1860, or any other corresponding law currently in force in a state or a public trust or a company registered under Section 25 of the Companies Act, 1956. In addition, there are three other types of university level institutions. A 'deemed-to-be university' refers to an institution that has been so declared by the union government under Section 3 of the UGC Act, 1956. The union government is also responsible for declaring an educational institution as 'deemed-to-be university' on the recommendation of the UGC. Today, we have deemed universities set up by state governments, some of which are financially supported by a state and some not. An institution of national importance is established by an Act of Parliament. An institution of a similar kind is also established or incorporated by a state legislature act.

In addition to the university and university-equivalent institutions mentioned in Table 7.2, higher education is offered in colleges, many of which offer undergraduate (bachelor's level) education and a few offer masters' level programmes. Among the colleges, there are

Table 7.2 *All Universities, by Type, from 2007–2008 to 2015–2016*

Type of Institution	2007–2008	2011–2012	2015–2016
Central Institutions			
Central Universities	28	42	43
Govt. Deemed Universities	(see below)	39	43
Central Open Universities	1	1	1
Institutions of National Importance	33	59	75
Others	–	–	6
State Institutions			
State Public Universities	222	284	329
State Deemed Universities	102*	91	32
State Open Universities	–	13	13
Institutions under State Legislation	5	5	5
State Private Universities	16	105	197
Private Deemed	–	–	79
Universities-aided	–	–	11
Private deemed (unaided)	–	–	79
State Private Open Universities	–	–	1
Others	–	3	13
Total	406	642	799

Sources: Ministry of Human Resource Development (MHRD), *Statistics of Higher and Technical Education, 2007–2008*. All-India Survey of Higher Education, 2015–2016.

Note: * Central government and state deemed universities combined.

government colleges, government-aided private colleges and private unaided or self-financing colleges. Every college is necessarily affiliated to one public—central or state university or other.

Except for about 100 colleges affiliated to (or constituents of) 2–3 central universities, namely, the University of Delhi, Banaras

Hindu University and Aligarh Muslim University, all other colleges in India are affiliated with state universities. In all, central institutions are relatively very few in number—162 university and university level institutions, with their 100 colleges—compared to nearly 600 state universities and university level institutions of higher education, with their 40,000 affiliated colleges. In this sense, the Indian higher education system is highly decentralized with the vast majority of students attending colleges that are affiliated with state universities or attending state universities themselves. Most of the colleges offer only first-degree courses of study, while universities mostly offer masters' level programmes and research studies in their campuses. Exceptions to both are very few.

The higher education system in India is dominated by under-graduate education—first-degree level studies. In 2014–2015, about 80 per cent of the students were enrolled in undergraduate programmes concentrated in colleges and about 20 per cent in master's level and higher-level programmes. A very small percentage (0.34%) of total students were enrolled in doctoral study programmes. There are a few postgraduate colleges that offer master's level and research programmes, and few universities offer bachelor's degree programmes in their teaching departments. Thus, in 2014–2015, a significant part of higher education took place in colleges (84.4% of the students enrolled) in India and only a small part (15.6%) directly in universities (MHRD 2015). But as we describe later, universities are responsible for curriculum and other academic aspects of colleges.

Though the growth in student numbers from less than 200 thousand in 1950–1951 to 34 million in 2015–2016 represents a massive increase in higher education, the proportion of the age cohort (18–23 years old) attending higher education institutions is relatively low: 24 per cent in 2015–2016, up from 9 per cent at the turn of the twenty-first century. This gross enrolment ratio varied greatly among states in 2014–2015, from 56 per cent in Chandigarh, above 40 per cent in Puducherry, Tamil Nadu and Delhi, and below 15 per cent in Chhattisgarh and Jharkhand, and between 15 per cent and 20 per cent in West Bengal, Madhya Pradesh, Assam, Tripura and Bihar, among major states (Table 7.3). Further, estimates in 2005–2006 placed the gross enrolment ratio

Table 7.3 Enrolment and Gross Enrolment Ratio in Higher Education, 2002–2003 and 2014–2015 (Distance Education Excluded)

State	Academic Year 2002–2003 Enrolment (000)	% 18–23 Years Old	Academic Year 2014–2015 Enrolment (000)	% 18–23 Years Old
Andhra Pradesh	751.5	9.51	1,367.0	29.9
Arunachal Pradesh	5.4	6.37	31.6	26.0
Assam	201.1	8.67	442.5	16.8
Bihar	494.0	7.30	1,314.0	12.9
Chhattisgarh	152.8	7.27	381.5	14.4
Delhi	172.2	10.94	364.2	43.3
Goa	19.4	13.47	38.4	27.7
Gujarat	519.0	9.65	1,352.4	20.1
Haryana	249.1	10.56	868.7	27.9
Himachal Pradesh	89.9	12.76	196.0	30.4
Jammu & Kashmir	59.6	4.95	260.4	26.0
Jharkhand	197.3	8.12	462.6	13.4
Karnataka	557.6	9.92	1,742.0	26.1
Kerala	251.2	7.66	673.6	27.0
Madhya Pradesh	474.8	7.77	1,491.7	19.6
Maharashtra	1,258.2	12.30	3,240.2	27.6
Manipur	36.4	13.19	104.8	38.5
Meghalaya	29.2	10.94	64.9	21.0
Mizoram	11.2	9.51	23.4	23.9
Nagaland	12.3	4.33	29.2	15.6
Odisha	345.1	8.71	781.0	17.5
Punjab	243.7	8.53	811.6	26.0
Rajasthan	363.2	8.77	1,593.0	19.7
Sikkim	4.1	6.29	15.7	29.4
Tamil Nadu	713.0	10.91	2,772.0	44.8
Tripura	20.1	5.84	61.7	16.4

(Continued)

Table 7.3 (Continued)

State	Academic Year 2002–2003		Academic Year 2014–2015	
	Enrolment (000)	% 18–23 Years Old	Enrolment (000)	% 18–23 Years Old
Uttar Pradesh	1,177.8	7.03	5,219.7	22.1
Uttaranchal	115.3	12.25	394.8	34.9
West Bengal	648.2	8.21	1,677.7	17.1
Chandigarh	33.9	26.68	65.7	55.6
Pondicherry	18.2	17.88	58.0	45.8
All India	9,227.8	8.97	29,383.8	23.6

Sources: UGC Annual Report 2002–2003; Education in India and All-India Survey of Higher Education 2014–2015.

in higher education at about 7 per cent in rural areas and 20 per cent in urban areas (MHRD 2009; UGC 2008).[11]

Central universities, institutions of national importance and other institutions (including institutions deemed-to-be universities), institutions of national importance, colleges normally affiliated to or constituents of central universities, research laboratories, social science institutions, Indian Institutes of Technology (IITs), Indian Institutes of Management (IIMs), etc., listed under the Union List are exclusively and totally under the jurisdiction of the union government. State universities, state institutions, deemed-to-be private universities and private universities broadly operate within the given framework of state legislation, and all traditionally enjoying institutional autonomy in governance. However, they are still subject to three-level structures of governance—institutional governance structure at the institutional level, control of the state government/state agencies and, ultimately, regulation by the union government through a variety of regulating agencies each devoted to a specific

---

[11] Other statistics worth noting: The gross enrolment ratio for women is somewhat lower than for men—24.5 per cent for men versus 22.7 per cent for women in 2014–2015—but this difference has closed over the years.

area like general university education, technical education, teacher education and so on. Some of these statutory professional councils are responsible for recognition of courses of study, promotion of professional institutions, and providing grants and rewards.

What are the regulatory agencies? The union government established several other central regulatory and funding agencies such as the UGC. Today, there are in all, as many as 15 regulating bodies, besides the UGC. They are All-India Council for Technical Education (AICTE), National Council for Teacher Education (NCTE), National Assessment and Accreditation Council (NAAC), National Board of Accreditation (NBA), Medical Council of India (MCI), Dental Council of India, Pharmacy Council of India, Indian Council of Architects, Bar Council of India, Council of Architecture, Veterinary Council, and so on, besides the Ministries of Human Resource Development (Education), Agriculture, Health, Science and Technology, Social Welfare, etc., which exercise direct and indirect supervisory and other regulating functions. Other organizations, such as the Association of Indian Universities, do not have any executive powers. Besides getting engaged in coordination, determination and maintenance of standards in higher education, particularly in universities and colleges, the UGC prescribes rules/regulations and other conditions for these institutions to follow. It also provides funds to these institutions. The AICTE is mainly concerned with regulation of technical education—engineering, technology architecture, management, pharmacy etc. Other professional bodies such as the MCI, the Bar Council of India and the Veterinary Council of India are concerned with their respective areas of study. They regulate the establishment of new institutions, determine standards and stipulate conditions for entry of graduates to specific professions. NAAC was set up by the UGC to assess and accredit institutions of higher learning in the country, and the National Board of Accreditation, created by the NAAC for the same purpose, concentrates on technical institutions. Thus, there are multiple organizations at the central level that are responsible for regulating growth as well as quality and standards in higher education. Both central and state institutions are subject to regulation by these central bodies. State institutions are subject to additional regulation by state governments—ministries/directorates of higher education and state level bodies such as the State Council of Higher Education.

Relative Priorities of the Union and the States: Quality and Quantity

In the first two decades after independence, the union government used its Constitutionally guaranteed powers to establish high quality central institutions, such as the IITs, IIMs, and science and research laboratories. Its interest in the quality and standards in university education was clear when it set up the University Education Commission immediately after independence in 1948, the UGC in 1956, and other institutions.[12]

Second, the union government established regulatory and funding bodies such as the UGC to ensure coordination, quality and standards in the higher education system. For the same purpose of better planning, coordination and maintenance of quality and standards in different areas of higher education, including in some cases relating to their concerned professions, several regulating bodies were set up. Third, the central institutions were relatively well funded, with the government paying, mostly through the UGC, all capital and operational costs. These institutions were encouraged to attract talented faculty and to devote time and resources to high quality research and high quality teaching programmes. Fourth, central universities having no burden of affiliated colleges (some have a few constituent colleges) and more importantly having mainly master's level teaching programmes and research programmes, as we describe later in detail, could concentrate on quality teaching programmes and advanced research activities.

Looking at these several efforts, it appears that the union government focused its attention on quality higher education at least during the initial decades after independence. The states, in turn, put a premium on expanding access rather than on maintaining quality. State governments established many state universities and government colleges and helped in the expansion of private colleges by providing finances to them through a mechanism of 'grants-in-aid'. A major part of the development expenditure of the state universities and colleges was met by the UGC, while state government financed most of the operational costs. The funds from the union government were used

---

[12] It also set up the Secondary Education Commission in 1952.

by the states primarily for the expansion of state systems of higher education and only secondarily for quality related programmes, while state funds were targeted for the maintenance of the institutions.

During the last several decades, both the union government and the states directly expanded higher education. But the union government is focused on producing graduates of adequate quality to meet the needs of the industrialized economy that was yet to emerge, a consideration which was partly shared by the states as well. On the other hand, states found expansion of higher education—public as well as government-supported private—more politically rewarding and hence adopted popular measure of expanding general, less expensive and even low quality higher education institutions (Carnoy and Dossani 2013).

The tension between the need to respond to democratic pressures for expansion of 'mass' higher education at the state level and the need to meet 'national objectives' by developing well-funded, high-quality higher education institutions at the central level managed by the Union Ministry of Education as well as using central agencies to regulate standards for the poorer-quality universities, run by the states has continued to the present day within the context of India's asymmetric federal system.

With governance structures controlled by local politicians and popular pressures, and with increasing budgetary constraints, states find no choice but to continue to expand higher education, specifically private unaided colleges and universities. In view of severe resource constraints, the union government has given tacit approval to the states to permit major growth such private institutions and, at the same time, tacitly approved increases in cost recovery through student fees and student loans in both state and central institutions. The result has been almost unfettered expansion without regard for greater equity or quality.

Equity: India's Affirmative Action

The union government also has a responsibility to promote the interests of disadvantaged groups (castes) and their economic opportunities. As in other countries—Brazil, Mexico and the United States—the union government in India responded to the demands of marginalized groups for greater access to higher education. The Constitution provides for reservation (quotas) of a good proportion of admissions in higher education to certain caste groups listed as scheduled castes, scheduled tribes and other backward communities (OBC).[13] Parliament made laws creating quotas for disadvantaged castes in both public and private institutions, including in employment, and required states to set lower standards for admission and lower tuition rates for such students. Based on population composition, scheduled castes have 15 per cent reservation, scheduled tribes 7.5 per cent, OBC 27 per cent, physically challenged 0.3 per cent, for a total of 49.8 per cent. Over the years, the overall size of the reserved categories in total admissions in higher education has increased. Further, the Constitution of India (1950) had provided for only a 10-year reservation period, up to 1960, but it has been continued indefinitely. Voting bloc politics is believed to be the main factor responsible for this situation—both for extension of the closing date and for expanding the group of 'backward classes' (see Gupta 2006).

In almost all cases, lower cut-offs in entrance test scores are used for admission of these students. Additional support is made available in terms of extra teaching in many public institutions as well as support in the form of special educators and rehabilitation professionals (for physically challenged students).

These provisions enacted by the national Parliament are applicable not only to central institutions of higher education but also to state institutions. They are, however, not applicable to private unaided institutions. A few states have introduced fee reimbursement/waiver system for disadvantaged groups, including in private institutions.

---

[13] The history of affirmative action of extending privileges to socially backward castes dates back to 1882 (as recommended by the Hunter Commission) and subsequently the Government of India Act, 1935 (based on the Poona pact between Mahatma Gandhi and Dr B. R. Ambedkar) (Basant and Sen 2011). Southern states were the front-runners in making their own list of backward castes. Moreover, affirmative action through scholarship schemes to increase access to tertiary education became more visible during the Ninth Five-Year Plan (1997–2002).

Thus, many private institutions get reimbursed for such students from the states, which is a major source of their institutional income. This also encourages opening of more private colleges, as the growth in government-aided private colleges has no longer been encouraged. State governments find this politically attractive, as it allowed expansion of higher education and through such expansion seems to have mobilized large voting blocs among students and private education entrepreneurs.

India's reservation policies are a matter of extensive research and discussion. Some studies have found that they have been very effective in improving access for disadvantaged groups (Weisskopf 2004), and argue in favour of caste-base reservations and their continuation (Deshpande 2006; Ghosh 2006). Other studies, however, suggest that these policies have been inadequate in improving completion rates either at high school or university levels or both. There are also the typical arguments against the policies as running counter to meritocratic admissions, there is no rationale for these policies to continue (Mehta 2004), and that reservation favours higher educational access for backward castes' elites, excluding the truly disadvantaged (Swaminathan 2006). The social class difference in individual characteristics of reservation eligible and non-eligible populations who graduate from secondary school appear to be negligible (e.g., Azam and Blom 2009). Finally, it is argued that addressing the issue of social equity in tertiary education through affirmative action is conditioned on the level of equity achieved in lower levels of schooling, and that reservation results in dilution, if not serious erosion, of the quality and standards in higher education and its overall competitive strength.

The reservation policy has therefore been highly controversial. The Supreme Court of India recently advised the union government not to relax admission criteria for disadvantaged groups, as it would dilute merit (DNA 2015). But both union government and the states find that it would be politically costly to go against the reservation policies. Some states vie with the union government and other states by providing reservations beyond the levels prescribed by the union government. For example, Tamil Nadu provides reservations for 69 per cent, while the Supreme Court put a cap at 50 per cent. Similarly, some states (e.g., Kerala and Andhra Pradesh) compete with other states to introduce reservations for minority religious groups, particularly Muslims, both in higher education and employment. In some cases, courts have turned down state legislation in this regard.

'Control' of Higher Education

It is generally interpreted that under the provision of coordination and maintenance of quality and standards in higher education, almost all aspects of higher education are, in practice, under the control of the union government. The 'guidelines' of the union government or UGC, which are *de facto* taken as prescriptions, are indeed too many. The UGC prescribes almost everything, from the pay scales for teachers in higher education and their eligibility requirements to teaching load (working hours). The UGC-prescribed pay scales are applicable to central as well as state institutions, including affiliated colleges. The teachers' salaries are uniform throughout the country. Teachers in the central universities are appointed by the universities. Not only their salaries but also their service conditions are uniform among all, since they are set by the UGC. But in the case of teachers in state universities, they are appointed by their respective universities, and the teachers in the colleges are appointed by their respective state governments. While pay scales are the same as for central universities, the service conditions in state institutions are decided by the respective state governments. The service conditions include allowances, age of retirement, retirement benefits, working days, leave and other benefits. While the salaries are prescribed by the UGC, and are periodically revised, the states find it often hard to pay those high salaries, and often opt only to delay implementing payment of the revised pay scales. No state can afford to reject these proposals outright.

The eligibility qualifications for all university teachers in higher education—central as well as state—and their promotions in their career are largely determined by the UGC. One of the eligibility conditions prescribed by the UGC for teachers is a pass in the National Eligibility Test in the concerned subject, conducted by a designated central agency on behalf of the UGC. Almost all states opted to conduct their own similar tests—the State Level Eligibility Test. Aspiring teachers in the states have an option to choose either the national test or the test prescribed by the given state. Graduates who pass in the National Eligibility

Test can apply for a teaching post in any central or state university or college in India, while those who succeed in a state eligibility test are eligible for employment in the given state only.

Similarly, national-level entrance tests are required for admission in higher professional education institutions, for example, the Joint Entrance Examination (JEE) for admission to engineering courses at the bachelor's level in central institutions such as the IITs; the National Entrance Eligibility Test (NEET) for courses in medicine for example, in the All-India Institute of Medical Sciences; and the Management Aptitude Test (MAT) for admission to management courses of study in, for example, IIMs. These test results/rank scores are also used by some states/institutions for admission in their own institutes. States also conduct similar entrance tests at state level for admission in state institutions—public and private. Students appear for national entrance tests and often for tests conducted by several states, as admission is not guaranteed in any institution. To avoid inconvenience to the students, in the recent past, there were moves to have only one national level test for a discipline, conducted by a central agency. States/institutions resent such a move, citing that it erodes their autonomy. Courts have entered the controversy about this proposal, and the issue is yet to be resolved.

Yet another example refers to State Councils of Higher Education. The union government suggested, as per the National Policy on Education 1986, setting up State Councils of Higher Education in every state. But until recently, just five states have done so—Tamil Nadu and Andhra Pradesh, Kerala, West Bengal and Uttar Pradesh. Now under a new centrally sponsored scheme called Rashtriya Uchchatar Shiksha Abhiyan, described later, the union government made it mandatory for every state to set up the Council. Similarly, until the UGC recently made accreditation and assessment by the NAAC mandatory for all universities and colleges, very few universities and colleges voluntarily opted for such accreditation. By December 2016, only 225 universities and 6,241 colleges were accredited (NAAC 2016).

When a UGC Committee (1993) suggested raising student fees to cover about 20 per cent of the current expenditure of the central universities, many states also welcomed this measure for implementation in the state universities. Although the recommendation of the UGC

(1993) committee, or a similar recommendation by the AICTE (1994) committee, are strictly enforced neither in the central universities nor in state universities, many universities did attempt to reach and even to exceed the goal provided by the committees of the central bodies.

Thus, in some cases, states look forward to the union government or central agencies for 'guidelines' or even 'orders' rather than doing the same on their own. This may be because that some of the states may be too weak to have their own long-term view in developing higher education, and/or because many of the central initiatives are followed by some funding support, and hence the states consider them worth waiting for.

Thus, although higher education is listed in the three lists in the Constitution, higher education has consistently been treated politically as the shared responsibility of both the union government and the states, and has been subject to the pushes and pulls of political power struggles between the union government and the states, with the union government playing a major role in policy-making, in prescribing rules and regulations, even curricula and other aspects, and the state governments playing an important role in implementing them.

It is telling, however, that over the years, the union government seems to have largely lost control over state policies, with the states setting up more and more state universities and colleges without necessarily strictly adhering to norms prescribed by UGC, ACITE, NCTE or MCI and allowing growth of private colleges, particularly 'unaided' colleges. At the same time, as the Supreme Court of India announced in its judgement in 2004 on private universities in Chhattisgarh, a gamut of higher education regulations, including teaching, quality of education, curriculum, standard of examination and evaluation and also research activity 'will not come within the purview of the state legislature, on account of a specific entry on coordination and determination of standards in institutions for higher education or research and scientific and technical education being in the Union List'.

Private Universities and Colleges

The emergence of private universities in India presents an interesting case in union–state power relations, in how the clause of concurrency has been used (or misused), and in how the role of the UGC, the main central body, has been minimized. Until a few years ago, there were only central and state (government) universities in the country, in addition to a few deemed universities. For a long period, private universities were not allowed at all, as per the union and state laws relating to higher education in India.

After the introduction of neoliberal economic policies in the early 1990s, pressures to open the higher education sector to private players became strong. Public universities had limited capacity to meet increasing demand. The union government felt the need to make legislation for the establishment of private universities. It prepared a Private Universities Bill (Government of India 1995) with a view to providing for the establishment of self-financing universities. The Bill was not passed in the Parliament for various political economy reasons.[14] But when the union government could not enact legislation allowing the establishment of private universities, some of the state governments, recalling the 'concurrent' nature of education in the Constitution that assigns higher education a joint responsibility of states and the national government, promulgated ordinances on their own and later enacted state legislation without waiting for the union government's Act. UGC was left only to formulate some regulations on the functioning of the private universities such as that they could not have any affiliated colleges and that their jurisdiction is limited to the state.[15] According to the UGC, there were 239 private universities in 2016 established by the Acts of the legislatures of different states. All these universities are in the state sector only; there is no single central private university. In addition, there are 90 private deemed universities—of which 11 receive direct financial support from the state, and 79 unaided in 2014–2015. In fact, there are a few types of private universities—all in the state sector—such as private universities, private open universities, and private deemed universities (aided, private deemed unaided

---

[14] There was an unsuccessful attempt to redraft the bill and present in the Parliament in 2005.

[15] UGC (Establishment of and Maintenance of Standards in Private Universities) Regulation, 2003. Available at http://www.ugc.ac.in/oldpdf/regulations/establishment_maintenance.pdf

universities, etc.) as shown in Table 7.2. The nomenclature of some of these universities does not seem to be clear.[16]

At the college level, there are exactly two types of private colleges, which are normally referred to as government-aided private colleges and unaided, or self-financing, private colleges that rely almost exclusively on tuition. Since all these colleges are in the state sector, UGC's role is limited mainly to providing regular development assistance to aided colleges and special assistance to unaided colleges, but, under special schemes, unaided colleges also receive several kinds of support such as for research projects.

An important feature of the pattern of growth in enrolments in recent years is the rapidly increasing number of self-financing private colleges. Such colleges formed 61 per cent of all colleges in India in 2014–2015. These so-called self-financing colleges largely offer accredited courses in high payoff fields of study, such as engineering, management and medicine. According to the Planning Commission (2013; Tilak 2011), private higher education accounts for about four-fifths of enrolment in professional higher education and 60 per cent overall higher education. Banerjee and Muley (2007, 69) also estimate that 76 per cent of annual student intake in engineering colleges was in private unaided institutions in 2006–2007. It also appears that enrolment in private institutions as a proportion of all enrolment continues to increase at a rapid rate. For example, the AICTE report of 2010–2011 shows that of those institutions that responded to their survey, 37 per cent of total enrolment in India was in private unaided colleges and 24 per cent in private aided colleges.[17] By 2014–2015, the proportion for enrolment in unaided private colleges had increased to 43 per cent, and, in aided private sector, it had dropped to 23 per cent, from a total of 66 per cent, with only 34 per cent in government colleges (MHRD 2009, 2015).

The rapid expansion of unaided colleges affiliated with universities is drastically transforming the landscape of higher education (Kapur 2010). State governments have control of not only the government

---

[16] There are differences in the data provided by the UGC and the MHRD.

[17] These seem to be under estimates. Note that these estimates are based on the institutions that responded to a survey.

colleges but also, through the grants-in-aid mechanism, they have been able to exert control over most aspects of private colleges—governance, appointment of teaching staff, tuition fees, teacher salaries and courses of study and the curriculum.[18] Since private colleges must be affiliated with a public university, they are subject to public university controls over curriculum and the examinations that students must pass to get credit for the courses. They are subject to assessment and accreditation by public agencies, the NAAC or NBA. They are also subject to other state controls, including in admissions and tuition policies. But the state public universities, with which these colleges are affiliated, are increasingly influenced and controlled by the heads of the private colleges, as these colleges, along with other government and government-aided private colleges, become members of the academic and other governing bodies of the respective universities. They are also acting as a strong pressure group working against many other aspects of university administration that affect their vested interests. All these adversely influence even the government colleges that are affiliated with the respective universities.

These complex public–private interactions that formally define the governance of the higher education institutions in the country makes it extremely difficult to define the meaning of *private* in Indian higher education. We have shown that government-aided private institutions are nearly totally financed by the state through development as well as maintenance grants. More importantly, the so-called unaided or self-financing private institutions also receive various development assistance, funds for research, scholarships including reimbursement of student fees, etc. They receive land at concessional prices and several tax concessions and rebates. Students are eligible to access subsidized loans from public sector banks. So strictly speaking, they cannot be described as 'unaided' or 'self-financing'. Hence, the meaning of *private* in Indian higher education needs to be interpreted carefully (Tilak

---

[18] During the 1960s and 1970s, a few state governments had taken over private-aided colleges in response to the violation of state rules and regulations by the colleges, including with respect to teacher recruitment and their salaries. But the phenomenon of private-aided colleges, which can be interpreted as an important form of public–private partnership, continues.

1999, 2010a). Some even argue that there is no 'private' educational institution in India, in its proper interpretation.

There are, however, many who find several positive factors associated with private institutions.

> These private institutions are helping to meet the growing demand that the public sector cannot. Private institutions are less subject to political instabilities and day-to-day political pressures that often bedevil public institutions in developing countries. They are also more nimble and able to respond to changes in demands from employers and labor markets. (Kapur 2010, 6)

This is not completely true. As most private colleges are set up or owned by politicians and big businessmen, they are not insulated from political pressures. The nexus between politicians, businessmen and government determines the nature and growth of these private institutions (see Tilak 1990). However, despite noting the positives, Kapur (2010, 6) also recognizes that 'these institutions are of highly variable—and often dubious—quality'. In fact, much of the deterioration in quality in higher education is felt to be attributable to the rapid increase in the number of private colleges.

It is difficult to imagine that universities and state and federal agencies such as the UGC and the AICTE or NCTE can keep track of this mass of self-sustaining private institutions and their academic operations satisfactorily. A significant percentage of private institutions do not even answer MHRD/AICTE/UGC surveys, so the statistics that we cited here on enrolments are probably under estimated. They exaggerate their performance and hide facts and often carry on misleading advertisements about their accreditation, pass percentages of students, placements of students on employment, quality of faculty and other aspects. Unaided institutions also have the freedom to accumulate surplus to expand operations with that surplus or siphon off the surplus.

While fees in government and government-aided colleges are set by the state governments, fees in universities—central and state—are set by the universities. The fees in private unaided colleges are controlled by the state, but are not set by the state. Normally a fee fixation committee headed by a judge of the high court sets these fees, based on the actual costs of education in those unaided professional colleges as reported by the respective colleges. Thus, private unaided colleges are somewhat, but not totally, free in fixing fee rates; however, they are mostly reported to be over charging the students outside the formal fee system.

As a good number of private universities and colleges are increasingly found to violate state rules and adopt unfair practices, the union government felt the need to intervene, although these universities are operating under state jurisdiction. The union government came with a draft bill, namely, 'Prohibition of Unfair Practices in Technical and Medical Educational Institutions and Universities Bill, 2010', which was criticized by state(s) as an attempt 'to frustrate rather than augment efforts being made by the state governments' and their control of these institutions (Baby 2010). This Bill, along with a few others on higher education, is still pending before the Parliament.

Thus, higher education has been subject to the pushes and pulls of political power struggles between the union government and the states, the union government dominating in some areas and states in others at various points of time. The lack of understanding and cooperation between the two is indeed an important issue of concern in a federal system. The changing political nature of the governments at the central and state levels is adding to this. The casualty is the higher education system. But for a few limited dimensions of higher education, the union government, as Carnoy et al. (2013) observed, transferred its responsibility of developing higher education to the states, and the states have further transferred it to private market forces.

Factors that make it possible for unaided private colleges to be such a major vehicle for growth in enrolments in India are the limited supply of undergraduate places in public and private aided colleges, the still rapidly expanding fraction of college-age youth in higher education, the high rate of earnings payoff for a college education, especially for graduates in professional and technical fields (Carnoy et al. 2013) and the relatively high social class of students currently in the market for college places. The parents of these students are willing and able to pay quite high tuition and even 'capitation'—huge lump sum, unauthorized fees—for their children's higher education.

TRENDS IN UNION-STATE FINANCES IN HIGHER EDUCATION

As already mentioned, development and maintenance grants are received by central universities and other institutions of higher education through the UGC, and/or directly, in some specific cases, from the MHRD (and/or other concerned ministries in the union government). The state universities and (other state institutions including colleges) receive development grants from the union government through the UGC, and maintenance grants directly from the state governments. As state universities depend upon both the state government and the union government (UGC and other ministries) for their funding, they are subject to regulation by both central and state agencies. Private aided institutions are also subject to the same pattern of funding. Self-financing private universities and colleges which are not expected to receive state support, receive special project-based grants from the union government through UGC and other bodies, and the students in these institutions may also receive scholarships and other financial support from state and union governments under various schemes.

UGC Funding of Central and State Universities/Colleges

Until now the UGC has been an important source of funding for India's higher education institutions.[19] A large share of the union government's funding for higher education flows through the UGC. Most central institutions—central universities and their constituent/affiliated colleges—are totally funded by the UGC for their plan (development) and non-plan (operating) expenditure, whereas state universities and their affiliated/constituent colleges are funded by the UGC and the respective state governments. UGC finances a high proportion of the plan expenditure of the state universities and their colleges, but a large part of the non-plan expenditure of the state institutions is met by the state governments, and the UGC finances only a small fraction of non-plan expenditure.

To illustrate the distribution of grants given by the UGC to central and state higher education institutions under plan and non-plan

---

[19] Very recently Higher Education Finance Agency (HEFA) has been created by the union government to take the responsibility of funding public and private higher education institutions in the country.

Table 7.4 Funding by University Grants Commission, 2005–2006 and 2014–2015 (₹ in 10 Million in Current Prices and %)

	2000–2001			2005–2006			2014–2015		
	Plan	Non-Plan	Total	Plan	Non-Plan	Total	Plan	Non-Plan	Total
Central									
Universities	83.0	621.7	704.7	222.3	878.7	1,118.2	2,316.3	3,462.9	5,779.2
Deemed Universities	17.9	59.4	77.3	29.4	83.1	117.4	106.3	247.9	354.2
Inter-university Centres	24.9	0.8	25.7	59.1	20.0	80.8	127.3	47.9	175.2
Colleges	6.4	243.2	249.6	15.1	315.2	330.5	46.6	1,556.9	1,603.5
Total	89.4	864.9	954.3	325.9	1,297.0	1,650.2	2,596.5	5,315.6	7,912.1
State									
Universities	164.1	28.5	192.6	266.9	13.5	270.0	489.0	140.3	629.3
Colleges	148.0	1.8	149.8	214.0	6.8	215.5	231.4	2.2	233.6
Total	312.1	30.3	342.4	480.9	20.3	485.5	720.4	142.5	862.9
Total (Central+State)	401.5	895.2	1,296.7	806.8	1,328.9	2,135.7	3,316.9	5,458.1	8,775.0
Grand Total[a]	447.9	1,004.0	1,451.9	808.7	1,389.8	2,198.5	4,178.5	5,536.1	9,714.6
Percentage									
Central	22.3	96.6	73.6	40.4	97.6	77.2	78.3	97.4	90.2
State	69.7	3.0	23.6	59.6	2.4	22.8	21.7	2.6	9.8

Source: UGC Annual Report, 2000–2001, 2005–2006 and 2014–2015.

Note: [a]Includes other items not listed here.

categories is shown in Table 7.4. Hardly 3 per cent of the non-plan grants of the UGC went to state universities and colleges in 2014–2015, and this was lower than in 2000–2001. The remaining 97 per cent went to central institutions. In case of plan grants, state institutions accounted for about one-fifth of the total non-plan grants in 2014–2015, but this figure was higher in the past. State governments and state institutions find the distribution skewed unfairly against them, and have argued for changes. Recently, the Yashpal Committee (Government of India 2009) and the National Knowledge Commission (2009) recommended increases in UGC allocations to state universities. The Twelfth Five-Year Plan promised action on this. It is widely observed that the UGC funding to different universities and colleges was not based on any sound criteria, although, in the recent past, there were serious discussions and initiation of some efforts to link funding to the performance of the institutions.

Centre-State Shares in Funding Higher Education

Thus, union and state governments both incur expenditures on higher education in India. The expenditure of the states increased (in 2004–2005 prices) from about ₹10,000 crore[20] in 2000–2001 to about ₹17,500 crore in 2011–2012, while the expenditure of the union government increased from about ₹4,500 crore to ₹13,500 crore during the same period (Figure 7.1). The expenditure of the states increased at an annual real (corrected for inflation) rate of growth of 6.2 per cent, and the union government's expenditure increased by 13.4 per cent. In case of technical education, the union government spent higher amounts than the expenditure incurred by the state governments from 2008–2009 onward, although in the earlier period, the states generally used to spend marginally more than the union government (Table 7.5).

Traditionally, state governments have met a much larger share of total public spending on higher and technical higher education. Nevertheless, the share of union government expenditures jumped in 2008–2009 from 30 per cent to 40 per cent of the total and has remained at that level since then.[21] The share of the union government

---

[20] 1 crore = 10 million.

[21] The *Analysis of Budgeted Expenditure on Education*, an important source of data on public expenditure on education, which is the source of data on expenditure on

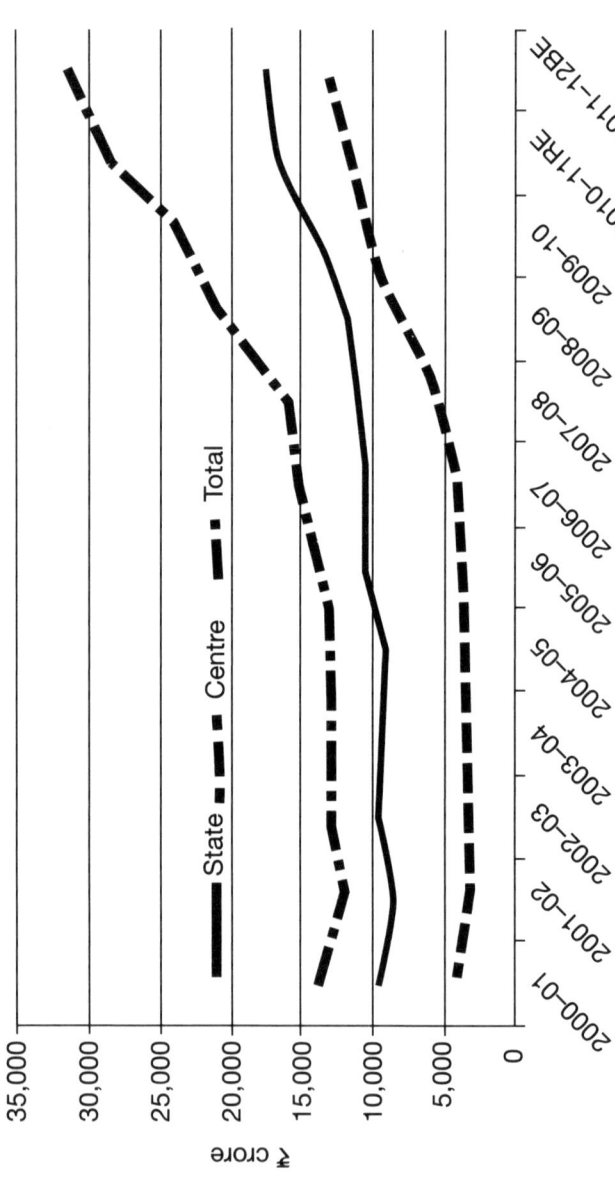

Figure 7.1 *Trends in Expenditure by Union and State Governments on Higher Education (in 2004–2005 Prices;* ₹10 Million)

Sources: Based on MHRD, *Analysis of Budgeted Expenditure on Education* (various years) and Ministry of Finance, *Economic Survey* (various years), both from Government of India, New Delhi.

Table 7.5 *Real Rate of Growth in Expenditure of the Union and State Governments on Higher Education, from 2000–2001 to 2011–2012 (%)*

Higher Education Category	Centre	State	Total
University and Higher Education	13.47	5.70	7.74
Technical Education	13.35	8.28	10.89
Total Higher Education	13.35	6.17	8.53

Source: Computed by the author, based on MHRD, *Analysis of Budgeted Expenditure on Education* (various years).

in public spending on 'university and higher education' increased from 25 per cent to 34 per cent, and on technical education, from 44 per cent to 58 per cent during this same period, 2000–2001 to 2011–2012. The increasing fiscal constraints that the states faced were probably the main factor in explaining why the states' role declined and why the union government increased its share in funding higher education, but the pressure on the union government for higher quality also played a role. The rapid expansion of low-quality private unaided education affiliated with state universities, especially in engineering and business management, took care of the exploding demand for greater access to higher education in these high payoff fields, but it also put pressure on the union government to provide more access to high quality institutions of national importance, such as the IITs and National Institutes of Technology (NITs), as well as IIMs. The union government's expenditure increased at almost double the rate of growth of state governments' expenditure on higher education between 2000–2001 and 2011–2012 (Table 7.5), resulting in a significant shift in the proportion of the union share in financing higher education by 2011–2012 (Figure 7.2).

---

higher education used in this chapter, provides data under two headings: 'university and higher education' and 'technical education'. A substantial proportion, but not all, of the former includes general higher education, and there is a small component of school education in the latter category. Both are generally considered in the context of higher education.

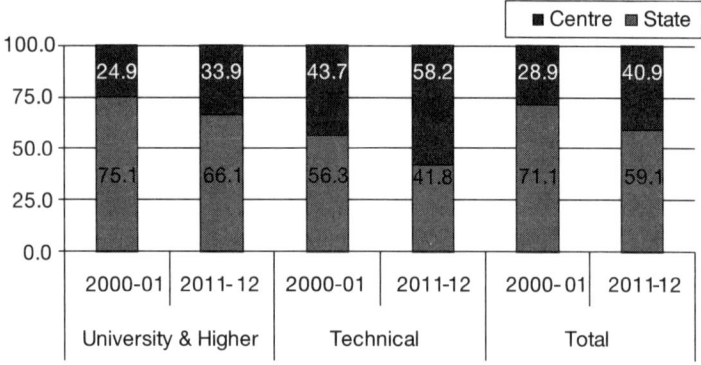

Figure 7.2 *Union–State Shares in Financing Higher Education (%)*
Source: Based on MHRD, *Analysis of Budgeted Expenditure on Education.*

Relative Priorities

As a proportion of GDP, the expenditures of the union government on higher education increased from only 0.3 per cent in 2005–2006 to a somewhat higher 0.5 per cent in 2011–2012. The expenditure of state governments were only 0.7 per cent of GDP in 2005–2006, and there was no increase in the relative spending on higher education by the states between 2005–2006 and 2011–2012 (Figure 7.3). The CABE Committee (2005) recommended an allocation of 1.5 per cent of GDP to higher education by the centre and state governments combined, so the total spent (1.2%) in 2011–2012 fell far short of that goal.

Further, the share of higher education is higher in the union government budget for education than in the total budget of the state governments on higher education. In 2010–2011, the union government spent nearly 30 per cent of its total education budget on higher education, while states allocated only 14 per cent. These figures reflect the relative responsibility of the respective governments for different levels of education and in that sense, the priority they give to primary plus secondary education and to higher education. Obviously, for the

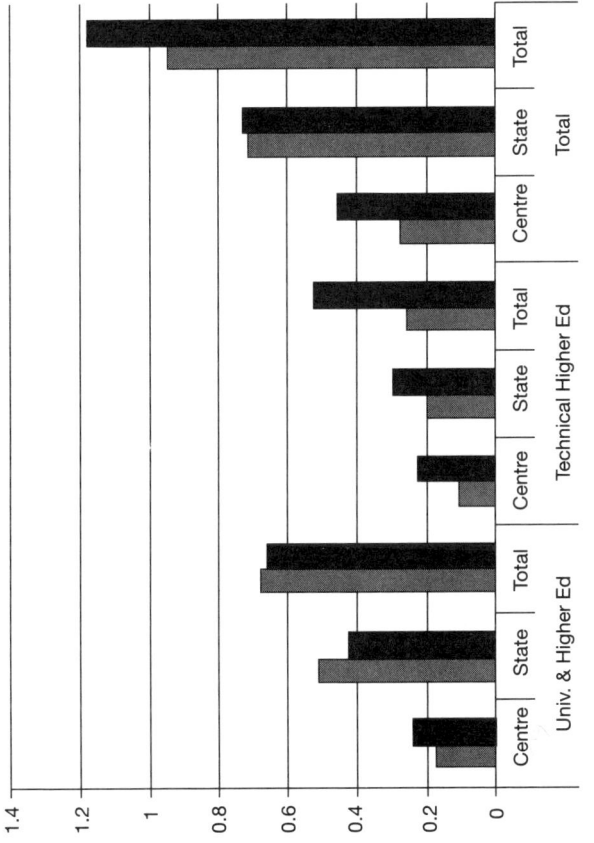

Figure 7.3 India: Financing of Higher Education as a Proportion of GDP, Centre and State Governments, by Type of Higher Education, 2005–2006 and 2011–2012 (% GDP)

Source: Based on MHRD, Analysis of Budgeted Expenditures on Education.

state governments, school education seems to be a priority, although both union and state governments spend less on higher education than on school education.

Even in case of the union government, its priorities have shifted as the low quality of primary and secondary education has received increasing attention. Thus, the relative share for spending on higher education of the union government's total education budget declined from 43 per cent to 29 per cent between 2000–2001 and 2010–2011, where states' spending only declined slightly, from 15.3 per cent to 13.6 per cent. These figures refer to total (plan and non-plan) expenditures.

Although plan expenditures in education are generally small compared to non-plan expenditures, allocations to plan expenditures in the five-year plans are important because they set new directions for future development—quantitative expansion, improvement in quality, innovations, as well as several other dimensions of education development. Until the Tenth Five-Year Plan, states used to account for about 40 per cent of the total plan expenditure on higher education, and the union government nearly 60 per cent. In the Eleventh Five-Year Plan (2007–2012), the union government suddenly increased its allocation to higher education by nearly nine times, and the state governments could not increase their allocations so significantly. Hence, the relative share of the union government increased to as high as 87 per cent and that of the states declined to 13 per cent. It is worth examining whether this trend is desirable and, if so, would continue into the Twelfth Five-Year Plan and beyond. Obviously it did not. A meaningful partnership between the union government and the states in financing higher education still seems to be elusive.

An important purpose of funding of higher education by the union government through devolution, grants and other mechanisms is to see that the interstate disparities in public expenditure on higher education, in enrolment ratios and thereby in overall development in higher education are minimized. The available evidence, however, shows that the results are far from satisfactory, although there has been some improvement. Although the coefficient of variation in enrolment ratio has declined very marginally from 0.43 to 0.40 between 2002–2003 and 2014–2015, variation in per capita public expenditure on education between different states, as measured by the coefficient of variation declined in a similar period, 2001–2002 to 2011–2012, from 1.10 to 0.85 (see Table 7.6).

SUMMARY, CONCLUSIONS AND EMERGING APPROACHES

One of the clear shifts in the past decade has been in the union government's share in public financing of higher and technical higher education. Reviewing the patterns of allocations made in the Eleventh and Twelfth Five-Year Plan periods, that is, during the last 10 years (2007–2017), it has been noted that the share of higher education public spending assumed by the state governments in terms of the proportion of GDP, plan outlays, total budget expenditure, etc., is much greater than the union government's share (note that the state allocations are inclusive of resources devolved through the Finance Commission). However, the relative share of the state governments in total expenditure on higher education has been declining over the years, from above 70 per cent in 2000–2001 to about 60 per cent in 2011–2012. Correspondingly, the relative share of the union government increased. This is true with respect to university and higher education and technical education. While the goal is to allocate 1.5 per cent of GDP to higher education by the union government and the states together, as per the recommendation of the CABE Committee (2005),[22] the states are not able to increase their share, while there has been a gradual but relatively small increase in the share of the union government. The rate of growth in the union government's expenditure on higher education is increasing at a high rate of growth of above 13 per cent, while in case of state expenditure the rate of growth has been around 6 per cent. Further, within the total education sector, the priority given to higher education by the union government is much higher than by the states. There are also frequent fluctuating trends in spending on higher education by the union government as well as the states.

Earlier research has shown that the allocations of the union government to state universities and other institutions of higher education are

---

[22] The goal does not specify the respective shares of the union and state governments.

Table 7.6 Budgeted Expenditures on Higher Education, by State, from 1990–1991 to 2011–2012 (₹ in Current Prices per Capita)

State/Union Territory	University & Other Higher			Technical			Total		
	1990–1991	2000–2001	2011–2012	1990–1991	2000–2001	2011–2012	1990–1991	2000–2001	2011–2012
Andhra Pradesh	31.68	112.19	224.50	4.22	11.23	81.66	35.90	123.42	306.16
Arunachal Pradesh	36.47	105.87	213.04	0.00	0.00	28.23	36.47	105.87	241.27
Assam	21.41	80.41	287.20	3.72	7.30	36.18	25.13	87.71	323.39
Bihar	14.92	1.29	171.79	2.51	1.14	5.32	17.43	2.43	177.11
Chhattisgarh	–	15.17	120.81	–	4.04	19.46	–	19.21	140.26
Goa	87.96	207.02	836.90	27.10	97.52	475.75	115.06	304.54	1,312.65
Gujarat	21.47	78.41	165.02	5.77	21.40	58.94	27.24	99.81	223.96
Haryana	27.83	102.27	307.87	4.51	18.92	100.31	32.34	121.19	408.18
Himachal Pradesh	28.47	106.22	295.29	3.79	11.95	34.42	32.25	118.17	329.70
Jammu & Kashmir	21.22	94.04	229.07	6.07	24.67	44.29	27.29	118.70	273.36
Jharkhand	–	–	133.20	–	–	19.24	–	–	152.43
Karnataka	24.86	104.47	262.37	4.95	11.73	65.18	29.81	116.20	327.55
Kerala	32.00	120.89	385.15	10.67	34.06	127.21	42.67	154.94	512.36
Madhya Pradesh	14.96	55.67	100.69	5.04	16.46	28.86	19.99	72.14	129.56
Maharashtra	27.20	116.00	237.13	9.17	35.19	101.14	36.37	151.19	338.27

Manipur	77.52	216.84	484.01	3.77	9.88	19.80	81.29	226.72	503.81
Meghalaya	31.93	96.94	294.30	2.71	6.29	44.47	34.64	103.23	338.76
Mizoram	57.08	173.67	687.60	5.65	21.30	55.68	62.73	194.97	743.28
Nagaland	28.19	63.23	264.35	7.73	14.94	45.79	35.92	78.17	310.14
Odisha	20.22	57.05	272.53	5.34	5.62	27.65	25.56	62.67	300.19
Punjab	35.59	89.12	139.44	4.38	12.95	27.44	39.97	102.06	166.87
Rajasthan	16.60	39.89	93.80	3.00	5.65	12.00	19.59	45.55	105.80
Sikkim	13.41	52.08	238.66	7.77	2.41	22.65	21.18	54.49	261.31
Tamil Nadu	23.46	82.64	209.01	7.70	22.03	94.14	31.17	104.67	303.15
Tripura	18.99	54.40	128.19	4.66	14.10	19.27	23.66	68.50	147.46
Uttarakhand	–	–	157.21	–	–	73.88	–	–	231.09
Uttar Pradesh	11.80	31.06	68.23	3.77	5.87	7.57	15.57	36.93	75.80
West Bengal	26.63	84.09	201.20	3.70	9.85	32.25	30.33	93.95	233.45
Chandigarh	331.94	611.23	913.89	66.28	166.43	395.45	398.21	777.66	1,309.34
Delhi	4.80	18.51	82.93	13.10	36.63	102.32	17.90	55.15	185.25
Puducherry	56.13	199.85	631.54	62.08	145.83	316.77	118.21	345.68	948.31
All-India	21.70	89.38	272.94	5.26	24.57	112.92	26.96	113.95	385.85
Coef. of Variation	1.47	1.01	0.75	1.55	1.51	1.37	1.42	1.10	0.85

Source: Based on *Census of India* and *Analysis of Budgeted Expenditure on Education*, MHRD, Government of India.

so small that they are not positioned to reduce regional or interstate inequalities in the development of higher education or even specifically in the expenditure or expenditure per capita on higher education. Neither inequalities nor concerns of quality could be adequately addressed by the central allocations to different states and their universities and higher education institutions (Tilak 1989, 2016). However, we find that interstate disparities in gross enrolment ratio in higher education and in public expenditure on higher education per capita (post-devolution) have been declining over the years. Nevertheless, affluent states with greater command over resources tend to be able to draw more funds from the union government by providing matching grants, while resource-poor states are not able to do so. In general, many poor states find that centrally sponsored schemes distort their priorities and dislocate their fiscal arrangements, depriving them of central funds when they were not able to match up to the advanced and richer states. The constant demand of some of the states, particularly economically less advanced states, was that centrally sponsored schemes should be fully (100%) centrally funded (Chaturvedi 2011, 66–68), but, at the same time, states should have a say in them. They also felt that centrally sponsored schemes are decided arbitrarily and unilaterally by the union government irrespective of whether they were relevant to a state or not, distorting the states' priorities and dislocating the states' spending on account of the requirement of counterpart share to the central schemes.

Often, state universities complain that although central universities account for only a small fraction of students in higher education in the country, about 5.9 per cent in 2014–2015, UGC funding is skewed in favour of central universities, and state universities receive very small amounts—no non-plan grants and small plan grants. Whereas central funding has been small, central/UGC intervention in the functioning of the higher education systems in the states is found to be significant. Although state universities are set up through state legislature, many of their core activities—recruitment of faculty, their promotions, salary structure, admissions including reservations, curriculum, assessment and accreditation, etc. are determined by the UGC. But state universities are primarily accountable to their respective state legislatures. States are indeed concerned with the increasing central control of higher education in the states. As no state has adequate resources of its own to develop higher education, the union government, which controls the purse strings, necessarily has the dominating voice in determining overall policies, priorities and programmes. In recent years, there has been an attempt to set up a National Commission for Higher Education and Research,[23] which was widely criticized as centralizing the powers of administration in higher education by taking away the powers from the state government in various ways, including the appointment of vice-chancellors of universities (see Tilak 2010a). There are several genuine and not so genuine political economy factors relating to the appointment of vice chancellors, over which states do not want to lose control.

Critics argue that the union government has appropriated all the rights in many sectors including in higher education. For example, Shankar Aiyar (2015) observed,

> in six decades, the Centre has appropriated the rights to design the political and fiscal anatomy of governance. In effect, the centre designs policies over which states have little or no say. States are tasked with implementing these policies and the Centre has little control over outcomes. India is trapped in a bipolar disorder—the overlap of authority and divorce of accountability.

Others have observed that 'there is no partnership between the Central Government and the state government and that is the heart of why we have not been able to move forward very quickly' (Sibal 2009).

The central government in federal systems may act to devolve functions, powers and funds to the federation's constituent members. That has not been the experience in Indian higher education. There is no matching of devolution of funds, powers and responsibilities. The phraseology of and the need for decentralization, delegation and devolution have appeared repeatedly in reports of the committees and commissions—including the Rajamanar (Centre–State Relations Inquiry) Committee, the Sarkaria Commission, the Administrative Reforms Commission and the 2010 report of the Inter-State Council

---

[23] This is one of the several bills on higher education, introduced in the Parliament by the last government, which were not passed by the Parliament (see Tilak 2010b).

on centre–state relations.[24] It is argued that the union government must let the states write their own playbook. As B. R. Ambedkar, the architect of the Constitution of India, has said, the union and states are created by the Constitution—one is not subordinate to the other in its own field, and the authority of one is required to coordinate with that of the other (as quoted in Aiyar 2015). This should be the guiding principle in developing cooperative federalism.

Emerging Approaches

The 1986 *National Policy on Education* (Government of India 1986) had referred to 'meaningful partnership' between the union government and the states. In recent years, the preference of the union government is to have 'co-operative federalism', not coercive federalism for a strong Republic (2012).[25]

Recent budgets of the union government are also indicative of two important likely trends. The union government seems to be favouring cuts in central/centrally sponsored schemes in general, including in the education sector.[26] Such a move has been preceded by a higher level of fiscal devolution of resources through the Finance Commission. As per the recommendation of the 14th Finance Commission, accepted by the government, as high as 42 per cent of the divisible pool of central revenues would be devolved to states during 2015–2016 to 2019–2020, against 32 per cent suggested by the previous (13th) Finance Commission. This is intended to allow states to have larger control over their desired fiscal direction, priorities and areas of improvement and is likely to increase states' fiscal autonomy to use the resources in any

---

[24] See 'Sarkaria Commission and Its Recommendations' (Inter State Council Secretariat, New Delhi) for reports and recommendations of these commissions. Available at http://interstatecouncil.nic.in/Sarkaria_Commission.html# (retrieved on 14 April 2016).

[25] Narendra Modi Blogs: Republic Day. Available at http://www.narendramodi.in/co-operative-not-coercive-federalism-for-strong-republic-3053

[26] Eight existing schemes, including, for example, the scheme for setting up of 6,000 Model Schools, have been delinked from the framework of the centrally sponsored schemes, according to the 2016–2017 budget proposals of the union government.

sector they would like to focus on. The trend is welcomed by many states, but, at the same time, some have apprehensions that the states may not necessarily spend the additional resources on the programmes of national priority currently funded by centrally sponsored schemes.

Another important development is the abolition of the distinction between 'plan' and 'non-plan' expenditure in making grants by the union government to the states. The Planning Commission, responsible for plan grants, has already been replaced by another organization, the NITI Aayog. Third, the union government also intends to scrap the development-planning framework based on five-year plans, and it intends to introduce medium-term fiscal framework planning (Sharma 2016).

Recently, the union government has launched the Rashtriya Uchchatar Shiksha Abhiyan (RUSA), aimed at providing strategic funding to eligible state higher educational institutions. The scheme involves sharing the funding responsibilities for the development of higher education in the ratio of 65 per cent (union government) and 35 per cent (state government), and in the ratio of 9:1 for special category states. The special features are that the funds from the union government would flow not from UGC but directly from the union government, and that they would be allocated not directly to universities and colleges, but through state governments/union territories to the State Higher Education Councils, based on critical appraisal of comprehensive state plans for higher education prepared by the state governments. Inter alia, this is argued to be recognizing the autonomy of the states in the development of higher education, and would promote state 'ownership' of higher education plans in a very effective way. However, many feel state universities and colleges would lose the fair degree of autonomy when they get funds not directly from the UGC, but from the union government through state governments, and would be subject to political factors at the state level, even in how they formulate development programmes and corresponding development expenditures. That higher education is politicized and more politicized at the state level in India is widely acknowledged. The role of the UGC in funding higher education might become confined to central universities, but the role of the union government—the MHRD—might substantially increase in shaping state plans for higher education. Even the role of the UGC in funding higher education is under question, as the newly created HEFA may take away the responsibility from the UGC of allocating resources to universities.

In the absence of a clear and cohesive policy statement making a firm commitment to state funding of higher education, the growth of higher education could be subject to all kinds of vagaries, uncertainties and instability. Principles of adequacy, equity, excellence and steady growth should guide the process of allocation of resources to higher education by the union government as well as state governments. In a federal system, it is also necessary to ensure that there is regionally balanced development. It is not clear whether the RUSA and/or HEFA would fulfil these criteria in ensuring a sound financial base for higher education. A long-term plan for the development of higher education that includes a long-term financial plan for higher education is critically needed. It should describe the relative roles of the union and state government, including their responsibilities for planning, funding and delivering higher education and how they complement each other.

REFERENCES

AICTE. 1994. *Report of the High-Power Committee for Mobilisation of Additional Resources for Technical Education* (Swaminathan Committee Report). All-India Council for Technical Education, New Delhi.

Aiyar, S. 2015. 'Centre vs. State'. *India Today*, 10 December. Available at http://indiatoday.intoday.in/story/india-today-40th-anniversary-centre-vs-state-shankkar-aiyar/1/543129.html

Altbach, P. G. 2012. *A Half Century of Indian Higher Education*. New Delhi: SAGE.

Azam, M., and Blom, A. 2009. 'Progress in Participation in Tertiary Education in India from 1983 to 2004'. *Journal of Educational Planning and Administration* 23 (2): 125–167.

Baby, M. A. 2010. 'The Bill on Prohibition of Unfair Practices and Inclusive Higher Education'. *The Hindu*, 2 April. Available at http://www.thehindu.com/opinion/op-ed/the-bill-on-prohibition-of-unfair-practices-and-inclusive-higher-education/article381696.ece

Baker, A. 1976. *The Union and the States in Education*. New Delhi: Shabd Sanchar.

Banerjee, R., and Muley, V. 2007. *Engineering Education in India*. Mumbai: Energy Systems Engineering.

Basant, R., and Sen, G. 2011. 'Access to Higher Education in India: An Exploration of its Antecedents'. Available at https://ssrn.com/abstract=2535644 or http://dx.doi.org/10.2139/ssrn.2535644

Basu, D. K. 1965. *Commentary on the Constitution of India*, 7th edition. Calcutta: S. C. Sarkar & Sons.

CABE. 2005. *Report of the CABE Committee on Financing of Higher and Technical Education*. New Delhi: Central Advisory Board of Education, Ministry of Human Resource Development, Government of India. Available at http://mhrd.gov.in/sites/upload_files/mhrd/files/document-reports/Report%20CABE%20Committee%20on%20Financing%20Higher%20and%20Technical%20EducationL.pdf

Carnoy, M., and Dossani, R. 2013. 'Goals and Governance of Higher Education in India'. *Higher Education* 65 (5): 595–612.

Carnoy, M., Loyalka, P., Dobryakova, M., Dossani, R., Froumin, I., Kuhns, K., Tilak, J., and Wang, R. 2013. *University Expansion in a Changing Global Economy: Triumph of the BRICs?* Stanford, CA: Stanford University Press.

Chaturvedi, B. K. 2011. *The Report of the Committee on Restructuring of Centrally Sponsored Schemes*. New Delhi: Planning Commission.

Deshpande, S. 2006. 'Exclusive Inequalities: Merit, Caste and Discrimination in Higher Education Today'. *Economic and Political Weekly* 41 (24): 2438–2444.

DNA. 2015. 'Supreme Court Tells Modi Govt to Scrap Reservations from Institutes of Higher Education. *DNA India*, 28 October. Available at http://www.dnaindia.com/india/report-supreme-court-tells-modi-govt-to-scrap-reservations-from-institutes-of-higher-education-2139383

Ghosh, J. 2006. 'Case for Caste-based Quotas in Higher Education'. *Economic and Political Weekly* 4 (24): 2428–2432.

Government of India. 1986. *National Policy on Education*. New Delhi.

———. 1995. *The Private Universities (Establishment and Regulation) Bill, 1995*. [Reproduced in *New Frontiers in Education* 25 (3): 290–308.]

———. 2009. *Report of the Committee to Advise on Renovation and Rejuvenation of Higher Education*. New Delhi: MHRD, Government of India. Available at http://mhrd.gov.in/sites/upload_files/mhrd/files/document-reports/YPC-Report.pdf

Gupta, A. 2006. 'Affirmative Action in Higher Education in India and US'. Occasional Paper Series, University of California, Centre for studies in Higher Education, Berkeley, US. Available at https://escholarship.org/uc/item/5nz5695t#page-1

Hardgrave, R. L., Jr., and Kochanek, S. A. 1986. *India—Government and Politics in a Developing Nation*, 4th edition. San Diego, CA: Harcourt Brace Jovanovich.

Kapur, D. 2010. 'Indian Higher Education'. In *American Universities in a Global Market*, edited by C. Clotfelter, 305–334. Chicago, IL: University of Chicago Press.

Kumar, V. 1975. *Committees and Commissions in India, 1947–1973*. New Delhi: D. K. Publishing House.

Mehra, P. 2016. 'NDC to be Scrapped, NITI Aayog Council Likely to Get Its Powers'. *The Hindu*, 1 January. Available at http://www.thehindu.com/news/national/ndc-to-be-scrapped-niti-aayog-council-likely-to-get-its-powers/article8051108.ece

Mehta, B. P. 2004. 'Affirmation without Reservation'. *Economic and Political Weekly* 39 (27): 2951–2954.

MHRD. 2009. *Statistics of Higher and Technical Education, 2005–2006.* New Delhi: Government of India, Ministry of Human Resource Development.

MHRD. 2015. *Analysis of Budgeted Expenditure on Education 2011–2012 to 2013–2014.* New Delhi: Ministry of Human Resource Development, Government of India. Available at http://mhrd.gov.in/sites/upload_files/mhrd/files/statistics/ABE_2011-14.pdf

————. 2016a. *All-India Survey on Higher Education 2014–2015.* New Delhi: Government of India. Available at http://mhrd.gov.in/sites/upload_files/mhrd/files/statistics/AISHE_2014-15%28P%29.pdf

————. 2016b. *Constitutional Provision: Centre-State Relations.* New Delhi: Government of India. http://mhrd.gov.in/centre-state-relations

————. 2017. *All-India Survey on Higher Education 2015-2016.* New Delhi: Government of India. Available at http://mhrd.gov.in/sites/upload_files/mhrd/files/statistics/AISHE_2015-16%28P%29.pdf

NAAC. 2016. *Annual Report 2016.* Bangalore: National Assessment and Accreditation Agency. Available at http://naac.gov.in/docs/Annual_Report_15-16.pdf

Naik, J. P. 1963. *The Role of Government of India in Education.* New Delhi: Ministry of Education, Government of India.

Naik, J. P., and Nurullah, S. 1945. *A Students' History of Education in India 1800–1973,* 6th edition, 1974. New Delhi: Macmillan.

Nair, J., and Jain, U. C. 2000. *Centre–State Relations.* Jaipur: Pointer Publications.

National Knowledge Commission. 2009. *Report to the Nation 2006–2009.* New Delhi: Government of India. Available at http://knowledgecommission-archive.nic.in/downloads/report2009/eng/report09.pdf

Planning Commission. 2013. *Twelfth Five-Year Plan (2012–2017): Faster, More Inclusive and Sustainable Growth.* New Delhi: Government of India.

Rao, V. K. R. V. 1972. 'Centre–State Relations in Education'. In *The Union and the States,* edited by S. N. Jain, S. C. Kashyap, and N. Srinivas, 178–186. New Delhi: National Publishing House.

Sharma, Y. 2016. 'Five Year Plans May Be Scrapped, Says NITI Aayog VC Aravind Panagariya'. *The Economic Times,* 3 March. Available at http://economictimes.indiatimes.com/news/economy/policy/five-year-plans-may-be-scrapped-says-niti-aayog-vc-arvind-panagariya/articleshow/51229645.cms

Sibal, K. 2009. 'There Is No Partnership Between the Centre and States. Solutions Are Needed Quickly'. *India Today,* 17 September. Available at http://india-today.intoday.in/story/there+is+no+partnership+between+the+centre+and+states.+solutions+are+needed+quickly/1/62291.html

Swaminathan, R. 2006. 'Assumptions and Arithmetic of Caste-based Reservations'. *Economic and Political Weekly* 41 (24): 2436–2438.

Tilak, J. B. G. 1989, November. 'Center–State Relations in Financing Education in India'. *Comparative Educational Review* 33 (4): 450–480.

Tilak, J. B. G. 1990. 'The Political Economy of Education in India'. Special Studies No. 24, Comparative Education Center, State University of New York at Buffalo (in collaboration with the University of Virginia).

———. 1999. 'Emerging Trends and Evolving Public Policies on Privatisation of Higher Education in India'. In *Private Prometheus: Private Higher Education and Development in the 21st Century*, edited by P. G. Altbach, 113–135. Westport, CT: Greenwood Publishing.

———. 2008. 'Transition from Higher Education as a Public Good to Higher Education as a Private Good: The Saga of Indian Experience'. *Journal of Asian Public Policy* 1 (2): 220–234.

———. 2010a. 'Higher Education in India: Emerging Challenges and Evolving Strategies'. In *The Search for New Governance of Higher Education in Asia*, edited by Ka-Ho Mok, 171–191. New York, NY: Palgrave Macmillan.

———. 2010b, May 1. 'The Proposed NCHER: A Solution Worse Than the Disease?' *Economic and Political Weekly* 45 (18): 10–13.

———. 2011. 'Private Sector in Higher Education: A Few Stylized Facts'. In *Quality, Access and Social Justice in Higher Education*, edited by K. N. Panikkar, Thomas Joseph, G. Geetha, and M. A. Lal, 11–33. New Delhi: Pearson/ Longman.

———. 2016. 'A Decade of Ups and Downs in Public Expenditure on Higher Education'. In *India: Higher Education Report*, edited by N. V. Varghese and G. Malik, 307–332. London: Routledge/National University of Educational Planning and Administration.

———. 2018. *Dilemmas in Reforming Higher Education in India*. New Delhi: Orient BlackSwan.

UGC. 1993. *UGC Funding of Institutions of Higher Education* (Justice K. Punnayya Committee, 1992–1992). New Delhi: University Grants Commission.

———. 2004. Supreme Court Judgment on Private Universities in Chhattisgarh. UGC, Government of India. Available at http://www.ugc.ac.in/subpage/ Supreme-Court-Judgment-Chhattisgarh.aspx

———. 2008. *Higher Education in India: Issues Related to Expansion, Inclusiveness, Quality and Finance*, 103–110. New Delhi: University Grants Commission.

Weisskopf, Thomas E. 2004, September 25. 'Impact of Reservation on Admissions to Higher Education in India'. *Economic and Political Weekly* 39 (39): 4339–4349.

Wheare, K. C. 1953. *Federal Government*, 3rd edition. London: Oxford.

Chapter 8

Mexico ·

Dilemmas of Federalism in a Highly Politicized and Semi-decentralized System

Imanol Ordorika, Roberto Rodríguez-Gómez and Marion Lloyd

INTRODUCTION

Modern federalism faces a central dilemma over competing demands for equity and efficiency. On the one hand, governments face pressure to become more equitable and democratic by expanding access and participation in the distribution of resources. On the other hand, society expects them to achieve economic growth and fulfil commitments to efficiency and transparency in public management. Much of the contemporary debate over governability centres on this dilemma, which forms part of a larger debate over democratic practices (Gibson 2004; Lechner 1997; Watts 2010).

The federation provides a functional, albeit far from complete, solution to the basic problems of democratic governance; it adds a new dimension to the traditional republican formula of the division of powers, and, in theory, facilitates the processing of local policies and government actions (Burgess 2003; Kramer 1994). In their day-to-day functioning, however, federalist systems are both highly complex and fraught with internal conflicts. They also face capacity constraints, particularly at the subnational levels (Flamand 2010). Implicit in the system is competition between the central power of a national character and the local associates, in this case the various subnational entities—regions, states, districts, municipalities, among others. According to William Riker (1964), all federalist regimes face a continued clash of interests of a political and economic nature. On the one hand, the local entities seek access to a growing share of resources distributed by the central power as well as increased influence in the decision-making processes affecting the entire group. On the other, the federal government tends to accumulate resources and attributions in a bid to ensure its control over the myriad subnational entities. When competing actors and forces with different political projects enter this competitive arena—the classic scenario of the transition from autocratic to more democratic regimes—the resulting instability threatens the original purpose of the federalist system.

To reduce those tensions, many governments have adopted legal norms that regulate the jurisdictions of the federation and the federated entities. Another common practice consists of the central authority setting national standards in certain areas and then empowering the entities to achieve those standards within their respective conditions and circumstances. In practice, the efficiency of such solutions depends primarily on three elements—the capacity of central and local authorities to avoid unnecessary overlap in the application of public policies; the adequate distribution of fiscal resources; and a system of economic resources and policies oriented towards achieving certain standards (Rodríguez-Gómez 2014).

Federalism in Mexico

In countries such as Mexico, in which the economy and the political structures are still undergoing significant transformations, the consolidation of such systems represents a challenge of extraordinary complexity. In addition to the problems of cost inefficiencies and bloated bureaucracies associated with the operation of federalist systems (Perotti 1996), policymakers must contend with scenarios of profound inequalities, weak democratic processes and institutions, governments that are divided along political lines and the existence of strong and constant political disputes over resources and spaces for political action (Majeed, Watts and Brown 2006). Such tensions necessarily limit the effective implementation of federalists systems, limiting the degree to which the federal government devolves power to the state and local levels.

Mexico first adopted a federalist system nearly two centuries ago, but later underwent long periods of de facto centralism. The process has been more cyclical than linear. During much of the twentieth century, the country was ruled by a highly centralized, authoritarian, one-party regime that was federalist mainly in name. In many cases, the states simply acted out the instructions of the federal government (Flamand 2010).

By the end of the last century, however, that panorama began to shift significantly. In 1997, for the first time since the Mexican Revolution, no party held a majority in the federal congress. Three years later, an opposition candidate won the presidency for the first time in 71 years, ending the decades-long stranglehold of the Institutional Revolutionary Party (PRI) at the national, state and municipal levels. The victory by President Vicente Fox, of the conservative National Action Party (PAN), culminated 11 years of opposition gains at the states level. At the same time, societal demands for greater democratization of both government and services have led to a devolving of federal power to the states in multiple areas—most notably in the political arena, but also in infrastructure, health care and education—a process we will refer to as *federalization*.

Arnaut (1994) notes that the term 'federalization' has been employed in government discourse to denote two opposite dynamics in Mexican history—the first is the recentralization of the system by the federal government, primarily during the first part of the twentieth century; and, the second and more recent phenomenon, is the decentralization of the system, with new powers and functions assigned to the state and municipal governments. In this chapter, we use the term to refer to the second trend, which reflects recent attempts in Mexico to shift both fiscal and administrative responsibility to authorities at the subnational level.

The process is by no means unidirectional or complete. It might seem as if the federal government were devolving ever more resources and control to the states and municipalities. In practice, decentralization coexists with centralizing trends in numerous areas. Examples include the new accountability rules imposed by the federal government on all state and municipal institutions and the new financing systems for public higher education institutions (HEIs).

The ongoing federalization process in Mexico is characterized by numerous contradictions, limitations and problems. These include the hyper-bureaucratization of the distributive and control mechanisms, which have diminished rather than increasing the level of autonomy enjoyed by state institutions (Ordorika 2010; Rodríguez-Gómez 2014). Second, while there has been a gradual shifting of resources to the local governments, the federal government still collects the vast majority of taxes and dictates most public policies, in effect reducing incentives for local governments to increase revenue and to remain accountable to their constituents. Finally, major discrepancies and inequalities persist in the distribution of resources among states and institutions; in many cases, the richest or most developed entities receive the greatest share of federal funds.

Furthermore, the return of the PRI to the presidency in 2012 has triggered a re-centralizing and neo-corporatist trend in Mexican politics. A day after President Peña Nieto took office, the PRI signed a pact[1] with the main opposition parties to push through a set of 'structural reforms' by 2018. Citing the need to strengthen key economic and social sectors—energy, telecommunications, law enforcement, education, and health among others—the government has since promoted policies and legal reforms that in practice entail recentralizing control over those sectors. As a result, Mexico has yet to reach the main goals of the federalist model—devolving real power to the states as a means of achieving greater accountability in government,

---

[1] On 2 December 2012, the presidents of the PRI, PAN and PRD parties signed the Pact for Mexico (*Pacto por México*), which outlined 96 goals to be completed by the time President Peña's term ends in 2018. The agreement was unprecedented in Mexico's fractured political landscape and sparked fears of a re-concentration of power in the executive branch (a process Mexicans refer to as *presidencialismo*).

promoting local and regional development and, above all, combatting widespread poverty and inequality, which varies considerably from state to state. For example, in 2014, the poverty rate in Chiapas, a low-income state in the south, was 76 per cent, whereas the higher income state of Nuevo Leon in the north had a poverty rate of 20 per cent (CONEVAL-INEGI 2014).

Higher Education in a Federalist Frame

In this chapter, we examine federalization of one strategic area of government influence—higher education. In the context of globalization and the knowledge society, the importance of higher education as an engine for economic and social change has perhaps never been greater. A surge in demand for college degrees has pushed many countries to expand and diversify their tertiary offerings, as part of the massification process underway since the 1970s. Nonetheless, in Mexico, as in other developing countries, access to higher education remains limited, while strong inequalities persist among social classes, regions and types of institutions. In 2015, gross enrolment was just 34 per cent, well below the Latin American average in 2012 of 41 per cent (Mendoza 2012). There are also major variations in the degree of autonomy among institutional types, unequal access to higher education among regions and socioeconomic levels and the heavy concentration of the country's science and technology research capacities in the capital, which has repercussions for regional development.

In recent decades, the government has embarked on a major expansion and decentralization of the system to render it more efficient, democratic and responsive to local needs. The states have become much more proactive in creating new institutions, with funding shared equally between the states and the federal government. The private sector has also contributed to greater decentralization of the higher education system, with the larger institutions establishing branch campuses and franchises throughout the country. Thus, the system is increasingly decentralized, in terms of basic funding, curricula and programme design, and the geographic location of institutions. Yet, the federal government retains control over the new sources of competitive funding—known as 'extraordinary funds'—available to finance this expansion as well as over strategic areas such as technological institutes and scientific research. The resulting panorama is highly complex, with often-contradictory results.

To place Mexico's federalist system in historic context, we begin by summarizing its origins and development from the early nineteenth century to the present. We then outline the main transitions and political processes that define the contemporary federalist framework, such as the fiscal reform, changes to the federal public administration, and the democratic transition, as well as the policies of control, transparency and accountability in the federal sector. Next, we provide a brief explanation of the Mexican fiscal system, with an emphasis on the funding mechanisms for education and higher education. We follow with an overview of the Mexican higher education system, focusing on the past six decades of growth and diversification, and then discuss some of the limits and contradictions of the Mexican brand of federalism, especially the persistence of inequalities, the hyper-bureaucratization of the funding mechanisms and the implications for university autonomy. Finally, we conclude with reflections on the current state of Mexico's higher education system and the prospects for change.

A BRIEF ACCOUNT OF FEDERALISM IN MEXICO
Earlier Developments

Mexico opted for a federalist system soon after achieving independence from colonial rule, even adopting the official name of the United States of Mexico. The Constitution of 1824 declares, 'The Mexican nation adopts for its government the form of a popular and federal republic'. However, the federalist principles first enshrined in the Constitution of 1824 have undergone major fluctuations and legal modifications over the past two centuries, depending on the group or party in power. For much of the nineteenth century, opposing factions fought over the degree to which the federal government should cede power to the states—or more precisely, the degree to which local entities should give up their power to the federal authorities—while the victors enshrined their preferences in successive constitutions in 1836, 1843 and 1857

(Valencia 2003). The dispute between federalism and centralism dominated the first three decades of Mexican independence, and was a recurrent source of conflict throughout the century (Vázquez 1993).

During the 1850s, Mexico adopted a set of liberal reforms, which resulted in the strongly federalist Constitution of 1857. A year later, Benito Juárez was elected for the first of five terms in office. However, war soon broke out between liberals and conservatives, followed by the French Invasion in 1861 and the three-year rule by Emperor Maximillian, starting in 1864. Juárez regained power in 1867 and began the period known as the Restored Republic, in which he sought to implement many of the modernizing reforms.

The federalist period did not last much longer than Juárez, who died in office in 1872. Four years later, Porfirio Díaz assumed the presidency, and the country embarked on a 35-year period of de facto dictatorship (1876–1911). Although Mexico remained constitutionally a federalist state, Díaz 'reduced the constitutional institutions to a purely semantic level. Federalism only existed on paper, while in reality the government was even more centralized' (Valencia 2003, 363).

Díaz's disregard for the federalist pact, and for democratic principles in general, finally led to his overthrow in 1911. However, the uprising against his government was also a testimony to the strength of the local and regional factions in a country whose population was still primarily rural and geographically dispersed. Under the slogan, 'effective suffrage, no re-election', local landowners and peasants took up arms against the government, triggering the decade-long civil war known as the Mexican Revolution. Finally, in 1917 and with an estimated 1 million casualties, the victorious side drafted a new Constitution based firmly on federalist principles, although fighting continued for several more years.

The 1917 Constitution, which is still in effect, states in Article 40:

> The will of the Mexican people is to constitute a representative, democratic, [and] federal Republic, composed of free and sovereign states in everything concerning their internal affairs; but joined in a Federation established according to the principles of this fundamental law. (Gobierno de México 1917)

The constitution itself opens the way to conflicting interpretations of Mexican federalism, including the provision for 'federal intervention' to re-establish order. That centralist mandate led to the establishment of an effective one-party system in 1929, under the National Revolutionary Party (later called the Institutional Revolutionary Party). As the party's name implies, it sought to cement and centralize the gains of the Revolution within a constitutional order. In practice, the party developed a complex corporatist system, which divided key sectors of society into different corporations under strict federal control. Yet, the president wielded considerable control over the state governments and, in many cases, handpicked the governors, acting essentially as federal delegates to the states (Carpizo 1978; Garrido 1982).

In sum, for most of the twentieth century, Mexico's system of government operated on the principles of 'theoretical federalism and *de facto* centralism' (Valencia 2003, 367–368). For example, a 1934 reform gave Congress sole power to legislate on electricity. Another reform in 1942 increased federal control over foreign investments, credit and insurance, the exploitation of natural resources and electricity taxes. Perhaps even more significant, for decades the federal government controlled 85 per cent of the national budget, with minimal input from the states (Valencia 2003). Even today, states only contribute 20–22 per cent to the national budget. In general, that arrangement has benefitted local politicians, who ceded their fiscal authority in exchange for federal (PRI) protection from local electoral competition (Díaz-Cayeros 2006).

Still, Mexican politicians were not blind to the contradictions between the constitutionally mandated federalism and the centralist reality, which had implications both for the legitimacy of the PRI and the country's governability. The National Fiscal Conventions of 1925, 1933 and 1947 sought to clarify the domains of the federal,[2] state and municipal governments in terms of tax collection and revenue sharing as well as to resolve competing demands from the wealthier north and the poorer south (Reyes 2004). In 1925, the system was so chaotic

---

[2] A fourth National Fiscal Convention, held in 2004, introduced mechanisms designed to channel more funding to poorer states. However, there is considerable debate as to the overall effects of the changes in terms of the equity of the fiscal system.

that the finance secretary, Alberto J. Pani, described it 'a fiscal anarchy' with 'innumerable sources of corruption' (Reyes 2004, 8). The first two conventions focused on simplifying tax collection to avoid double-taxation and increase revenue. However, the process was interrupted by the onset of World War II. By the third convention, the system had become so complex that the delegates had to start virtually from scratch in defining fiscal responsibilities—efforts that were only partially successful from a federalist perspective (Reyes 2004).

With the financial and political crises of the late 1970s, Mexico embarked on an era of 'new federalism' (Valencia 2003). In contrast to classical federalism, which distinguished between two orders in juxta-position with each other, this new approach operates on the principle of the distribution of power, conducted through mechanisms of coop-eration and coordination. Among major changes were fiscal reforms and modifications to the federal public administration. The political alternation at the state and later federal level, starting in the late 1980s, was also fundamental in shifting the power balance between the federal and state governments, as was the creation of the autonomous Federal Electoral Institute in 1990. In the following section, we review the key reforms that have served as catalysts for the 're-federalization' of Mexico, a process that, while far from complete, had major implica-tions for the country's higher education system.

From Theoretical Federalism to New Federalism

Over the past three decades, the Mexican political system has under-gone major transformations, which are the result of processes underway at the national and local levels. Four trends are particularly significant. Starting in the late 1970s, the country adopted major reforms in public administration, through the creation of new agencies, rules and criteria affecting both the federal and local governments. Second, the introduc-tion of a new tax system starting in 1978, and particularly after 1997, has transformed the collection, distribution and supervision of federal revenue. Third, as part of the decentralization process, the government transferred administrative control of the health and basic education sys-tems to the state governments. Finally, the political gains by opposition parties starting in the late 1980s culminated in the collapse of one-party rule in 2000, ushering in new processes of democratic transition. While these processes occurred with relative independence, they form part of efforts to address the economic and social problems that have emerged in Mexico since the 1980s.

In response to the severe economic crisis triggered by plummeting world oil prices and the debt crisis of the 1980s, the federal government pursued a series of strategies intended to insert Mexico into the dynamics of globalization. As with other Latin American countries, the country acted in accordance with the structural adjustment plans stipulated by the international finance agencies. Starting with the presidency of Miguel de la Madrid (1982–1988), the government experimented with formulas for re-activating the national economy. Over the next two decades, however, the anti-crisis programmes shifted from monetary and fiscal control to the reorganization of public finances; from programmes designed to lure foreign investment and international commerce to the redefinition of the role of the state and in the economic sphere; and from fiscal austerity programmes to regional and economic development policies.

Underlying all these changes was a new emphasis on government planning, with increasing collaboration between the federal and state governments. While initially many of the planning functions were concentrated in the executive branch under the Secretariat for Programming and Planning (1976), the government has since created a series of autonomous institutions to monitor the work of the federal and state governments and devolve more power to the latter. These include the Superior Auditor of the Federation and parallel offices at the state level, the National Council for the Evaluation of Social Development Policy and the Federal Institute for Access to Public Information (now National Institute for Transparency, Access to Public Information and the Protection of Personal Data), which has promoted the development of transparency laws at the local level.

The government has also undergone major changes in terms of fiscal responsibility. In 1978, the congress approved the Fiscal Coordination Law, which led to the creation of the National System for Fiscal Coordination. The system had the dual goal of increasing tax collection and empowering the states to distribute a larger share of the resulting revenue. Even more relevant for higher education financing was the 1997 amendment to the Fiscal Coordination Law, which introduced the concept of 'support funds' for strategic areas, including technology education and teacher training. The new budget framework also specified federal and state responsibilities and oversight for spending programmes; federal agencies are accountable for calculating the total budget to be transferred to each state, and the state then records the funds received in their own accounting systems (Rodríguez 2007).

To reduce the risk of state or municipal entities using the funds for other purposes, the law introduced a system for earmarking funds and other control mechanisms. The government also implemented more flexible systems and joint funding for specific projects, such as the creation of new university campuses at the state level. The changes have had major implications for the federal funding of higher education, as we will discuss later on in this chapter.

A third landmark in the federalization process was the decentralization of Mexico's basic education system starting in the 1980s. The process accelerated in 1992, when the federal government and the National Union of Education Workers (SNTE) signed the National Accord for the Modernization of Basic and Teachers' Education (ANMEB). The agreement had three main objectives—to shift administrative control of the education system to the states (in part in a bid to reduce the negotiating power of the teacher's union, which is the largest in Latin America); to reform the curriculum; and to implement a new incentive system for teachers to improve their on-the-job qualifications. In practice, however, the federal Public Education Secretariat (SEP) retained control over school curricula and salary negotiations with the union, while it only devolved administrative control to the states (Arellano 2012). As a result, 'negotiations on wages take place at the federal level, but the additional fiscal burden is borne by the states' (World Bank 2012, 9). Some observers have suggested that the decentralization of the education system, like that of the health care system in the 1980s, had more to do with image than substance; the PRI needed to boost its democratic credentials following mounting allegations of electoral fraud and corruption (Martínez 2001).

If the strategy paid off, however, the dividends were short-lived. Opposition parties won their first governorship in 1989. Then, in 1997, for the first time since the Mexican Revolution, no party held a majority in the lower chamber of Congress and an opposition candidate was elected the Mayor of Mexico City.[3] The victories paved the way for the election of President Fox in 2000 and subsequent opposition gains at the state and municipal levels. The resulting political competition has led to greater activism at subnational level, including the now common practice by which state legislators and university officials lobby Congress for more funding for existing or new institutions. In the following section, we provide a brief overview of the structure of the country's fiscal system, with details on the funding system for basic and higher education.

THE MEXICAN FISCAL SYSTEM

Mexico's fiscal system is extremely centralized (Díaz-Cayeros 2006). In general terms, the federal government is responsible for collecting taxes on all movable sources of income, including income, sales and capital gains tax, which together account for roughly 90 per cent of all tax revenue. Local governments, meanwhile, collect from immovable sources, such as land and real estate, and locally registered vehicles. In comparison, local tax revenue accounts for 17 per cent of total public revenues in Argentina and 30 per cent in Colombia (World Bank 2012).

Under the Mexican system, the local governments cede tax collection powers to the federal government, which then channels 60 per cent of the resulting revenue back to the local entities. Of that share, 80 per cent goes to the states and 20 per cent to the municipalities (Reyes 2014). In theory, the mechanism enables the federal government to combat inequalities at the state levels by diverting a proportionally larger share of tax revenue to poorer states. However,

---

[3] As part of the federalization process, a January 2016 amendment to the Constitution transformed the Federal District (Distrito Federal) into the equivalent of Mexico's 32nd state. The capital is now known simply as Mexico City (Ciudad de México).

that is not always the case, as roughly 10 per cent of total funding is disbursed through agreements (known as *convenios*) negotiated on a case-by-case basis between the states and the federal government (CEEY 2013; World Bank 2012). The heavy dependence of local governments on federal funding in Mexico also serves as a disincentive for states to increase local tax collection, while making local officials less accountable to their constituents (World Bank 2012).

As a part of the decentralization process, total federal funding for local governments nearly doubled between 2000 and 2012, from 776 billion pesos to 1.3 trillion pesos (Auditoría Superior de la Federación 2013), increasing the overall spending capacity of the subnational governments. In addition, in recent years, the government has created special funds to strengthen development projects and administrative management capacity at the regional, state and municipal levels. However, the increase in federal funding comes with strings attached. Under the new system of categorical or 'extraordinary' funding in place since the late 1990s, the federal government disburses nearly half of its funding for the states in the form of conditioned funds known as *aportaciones*. The federal government transfers the rest in the form of *participaciones*, which is to be used at the states' discretion and which derive from federal tax collection at the state and municipal levels. The *aportaciones* go towards specific areas, such as education, health, road-building or environmental conservation, an arrangement that limits the degree of autonomy of local governments. In fact, the share of conditioned federal funding to state governments in Mexico is among the highest in the world—about 48 per cent compared with 25 per cent in the United States and 2.5 per cent in Russia (CEEY 2013; World Bank 2012).

Education Funding

The Mexican government spent approximately 5.5 per cent of GDP on education in 2014 (Peña Nieto 2015), slightly above the average of fellow members of the Organization for Economic Co-operation and Development (OECD 2015). As is the case with other sectors, the federal government accounts for most education spending—79.2

per cent, compared to 20.7 per cent by the states and 0.01 per cent by the municipalities in 2014 (Peña Nieto 2015). These percentages have varied little since 2000, when the breakdown was 80.8 per cent federal, 19.0 per cent state, and 0.2 per cent municipal. The bulk of the federal share is assigned through branches 11, 25 and 33 of the federal budget, the first of which is administered directly by the federal SEP and the rest by the states. However, in the case of basic education, about 80 per cent of funding is tied up in teachers' salaries, and another 17 per cent in other fixed spending areas, leaving states with little margin for determining spending priorities (México Evalúa 2011).

Compared with public primary and secondary schools, HEIs have greater discretion over how they spend their budget, which has grown significantly in recent years. Total public higher education spending nearly doubled between 2006 and 2015, from 73 billion pesos to 126 billion in the 2016 budget. State expenditure has also grown significantly, from 24 billion pesos in 2006 to 38 billion in 2015. As a result, the share of state funding compared with federal funding has remained relatively constant over the same period, ranging from 29.9 per cent to 34.8 per cent (Table 8.1). However, as we show later in this chapter, HEIs, including those with autonomous status, have become increasingly dependent on discretionary, competitive funds, whose share of institutional budgets has averaged about 20 per cent in recent years (Mendoza 2015a). In addition, in the context of political pluralism and decentralization, institutions must negotiate for funding with an increasingly broad array of actors; these include the local legislatures, governors, the federal congress, the executive branch, the National Council for Science and Technology (CONACYT), among others.

The changes mentioned in Table 8.1 have also impacted the private sector. Under the pro-business administrations of the PAN (2000–2012), the federal government increased funding to private institutions to support technology and business incubators. In addition, in 2008, the Fox Government agreed to cover 30 per cent of salary bonuses for academics at private institutions that are members of the National Researchers System (SNI). Then in 2014, CONACYT announced that it would cover the full cost of the stipends in the private sector in a bid to expand the country's research capacity (CONACYT 2014).

Table 8.1 Higher Education Spending (in Million Pesos), 2016

Year	Federal Higher Education Spending^a ($)	State-level Higher Education Spending^b ($)	States/ Federal (%)
2006	73,958.70	24,663.10	33.3
2007	82,437.23	26,985.19	32.7
2008	91,744.71	28,861.10	31.5
2009	100,724.07	30,261.01	30.0
2010	104,144.74	33,835.12	32.5
2011	106,917.74	31,917.80	29.9
2012	109,287.25	33,226.40	30.4
2013	114,881.49	34,746.60	30.2
2014	124,100.38	43,134.53	34.8
2015	125,719.86	38,360.00	30.5
2016	125,875.34	n.a.	–

Source: Dirección General de Planeación y Programación de la SEP.

Note: The figure for 2015 corresponds to the authorized federal budget, and for all other years, to the actual spending.

^a *Federal* Budget approved for higher education.

^b *Figure* reported by the Questionnaire on State Education Financing (Cuestionario sobre Financiamiento Educativo Estatal).

MEXICAN HIGHER EDUCATION FROM 1950 TO THE PRESENT

Growth

Mexico is home to one of the first HEIs in the Americas. In 1551, the Spanish crown established the Royal and Pontifical University of Mexico. After Mexican Independence, liberals who opposed the university's ties to the Catholic Church closed it down in 1867, and it was not until 1910 that the institution was reborn as the National University of Mexico (Ordorika 2006). During the first half of the nineteenth century, higher education remained the province of the privileged elite. In 1950, Mexico had just 23 HEIs. These included two federal institutions—the National Autonomous University of Mexico (UNAM), the modern successor of the Royal and Pontifical University of Mexico, and the National Polytechnic Institute (IPN). In addition, there were 12 public, state-run universities, 3 regional technological institutes and 6 private universities. Total enrolment at the time was approximately 50,000 students.

Starting in the 1950s, the government embarked on the first major expansion of higher education in Mexico with the creation of 10 new public state universities throughout the decade and seven more in the 1960s, all of them located in the state capitals. To decentralize the system, the government expanded the number of regional technologi-cal institutes, many of which opened in cities and municipalities with growing demand for industrial and agricultural production. Thanks to a major investment by the federal government, the HE system under-went a period of extraordinary expansion in the 1970s. By the end of the decade, total enrolment had reached 800,000 students—16 times the number of students in 1950—and net enrolment (as a proportion of students between the ages of 19 and 23) had reached 10 per cent. For the first time in Mexican history, HEIs outside the capital enrolled a majority of students (Rodríguez 2009).

Most of the initial growth in the system was in the public sector. Private higher education accounted for a limited share of enrolment for much of the last century. This was largely due to the onerous and highly centralized government licensing process for private HEIs. Although the first private institutions began in the 1910s, they did not gain gov-ernment recognition for another two decades (Rodríguez and Ordorika 2012). Similarly, the country's leading private institutions, including the Monterrey Institute for Technology and Higher Studies (Tec de Monterrey 1952), the Autonomous Technological Institute of Mexico (1963), the Ibero-American University (1981) and the Autonomous University of Guadalajara (1982), received authorization by presidential decree (Rodríguez and Ordorika 2012). However, during the debt crisis of the 1980s, the government relaxed controls on the private sector in a bid to increase higher education places to compensate for major budget cuts for public higher education.

The decentralization of the education system starting in 1991 further fuelled the expansion of the private sector by increasing the number of licensing entities. In addition to public universities, state governments were now empowered to issue licenses for academic programmes (known as RVOEs) to private universities. In the later part of the decade, the government of Ernesto Zedillo (1994–2000) negotiated a new legal framework for the RVOE system with the Federation of Mexican Private Higher Education Institutions (FIMPES), which simplified the licensing process even further. The result was a surge in the number of new private institutions, many of questionable quality.

That trend changed somewhat under Zedillo's successor, Vicente Fox, who sought to stem the proliferation of low-quality institutions. His government pushed for new common academic criteria among the federal government and the states in issuing RVOEs, and, by 2004, all 32 states had an agreement of this kind in place. The government also encouraged public universities to stiffen their standards for issuing RVOEs. As a result, some 201 programmes lost their licenses during the Fox period (Rodríguez and Ordorika 2012). Nonetheless, the government crackdown on 'junk universities' may have facilitated the growth of the largest private institutions as part of a broader diversification of the country's higher education system.

The following factors were decisive in fuelling the expansion and de-concentration of higher education in the country:

1. *Private investment.* Bolstered by unmet demand in the public sector as well as government support (through weak regulation and favourable fiscal policies), private enrolment expanded heavily in the 1980s and 1990s. By the end of the 1990s, 30 per cent of total enrolment was private. It then flattened out at the current 33 per cent of undergraduate and 40 per cent of graduate enrolments (Rodríguez 2009). However, some of the biggest and most established providers have expanded nationwide. The largest private institution, the Tec de Monterrey, has established branches in virtually every state in Mexico, while several of the leading Catholic institutions have opened universities in the major provincial cities. By far, the largest

expansion has come from proprietary (for-profit) institutions,[4] which now comprise an increasing share of the private market and of total tertiary enrolment. For example, Laureate International Universities, the US based for-profit education giant, operates three universities in Mexico, including the second-largest private institution in the country, the University of the Valley of Mexico, with 70,000 students (ExECUM 2016).

2. *The growth of publically funded technological institutions.* In 1991, the federal government established the first technological universities, which offered superior technical degrees (i.e., Técnico Superior Universitario or TSU) after 2–3 years of coursework. These universities are similar to community colleges in the United States, in that they cater to working students from less affluent families and, theoretically, serve as stepping-stones to higher-level degrees. Starting in 1994, the government reinforced the system of technological institutes (which offer undergraduate engineering degrees of 4–5 years), through the creation of a subsystem of decentralized technological institutes to complement the existing federal technological institutes. In addition, starting in 2001, a new subsystem of institutions, the polytechnic universities, began opening across Mexico (De la Garza 2003). The new model offers a variety of engineering degrees and seeks to strengthen ties with industry by requiring students to undergo intensive internships and linking study plans to local technological needs. Finally, in 2014, the government created the National Technological Institute of Mexico to strengthen (and recentralize) coordination of the rapidly expanding system of technological institutes.

3. *The creation of new public HEIs in the states.* Since 2001, the federal government, in conjunction with the state governments,

---

[4] Traditionally, most private universities have operated as non-profit institutions, a status which requires them to reinvest all profits in the institution in exchange for tax breaks. However, in recent years, there has been a boom in for-profit education providers, which are often subsidiaries of large corporations and many of which are listed on the stock market. The for-profit sector has come under fire in recent years in the United States and Chile, among other countries, for adopting dishonest business practices in a bid to lure students and skirt government restrictions (Ordorika and Lloyd 2015).

has established 23 new institutions under the name of 'public universities with solidarity support' (UPEAS) and 12 'intercultural universities' (UIs). In both cases, the universities typically receive half of their funding from the federal government and the other half from the states, in contrast to the funding systems for the traditional state universities, in which the federal-state ratio varies considerably (Mendoza 2015a).

4. *The decentralization of public state universities.* To expand higher education coverage in smaller cities and municipalities, the state universities created new campuses and centres in the interior of the respective state. While examples vary significantly, the new facilities opened outside the state capitals and in areas with large demand for tertiary studies in most cases. That trend has accelerated in recent years, with state universities opening 45 new campuses or extension centres between 2007 and 2012 (Mendoza 2012).

5. *The incorporation of public teachers' colleges into the higher education system.* In the 1980s, the government determined that institutions dedicated to training primary and middle school teachers, known as *normales* in Mexico, could award degrees at the tertiary level. However, it was not until 2005, following the restructuring of the SEP, that the teachers' colleges were officially incorporated into the higher education system (Rodríguez 2009).

6. *Distance education.* In 2002, the private Monterrey Technological Institute of Superior Studies (ITESM) became the first institution in Mexico to offer distance education at the tertiary level, through its TECMilenio subsidiary. A year later, the UNAM added the term 'distance education' to its open university, and, in 2005, it began offering the first six undergraduate degrees to 300 students (Andrade 2011). Other universities quickly followed the suit, and, in 2012, after several years of piloted programmes, the government created the Open and Distance University of Mexico. Today, there are more than 460,000 students enrolled in distance higher education programmes, accounting for 11 per cent of tertiary enrolments (SEP 2014).

7. *New funding models for institutions.* In 1991, the federal government introduced a system of conditioned funding to state universities, as a supplement to regular funds for operating costs. The new

'extraordinary' funds cover infrastructure expansion (including the construction of new campuses) as well as costs incurred by increasing student enrolment, scientific programmes and other areas deemed strategic by the federal government. Universities must demonstrate that they used the funds for the stipulated purpose, in order to be eligible for future funding.

Fuelled by these changes, tertiary enrolment in Mexico nearly tripled between 1990 and 2015, from 1.3 to 3.5 million students, re-accelerating the trend of enrolment growth that slowed in the 1980s (from 0.9 million in 1980 to 1.3 million students in 1990). Net enrolment increased from 15 per cent in 1990 to about 29 per cent today. The percentage of students undergoing degree programmes is as follows: TSU, 4.3 per cent, *normales*, 3.9 per cent, undergraduate programmes (called *licenciatura* in Mexico), 85.1 per cent, and graduate programmes, 6.7 per cent (SEP 2014).

Growth has been largest in the state-controlled institutions (decentralized technological institutes, technological universities, polytechnic universities, UPEAS and UIs), whose combined enrolment grew six-fold between 2000–2001 and 2014–2015 (see Table 8.2), while their share of the total tertiary enrolment more than tripled, from 5.8 per cent to 18.6 per cent (SEP 2016), largely due to increased lobbying on the part of local officials.

There are also large variations among states, both in the size of enrolment and in the concentration of students among different institutional control types and sectors. For example, in Chiapas, Mexico's poorest state, a third of tertiary enrolment was in the private sector in 2015, while in Baja California, a relatively wealthy state, the private share was just one-fifth.

The Higher Education System Today

In 2014, there were 2,790 HEIs in Mexico, of which 868 were public and 1,930 were private (Table 8.3). In terms of enrolment, the ratio reverses with approximately 66 per cent of students enrolled in public institutions and 33 per cent in private (ExECUM 2016).

Table 8.2 Undergraduate Enrolment Growth by State and Administrative Control Type

State	2000-2001					2014-2015				
	Total	Federal	State	Autonomous	Private	Total	Federal	State	Autonomous	Private
Aguascalientes	16,992	2,890	1,468	9,318	3,316	40,821	6,740	8,996	14,910	10,175
Baja California	39,570	7,947	700	23,023	7,900	94,115	11,754	6,159	57,619	18,583
Baja California Sur	6,633	2,089	434	2,132	1,978	18,219	3,025	4,814	5,362	5,018
Campeche	11,237	2,726	1,195	6,729	587	24,524	2,914	7,228	11,514	2,868
Coahuila	52,688	9,448	4,899	23,188	15,153	84,442	13,662	20,083	26,786	23,911
Colima	12,934	1,741	0	10,571	622	19,462	3,151	1,598	12,264	2,449
Chiapas	37,111	3,933	1,939	14,275	16,964	71,029	8,182	17,909	20,760	24,178
Chihuahua	52,887	15,670	1,806	25,174	10,237	110,932	19,541	23,054	51,519	16,818
Ciudad de M	336,695	86,360	0	129,765	120,570	481,142	139,702	0	164,775	176,665
Durango	20,021	5,737	1,785	8,503	3,996	38,821	7,058	11,611	13,407	6,745
Guanajuato	49,037	7,642	4,543	7,743	29,109	103,185	13,355	29,759	19,598	40,473
Guerrero	38,779	8,003	1,561	26,017	3,198	57,054	12,210	11,486	27,503	5,855
Hidalgo	24,656	3,773	4,215	9,970	6,698	79,873	5,708	30,645	25,845	17,675
Jalisco	111,903	5,456	1,670	55,182	49,595	209,785	8,740	20,442	102,429	78,174
México	153,923	11,057	14,241	71,209	57,416	370,364	12,728	91,887	119,897	145,852
Michoacán	49,219	8,709	5,351	28,014	7,145	90,339	13,111	23,867	39,467	13,894

Morelos	22,309	4,479	144	9,337	8,349	44,107	6,419	6,597	18,028	13,063
Nayarit	12,564	2,880	0	8,617	1,067	30,792	5,377	7,344	15,430	2,641
Nuevo León	98,445	2,847	910	53,020	41,668	158,883	4,319	7,284	91,815	55,465
Oaxaca	41,827	12,908	1,398	22,541	4,980	58,486	18,169	11,326	15,904	13,087
Puebla	87,895	7,806	9,888	28,703	41,498	181,474	10,277	42,055	56,425	72,717
Querétaro	24,397	5,345	3,145	7,741	8,166	55,885	7,674	13,159	18,032	17,020
Quintana Roo	8,194	3,965	2,744	0	1,485	31,802	6,384	16,555	0	8,863
San Luis Potosí	30,562	6,116	1,784	17,506	5,156	62,044	7,509	13,157	25,629	15,749
Sinaloa	68,215	8,474	9,324	43,670	6,747	104,151	13,223	18,084	59,434	13,410
Sonora	54,335	7,736	7,904	33,571	5,124	95,641	11,699	23,041	45,364	15,537
Tabasco	41,230	4,922	6,059	26,262	3,987	67,490	6,563	23,121	28,681	9,125
Tamaulipas	64,878	16,183	217	28,419	20,059	99,859	21,837	13,447	34,531	30,044
Tlaxcala	15,936	3,627	1,219	9,165	1,925	27,640	4,086	7,021	13,435	3,098
Veracruz	88,801	17,418	5,469	38,378	27,536	168,178	20,519	57,950	54,113	35,596
Yucatán	26,933	6,188	1,532	7,526	11,687	61,186	8,142	11,566	14,612	26,866
Zacatecas	17,211	2,680	2,742	10,649	1,140	39,782	3,310	10,640	22,153	3,679
National Total	1,718,017	296,755	100,286	795,918	525,058	3,181,507	437,088	591,885	1,227,241	925,293

Source: Secretaría de Educación Pública [Public Education Secretariat] (SEP) (2016). Sistema Nacional de Información Estadística Educativa [National System of Education Statistics]. Database.

Table 8.3 Mexican HEIs by Type and Control Regime, 2014

Federal HEIs	**147**
Federal Universities	9
Federal Technological Institutes	132
Federal Teachers' Colleges (Normales)	6
State HEIs	**634**
State Universities	34
State Universities with Solidarity Support (UPEAS)	23
Decentralized Technological Institutes	134
Technological Universities	109
Polytechnic Universities	58
UIs	12
Federal Teachers' Colleges (Transferred to State Control)	121
State Teachers' Colleges	143
Other Public HEIs (Federal or State)	**88**
Private HEIs	**1,929**
Universities, Schools and Centres	1,755
Teachers' Colleges	174
Total Higher Education System (Federal, State and Private)	**2,798**

Sources: Secretaría de Educación Pública (SEP), Sistema Nacional de Información Estadística Educativa. Database. Asociación de Universidades e Instituciones de Educación Superior (ANUIES). 2014. Anuario Estadístico 2013–2014. Database.

Note: Does not include institutions that offer solely graduate studies.

The Mexican higher education system is comprised of various subsystems—universities (both public and private), technological institutes, teachers' colleges (*normales*) and public institutions tied to specific government entities. The private system includes a handful of high quality and high tuition institutions, including the Tec de Monterrey, the Ibero-American University, and the Mexican Autonomous Technological Institute (ITAM). There are also a number of second-tier institutions, both Catholic and for-profits, while the rest tend to be of mediocre or low quality and conduct virtually no research. The public universities, in turn, are divided into five broad groups—federal universities, state universities, UPEAS, UIs (which are often grouped together with the UPEAS for administrative reasons) and technological and polytechnic universities. Both admissions standards and the profile of students vary significantly among the institutions, with the federal universities and a handful of state universities among the most competitive.

There are nine federal institutions of higher education, of which four, all located in Mexico City, account for 12 per cent of total tertiary enrolment and employ 13 per cent of university professors. They are the UNAM, the Autonomous Metropolitan University (UAM), IPN and the National Pedagogical University (UPN). The first three are the most competitive HEIs in Mexico. The UNAM, for instance, accepts roughly 9 per cent of regular applicants (Olivares 2015), although students that attend its high school system are guaranteed admission with a minimum grade point average. The exact cut-off varies, depending on demand for the programme of study. Medicine, engineering and architecture are the most competitive. The other five federal institutions cater to specific sectors—two agricultural universities, two small research universities and the military university. Together, the federal universities accounted for 27 per cent of total tertiary enrolment.

There are also 34 state universities. Most are autonomous and receive a significant share of their budget from the federal government. As with the federal universities, the state universities apply a standardized entrance exam, and the degree of competitiveness varies greatly depending on the institution. These accounts for 22 per cent of tertiary enrolment. There are another 23 UPEAS, which were created over the past 15 years to satisfy unmet demand at the traditional state universities. Admissions requirements tend to be relatively lax. Together, these institutions accounted for 3 per cent of total tertiary enrolment (ExECUM 2016).

In addition, there are 12 UIs, which cater to the country's minority indigenous population. They represent roughly 10 per cent of the country's 122 million people, but, because this group has traditionally been excluded from higher education, they account for an estimated

0.7 per cent of enrolment in 1990 (Carnoy et al. 2002) and 1.5 per cent of all tertiary-level students in 2014 (Universia 2014). The first UI opened in 2002 in northern Sinaloa state, and since then, another 11 institutions have opened in different states. Their curriculum targets local development needs and the preservation of indigenous languages. Together, these institutions accounted for just 0.3 per cent of enrolment in 2014 (ExECUM 2016).

The technical universities, which are divided into technological universities and polytechnic universities, enrolled 4.5 per cent and 1.4 per cent of students, respectively, in 2014 (ExECUM 2016). According to the web site of the Undersecretariat for Higher Education (SES) of the SEP, there are currently 61 technological universities and 48 polytechnic universities in 2015 (SEP), although only 30 reported enrolment statistics to the SEP in 2013 (ExECUM 2016). In addition, there are 249 technological institutes, accounting for 12.5 per cent of enrolments. Former President Lázaro Cárdenas (1936–1942) created the first technological institutes as part of an industrialization strategy in the early 1940s, and the sector has undergone a major resurgence in the past two decades. Together, the three types of technical institutions, which tend to cater to less affluent students in search of job security, accounted for a combined 17.5 per cent of enrolments (ExECUM 2016).

Finally, there were 127,000 students enrolled in more than 450 teachers' colleges in 2013, accounting for 3.7 per cent of tertiary enrolment in that year (SIBEN/SEP 2015). This sector, which has a long history of political activism, is comprised of both public and private institutions. As is the case with the UIs, students attending the teachers' colleges tend to be among the poorest of the university-going population.

Expansion of the System

The significant expansion of the Mexican higher education system in recent decades has not occurred equally across sectors. Of all the sub-systems, the technological sector has experienced the greatest growth. During the administration of Vicente Fox (2000–2006), the government created 95 new HEIs, 73 of which offer primarily engineering and other technical degrees. The breakdown was as follows: 24 technological universities, 21 polytechnic universities, 28 technological institutes, 14 UPEAS and 7 UIs (Mendoza 2015b). This period was particularly noteworthy for the creation of two new subsystems, the polytechnic universities and the UIs, which formed part of a government strategy to democratize and decentralize the system as well as to expand ties between HEIs and local industries. In addition, the state universities, aided by federal support, created 13 new campuses outside the state capitals.

Under Fox's successor, Felipe Calderón (2006–2012), the government continued the expansion of the public higher education system, with an even greater emphasis on technological degrees. The SEP reported the creation of 140 new institutions—43 technological universities, 34 polytechnic universities, 23 state technological institutes, 22 federal technological institutes, 13 public state universities (state, federal and intercultural) and 5 regional centres for teacher training (Mendoza 2015b). Of the total, 100 were technological institutions, a focus whose implications we will discuss later on in this chapter.

The current administration of Enrique Peña Nieto (2012–) has set even more ambitious goals for higher education expansion than its predecessors. His Sectoral Program for Education (2013–2018) calls for gross tertiary enrolment to reach 40 per cent, up from the current 314 per cent (SEP 2014). Unlike net enrolment, gross enrolment, which is computed by dividing the total number of students of any age by the share of the population aged 19–23, incorporates overage students—a sizable portion of the tertiary population in Mexico and in other developing countries. So far, the government has met its annual goals. However, major federal budget cutbacks for 2016, due to plummeting world oil prices, may well have limited the government's ability to continue to invest in the sector for the short term.

Despite recent gains in coverage, Mexico remains far behind many Latin American countries in higher education enrolment. Argentina, the regional leader, reports gross enrolment of 80 per cent (2012 figures), Chile, 79 per cent; Uruguay, 63 per cent; and Colombia and Costa Rica, 48 per cent (World Bank 2015). Of equal importance, the

Mexican higher education system is highly inequitable and stratified along class and regional lines.

THE LIMITS TO FEDERALISM IN HIGHER EDUCATION

In broad terms, the federalization of higher education occurs across two dimensions—the devolution of academic, financial and administrative control and geographic decentralization, which refers to the distribution of educational opportunities throughout the country. In both those dimensions in Mexico, significant tensions and contradictions remain. The Mexican higher education system has expanded and diversified over the past two decades, both in terms of institutional type and geographic location. However, there has been a simultaneous loss of institutional autonomy, due to the introduction of higher education policies dictated at the supranational level and an increase in federal control over budgeting, in the case of all institutions, and curriculum, in the case of the technological and teacher-training sectors. Perhaps of most concern, the federalization process has done little to reduce inequalities among states and institutions in terms of resources and knowledge-production capacities, neither has it significantly improved access to high-quality education for low-income and indigenous students.

Institutional Autonomy and Federalism in Higher Education

The federalization of higher education in Mexico has affected some subsystems more than others, and in different ways. There is almost no federal or state intervention in student admissions and faculty hiring across institutional types or state or federal regimes. Notwithstanding, some institutions have gained increasing control over their administration and curricula, most have become more dependent on state and federal authorities in determining budgetary priorities, despite receiving a larger amount of overall funding. The process has also resulted in the increasing bureaucratization of the financing process, as institutions seek to respond to state or federal demands for accountability and transparency.

In the case of the public teachers' colleges and the technological sector, federalization has primarily translated into administrative decentralization, with the SEP still dictating much of the curricula and financial policies from the capital. However, there are exceptions. The recent expansion of the technological institutions at the state level as well as the diversification of the sector with the creation of the polytechnic universities has resulted in greater freedom for institutions to design their own curricula. Furthermore, in 2011, the SEP authorized the technological universities to offer 4-year engineering degrees, in addition to 2-year technical degrees—a long-time demand of students at those institutions.

Another example in which federalization has had mixed results is that of the UIs. Overall, these institutions receive by far the largest per-student share of funding of any public universities in Mexico. The most well-funded of these, the Intercultural University of Puebla State, received 50 million pesos in government funding in 2013 and enrolled just 214 students—the equivalent of $234,000 pesos per student (US$12,700 at 2016 exchange rates). In practice, however, these universities enjoy very little institutional autonomy from either level of government. The SEP is responsible for approving their study plans, and extraordinary funds (both federal and state) represent 50 per cent of their budgets—the largest share of any type of institution—meaning that many administrative and academic decisions are made outside university walls. Similarly, while in theory the institutions are responsible for choosing their own rectors and top officials, in practice the state governments often intervene directly or indirectly in the succession process.[5]

Especially relevant are the effects of federalization on the traditional public university sector, which includes both federal and state universities and accounts for 39 per cent of tertiary enrolment and 80 per cent of scientific production, as measured by the number of indexed articles in the Thomson Reuters Web of Knowledge (ExECUM 2016). In theory, these institutions—most of which have official autonomous

---

[5] Interview with a former professor from the Intercultural University of Chiapas and a former member of the federal General Coordinating Office for Bilingual and Intercultural Education, who spoke on the condition of anonymity on 25 September 2015.

status and bear the word 'autonomous' in their names—have virtually total control over the design of their academic programmes and in the use of their budgets. Similarly, by law, professors and researchers employed in those institutions enjoy significant academic freedom in terms of the content of their teaching and research. A 1980 amendment to the Constitution outlines those rights:

> Universities and other higher education institutions that are legally granted autonomy will have the power and responsibility to govern-ment themselves; to fulfill their educational goals, to research and dis-seminate culture under the principle of academic freedom, with the free and open debate of ideas; to determine their plans and programs; to determine their own policies governing faculty hiring and retention; and to administer their own patrimony. (Mexican Constitution Article 3, Fraction 7)

Yet, the degree of autonomy exercised by the public universities varies significantly among institutions and, over time, in part because the government has yet to issue the regulations to accompany the con-stitutional amendment. This leaves its application to the discretion of political and higher education actors (Villa 2013). More importantly, changes in the federal budgetary process have made institutions and academics more dependent on conditioned sources of funding. Such contradictions are typical of Mexico's federalist pact, in which historic notions of university autonomy[6] clash with more recent policies favour-ing greater government oversight of public institutions.

Thus, the public universities—and the state universities in particular—have had to adjust to competing for a sizable share of budgets, and many institutions have reacted by dramatically increasing the number of administrators whose main job entails soliciting and justifying federal and state funding. This new class of administrators play an increasing role in determining institutional policy (Acosta 2009). In

---

[6] The 1918 reform movement at the University of Córdoba, Argentina, gave root to a tradition of university autonomy in Latin America, which has remained the dominant model until recently. The movement also promoted the role of public universities as agents of social change, a goal that was incorporated into the missions of the UNAM and the public universities that followed in Mexico.

addition, significant fluctuations in the amount of federal- and state-extraordinary funds have an impact on universities' planning capacity.

The new policies form part of the raft of changes in higher education policies implemented on a global scale starting in the 1980s. The structural adjustment measures, and the so-called neoliberal[7] policies that accompanied the globalization trends towards the end of the century, had a major influence on public universities in Latin America. Higher education policies adopted during the period included the massive reduction of public financing and the establishment of accountability measures; institutional diversification and decentralization; a new emphasis on 'excellence'; the evaluation and adoption of new market-based competitive models as well as the privatization and commercialization of the educational providers; and a new emphasis on 'university production' (Mendoza 2002). Together, these policies opened a new era in the relationship between the universities and the state (Rodríguez 2002), characterized by an intense and growing competition for individual and institutional resources (Marginson 1997; Marginson and Considine 2000). Such changes dramatically reduced the traditional autonomy of academic institutions (universities and other postsecondary institutions) and their professionals vis-à-vis the state and the market (Ordorika 2004; Rhoades 1998; Slaughter and Leslie 1997).

Mexico first adopted neoliberal policies following the debt crisis in the early 1980s, which triggered a period of fiscal austerity and negative growth known as the 'lost decade'. As part of the fiscal austerity measures dictated by the International Monetary Fund and the World Bank, the government slashed spending on education and health care, among other social services. It also introduced new measures designed to increase accountability, efficiency and competitiveness, as part of the neoliberal logic promoted by the international agencies.

An example of such policies at the individual level is the SNI, which was created in 1984 to staunch the faculty income loss due to the

---

[7] We ascribe to Harvey's (2005, 3) definition of neoliberalism, as a philosophy that 'holds that the social good will be maximized by maximizing the reach and frequency of market transactions, and it seeks to bring all human action into the domain of the market'.

financial crisis and to promote competition among top scholars. The system provides financial incentives for academics with a demonstrated capacity for scientific research, measured in terms of the number of articles published in international peer-reviewed journals, patents produced, doctoral theses directed, etc. (Ordorika 2004). Currently, there are more than 22,000 members of the SNI, whose salaries are largely conditioned by their adherence to research quotas—either publish or perish dynamics, which has implications for academic autonomy.

At the institutional level, the government of Carlos Salinas de Gortari (1990–1994) approved the first extraordinary fund in 1991, the Fund for the Modernization of Higher Education (FOMES), followed five years later by the Program for the Improvement of the Professorship (PROMEP), which supports postgraduate programmes for academics who lack master's or doctoral degrees. The number of such funds increased significantly in the first decade of the twenty-first century. By 2010, there 10 extraordinary funds directed at the state universities, with the highest level of funding disbursed in 2007 and 2008, when such funds represented 34 per cent of state university budgets (Mendoza 2015a).

The federal government also exerts control over institutions through the certification process. The SEP is responsible for licensing the majority of HEIs both in the capital and at the state level, through the issuing of certificates known as Official Recognition of Educational Validity (RVOE in Spanish), which in turn empower institutions to award degrees. However, public universities of recognized quality and the state educational secretariats are also empowered to award degrees.

In sum, the neoliberal policies implemented over the past few decades have run counter to the decentralization process by introducing new administrative and fiscal controls at the federal level. The state universities have been the most affected, as the new policies run counter to the century-old tradition of university autonomy in Mexico.

Equity in Mexican Higher Education

The federalization of higher education in Mexico has not been a linear process, nor has it affected all regions and institutions equally. Both in terms of funding and coverage, huge disparities remain, particularly between the richer and poorer states and between urban and rural areas. Variations in higher education enrolment tend to mirror income disparities among states. For example, Chiapas ranks at the bottom of Mexico's 33 states, both in terms of the share of the population living in poverty (76%) and its ranking on the country's human development index—at 0.667, it is at par with the African nation of Gabon (CESOP 2013; PNUD 2015). It also has the lowest tertiary enrolment rate, 14.8 per cent (CONAPO/SEP 2016). In contrast, the Federal District has a poverty rate of 28.5 per cent and a human development index of 0.83, on par with Andorra (CESOP 2013; PNUD 2015). Gross tertiary enrolment in the capital is 60 per cent, higher than most European nations (Table 8.4). The closest rivals to the capital are the relatively prosperous northern states of Sinaloa, Sonora and Nuevo Leon, which have gross enrolment rates of 43 per cent, 41.9 per cent and 41.6 per cent, respectively (Mendoza 2012).

A similar gap exists between urban and rural areas. Two factors explain the disparity—the lack of institutions and the smaller share of students graduating from high school in the poorer regions. In 2012, just 23 per cent of all municipalities offered some form of tertiary education. In Oaxaca state, which concentrates the country's largest indigenous population and is among the poorest entities, HEIs were concentrated in just 5 per cent of municipalities; while in Baja California, along the border with the United States, every municipality had at least one HEI institution. The type of institutions also varied greatly depending on the type of locality. Despite the decades-long process of decentralization, a majority of the public universities are still located in the state capitals. Meanwhile, in many small cities, the only options available to students are technological institutions, teachers' colleges, private institutions of often questionable quality and, increasingly, distance education programmes (Ordorika and Rodríguez 2012).

The share of students eligible to attend college also varies by region and socioeconomic condition. A year after a constitutional amendment made secondary education mandatory in 2011, gross enrolment at the level was just 71 per cent and net enrolment around 50 per cent in the 2012–2013 school year. That proportion is not expected to increase

Table 8.4 Gross Enrolment in Higher Education by State

	2000–2001	2005–2006	2010–2011	2011–2012	2012–2013
Aguascalientes	20.2	26.7	32.1	33.1	34.7
Baja California	17.4	21.8	27.1	29.1	30.7
Baja California Sur	15.5	26.2	27.3	29.4	29.4
Campeche	22.0	26.2	29.9	30.0	29.9
Coahuila	24.4	27.5	32.1	32.5	32.4
Colima	24.6	26.5	30.0	30.8	32.6
Chiapas	10.6	12.9	14.2	14.7	14.8
Chihuahua	19.4	25.1	30.6	32.0	34.0
Ciudad de México	39.5	43.8	53.3	56.6	60.1
Durango	17.2	20.6	24.1	24.5	26.0
Guanajuato	11.2	14.7	17.5	18.2	19.0
Guerrero	17.2	17.0	17.0	17.3	17.4
Hidalgo	14.1	21.8	26.5	27.6	29.5
Jalisco	19.4	22.2	26.1	27.5	28.1
México	12.9	17.8	21.2	22.5	23.7
Michoacán	13.3	18.3	20.3	21.0	22.1
Morelos	18.6	23.7	24.7	26.2	27.9
Nayarit	27.1	23.9	29.8	27.7	29.2
Nuevo León	27.0	31.5	35.7	38.3	38.8
Oaxaca	14.0	16.4	16.9	16.8	17.4
Puebla	20.2	25.8	30.5	31.7	32.4
Querétaro	16.8	21.5	26.5	27.9	29.3
Quintana Roo	8.6	13.2	17.6	17.8	19.0
San Luis Potosí	15.7	21.3	24.6	25.4	26.0
Sinaloa	28.2	29.5	32.9	36.7	38.2
Sonora	26.6	30.9	35.5	37.8	38.6
Tabasco	21.2	26.5	29.7	29.7	30.5
Tamaulipas	32.6	30.7	33.2	34.3	34.8
Tlaxcala	17.7	20.6	23.2	24.1	24.6

	2000–2001	2005–2006	2010–2011	2011–2012	2012–2013
Veracruz	14.2	18.8	22.1	23.0	22.9
Yucatán	19.2	24.5	29.0	29.4	30.8
Zacatecas	13.8	19.4	24.5	25.2	26.4
National Average	19.5	23.3	26.9	28.1	29.1

Sources: (a) Consejo Nacional de Población [National Population Council] (CONAPO). Proyecciones de Población 1990–2030 [Population projections 1990–2030]. Database. Accessed at: http://www.conapo.gob.mx/es/CONAPO/Proyecciones_Datos. (b) Secretaría de Educación Pública, Serie Histórica de Matrícula, Database.

significantly in the near future, given the shortage of high schools in many municipalities (Ordorika and Rodríguez 2012).

The direct link between poverty and educational attainment starts at the basic education level. In Chiapas, 14 per cent of the population aged 15 and above was illiterate in 2015, and 51 per cent had not completed ninth grade—the mandatory minimum education level prior to 2011. In contrast, illiteracy in Mexico City was 1.4 per cent and ninth grade completion was almost 80 per cent (SEP 2015).

Not surprisingly, there is also a direct relationship between socio-economic class and access to higher education, with students in the top income brackets far more likely to attend university than their poorer peers. According to the National Surveys of Income and Household Spending[8] (for years 2000, 2006 and 2010), in 2000 just 2.76 per cent of college-age students in the bottom income quintile were enrolled in higher education, compared with 63.5 per cent in the top quintile. However, that panorama may be starting to change. In 2010, the enrolment rate among the bottom quintile of the population had reached 14.4 per cent and the top quintile hit 78.4 per cent. Nonetheless, a

---

[8] Household surveys tend to yield higher estimates of school attendance than data on the educational system, as families often report part-time or sporadic students as being enrolled in college. However, the Education Secretariat does not provide data on tertiary enrolment by income bracket.

large share of lower-income students is enrolled in the technological and private sectors, since competition has become increasingly fierce at the top institutions (Table 8.5).

The federal government has attempted to address some of the inequalities through compensatory funding programmes for poorer institutions and regions. In 2001, the Fox government created a national scholarship programme for higher education, known as, Pronabes, issuing the first 44,000 scholarships to low-income students. By 2011, the number of scholarships had more than quadrupled, and the government created an additional funding programme, bringing the total number of scholarships in that year to 813,000 (Villa 2013). However, like other government funding programmes, Pronabes has disproportionately benefited residents of the capital; during the 2010–2011 school year, Mexico City accounted for a fourth of all the scholarships, despite representing just 16 per cent of the country's total public tertiary enrolment (Rodríguez 2012). Similarly, while the states of Mexico[9] and Michoacán enrolled almost the same proportion of public university students in 2010–2011 (12.9% and 12.5%, respectively), the former state received three times as many Pronabes scholarships, 24,218 compared with 8,854 (Rodríguez 2012). The different degrees of political influence of the two states—Mexico state is adjacent to the capital—go a long way in explaining the discrepancy in funding patterns.

Inequalities among institutions

There are also major inequalities among institutions and institutional types in Mexico. Particularly noteworthy is the lack of a clear and uniform set of criteria for apportioning federal funding to the 34 state universities (Mendoza 2015a). Instead, each institution has its own agreement with the federal government that determines the share of federal funding in the overall budget, with significant variations depending on the institutions' degree of bargaining power in the federal

---

[9] The name 'Mexico' is used to denote three different geographic areas— Mexico (the country), Mexico State (one of the country's 32 federated entities) and Mexico City (the capital, which, making things somewhat more confusing, became its own state as of January 2016).

Table 8.5 *Higher Education Age Group Participation by Income Quintile, 2000–2010, Only Undergraduate, TSU and Normal*

Income Quintile	Population 19–23 Years Old	Total Enrolment	% Coverage
2010			
Total	9,917,474	3,787,293	38.19
I	1,716,583	247,930	14.44
II	2,092,248	551,472	26.36
III	2,211,953	792,280	35.82
IV	2,395,955	1,018,490	42.51
V	1,500,735	1,177,121	78.44
2006			
Total	9,071,659	3,155,394	34.78
I	1,608,601	202,173	12.57
II	1,878,508	311,677	16.59
III	2,025,247	642,074	31.70
IV	2,170,512	1,021,861	47.08
V	1,388,791	977,609	70.39
2000			
Total	8,487,381	2,041,421	24.05
I	1,420,714	39,221	2.76
II	1,766,078	148,748	8.42
III	1,950,223	364,333	18.68
IV	1,836,393	527,157	28.71
V	1,513,973	961,962	63.54

Source: Estimates by the Subsecretaría de Educación Superior (SES), based on the National Household Survey of Income and Spending (ENIGH), 2000, 2006 and 2010.

congress as well as the particular moment in time in which the institu- tions first negotiated their funding structure. Once set, these agree- ments have proved difficult to modify, despite a series of short-term measures on the part of the federal government designed to minimize the inequalities.

For example, while some universities, such as the Autonomous University of Guerrero and the Autonomous Benito Juarez University of Oaxaca, depend almost entirely on federal funding for their budg- ets, others, such as the University of Guadalajara, receive a majority from their respective states (ExECUM 2016). Nevertheless, a majority receive a greater share of federal funding than state funds, a reliance that reflects the institutions' financial dependence on the federal government (Mendoza 2011). In general, the universities in poorer states rely more heavily on federal subsidies, although there are some exceptions, such as the Autonomous University of Nuevo Leon, which receives three times more from the federal government than from the state (ExECUM 2016), despite Nuevo Leon's role as the country's main industrial hub.

There are also considerable inequalities in the share of funding per student. In 2007, this figure varied more than threefold, depending on the institution, from 23,187 pesos (US$2,070 at 2007 exchange rates) at the Autonomous Benito Juarez University of Oaxaca to 70,658 pesos (US$6,300) at the Autonomous University of Yucatan. In gen- eral, the amount of funding corresponds directly with the economic situation of the respective state, although there are some exceptions, such as the University of Guadalajara, whose low share of spending is primarily a reflection of its large enrolment—with 103,000 students, it is the second largest public university in Mexico, surpassed only by the UNAM, with 217,000 students in 2013 (ExECUM 2016). Those differences not only have impacts on the teaching conditions but also on the capacity of the institutions to conduct research.

The decentralization of the higher education system starting in the 1990s sought to address such inequalities, through a series of compensatory funds for poorer states and institutions. One such fund was designed to increase per student spending at institutions that fell below the national average, with the largest such fund assigned during the government of Felipe Calderón (2007–2012). The programme resulted in significant funding increases at a majority of the targeted institutions. However, starting in 2009, the share of total contingent extraordinary funds has steadily decreased. In 2013, federal extraordinary funds represented 17 per cent of federal ordinary funding to the 34 state universities.

Such fluctuations have major implications for the capacity of state universities to plan their budgets and invest in long-term expansion. Similarly, while part of the funds are earmarked for increasing student enrolment and the construction of new facilities, there has been no corresponding increase in ordinary funding for the new campuses or centres (Mendoza 2015a). Finally, the universities' ability to secure extraordinary funding varies, as does the degree to which institutions depend on these resources. For example, in 2013, extraordinary funds represented 71 per cent of the ordinary budget of the University of Quintana Roo, equivalent to 41 per cent of the total institutional budget. In eight other universities, the funds represented between 31 per cent and 44 per cent of the ordinary funding. At the other end of the spectrum were the large state universities for which extraordinary funds were just 20 per cent of ordinary funds and 16 per cent of their total budgets.

Inequalities among faculty

A final area where federalization has yet to achieve equity is in terms of the country's scientific research system, which remains heavily centralized in the capital. In addition, a small share of researchers at top universities receive a majority of research funding, while many state universities and a majority of private ones—not to mention the technological sector and the teachers' colleges—conduct virtually no research.

One of the best indicators of the distribution of S&T capacities and investment in Mexico is the SNI. Members of the SNI represent a privileged and tiny minority of university professors—just 3.7 per cent of the 380,000 professors employed nationwide (ExECUM 2016). While the system also has members in private universities and research institutes, the vast majority of SNI members work in a handful of public universities, with three main universities in the capital accounting for nearly 30 per cent of the total (ExECUM 2016). The system has four levels, with bonuses (extra salaries) ranging from 5,906 pesos (US$450) to 27,561 pesos (US$2,090) per month in 2014 (Olivares 2014), meaning that SNI members often earn double the salary of non-members. The result is a highly stratified system of teachers and researchers, with the latter considered more valuable, and between academics at different types of institutions (Bensimon and Ordorika 2006; Ordorika 2004). The concentration of top-ranked SNI members (Level III) in the capital is noteworthy, as these academics command the largest share of research funding.

The country's scientific production in terms of articles and other documents published in internationally indexed journals is even more concentrated in the capital. Researchers based in Mexico City were responsible for publishing nearly half (48%) of all the Mexican documents indexed by the Thomson Reuters Web of Science in 2004, while the second closest state, Morelos, accounted for just 7.3 per cent of the total (ExECUM 2016). The concentration of international-level research in few institutions has implications for the government's stated goal of expanding and decentralizing Mexico's science and technology research capacities.

The heavy concentration of research centres in the federal capital and a few states also has implications for regional technological development. For example, two institutions—the National Petroleum Institute and the UNAM—have produced nearly half all the patents issued to HEIs in Mexico (ExECUM 2016).

FINAL COMMENTS

To understand the dynamics and organization of the country's higher education system, we have analysed the emergence, historical transformations and characteristics of Mexican federalism in order. In particular, we have assessed the extent to which higher education policies, funding, decision-making, administration and coverage are effectively decentralized to the subnational level.

Two centuries have passed since Mexico first adopted federalism as its form of government. During the nineteenth century, opposing

Table 8.6 Total SNI Members, SNI Level III, and Indexed Documents, by State, 2014

	Total		Level 3			Indexed Documents	
	No.	% National	No.	% National	% Inst.	No.	% Total
Mexico	21,358	100	1,842	100	8.6	11,946	100
Ciudad De Mexico	7,482	35	1,105	60	14.8	5,738	48
Estado De México	1,208	5.7	45	2.4	3.7	796	6.7
Jalisco	1,087	5.1	52	2.8	4.8	607	5.1
Morelos	946	4.4	111	6	11.7	869	7.3
Nuevo Leon	857	4	34	1.8	4	765	6.4
Puebla	799	3.7	62	3.4	7.8	707	5.9
Guanajuato	720	3.4	55	3	7.6	632	5.3
Baja California	661	3.1	58	3.1	8.8	583	4.9
Veracruz	631	3	27	1.5	4.3	585	4.9
Michoacán	626	2.9	42	2.3	6.7	511	4.3
Queretaro	549	2.6	50	2.7	9.1	501	4.2
San Luis Potosi	512	2.4	36	2	7	492	4.1
Yucatan	508	2.4	34	1.8	6.7	462	3.9
Sonora	454	2.1	17	0.9	3.7	323	2.7
Chihuahua	340	1.6	9	0.5	2.6	258	2.2
Sinaloa	339	1.6	6	0.3	1.8	221	1.8
Coahuila	298	1.4	8	0.4	2.7	299	2.5
Hidalgo	283	1.3	0	0	0	208	1.7
Chiapas	243	1.1	4	0.2	1.6	178	1.5
Oaxaca	242	1.1	5	0.3	2.1	194	1.6
Baja California Sur	228	1.1	18	1	7.9	132	1.1
Zacatecas	186	0.9	6	0.3	3.2	107	0.9

(Continued)

Table 8.6 *(Continued)*

	Total		Level 3			Indexed Documents	
	No.	% National	No.	% National	% Inst.	No.	% Total
Tamaulipas	178	0.8	2	0.1	1.1	172	1.4
Colima	175	0.8	4	0.2	2.3	113	0.9
Aguascalientes	138	0.6	2	0.1	1.4	87	0.7
Durango	138	0.6	5	0.3	3.6	150	1.3
Tabasco	130	0.6	2	0.1	1.5	110	0.9
Tlaxcala	128	0.6	4	0.2	3.1	96	0.8
Quintana Roo	127	0.6	3	0.2	2.4	126	1.1
Campeche	112	0.5	1	0.1	0.9	101	0.8
Nayarit	107	0.5	0	0	0	76	0.6
Guerrero	90	0.4	0	0	0	71	0.6

Source: ExECUM (2016).

political projects overtly challenged or promoted federalism. After the Mexican Revolution (1910–1917), the system was legally adopted and enshrined in the current Constitution. In spite of its legal standing and centrality in official political discourse, however, federalism has been hampered by the realities of an authoritarian political regime, *priismo*, which gained prevalence starting in the 1920s.

The weakening of authoritarianism since the 1970s, internal needs for political stability and economic growth as well as modernization policies aligned with international trends have given federalization attempts renewed political currency and administrative relevance. These trends have been strengthened by the new realities of party transitions and multiparty government at the state and national levels.

Federalism in Mexico is far from being a complete or unified reality. Beyond ideological depictions and political claims, it is possible to argue that during the last four decades, movements towards decentralization and federalism have been as strong as those seeking the preservation of authoritarian centralism or the recentralization of key sectors and structures. The contradictory dynamics between federalization and decentralization, on the one hand, and centralization and control, on the other, are a consequence of and shape the modernization of the authoritarian regime, as well as contemporary models for accumulation. These processes have become crucial to the establishment of new political arrangements and commitment to structural reforms (fiscal, oil and electricity and education, among others) between political parties across the spectrum, which have become institutionalized in the *Pacto por México*.

The tensions and contradictions surrounding federalization and centralization are evident in the case of Mexican higher education, in which deep-rooted inequalities and conflicts persist in the forms of funding, administration and the geographic distribution of institutions. The discourse of decentralization and diversification of higher education, prevalent since the 1980s, preceded the new emphasis on federalization starting in the late 1990s. In practice, outcomes have been contradictory.

On the one hand, the federal government has strengthened its control over HEIs and faculties. In 1980, university autonomy was raised to the constitutional level, as part of government efforts to impede the nationwide unionization of faculty and staff. A few years later, merit pay and incentive systems were introduced at the federal and institutional levels. These policies, which included centralized research funding through CONACYT and performance-based subsidies, were designed to reign in autonomous universities and an ill-coordinated conglomerate of tertiary institutions.

On the other hand, the government's decentralization and diversification policies have relied almost entirely on increasing enrolment in the private sector, during the 1990s, as well as the creation of two- and four-year public vocational institutions over the past two decades. Many of these private and public institutions were established in mid-sized urban areas, outside Mexico City and the state capitals. However, while decentralization and expansion have increased tertiary enrolment rates, diversification and privatization have reproduced inequalities among students. This is due to the stratified access to different types of tertiary education institutions, which vary greatly in terms of resources and the quality of teachers and programmes.

Recent government financing policies also reveal numerous contradictions and limitations in the federalization process. Total public expenditure on higher education increased 70 per cent in real terms from 2000 to 2016, while state-level participation has remained relatively constant at around 30 per cent of the total. Federal and state subsidies are still unevenly distributed geographically and by institutional type. Financial resources are heavily centralized in federal universities and to a minor extent in public state institutions (UPES), policies that cater to more affluent students in traditional universities in Mexico City and the state capitals. In addition, federal and state performance-based subsidies as well as faculty participation in national merit-pay programmes such as the SNI, further reinforce inequalities.

While Mexico's government continues to tout the merits of federalization in many spheres, including higher education, the reality is far more complex. Throughout this chapter, we have provided numerous examples of the contradictions and limits inherent to Mexico's brand of federalism in general, and with regard to higher education, in particular. Effects of these tensions between federalization and centralization on higher education can be summarized in three broad dimensions. First, despite the constitutional guarantees of university autonomy (as with state autonomy), the effective exercise of that right has waxed and waned depending on the policies of the federal government. Second, while state governments are playing an increasing role in creating new institutions outside the capital, a majority of those institutions fall under centralized control, as in the case of the technological institutions and the indigenous universities. Third, while the overall federal budget for higher education has increased dramatically in recent years, the federal government dictates spending priorities for a greater share of that funding than it did in the 1950s.

While the newly pluralistic political system has devolved significant power to the states—often by mere necessity, given the impossibility of ruling the opposition states from the centre, or out of political expediency—in many spheres the system remains highly centralized.

Major challenges also persist in terms of equity, both in overall access to higher education and in the types of educational offerings at the state and municipal levels, particularly in the poorer regions. Nonetheless, financing is only one piece of the federalization process, the success of which depends just as much on administrative capacity and political will. In developing countries such as Mexico, which are still in the process of democratic and institutional consolidation, such elements are in short supply.

REFERENCES

Acosta Silva, A. 2009. *Príncipes, burócratas y gerentes. El gobierno de las universidades públicas en México*. México City: ANUIES.

Andrade Díaz, G. E. 2011. 'La educación superior pública a distancia en México. Sus principales desafíos y alternativas en el siglo XXI'. *Reencuentro* 62: 20–29.

Asociación Nacional de Universidades e Instituciones de Educación Superior (ANUIES). 2014. *Anuario Estadístico 2013–2014*. Available at http://www.anuies. mx/iinformacion-y-servicios/informacion-estadistica-de-educacion-superior/ anuario-estadistico-de-educacion-superior

Arellano Ramos, E. 2012. 'Evaluación del Fondo de Aportaciones para la Educación Básica' (FAEB). *Journal of Economic Literature* 9 (26): 82–95.

Arnaut, A. 1994. 'La federalización de la educación básica y normal (1978)'. *Política y Gobierno* 1 (2): 237–274.

Auditoría Superior de la Federación. 2013, June. *Diagnóstico sobre la opacidad en el gasto federalizado*. Available at http://www.asf.gob.mx/uploads/56_Informes_ especiales_de_auditoria/Diagnostico_sobre_la_Opacidad_en_el_Gasto_ Federalizado_version_final.pdf

Bensimon, E. M., and Ordorika, I. 2006. 'Mexico's Estímulos: Faculty Compensation Based on Piecework'. In *The University, State, and Market: The Political Economy of Globalization in the Americas*, edited by R. A. Rhoads & C. A. Torres, 250–274. Palo Alto, CA: Stanford University Press.

Burgess, M. 2003. 'Federalism and Federation'. In *European Union Politics*, edited by M. Cini, 65–80. Oxford: Oxford University Press.

Carnoy, M., Santibañez, L., Maldonado, A., and Ordorika, I. 2002. 'Barreras de entrada a la educación superior y a oportunidades profesionales para la población indígena mexicana'. *Revista Latinoamericana de Estudios Educativos* 32 (3): 9–43.

Carpizo, J. 1978. *El presidencialismo mexicano*. México: Siglo Veintiuno Editores.

Centro de Estudios Espinosa Yglesias (CEEY). 2013. *El México del 2013: Hacia una reforma del federalismo fiscal*. Available at http://www.ceey.

org.mx/site/politicas-publicas/propuestas-politicas-publicas/mexico-2013-hacia-reforma-federalismo-fiscal

Centro de Estudios Sociales y de Opinión Pública (CESOP). 2013. *Medición de la pobreza por entidad federativa 2012.* Available at http://cesop.blogspot.mx/2013/08/medicion-de-la-pobreza-por-entidad.html

CONEVAL-INEGI. 2010, 2012 and 2014. *Encuesta Nacional de Ingresos y Gastos de Hogar (MSC-ENIGH).* CONEVAL-INEGI. Available at http://www.inegi.org.mx/est/contenidos/proyectos/encuestas/hogares/modulos/mcs/

Consejo Nacional de Ciencia y Tecnología (CONACYT). 2013. *Actividad de CONACYT por Entidad Federativa 2013. Morelos. Conacyt/Gobierno de México.* Available at http://www.conacyt.mx/siicyt/index.php/centros-de-investigacion-conacyt/actividad-de-conacyt-por-estado-1997-2013/actividad-conacyt-por-estado-2013/2370-morelos-2013/file

————. 2014, January 20. 'Firma de convenio entre el Conact y universidades particulares para fomentar el desarrollo científico y tecnológico de México'. Press release. Available at http://www.conacyt.mx/index.php/comunicacion/comunicados-prensa/293-firmade-convenio-entre-el-conacyt-y-universidades-particulares-para-fomentar-eldesarrollo-cientifico-y-tecnologico-de-mexico

Consejo Nacional de Población (CONAPO). *Proyecciones de Población 1190–2030.* Database. Available at http://www.conapo.gob.mx/es/CONAPO/Proyecciones_Datos

De la Garza Vizcaya, E. L. 2003. 'Las Universidades Politécnicas. Un nuevo modelo en el sistema de educación superior en México'. *Revista de la Educación Superior* 333 (126): 75–81.

Díaz-Cayeros, A. 2006. *Federalism, Fiscal Authority, and Centralization in Latin America.* Cambridge: Cambridge University Press.

ExECUM. 2016. *Explorador del Estudio Comparativo de Universidades Mexicanas.* Available at http://www.ExECUM.unam.mx/

Flamand, L. 2010. 'Sistema federal y autonomia de los gobiernos estatales: Avances y retrocesos'. In *Los grandes problemas de México. Políticas públicas,* edited by J. L. Méndez Vol. XIII, 495–522. Mexico City: Colegio de México.

Garrido, L. J. 1982. *El partido de la revolución institucionalizada (medio siglo de poder político en México): La formación del nuevo estado, 1928–1945.* México, D.F.: Siglo Veintiuno Editores.

Gibson, Eduard L. 2004. *Federalism and Democracy in Latin America.* Baltimore, MD: Johns Hopkins University Press.

Gobierno de México [Mexican government]. 1917. 'Constitución Política que los Estados Unidos Mexicanos, que reforma la de 5 de febrero de 1857'. *Diario Oficial,* 5 February. Available at http://www.diputados.gob.mx/LeyesBiblio/ref/cpeum/CPEUM_orig_05feb1917_ima.pdf

Harvey, D. 2005. *A Brief History of Neoliberalism.* Oxford: Oxford University Press.

Kramer, L. 1994. 'Understanding Federalism'. *Vanderbilt Law Review* 47: 1485–1561.

Lechner, N. 1997. *Las condiciones de gobernabilidad democrática en la América Latina de fin de siglo.* Buenos Aires: Flacso.

Majeed, A., Watts, R. L., and Brown, D. M., eds. 2006. *A Global Dialogue on Federalism: Distribution of Powers and Responsibilities in Federal Countries*, Vol. 2. Montreal and Kingston: McGill/Queen's University Press.

Marginson, S. 1997. *Markets in Education.* St. Leonards, N.S.W.: Allen & Unwin.

Marginson, S., and Considine, M. 2000. *The Enterprise University: Power, Governance, and Reinvention in Australia.* Cambridge, UK & New York, NY: Cambridge University Press.

Martínez Rizo, F. 2001. *La federalización de la educación superior en México. Alcances y limitaciones del proceso en la década de los años 90s.* Draft of book by the same name published in 2002 by the ANUIES. Available at http://www.fmrizo. net/fmrizo_pdfs/libros/L%2029%202002%20Federalizacion%20de%20la%20 ES%20en%20Mexico%20ANUIES.pdf

Mendoza Rojas, J. 2002. *Transición de la educación superior contemporánea en México: de la planeación al Estado evaluador.* México City: UNAM-Centro de Estudios Sobre la Universidad/M.A. Porrúa.

———. 2011. Financiamiento público de la educación superior en México: Fuentes de información y cifras del periodo 2000 a 2011. Cuadernos de Trabajo de la Dirección General de Evaluación Institucional, vol. 6. Mexico City: UNAM/DGEI.

———. 2012. Cobertura de educación superior en México. Power point presentation to the Sixth Inter-institutional Course 'Problems and Current Debates in Higher Education: International Perspectives' at the Institute for Economic Research, National Autonomous University of Mexico, 26 October. Available at http://www.ses.unam.mx/curso2012/pdf/Mendoza_M5S1.pdf

———. 2015a. *Una aproximación al análisis de los fondos de financiamiento extraordinario para las universidades públicas estatales. Cuadernos de Trabajo de la Dirección General de Evaluación Institucional*, Vol. 13. Mexico D.F.: UNAM/DGEI.

———. 2015b. 'Ampliación de la oferta de educación superior en México y creación de instituciones públicas en el periodo 2001–2012'. *Revista Iberoamericana de Educación Superior* 16 (6): 3–32.

México Evalúa. 2011. *10 puntos para entender el gasto educativo en México: Consideraciones sobre su eficacia.* Available at http://www.mexicoevalua.org/wp-content/uploads/2013/02/MEX_EVA-INHOUS-GASTO_EDU-LOW.pdf

Olivares Alonso, E. 2014. 'Destinará Conacyt 120 millones de pesos a académicos de 39 instituciones privadas'. *La Jornada*, 31 March.

———. 2015. 'Quedan 117 mil 29 aspirantes sin lugar para estudiar en la UNAM'. *La Jornada*, 30 March.

Ordorika, I. 2004. 'El mercado en la academia'. In *La academia en jaque: perspectivas políticas sobre la evaluación de la educación superior en México*, edited by I. Ordorika, 35–74. Mexico: UNAM-CRIM/Miguel Ángel Porrúa.

———. 2006. *La disputa por el campus: poder, política y autonomía en la UNAM.* México D.F.: UNAM-Centro de Estudios sobre la Universidad/ Plaza y Valdés Editores.

Ordorika, I. 2010. 'La autonomía universitaria: Una perspectiva política'. *Perfiles Educativos* 32 79–93.

Ordorika, I., and Rodríguez Gómez, R. 2012. 'Cobertura y estructura del Sistema Educativo Mexicano: problemática y propuestas'. In *Plan de diez años para desarrollar el Sistema Educativo Nacional*, edited by J. Narro Robles, J. Martuscelli Quintana and E. Bárzana García, 197–222. Mexico City: UNAM.

Ordorika, I., and Lloyd, M. 2015. 'Critical Theories of the State and Contest in Higher Education in the Globalized Era'. In *Critical Approaches to the Study of Higher Education: A Practical Introduction*, edited by A. Martínez-Alemán, E. Bensimon and B. Pusser, 130–152. Baltimore, MD: The Johns Hopkins University Press.

Organisation for Economic Coordination and Development (OECD). 2015. *Education at a Glance 2015*. OECD Indicators. Available at http://www.oecd-ilibrary.org/education/education-at-a-glance-2015/indicator-b2-what-proportion-of-national-wealth-is-spent-on-education_eag-2015-18-en

Peña Nieto, E. 2015. *Tercer informe de gobierno 2014–2015*. Anexo estadístico. Mexico City: Presidencia, Gobierno de Los Estados Unidos Mexicanos.

Perotti, R. 1996. 'Growth, Income Distribution and Democracy: What the Data Say. *Journal of Economic Growth* 1 (2): 149–187.

Programa para las Naciones Unidas para el Desarrollo (PNUD). 2015. *Índice de Desarrollo Humano para las entidades federativas*. México 2015: Avance continuo, diferencias persistentes. Available in http://www.mx.undp.org/content/mexico/es/home/library/poverty/indice-de-desarrollo-humano-para-las-entidades-federativas–mexi.html

Reyes Tépach, M. 2004. *Las Convenciones Nacionales Fiscales y Hacendaria de 1925, 1933, 1947, and 2004*. Mexico City: Mexican Chamber of Deputies.

———. (2014). *Distribución de los flujos de participaciones y de aportaciones federales de México, 2000–2014*. Available at http://www.diputados.gob.mx/sedia/sia/se/Inv_Part_y_Aport_2014/AANACIONAL_28_33.pdf

Rhoades, G. L. 1998. *Managed Professionals: Unionized Faculty and Restructuring Academic Labor*. Albany, NY: State University of New York Press.

Riker, W. 1964. *Federalism: Origin, Operation, Significance*. Toronto: Little, Brown & Co.

Rodríguez-Gómez, R. 2002. 'Continuidad y cambio de las políticas de educación superior'. *Revista Mexicana de Investigación Educativa* 7(14): 133–154.

———. 2007. Higher Education Decentralizes. *Federations* (June/July): 21–23.

———. 2009. 'La coordinación de sistemas universitarios en la transición federalista. Panorama internacional y el caso de México'. In *Memorias de la Universidad: Otras perspectivas para una nueva Ley de Educación Superior*, edited by M. Mollis, 161–188. Buenos Aires: Ediciones del Centro Cultural de Cooperación Floreal Gorini/CLACSO.

Rodríguez-Gómez, R. 2012. 'El lado oscuro del PRONABES'. *Campus Milenio* 455: 7–8.

Rodríguez-Gómez, R. (2014). 'Educación superior y transiciones políticas en México'. *Revista de la Educación Superior* 43: 9–36.

Rodríguez Gómez, R., and Ordorika, I. 2012. 'The chameleon´s agenda: Entrepreneurial adaptation of private higher education in Mexico'. In *Universities and the Public Sphere: Knowledge Creation and State Building in the Era of Globalization*, edited by B. Pusser, K. Kempner, S. Marginson, and I. Ordorika, 219–241. New York, NY: Routledge.

Secretaría de Educación Pública (SEP). 2014. *Sistema educativo de los Estados Unidos Mexicanos. Principales Cifras 2013–2014*. Mexico City: SEP.

———— (2016). Serie Histórica de Matrícula. Database.

SIBEN/SEP. 2015. *Sistema de Información Básica de la Educación Normal (SIBEN), Secretaría de Educación Pública (SEP)*. Available at http://www.siben.sep.gob.mx/

Slaughter, S., and Leslie, L. L. 1997. *Academic Capitalism: Politics, Policies, and the Entrepreneurial University*. Baltimore, MD: Johns Hopkins University Press.

Universia. 2014, June 6. *Menos del 2% de la población indígena ingresa a la educación superior*. Available at http://noticias.universia.net.mx/vida-universitaria/noticia/2014/06/1098394/menos-2-poblacion-indigena-ingresa-educacion-superior.html

Valencia Carmona, S. 2003. 'En torno al federalismo mexicano'. In *Estudios sobre federalismo, justicia, democracia y derechos humanos*, edited by A. M. Hernández and D. Valadés, 359–380. Mexico City: UNAM/Instituto de Investigaciones Jurídicas.

Vázquez, J. Z. 1993. 'Un viejo tema: El federalismo y el centralismo'. *Historia Mexicana* 42: 621–631.

Villa Lever, L. 2013. 'Modernización de la educación superior, alternancia política y desigualdad en México'. *Revista de la Educación Superior* 42 (67): 81–103.

Watts, R. L. 2010. 'Comparative Reflections on Federalism and Democracy'. In *Federal Democracies*, edited by M. Burgess and A. Gagnon, 335–346. London: Routledge.

World Bank. 2012. *Strengthening Subnational Public Finance*. Mexico Policy Note 10. Available at http://www.worldbank.org/content/dam/Worldbank/document/Policy%20Note%2010_0118.pdf

————. 2015. *World Bank Indicators*. Available at http://data.worldbank.org/indicator

Chapter 9

The Russian Federation
Pragmatic Centralism in a Large and Heterogeneous Country

Isak Froumin and Oleg Leshukov

INTRODUCTION
A Centralized Country

Higher education system in the Russian Federation is one of the most centralized in the world. The federal government controls and in large degree directly manages 91 per cent of all public universities in the country. The Russian Federal Ministry of Education and Science (MoES) is the world leader in the number of higher education institutions (HEIs) under its direct jurisdiction—274 in total.

This is a result of the long history of highly centralized Russian governance. The complex and heterogeneous range of 85 Russian regions reflects a history of inclusion of new regions, and even countries, throughout the formation of the Russian and Soviet state. Russia is a federation that emerged from an empire which was a unitary state. Its power distribution model is favourable to the national authorities and is primarily defined by the central government.

The central authorities in Russia have always tried to use the federal structure to increase the efficiency and effectiveness of the state as a whole. They have been able to modify the rights and obligations of the regions and their legal relationships with the central state in order to get better results in particular sectors of social and economic life. This is why the term pragmatic federalism (Hollander and Patapan 2007) suggested by Australian higher education researchers could well be applied to the Russian higher education system too.

The Chapter

This chapter begins with a description of the main features of Russian federalism that affect the higher education sector. It argues that the Russian state has always tried to achieve three often-conflicting objectives—to preserve the unity of the state, to support regional economic development and to ensure targeted support for the development of selected parts of the country's vast territory (Decree of President 1996). This section also highlights the heterogeneous structure of the Russian Federation, where different types of regions have different capacities with regard to education and culture. These unique features of the Soviet and Russian state have had profound importance for the development of higher education.

The second and third sections of the chapter discuss the history of Russian higher education in the context of federal relationships. Russian higher education has a history over 300 years in length. From the very beginning, the establishment of new universities and control over their operation was the responsibility of the central government. At the same time, the central authorities experimented with various different ways of involving the regional authorities in the governance and operation of the higher education system. In each period, the role of the regional authorities reflected the specific objectives of higher education within the context of nationwide social and economic development. The search for new models of federal–regional interaction in higher education was particularly active after the collapse of the Soviet Union.

The fourth and fifth sections of the chapter describe the current regulatory, structural and financial aspects of national–regional relationships in higher education. These reveal a unique level of centralism in the governance of higher education and the lack of regional government involvement in university development.

The sixth section of the chapter discusses how centralism in national–regional relationships in higher education affects the achieving of such objectives of pragmatic federalism as the active and balanced development of regional higher education systems. It shows that inter-regional differences are growing.

The final section of the chapter discusses the trends in federal–regional relationships in higher education in the search for an optimal higher education governance model in the context of a large and heterogeneous country undergoing political, cultural, economic and geopolitical transformations. It suggests possible approaches to the development of these relationships.

FEDERALISM IN THE RUSSIAN FEDERATION

The Russian Federation is the largest (by territory) country in the world, encompassing 11 time zones. The administrative structure of such a large territory is complex. There are three main levels of governance: the state comprises two levels of governance—federal (national) and regional authorities (analogues of US states, German *Länder*, Canadian provinces, etc.). The third separate level of govern-ance is represented by the municipal authorities. This level is not *de jure* considered part of the state, but rather a form of local administration representing the people's self-government.

The federal structure of Russia includes 85 Federation subjects (enti-ties)—which we will refer to as regions.[1] According to Article 5 of the Constitution, 'in relations with federal bodies of state authority all the subjects of the Russian Federation shall be equal among themselves'.

The following *administrative* or *legal* types of regions exist in the current version of the Constitution:

- *Republic* (22 regions). Unlike other regions, republics have a name that reflects the particular ethnic group ('titular nation') that his-torically populated the territory. The republics have the right to

---

[1] Including Crimea and Sevastopol; further analyses will include these regions where data is available.

establish their own constitution (which may not contradict the federal constitution) and designate additional (to Russian) national languages.

- *Province/oblast* (46 regions). The most numerous and typical type of administrative units.
- *Territory/krai* (9 regions). There are currently no real legal differences between territories and provinces. The different name is a legacy of the Soviet model of federalism, when the territories included special 'ethnic' districts.
- *Cities of federal significance* (3 regions—Moscow, St. Petersburg and Sevastopol). Their status represents the social, economic and cultural significance of these particular cities for the country's development, and they are endowed with the same powers as territories and provinces.
- *Autonomous province* (1 region—the Jewish Autonomous Province, established by Stalin in 1934 in the Far East of Russia as an attempt to give the Jews an autonomous territory). It has the right to adopt local basic law (analogous to the republic constitutions).
- *Autonomous district/okrug* (4 regions). These have the right to adopt special laws reflecting the specific role of the particular ethnic group that historically populated the territory. These regions were historically associated with adjoining *krai* territories.

This variety of legal types of regions can be reduced to two main groups—the 'ethnic' regions (27) and other regions (58). The main difference between these types of regions is the legal capability to protect linguistic and cultural heritage. In some 'ethnic' regions, the proportion of representatives of the 'titular nation' within the total population of the region is less than 1 per cent, while in others it is more than 85 per cent. The population inhabiting regions that can be marked as 'ethno-regions' (Treyvish 2009, 369) makes up more than 15 per cent of the country's total population. This means that the Russian Federation exhibits the features of asymmetric federalism (Watts 2005). As we shall discuss, this legal asymmetry does not play a major role in higher education development. Other differences are more important. We shall come back to the issue of the regional heterogeneity later in this section.

The basic features of modern federalism were inherited from the Soviet period. The Soviet Russian state—the 'Russian Soviet Federative Socialist Republic'—emerged from the ruins of the Russian Empire and was defined as a federation in order to emphasize the ideological shift from imperial control (Lenin had called the Russian Empire a 'prison of nations') to a system wherein the different people had voluntarily joined together. This federation inherited the complex nature of the former empire's provinces, including both provinces with an ethnic Russian majority ('old Russia') and territories (countries) acquired by the empire during its expansion. The Soviet Union was established by the Union Treaty of 1922, signed by the Russian Federation, Ukraine, Byelorussia and the Caucasian Federation.

The sheer size of the country and its regional heterogeneity (ethnic, economic and cultural) were, from the first days of the Russian Soviet Federation, considered risks to the unified development of the state. Formal structure of the Soviet Russian state was federative. There were central government, national parliament and Supreme Court. At the same time, the local population elected representative authorities (councils) in each region that appointed the highest executives. This presented a certain risk to the power of the centre. To mitigate this, the Communist Party became highly centralized, ensuring that central policy was implemented at the lower levels of government. The charter of the Communist Party included the principle of democratic centralism, assuming that the decisions of the higher authorities are obligatory for the lower bodies (CCC, CPSU 1939). Leaders of the regional Communist party committees were real bosses. Thus, the Soviet Russian state was a federation according to a number of formal features but was in reality characterized by an extremely high level of centralization of power and a rigidly hierarchical management structure (Gaman-Golutvina 2015, 752).

The Russian Soviet Federative Socialist Republic was the only republic of the Soviet Union to be proclaimed, by the Constitution of the USSR in 1936, as a federation in itself. There were a number of discussions about the possible nature of the Russian state after the collapse of the Soviet Union in 1991. Some voices called for the institutionalization of the idea of a unitary state where the regions would not have significant legal autonomy or mutual asymmetry. The complex political process resulted in the compromise reflected in the Constitution of 1993. The federative structure of Soviet Russia survived. At the same time, the Russian state became a presidential republic with very strong power in the hands of the president.

The young Russian state searched for the right implementation of its constitutional federal principles since the collapse of the Soviet Union in 1991. The transformation of federal–regional relationships went through three main stages (Valentey 2012, 57). Each stage is characterized by its specific distribution of power between federal and regional authorities, and by different tax regimes.

The main feature of the first period of the development of the Russian federalism (1991 to the early 2000s) is the growth of differentiations between regions and, in some cases, the strengthening of regional power. Often this period is called the 'war of sovereignties', in which (Valentey 2012, 57):

- the constitutions and laws of many regions contradicted federal legislation;
- several regions (mainly republics) appropriated additional powers without ensuring that adequate financial capabilities were in place;
- some regions conducted special popular votes regarding their legal sovereignty; and
- the titular nations in the 'ethnic' regions gained special rights and privileges.

During this period, regional leaders (governors) were elected by the regional populations, without the approval of the federal centre. This was key in the new regional autonomy.

At the same time, the federal government did not restrain, but actually encouraged the ambitions of a number of regions (especially republics) regarding the arbitrary expansion of their powers. 'Take as much sovereignty as you can swallow', President Yeltsin's famous quote. This led to the expansion of the bilateral negotiations and contractual process between the federation and its regions. Obviously, such practices increased asymmetry within the Federation. This system of 'asymmetric' federalism led to a situation in which those regions with the greatest ability to make trouble for Moscow received the best fiscal deals (de Figueiredo and Weingast 2002; Solnick 1995; Treisman 1999).

This first stage of the development of federalism in modern Russia can be interpreted from the perspective of the theory of cooperative federalism (Elazar 1991). Cooperative federalism can be distinguished by a special type of cooperation between national and regional governments. The model lacks administrative hierarchy or pressure from higher levels. The centre and the periphery interact through negotiations, which turn governance into a shared function that is distributed among all decision-makers. Certain features of this model can be found in Germany (see U. Teichler's chapter in this book). The cooperative approach led to growing differences of regional policies and governance structures, and in the level of regional economic performance and development. In some regions, it also led to the growth of separatist movements, including the war in Chechnya (Pain 2003).

The central government increasingly perceived these trends as a threat to the integrity of the country. It initiated legal actions and policy changes that marked the second period of the development of Russian federalism (the 2000s to the beginning of 2010)—the concentration of power and resources at the federal level.

In 2000, the federal districts as special level of state administration and positions of Plenipotentiary Representatives in the federal districts were established by Presidential Decree 'to ensure implementation of the President of the Russian Federation's constitutional powers'. The role of the representatives was 'to discipline' the regional authorities.

In 2001, the aforementioned bilateral agreements were deemed illegitimate. A clear mechanism for the distribution and execution of powers between the federal and regional levels was introduced through a set of new laws. These marked the transition to a symmetric model of centre–periphery relations, according to which the regions were put on equal terms with one another in their rights when interacting with the federation. The key legal document that strengthened the role of the federal centre was the 'Federal Concept for Increasing the Efficiency of Intergovernmental Relations and Improving Subnational Finance

Management' (2005). This document significantly ensured that regional authorities follow the new strict federal regulations on subnational fiscal relations (De Silva et al. 2009).

Another important action was the 2004 abolition of elections for regional leaders and the introduction of procedures for their appointment directly by the President. The regions came under the full control of the federal government and had weak incentives to choose their own development models. The rigid governors' performance monitoring was implemented to keep the governors tightly accountable to the centre—not to 'their' regional population. There were no indicators of the performance related to higher education in this monitoring.

Besides the objective of strengthening the integrity of the country, the central government aimed to foster more balanced development between different regions, initiating a number of so-called 'national projects'. National projects were countrywide programmes in areas such as health care, housing and communal services, road construction and education, including the establishment of a group of strong universities outside Moscow and Petersburg (so-called 'federal universities' that will be discussed in details later in the chapter). These projects manifested a more active role of central government in the social development of the regions. At the same time, it promoted passivity and paternalistic behaviour on behalf of regional leaders.

The third stage of development of the federal–regional relationships (from 2010 to the present) is associated with the search for a new model of federalism that would force the regions to be proactive in their development, while maintaining a high level of the control from the centre.

The reinstating of the system of electing governors provides a good example of this transformation. Popular elections were reintroduced but they were restricted by special filtering mechanisms that favour candidates loyal to the central authorities. Another example of the new approach was the introduction of transparent competitive mechanisms to distribute 'federal development grants' between the regions (instead of directly imposing uniform development models on all regions). This led to growing differences between the regions in economic performance and living standards.

The government continues to maintain tight control over regional incomes and continues to concentrate financial resources in the centre. Major taxes—value added tax and customs duties—have been transferred completely to the federal budget. Together, these taxes generate 46 per cent of tax revenues for the general consolidated budget of the Russian Federation. In the Russian Tax Code, the regions only administer the transport tax, property taxes and the tax on the gambling industry. The distribution of tax revenues between the federal and regional budgets is shown in Figure 9.1.

The share of regional taxes in the consolidated budget of the Russian Federation is extremely low. The basic tax revenues of the regional budgets are accounted by federal taxes—personal and corporate income tax (Table 9.1).[2] The federal tax authority administrates these taxes, and regions cannot change them. That being so, all revenues from personal income tax are transferred to the regional budget (Figure 9.1). This means, in fact, that any changes in the regions' fiscal policy have little effect on their financial condition.

Increased centralization of federal fiscal power is clearly demonstrated in Figure 9.2.

It is interesting that in 1997 (during the aforementioned 'war of sovereignties'), about 30 per cent of regions had a positive financial balance with federal budgets. The number of such 'donor regions' (budgetary self-sufficient) dropped from 18 in 2000 to 13 in 2010 (about 15 per cent of all regions), although these regions continued to generate more than 52 per cent of GDP. The majority of the fiscal surplus regions of the Federation are those where oil and gas production dominates the economy. Only these regions can afford 'modernization experiments' that might include reforms in research and development and in higher education.

This historical analysis confirms that, during the 25 years since the collapse of the Soviet Union, Russia has experimented with different

---

[2] Personal income tax (13%) is a tax levied on the income (salary plus additional sources of income, such as renting, deposit income, etc.) of individuals. Corporate income tax is a tax on company profits (20%).

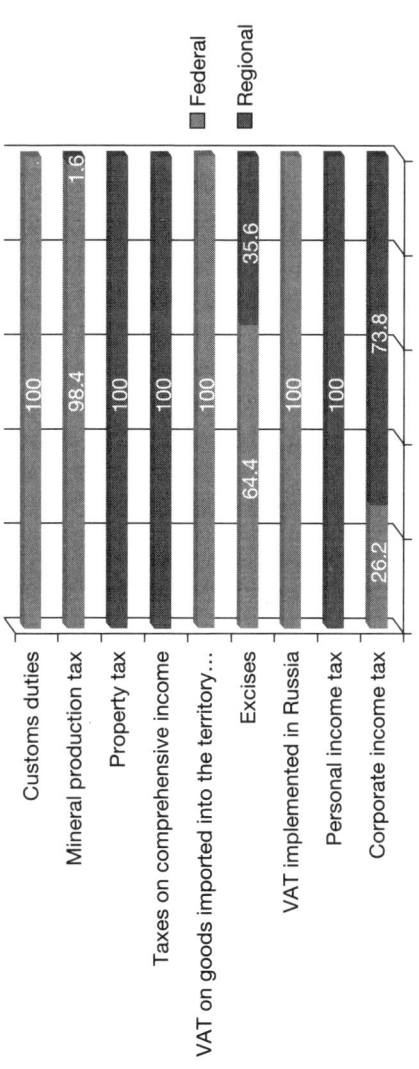

Figure 9.1 *The Structure of Tax Revenues by Levels of the Budget System, 2015*
Source: Ministry of Finance.

Table 9.1 *The Structure of Tax Revenues for the Consolidated Budgets of the Regions of the Russian Federation, 1 March 2014 (%)*

Personal Income Tax	39.5
Corporate Income Tax	30.7
Property Tax	10.8
Excises	7.5
Mineral Production Tax	0.7
Other Tax Revenues	10.8

Source: Ministry of Finance.

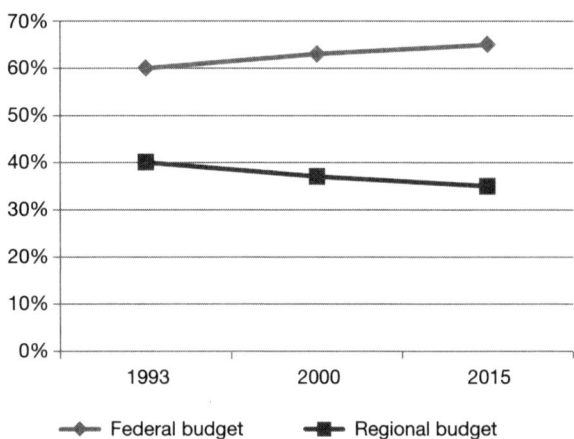

Figure 9.2 *Federal and Regional Budgets as a Share of the Consolidated Budget*

Source: Sadkov (2007) and authors' calculations.

models of federal–regional relations to find the right balance between the following three objectives:

1. The preservation of the unity and integrity of the state (social, economic, administrative and political)
2. Creating conditions for self-sufficient economic development of the regions

3. Targeted development (modernization) of some backward parts of the country

The problem is that these three objectives often contradict one another. If Russia chose to focus on the second objective, it would build market-preserving federalism (de Figueiredo and Weingast 2002). The framework of market-preserving federalism includes four main elements: (a) subnational governments have primary regulatory authority over their economy; (b) the existence of a common market—absence of restrictions for different higher education consumers; (c) hard budget constraints in the fiscal system; and (d) institutional protection of the federal arrangement. Market-preserving federal systems are likely to exhibit competition among subnational governments that enables them to foster good economic results.

The attempts of the central authorities to combine the principles of market-preserving federalism, while retaining the 'one-size-fits-all' policy for the regions, have created what Slider (1997) called 'market-distorting' federalism. Regulatory and fiscal regulation of national–regional relationships impedes regional development, including that of higher education as part of the public sector. Russia has suffered significant losses due to Moscow's attempts to keep strong political and fiscal control over the regions. This has led to a striking lack of cooperation between the centre and the regions, yielding considerable losses in social surplus (de Figueiredo and Weingast 2002; Zhuravskaya 2010).

Following the definition suggested by Hollander and Patapan (2007) for Australia, the Russian model of federalism could also be called 'pragmatic'. This model of federal–regional relationships is not a stable agreement between the subjects of the federation but a governance mechanism chosen by the central government. Pragmatic federalism is considered here as *ad hoc* direct resolution of particular national problems in the context of specific policy agendas. Pragmatic federalism is problem-driven in a particular period of government development and does not especially require the strengthening of the powers of the centre—depending rather on the most effective way of solving the problem.

As a result of the implementation of the pragmatic federalism model aimed to three mentioned objectives, there has been no significant reduction in the heterogeneity of the Russian regions. The Russian regions vary significantly not just in their legal type but also in their geographical and demographic characteristics. They are also very different in levels of social and economic development (see Table 9A.1). A total 36 per cent of the population lives in the central and southern parts of the country, covering only 14 per cent of the territory of the Russian Federation. The two largest Russian regions—Krasnoyarsk Krai and Yakutiya—occupy 32 per cent of the country's territory, although their population is just 2.6 per cent of the whole. The differences in terms of density (population per square kilometre) between the most populated regions of the Central Federal District and the regions of the Far Eastern Federal District are very large.

The big issue is differentiation of economic potential. The City of Moscow and Tyumen Region (Russia's main oil-producing region) combined produce 35 per cent of the total GDP of the country. The data shows that the differentiation by gross regional product per capita can reach more than 65 times between different regions. Disparities in terms of the Gini coefficient of per capita income and the level of poverty (Zubarevich 2009) have not changed much during the last few years. They exist because the model of income redistribution does not have a significant positive influence on regional equalization.

THE RUSSIAN HIGHER EDUCATION SYSTEM

Russia inherited a well-developed and highly centralized system of public HEIs from the Soviet Union. This section of the chapter describes the transformed system—its structure, accessibility, funding and regulatory framework.

By 2012, this system had not changed much in structural terms since 1939 (Kouzminov, Semyonov and Froumin 2013). Only 15 per cent of the new public universities were established between 1939 and 2012. Most Soviet universities were (at least formally) highly specialized in a particular sector of economy. By 2012, most remained specialized (even after opening low-quality programmes in management and social sciences) as universities of medical sciences or transport and agricultural universities.

Four major developments since the collapse of the Soviet Union have been (a) the possibility for public HIEs to open new vacancies for fee-paying students; (b) the emergence and rapid growth (in the mid-1990s) of private universities; (c) Russia joining the Bologna process and replacing the traditional five-year specialist training with a two-tier degree system; and (d) introduction of the national university entrance exam, allowing prospective students to apply to a number of universities.

While the third and the fourth reform significantly increased opportunities for student mobility, the first and the second gave a strong impulse to *increase access* to achieve a great expansion of higher education opportunities in both public and private institutions. All four major reforms led to greater vertical differentiation of the national higher education landscape.

At present, there are 950 HEIs in the Russian Federation, 548 of which are public (see Figure 9.3). This figure also shows that, during recent years, the number of universities has decreased due to demographic decline and government-pushed mergers of public universities.

High demand for higher education also encouraged universities (both public and private) to open branches in different locations, in order to bring the services closer to potential customers. The branch is a full-scale university (usually small in student numbers) that operates under the brand name of its parent university. Branches have limited autonomy, they have to get a separate state license and undergo state accreditation. A total of 1,319 branches operated in Russia in 2014 (843 of which were public and 476 private).

The branches helped moderate the inequality in the territorial distribution of universities (Table 9A.1). Twenty-three per cent of all universities in the country are located in Moscow. In contrast, a mere 4 per cent of universities are situated in the nine Far Eastern Russian regions. The higher education systems in two regions consist of several branches and do not include any independent institutions.

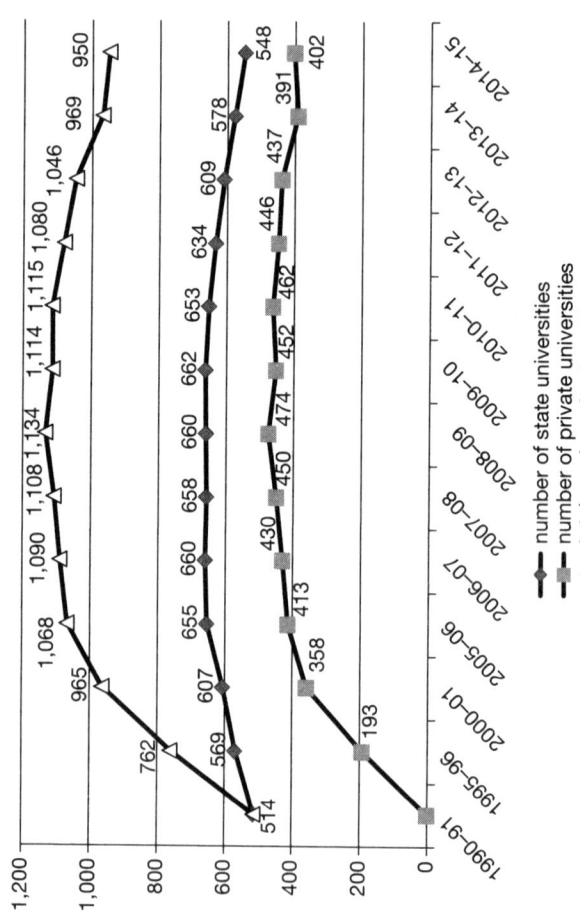

Figure 9.3 *The Total Number of HEIs in Russia*

Source: Federal State Statistics Service.

Growth of enrolment in both public and private universities is demonstrated in Figure 9.4. The variety of programmes and prices could satisfy almost any demand. The proportion of students in the 17–22 years age cohort has reached 84 per cent (Nikolaev and Chugunov 2012, 85). By the number of higher education students per 10,000 population, Russia ranked second in the world in 2010 (Klyachko 2011). Combining these figures with students of vocational colleges (tertiary level), the Russian higher education system stands among the world leaders, with 585 students per 10,000 population (2013–2014). The number of first-year students is now greater than the number of school leavers, and this gap is increasing. This is due to changes in the structure of the student contingent entering universities. It is influenced by the growing demand for higher education from other groups. Many people were studying to get a second or even third higher education diploma. Many graduates of two- and three-year colleges have also entered the HEIs. In 2014, the total enrolment to HEIs was 5.2 million,

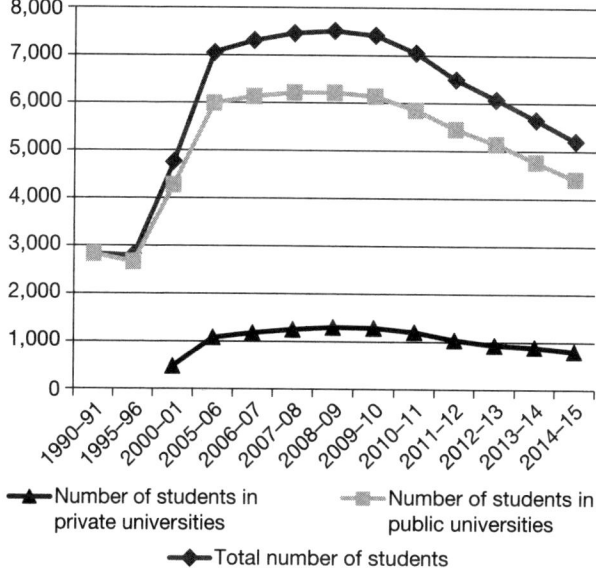

Figure 9.4 *The Total Number of Students at HEIs*

Source: Federal State Statistics Service (2015).

of which 803,500 were enrolled in private institutions. The decline in enrolment from 2009 onward could be explained by the decreasing demographic base. The number of school graduates declined by 45 per cent from 2005 to 2010.

An important feature of the Russian higher education system is the high proportion of part-time students. In 2014, only 50 per cent of the total number of students were enrolled in full-time programmes. The remaining 2.6 million were studying in part-time educational programmes, enabling them to work full-time.

In accordance with Article 43 of the Constitution of the Russian Federation, citizens have the right to a free vocational education and a free first time higher education (through the competitive admission process). However, the rapid expansion of higher education has not imposed much burden on the public budget. Currently, on average, 45 per cent of students in public universities are studying at their own expense. The share of budget financing in the total funding of the higher education system dropped from 100 per cent in 1990 to 58 per cent in 2014 (Table 9.2).

At the end of this section, it is important to highlight the issue of university autonomy. In accordance with the Law on Education, universities' relations with the state should be guided by the principle of autonomy, academic rights and the freedoms of teachers and students. However, the real impact of the federal government on the activities of

Table 9.2 *Sources and Scale of Higher Education Financing*

	2010 (%)	2011 (%)	2012 (%)	2013 (%)	2014 (%)
Budget Financing of HE Sector	53.5	55.1	56.0	56.3	57.7
Non-Budgetary Financing of HE Sector	46.5	44.9	44.0	43.7	42.3
Public Spending on Higher Education (Expenses on Education)	20	19	18	18	17

Source: Federal State Statistics Service.

universities remains significant. Requirements of common federal state educational standards, rectors' appointment procedures, national-level state accreditation and licensing, and stringent conditions for expenditure and financial management are just some examples of external authorities' direct control over the operation of universities. However, the federal involvement mostly is limited by control rather than strategic influence. Public universities do not enjoy strong supervision of their strategic development at the national level. It could be explained in a simple way—the direct guiding the strategic development of hundreds of universities is an impossible mission for the national level bureaucracy. At the same time, the alternative governance structures that allow the involvement of local authorities and business into the strategic development of universities (e.g., governing boards in the Western sense) do not exist yet.

THE TRANSFORMATION OF NATIONAL–REGIONAL RELATIONSHIPS IN HIGHER EDUCATION IN THE RUSSIAN FEDERATION

Higher education, along with all the other social sectors in the Soviet Union, was regarded as a part of the unified public economic system. In essence, HEIs were manpower producers for various sectors of the Soviet economy (Froumin and Leshukov 2015). The major features of the design of the Soviet higher education system were specialization, targeted spatial location and manpower planning, and job placement. The mechanisms of specialization included a narrow curriculum and subordination of universities to sectoral ministries. Late in the Soviet period, in 1988, the USSR had 896 HEIs under the jurisdiction of over 70 government agencies.

The special Soviet Central Planning Authority created strict rules for defining HEIs' specialization, size and location. For example, there were rules regulated the rights of the regions to have comprehensive university or conservatory. Some types of HEIs—for instance, teacher training institutes—were created in every region in order to meet the local demands for certain professionals. Other HEIs—cultural and arts institutions, for example—served multiple regions officially assigned for the job placement of their graduates (Kouzminov et al. 2013). Universities for sciences and humanities (comprehensive universities), in turn, were located in the largest cities and the capitals of all 'ethnic' regions. Highly specialized universities were established near big enterprises and operated in close connection with 'parent' plants, maximizing the integration of production processes and training a secured cycle of employee preparation for particular workplaces. Graduates were assigned to particular jobs by the state, and this allowed the government to concentrate universities in certain regions even if there was no adequate demand from the local labour market. After leaving school, a prospective student could move away from home in order to enter a university and later on, after graduation, could be sent to work in another city. Centralized student job placements made it almost redundant for most HEIs to take into account the specific features and demands of their own region's economy and labour market. For example, in the 1930s, Moscow experienced a surge in the number of engineering HEIs (such as the water transport institute, mining institute, etc.), even though the city lacked the jobs needed to employ the graduates of these institutions. After completing their studies, they received work assignments that required them to move to other city that had an appropriate job opening.

The planned nature of the national economy also led to an underrepresentation of the regional development agenda in higher education policy (Kinelev 1993). The spatial aspect of the higher education development system adjusted to issues of the economic and administrative development of the whole country, rather than individual regions (Katrovsky 2003, 200). Centralization was further supported by hierarchical relationships within the networks of specialized universities. Selected universities in the capital cities were officially assigned to provide quality assurance and staff development support to universities with similar specialization in the regions (Kouzminov et al. 2013).

Some researchers suggest that no local initiative in higher education was tolerated (Kuhns 2011). There is evidence, however, that local (regional) committees of the ruling Communist Party provided some links between nationally subordinated universities situated in a particular region and certain regional needs. This was particularly evident in 'ethnic' regions where the regional party authorities considered universities as a tool for building ethnic elites and fostering cultural development (Hrenov 1974).

The socialist regime dictated that all regional and local authorities faithfully follow the directions and policy of the national government in accordance with the principle of democratic centralism. The Soviet higher education governance model was to some degree effective for the Soviet type of economy and society, but it largely neglected the importance of local activism on behalf of HEIs, effectively turning the system into a passive tool of the state economy and political agenda (Dneprov 2011).

After the Soviet Union's collapse, HEIs on the territory of the Russian Federation, including a majority of the Soviet Union's sectoral institutions, were claimed as the property of the Federation and in December 1991. Most of them became subordinates of the MoES. Other stayed under the sectoral ministries (major regulatory framework including curriculum development and quality assurance remained under the control of the MoES).

Education reformers claimed that the main directions of changes in the early post-Soviet period were 'decentralization and democratization of governance and the delegation of greater autonomy to HEIs and their regional associations' (Kinelev 1993). This intention led to a greater openness from the federal authorities towards regional initiatives in higher education.

Many agreements between the centre and regions during the 'war of sovereignties' (see second section) included provisions for regional higher education development programmes and responsibility sharing between the region and the centre for federally controlled HEIs.

From 1992 until 1996, the regions were granted the right to license new HEIs. Before the year 2000, more than 40 public universities had been established by the regional authorities in less than a third of the regions. In some cases, the federal government transferred HEIs or their parts to the regional jurisdiction. This led to the creation of a new layer within the higher education system. Some regions were allowed to spend a portion of their tax revenue on funding higher education. The strengthening of fiscal federalism in the years to come would put an end to all these financial opportunities. In this period, it was mostly the wealthier regions that had the opportunity to open their own universities (e.g., oil-producing Tyumen Region). Also during this period, departments for the supervision of higher education were created within some regional governments.

During this stage of federation construction, the HEIs that had been established under the Soviet government had to adapt to a completely new environment. They were forced to act quickly to adjust to the economy's rapid shift to a market-based system of labour allocation, to a decline of public funding for higher education caused by a deep and long economic recession and to the necessity to raise revenues through fee-based services.

The disappearance of the countrywide graduate placement system inevitably led to a sudden 'regionalization' of the education system. Graduates did not have to go to other regions for assigned jobs. This meant that HEIs lost their nationwide labour market context. In order to survive, they were forced to look for ways to establish stronger economic connections with the regions (Katrovsky 2003, 200). They also had to work with local school systems and to market themselves locally to get more fee-paying students. The central authorities did not interfere much with revenue-generating activities, and the regional authorities did not have any right to regulate these activities. The universities therefore won more autonomy and flexibility. In these conditions, the higher education system became even more diverse (Bain 2003), while some HEIs found themselves in isolation, unable to adapt to the new social and economic demands of the regions (Leshukov and Lisyutkin 2014). The expansion of branches is a good example. It was not the initiative of the central government. Market forces drove universities to talk to the regional or municipal authorities to get their support for opening the branches.

The government also outlined a draft for a new policy aimed at strengthening the regionalization of higher education (Bain 2003). This effort aimed at aligning higher education with the needs of local labour markets. The main rationale behind this attempted reform was the challenging social and economic environment of the time. It was assumed that the regions' financial contribution would ease the burden on the federal budget. From the regions' perspective, this was supposed to make them more accountable and flexible to the needs of their educational institutions (Bain 2003). The drafted legislation suggested that the regional governments finance higher education, and that the central government would only fund the education of specialists deemed necessary by the federal government (Jones 1994). University rectors and the academic community in the regions were sceptical that the regions alone had the prospect of supporting universities. They threatened the central government that the regionalization of higher education would lead to the cultural and political disintegration of the country (Bain 2003). Resistance was strong, and this attempt at reform failed.

As a result, the regionalization process affected only secondary vocational education institutions. These required far less budget expenditure, enabling the regions to take responsibility for their funding. The subordination of almost all colleges and technical schools was transferred from the national to regional authorities. The reform gave the regions an incentive to restructure the system and to make it more relevant to the local labour market. The universities survived this attempt at regionalization. This is a good illustration of pragmatic federalism where the federal centre allocates regional competencies based on the considerations of the national social and economic development agenda and the unity of the country.

The early 2000s were characterized by a trend to restore state or federal power over the public sphere (including higher education) that it had lost in the 1990s (Johnson 2008). It was part of a 'compensatory legitimation' agenda (Weiler 1983). The federal government was attempting to regain authority and influence by controlling the provision of public goods (Kuhns 2011). The discussion about the growing influence of the regional authorities on HEIs essentially came to an end.

NATIONAL-REGIONAL RELATIONSHIPS IN HIGHER EDUCATION IN THE RUSSIAN FEDERATION: THE REGULATORY AND STRUCTURAL ASPECTS

When speaking of the regional system of higher education, we refer to the range of public universities (federal, regional and municipal), private universities and branches of public and private universities situated in the regions. The compositions of these systems and their scale depend on the earlier history of the development of HEIs in each region and economic and geographical factors. The scale varies dramatically from region to region. In this section, we discuss these differences and the regulatory frameworks for different types of universities—public regional, private and public national.

Regulatory Aspects

The Russian Constitution of 1993 only defines the overall framework of joint responsibilities between the centre and regions regarding educational provision, without any specifics for higher education. In contrast, many other federal countries have constitutionally established the power of the regions to manage higher education.

The basic legislative act for higher education governance is the Federal Law of the Russian Federation dated 29 December 2012 No. 273-FZ 'On Education in the Russian Federation' (henceforth—the Law on Education). In accordance with this law, chief responsibilities for higher education relegated to the Federal authorities are as follows:

- Establishing, reorganizing and closing universities
- Accreditation, licensing and control over universities and educational programmes
- Basic financing of HEIs, including provision of state guarantees of the right to free higher education on a competitive basis
- Development of educational standards, etc.

The main managerial functions at the national level are distributed among several agencies. The MoES of the Russian Federation carries out the general management of the universities; develops and implements the national policy, including financial policy and legal regulation; and sets education standards and provides financial and methodological support for the institutions' activities. Sector-specific ministries are responsible for the development of their subordinate universities, financing their activities, and supporting and controlling educational standards and requirements. The Federal Supervision Service for Education and Science performs the functions of controlling and supervising HEIs and responding to issues of accreditation and licensing of educational institutions (Froumin and Leshukov 2015).

The regions have the right—not actually explicit in the new Law—to create and finance their own regional universities. At the same time, the regional authorities have several other legal channels to influence federal and private HIEs within their territories (Froumin and Leshukov 2015). Most of these channels were created relatively recently (during the third development period of federal–regional relationships) when the federal authorities realized that they could not effectively manage hundreds of universities. These other legal channels include the following:

- Influencing the appointment of university presidents through lobbying on the federal level
- Providing regional approval for the central government's allocation of 'free' student places funded from the federal budget
- Appointing regional representatives on the supervisory boards of the universities
- Contracting federal universities to train additional students and to do research and development (about 30% of the regions have such contracts with federal universities)
- Transferring region-owned properties (buildings) to universities
- Creating special agencies or departments within regional governments to supervise higher education (about 20% of the regions have such agencies)[3]
- The possibility for targeted financing of HEI with special status of 'federal universities' (to be described in further later) from the regional budget
- Some federal higher education development programmes envisage co-financing of their initiatives by regional authorities

Structural Aspects

The ratio of *regional* (subordinated to the regional authorities) to federal (national) universities has remained almost unchanged over the past 20

---

[3] Our analysis suggests that these regions have stronger engagement with the universities than the regions that do not have such agencies. Notably, the Moscow City Government does not have a department to coordinate or supervise the activities of the approximately 300 public and private universities in its region.

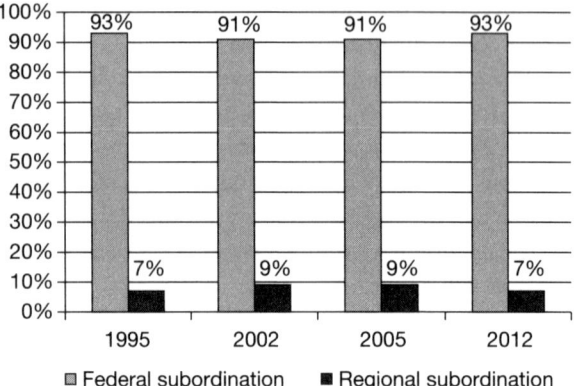

Figure 9.5 *The Number of HEIs Controlled by Federal and Regional Authorities*

Source: Federal State Statistics Service.

years (see Figure 9.5). In 2014, only around 9 per cent of all public universities (49 HEIs) were controlled by regional authorities. These universities had to pass national accreditation in order to award degrees recognized countrywide. They also have to follow federal law on higher education. However, they are fully dependent financially on the regional authorities. They also have to demonstrate a positive impact on the region's economic and social development in order to survive. Of all the regional universities, 20 per cent are of arts that reflect the cultural identity and needs of their particular region.

Private universities are regulated on the federal level. Public and private universities have equal rights according to the Law on Education and have to follow the uniform requirements of the federal state educational standards. The government influences private education through accreditation and licensing as well as by setting a rule that the price paid by students for commercial places cannot be lower than the state pays for a budget place on the same programme. This allows the sector to protect against dumping prices and selling diplomas. At the same time, the mission of the majority of private institutions is 'demand absorption'. From the very beginning, they were considered a kind of 'employment agency for young people saving them from being unemployed and falling into criminal structures' (Ilyinsky 2004). This led to a situation wherein the vast majority of private universities concentrated on economics, management and the humanities. There is no common pattern for relationships between private universities and the regional authorities. In most cases, the regional authorities do not care about the private institutions—they consider them part of the service sector. In some cases, former regional leaders or their relatives have created these institutions. In these circumstances, the private universities could become an important part of the regional higher education system. In general, one can conclude that the potential of private higher education for the regional development has not yet been fully explored.

The structural policy (institutional landscape) of the *Russian public universities system* has played a critical role in federal–regional relationships in higher education. This includes three aspects—subordination of universities to different national-level authorities; branches of universities; and vertical stratification of universities.

The Soviet legacy of industry-oriented governance in higher education continues to exist. There are 24 national executive authorities that finance and control public HEIs. The distribution of universities according to their subordination is presented in Table 9.3.

It is clear from Table 9.3 that, in addition to the issue of effective vertical cooperation between the centre and regional powers, it is important to keep in mind the issue of the horizontal coordination between different agencies of the central government (Froumin and Leshukov 2015). Sectoral federal agencies have managed to keep 'their' universities despite many attempts by the MoES and Ministry of Finance to put all national universities under the direct control of one ministry. Such a distribution of national universities, inherited from the Soviet past, creates considerable inconsistencies and conflicts within the higher education system (Kouzminov et al. 2013). It also leads to the precedence of the needs of particular industries over the needs of the general population.

The territorial (geographic) inequality and inconsistency in the distribution of HEIs stimulated the creation of a wide network of branches of universities, as mentioned in the third section. For many remote

Table 9.3 *The Distribution of HEIs (Without Branches) by Controlling Agency (2014–2015)*

Department	Number of HEIs	Percentage of Total Number of HEIs (%)	Share of Total Number of Students (%)
Regional (and Municipal) Authorities	59[a]	11	3
Ministry of Education and Science	274	51	69
Ministry of Agriculture	55	10	9
Ministry of Health and Social Development	46	9	5
Ministry of Culture	45	8	2
Ministry of Sport	14	3	1
Ministry of Railway Transport	9	2	3
Others (Including Defence, Security, Customs, etc.)	121	6	8

Source: The monitoring of HEIs efficiency, organized by the Ministry of Education and Science of the Russian Federation (http://indicators.miccedu.ru/monitoring/).

Note: [a]Including 10 municipal higher education institutions—municipal authorities do not constitute a direct part of the state system. They are directly responsible to their local voters.

regions with a lack of universities, the branches have solved the access problem. The current total number of students at such branches is 17 per cent of the total number of students. The majority of students in the branches pay their tuition fees. The number of part-time students exceeds 50 per cent in 90 per cent of university branches. The federal authorities found that many branches became just revenue-generating machines for the parent university and started to employ licensing and accreditation instruments to close these branches. During the period 2008–2015, the total number of branches fell by over 20 per cent. Currently, the regional authorities play a more important role in the process of the closing the branches. If a governor confirms the importance of a branch in ensuring access to higher education, it can remain in operation.

The first structural reform aimed at creating a leading group of universities consisted of two parts—creating the group of the so-called 'federal universities' and creating the group of the so-called 'national research universities'. The objective of the 'federal universities' project was the creation of strong centres of higher education and research in provincial cities in each geographical part of Russia—the South, Siberia, the Far East, etc. Such universities were to become globally competitive research universities and, at the same time, drivers of regional (macro-regional) economic, social and cultural development. They were supposed to keep the best students in the regions and to break the trend for depopulation of the northern and eastern parts of the country. Ten 'federal universities' were created within this programme through merging the existing institutions (from two to five) found in a single city in a given region. These universities were not selected competitively. At the same time, they were granted additional autonomy and awarded huge development grants by the central government. One of the conditions was that they received significant co-financing from the regional authorities. The Supervisory Boards of regional federal universities included high-level officials from Moscow, regional governors and representatives of big business.

Thus, according to the pragmatic federalism model, the central state chose a path leading towards educational regionalization, but retained a highly centralized management system and federal control. The results of the programme are ambiguous. On the one hand, these universities developed closer links with their regional economy, improving the quality of incoming students and research outputs; on the other hand, the majority of them are still not really competitive in comparison with the leading research universities in Moscow and St. Petersburg (Froumin and Povalko 2014). This project showed that it is difficult to achieve both objectives—research excellence and regional relevance—in a short period. This lesson helped to design the second structural reform project differently.

The government tried to transform a group of Russian universities into globally competitive research universities using the 'global research university model' (Mohrman, Ma and Baker 2008). This task proved very difficult due to the long-standing Soviet tradition of separating higher education and research, concentrated in the Academy of Sciences. In 2009 and 2010, 29 universities won a competition to acquire the status of national research universities and receive special grants. The regional authorities were not involved in this project. As a result, it did not have a serious impact on federal–regional relationships in higher education.

The next stage of the project changed the attitude of the regions. In 2012, 14 of the 'national research universities' won a new competition conducted by the MoES to get special grants to improve their global competitiveness, with the aim of filling five positions in the top 100 universities rankings by 2020—this project was called the 'Russian Excellence Initiative' or 'Project 5-100'. In 2015, seven more universities were added to this group.

The regional authorities noticed that such universities could bring talents and money to their regions. Many governors lobbied for 'their' universities during the competition. As a result, such universities, even with relatively low capacity, appeared in 13 regions. The distribution of such universities is shown in Figure 9.6.

At the same time, the global orientation of this project means that the immediate linkages between these universities and local economic and social systems are becoming even weaker.

One could say that the regulatory and structural policies of the Russian government lead to the strengthening of the role of the centre in higher education. Higher education has become more rather than less centralized under pragmatic federalism, weakening the role of the regions. Even the 'federal universities', designed to become drivers of regional development, were established and managed by a central ministry.

Figure 9.6 *The Location of Universities Participating in the Russian Excellence Initiative*

Source: Prepared by authors based on information of the Ministry of Education and Science of the Russian Federation.

NATIONAL-REGIONAL RELATIONSHIPS IN HIGHER EDUCATION IN THE RUSSIAN FEDERATION: THE FINANCIAL ASPECTS

As previously mentioned, 58 per cent of the income of the higher education system comes from the public budget, and 96 per cent of these public funds come from the federal budget (Figure 9.7).

The reason behind this low level of participation of the regions in funding higher education is the lack of regions with sufficient revenues. As we discussed, 72 of the 85 regions are subsidized by the federal government. It is strictly prohibited to spend the subsidies on higher education. The regions are thus forced to look for alternative ways to finance the local universities when they want to include the higher education sector in their economic development plans (Kuhns 2011). These features of fiscal federalism therefore provide no incentives for regions to put their money into universities. Furthermore, the presence of universities financed solely from the federal budget is, primarily from an economic viewpoint, advantageous for regional governments (Leshukov and Borisova 2014). The regions compete with each other to receive more federal and private money for their higher education systems. The amounts obtained depend on the number of student places allocated to each university, funding for construction and equipment and specially targeted grants for the leading universities. The main part of federal funding comes to the HEIs through per-student allocation. The formula for such per-student allocation recently was established (in 2014). It is relatively clear (the amount depends on the area of training, coefficient for the category of the institution, and form of instruction, part-time or full-time). However, the number of places in different programmes is defined by the MoES without substantial analysis and involvement of the regions. The regional governments and universities have an incentive to increase the requests for student places regardless of the real labour market demand for graduates. This leads to universities not actively analysing regional labour markets to bring their educational programmes in alignment with them (Kuhns 2011). The regional authorities bargain with the federal centre on the allocation of this funding. The current distribution of federal funding for higher education depends on Soviet Era decisions on university location and the bargaining power of the present-day governors.

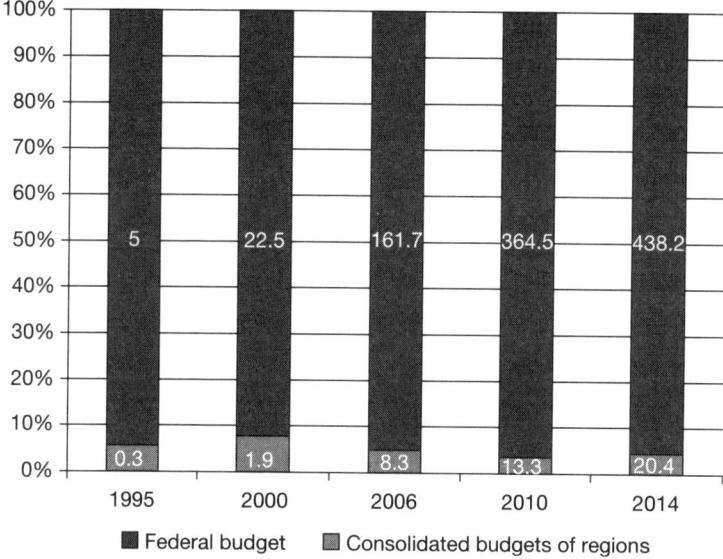

Figure 9.7 *The Total Funding of Higher Education System from Public Sources (in Billion Roubles)*

Source: Federal State Statistics Service.

The distribution of per student funding from the federal budget to the regions demonstrates significant asymmetry in the financial subsidies of universities of different regions (Figure 9.8, X axis).

Such disparities may be caused by the different economic contexts of the regions. For example, the cost of living and economic potential varies considerably in different regions. We therefore compared indicators of regional funding of higher education systems per student with parameters of regional economic potential measured by gross regional product per capita adjusted by the regional consumer price index (Y axis)—see Figure 9.7.

Figure 9.8 suggests that even when we adjust GRP for the regional price index, there is high heterogeneity in federal funding for regional higher education systems. The regions in Quadrant I have low financial capacity for higher education because they receive low funding per student adjusted for higher cost of living. In contrast, several regions

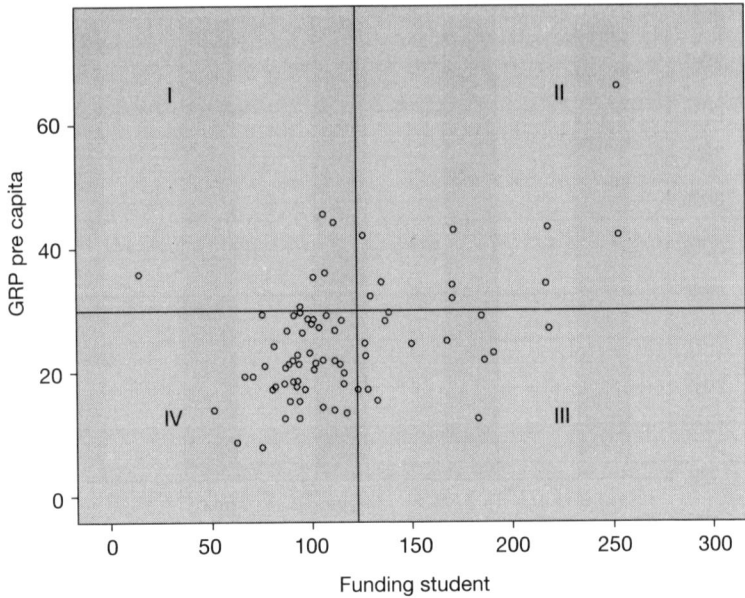

Figure 9.8 *Average Funding per Student in the Region (Thousands of Roubles) and the Index of GRP per Capita Adjusted by Regional Consumer Prices, 2011*[a]

Source: Federal State Statistics Service.

Note: [a]Statistical outliers were excluded from the calculation.

of the third quadrant have relatively high levels of funding. On average, the more prosperous regions attract more federal funding for the higher education sector. In fact, the federal government provides special support for the most advanced regional systems of higher education. In 2015, the leading and largest 12 per cent of universities received 42.5 per cent of the total budget funding from various funding sources of the MoES.[4] These universities are concentrated in less than 20 per cent of Russian regions. In contrast, the universities from 15 regions of the Russian Federation (about 20% of the regions with universities) have not received any development grants from the federal centre during the last 10 years.

---

[4] Calculations of experts from the Institute of Education of HSE.

However, the current financing system of universities is changing. In particular, differences of regional resource sufficiency and economic potential are being considered in the allocation of federal subsidies to universities. According to a recent federal regulation, the norms of public funding of universities include territorial correction coefficients measured by average wage level in the region. These territorial coefficients take values ranging from 1 to 4.147.

Despite the intention of pragmatic federalism to develop all regions more or less uniformly, the federal policy of financing higher education is not consistent with this objective. Rather, it has primarily been aimed at supporting certain leading universities located in a small number of regions.

IMPACT OF NATIONAL-REGIONAL RELATIONSHIPS ON HIGHER EDUCATION

In this section, we discuss how the federal policy in higher education works to achieve one of the most important objectives of pragmatic federalism in higher education—balanced regional development and the equal provision of basic social services in different regions. We shall look at educational migration (interregional mobility), access to higher education and the competition between universities.

Federal policy aimed at strengthening the attractiveness of the regions for young talent. What is the impact of the federal–regional relationships on the achieving this objective? Unfortunately, Russian regional higher education systems lack data on *education migration* after students enter the first year of university. That is why our analysis of education migration does not include graduate programmes. It is based on the regional ratio of the number of high school graduates to the number of those who entered HEIs. This approach could be considered valid because of the aforementioned almost universalization of higher education in Russia. A value greater than 1 (Figure 9.9) means that the region has a positive balance of migration and attracts high school graduates from other regions. Data shows that no more than 13 per cent of the regions attract students from other regions, that is, that they show a surplus of university freshmen on full-time programmes

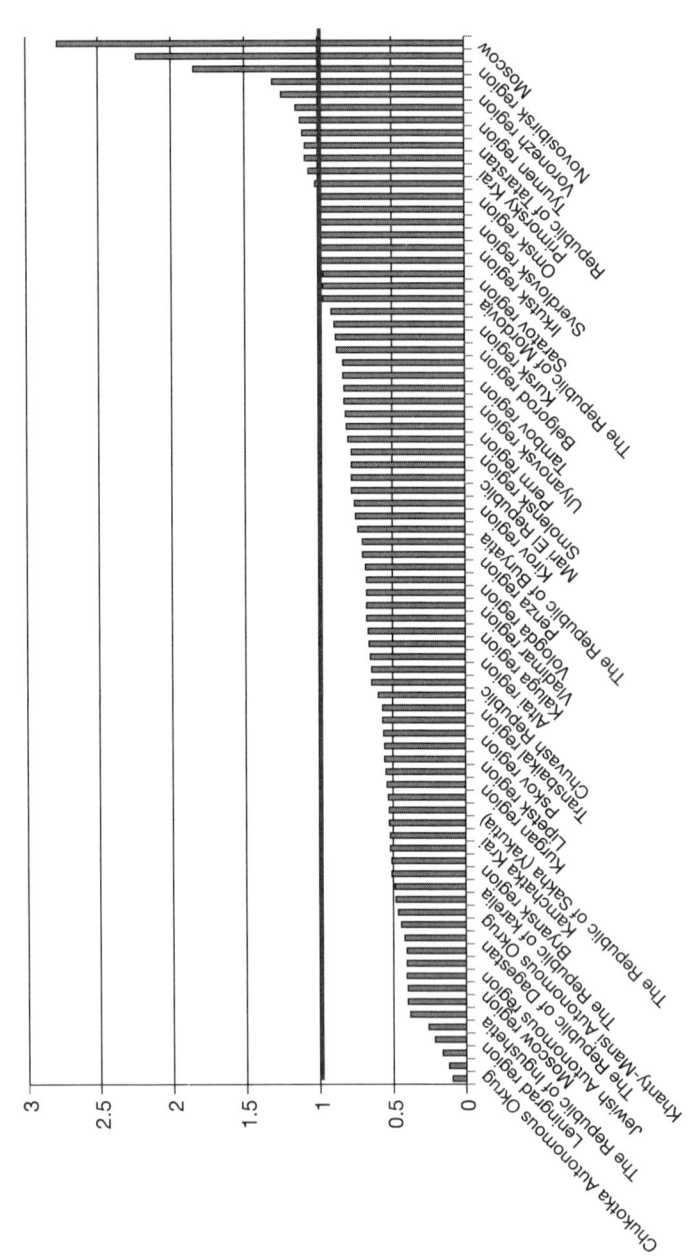

Figure 9.9 *Russia: Level of Interregional Higher Education Migration, 2013*

Source: Federal State Statistics Service, 2013.

relative to the number of high school graduates planning to continue their education at the university (Leshukov and Lisyutkin 2014).

The data demonstrates a low level of educational migration and actually indicate the territorial 'closedness' (Andruschak, Novikov and Pavlyutkin 2010) of the regional higher education systems in their borders. The current model of higher education governance does not contribute to the development of educational mobility through the creation of an open competitive environment among universities seeking students. It facilitates the outflow of young talent from the overwhelming majority of regions.

How has pragmatic federalism influenced *access to higher education* in different regions? As stated here, Russia has undergone rapid massification of higher education since the collapse of the Soviet Union. The national average level of access to higher education estimated by the number of students per 10,000 population was 356 in 2014. However, regional differences in this indicator among the regions are quite significant (for example, 606 for Tomsk versus 95 for Chukotka).

Another indicator of access is the proportion of youths aged 17–25 years in higher education programmes (free and fees-based). For Russia, this indicator is 33 per cent—one of the highest in the world. The disparities between the leading regions and the outsiders are also high (see Figure 9.10), reaching as much as an eleven fold difference.

These facts show that Russia has achieved a very high average level of access to higher education. At the same time, interregional differences can be very high.

We do not have data to estimate access to higher education for socially disadvantaged students. However, we could estimate the access to higher education depending on geographic factors. The question of whether students from remote regions of Russia have real opportunities for studying at university becomes very important in strategic planning of regional development.

One of the possible indicators of geographical access to higher education could be a minimum distance from the district centres located in the region to the nearest town with a university or a university branch

Figure 9.10 *The Level of Higher Education Access (Equity) by Regions*

Source: Federal State Statistics Service, 2014.

within the region, averaged over all the district centres of the region (Gromov et al. 2016).

The regions of Siberia and the Far East have serious problems with geographical access (the average distance to universities towns there is about 300 km, compared with a figure of about 50 km in the central regions). The federal authorities do not pay any attention to these interregional differences. The problem looks solved by the provision of fee-paying distance higher education. However, geographical access to full-time programmes remains very uneven.

One of the important reasons for growing differentiation in access to higher education among the regions is that of uneven demographic trends in the regions. The system as a whole is expecting a sharp decline in student population. Student enrolment forecasts (Figure 9.11) show the largest decline in the student body will come in the 2021–2022 academic year—a drop of over 35 per cent relative to the highest level in 2008–2009. This trend, however, is not the same for all regions. There are no federal instruments to adjust the capacity of the regional higher education systems according to demographic trends. This is a good example of pragmatic federalism not working to equalize access to higher education. One might consider the idea of introducing various regional norms for access to higher education. However, this idea at least deserves to be discussed and reflected in the federal educational policy.

At the end of this section, we will try to combine different indicators of heterogeneity for the regional systems of higher education into a coherent typology of these systems. We used such indicators as the level of competitiveness in the regional higher education market, the level of attractiveness of regional higher education systems (educational migration balance) and the distribution of students attending different types of universities in the region (research universities, specialized universities, etc.). Based on a cluster analysis technique, we identified several types of regional higher education system. Detailed explanations of the methods have been published in (Leshukov and Lisyutkin 2014). Here we consider the more generalized types; these are as follows:

1. *Metropolitan higher education systems (Moscow and Moscow Region, St. Petersburg and Leningrad Region).* These regions have the highest

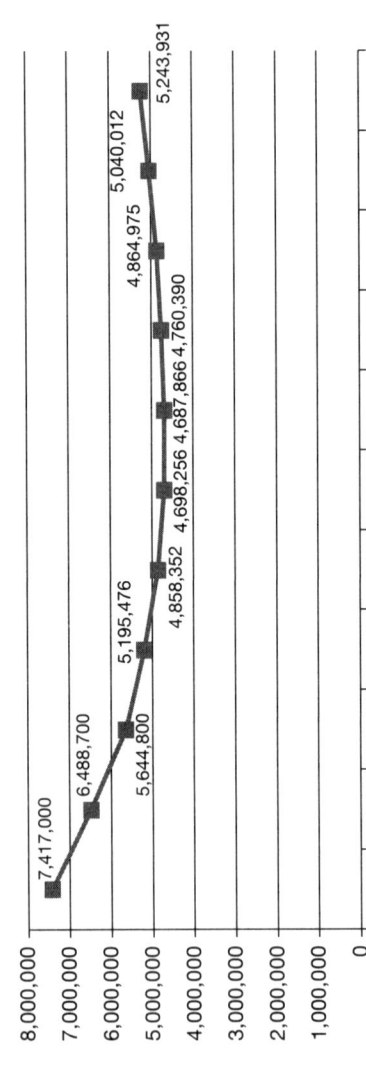

Figure 9.11 *Forecast of the Number of HEI Students*

Source: Calculated by the authors. Data from Population in Russia 2015.

concentration of educational and research organization, and they attract talented students from all over the country and from abroad. They include the majority of globally oriented universities of the country. The highest density of universities engenders a high level of competitive environment. In addition, the leading position of these regional systems of higher education is supported by the much higher standards of living of these metropolitan areas.

2. *Developed regional systems of higher education (the regions of Tomsk, Novosibirsk, Sverdlovsk, Nizhny Novgorod, etc.).* Historically, these regions (about 15–20% of the total number of regional higher education systems) have been developed as centres of military and heavy industries. They had very developed networks of applied research and development institutes and centres of the Russian Academy of Sciences. These regions are still attractive on a national scale. They pull in the talented students of the neighbouring regions. There is high competition among the HEIs located in each of these regions.

3. *Balanced and sustainable regional higher education system (Republic of Bashkortostan, Krasnodar Territory, Omsk Region, etc.).* The majority of these regional higher education systems (more than 50% of the total number of regional higher education systems) are oriented to the basic manpower needs of the regional economy. The main entrants to these universities are graduates of high schools in these regions, and inflow of students is almost absent. At the same time, these systems include different types of universities (classical, sectoral, technological, etc.) that produce some intraregional competition.

4. *Weak regional higher education systems (the regions of the Amur, Sakhalin, Magadan, etc.).* This type (about 20–25% of the total number of regional higher education systems) is characterized by mass low-cost higher education. Most of the HEIs in these regions fall into the category of low-quality education according to the monitoring of HEIs organized by the MoES of the Russian Federation. These regional systems are highly monopolized and unattractive for high school dropouts, as evidenced by high rates of student outflow. Most of these regions are in underdeveloped territories of the country. The low level of social and economic development of these regions complicates the development of higher education.

The allocation of the regional higher education systems within this typology suggests that pragmatic federalism in higher education does not help to create vibrant and strong higher education systems in the majority of regions. It can be explained by the inability of the federal centre to act *ad hoc*, solving new problems of higher education sector. The national system of higher education is so huge and diverse that managing it *in real time* is impossible.

TRENDS OF DEVELOPMENT OF HIGHER EDUCATION FEDERALISM IN THE RUSSIAN FEDERATION

As has been shown, the Russian higher education system is highly centralized, although this centralism does not ignore regional needs and interests. Moreover, one of the reasons behind this pragmatic centralization is to ensure the active and balanced development of higher education in the regions. However, as was shown in the previous section, the differentiation of the regions in terms of the development of higher education systems is very high. We could observe that it is higher than in Soviet times. There are some mechanisms for the regions to influence the development of their higher education systems. Paradoxically, all these mechanisms were created by the federal government: They are not the result of initiatives from the regions themselves. The regional governments as a rule have no incentives to be active in the field of higher education and have no responsibility for this sector. Even during radical changes in the way society and the economy are organized, the system of national–regional interaction in higher education governance still remains almost untouched.

The problem is that the Russian model of pragmatic federalism responds mainly to the objective of maintaining the political and economic unity of the country. It partially responds to the objective of targeted development of some regions and barely responds at all to the goal of facilitating competition among regions and facilitating their economic development.

Even when national higher education policy does focus on the role of higher education in regional social and economic development, it acts blindly, using a 'one-size-fits-all' principle, and *ad hoc*, avoiding long-term vision and strategy.

The role of decentralization of public services in increasing overall efficiency of the public sector has been shown in a number of international studies (Lobo et al. 1995). But Russia still has not found the appropriate way to decentralize control over its higher education system to give more rights and responsibilities to the regions.

Some recent reform attempts show that the Russian government continues its search for the best implementation of the ideas of pragmatic federalism. In 2014, the MoES started the project aimed at establishing 100 regionally oriented 'flagship' universities, oriented on the facilitation of social and economic development in the regions. Moreover, many regional governments are already taking a proactive role and providing all negotiations between the interested parties of the project (universities, the federal ministry, and main regional employers). It can therefore be expected that regional influence on the development of higher education will increase, but the high level of centralization needed for adaptation of the public sector to pragmatic federalism remains at the core of these reforms.

REFERENCES

Andruschak, G. V., Novikov, A. V., and Pavlyutkin, I. V. 2010. Regionalny atlas ekonomiki vysshego obrazovaniya (pokazately rynka) [Regional atlas of higher education economy (market data)], 80. M.-Yoshkar-Ola: Poligraficheskoye Predpriyatiye Centr Print [Center Print Printing Enterprise] OJSC.

Bain, O. 2003. *University Autonomy in the Russian Federation Since Perestroika*. New York, NY: RoutledgeFalmer.

Commission of the Central Committee of the Communist Party of the Soviet Union (CCCCPSU). 1939. *History of the Communist Party of the Soviet Union (Bolsheviks)*. New York, NY: International Publishers.

de Figueiredo, R. J. P., and Weingast, B. R. 2002. *Pathologies of Federalism, Russian Style: Political Institutions and Economic Transition*. Available at http://faculty.haas.berkeley.edu/rui/mpfrussia.pdf

De Silva, M. O., Kurlyandskaya, G., Andreeva, E., and Golovanova, N. 2009. *Intergovernmental Reforms in the Russian Federation: One Step Forward, Two Steps Back? Directions in Development; Public Sector Governance*. Washington, DC: World Bank.

Decree of President. 1996. 'On Basic regulations of Regional Policy in the Russian Federation'. N 803. 3 June. Government of Russian.

Dneprov, E. 2011. *Noveishaya politicheskaja istorija rossijskogo obrazovanija: opyt i uroki*. [Contemporary Political History of Russian Education: Experience and Lessons]. Moscow Marios, 456.

Elazar, D. J. 1991. 'Cooperative Federalism', In *Competition Among States and Local Governments: Efficiency and Equity in American Federalism*, edited by D. A. Kenyon and L. Kincaid, 65–86. Washington, DC: Urban Institute Press.

Froumin, I., and Leshukov, O. 2015. 'National–Regional Relationships in Federal Higher Education Systems: The Case of Russian Federation'. *Higher education forum Hiroshima University* 12: 77–94.

Froumin, I., and Povalko, A. 2014. 'Top Down Push for Excellence: Lesson from Russia'. In *How World-class Universities Affect Global Higher Education. Influences and Responses*, Vol. 30, 47–64. Boston, Rotterdam, Taipei: Sense Publishers, P.

Gaman-Golutvina. 2015. *Comparative Politology*. Musco: Aspect Press Publishing.

Gromov, A., Platonov, D., Semyonov, D., and Pyurova, T. 2016. Dostupnost' vysshego obrazovaniya v regionah Rossii: kompleksnyy analiz [Accessibility higher education in the Russian regions: comprehensive analysis]. Series 'Modern Analytics Education', N8. Musco: Institute of Education, National Research University Higher School of Economics.

Hollander, R., and Patapan, H. 2007. 'Pragmatic Federalism: Australian Federalism from Hawke to Howard'. *Australian Journal of Public Administration* 66 (3): 280–297.

Hrenov, N. I. 1974. *Iz opyta deyatelnosti KPSS po razvitiju vysshej shkoly* [From the Experience of Communist Party on the Development of Universities], M.: "Znanie" [Knowledge].

Johnson, M. 2008. 'Historical Legacies of Soviet Higher Education and the Transformation of Higher Education Systems in Post-Soviet Russia and Eurasia'. In *The Worldwide Transformation of Higher Education*, edited by D. P. Baker and A. W. Wiseman, 159–176. Emerald Group Publishing Limited. Available at https://www.emeraldinsight.com/doi/full/10.1016/S1479-3679%2808%2900006-6

Jones, A. 1994. 'The Educational Legacy of the Soviet Period'. In *Education and Society in the New Russia*, 3–23. Armonk, New York: M. E. Sharpe.

Ilyinsky, I. M. 2004. *Private Russian Universities: The Experience of Self-identification*. Mosco: Moscow University for the Humanities.

Katrovskiy, A. P. 2003. *Territorial'naya organizaciya vysshey shkoly Rossii* [Territorial Organization of Russian Higher Education System]. Monografiya [Monograph]. Smolensk: Oykumena.

Kinelev, V. G. 1993. 'Regional'naja politika v oblasti vysshego obrazovanija: kakoy ey byt?' [Regional Policy in the Field of Higher Education: How it Should be?]. *Vysshee obrazovanie v Rossii* [*Higher Education in Russia*] 4: 14–24.

Klyachko, T. L. 2011. 'Obrazovanie v Rossiyskoy Federacii: problemy i tendencii razvitiya v nachale XXI veka'. [Education in the Russian Federation: Problems and Trends in the Early XXI]. *Mir Rossii: Sociologiya, ehtnologiya* [*The World of Russia: Sociology, Ethnology*] 20 (1): 88–124.

Kouzminov, Y., Semyonov, D., and Froumin, I. 2013. 'Struktura vuzovskoi seti: ot sovetskogo k rossiyskomu masterplanu'. [HEIs Network Structure: From the Soviet to the Russian Masterplan]. *Voprosy obrazovania* [*Educational Studies*] 4: 8–63.

Kuhns, K. 2011. *Globalization of Knowledge and its Impact on Higher Education Reform in Transitioning States: The Case of Russia.* Dissertation, School of Education, Stanford University.

Leshukov, O., and Borisova, L. 2014. 'Vysshie uchebnye zavedenija v social'no-jekonomicheskom prostranstve'. [*Higher Education Institutions in the Socio-economic Environment*]. *Vysshee obrazovanie segodnja* [*Higher Education Today*] 12: 89–95.

Leshukov, O., and Lisyutkin, M. 2014. 'Modern Approaches to the 'Regionalization' of Federal Policy in Russian Higher Education'. Working papers, NRU Higher School of Economics. Series PA, 'Public Administration'.

Lobo, T., Guedes, A., Amaral, A. L., and Walker, R. (1995). *Decentralized Management of Education in Minas Gerais, Brazil.* Washington, DC: World Bank, Human Development Department.

Mohrman, K., Ma, W., and Baker, D. 2008. 'The Research University in Transition: The Emerging Global Model'. *Higher Education Policy* 21 (1): 5–27.

Naselenie, R. 2013. *dvadcat' pervyy ezhegodnyy demograficheskiy doklad* [*The Population of Russia 2013: Twenty-first Annual Demographic Report*]. Edited by S. V. Zaharov. Mosco: National Research University Higher School of Economics.

Nikolaev, D., and Chugunov, D. 2012. *The Education System in the Russian Federation Education Brief.* The World Bank Study. Washington, DC: World Bank.

Pain, E. 2003. 'Federalizm i separatizm v Rossii: mify i real'nost' [Federalism and Separatism in Russia: Myths and Reality], *Kosmopolis* 1 (3): 39–58.

Sadkov, A. 2007. *Byudzhetno-nalogovyj federalizm v Rossijskoj Federacii i nalogovaya politika* [*Fiscal Federalism in the Russian Federation and Fiscal Policy*]. Mosco: Nalogy.

Slider, D. 1997. 'Russia's Market-distorting Federalism'. *Post-Soviet Geography and Economics* 38: 489–504.

Solnick, S. L. 1995. 'Federal Bargaining in Russia'. *East Europe Constitutional Review* 4 (4): 52–58.

Treisman, D. 1999. *After the Deluge: Regional Crises and Political Consolidation in Russia.* Ann Arbor: University of Michigan Press.

Treyvish, A. 2009. *Gorod, rayon, strana i mir. Razvitie Rossii glazami stranoveda* [City, region, country and the world. The development of Russia through the eyes of a geographer]. M. Novyy hronograf [The New Chronograph].

Valentey, S. D. 2012. *Simmetriya i asimmetriya·v rossiyskoy modeli federativnyh otnosheniy* [Symmetry and asymmetry in the Russian model of federal relations]. Institute of Economics RAN.

Watts, R. L. 2005. 'A Comparative Perspective on Asymmetry in Federations'. *Asymmetry Series*, 4. IGR, Queen's University

Weiler, H. 1983. 'Legalization, Expertise, and Participation: Strategies of Compensatory Legitimation in Educational Policy'. *Comparative Education Review* 27 (2): 259–277.

Zhuravskaya, E. 2010. 'Federalism in Russia'. Working Paper No. N141, CEFIR/ES Working Paper series, Moscow.

Zubarevich, N. V. 2009. 'Regional'noe razvitie i regional'naya politika za desyatiletie ehkonomicheskogo rosta'. [Regional Development and Regional Policy in a Decade of Economic Growth]. *Voprosy ekonomicheskoj politiki* [Issues of economic policy]. 1–2(1–2): 161–174.

APPENDIX

Table 9A.1 *The Indicators of Regional Variations, Federal State Statistics Service (2015)*

	The Share of Population (%)	The Size of the Territory, % of the Entire Territory of the Russian Federation	GRP per Capita (2014), Rouble	Number of HEIs			Number of Branches	Number of Students		
				Total	Public	Private		Total	Public	Private
Russian Federation	**100.0**	**100**	**403,178.90**	**896**	**530**	**366**	**1,079**	**4,766,479**	**4,061,402**	**705,077**
Central Federal District	**26.7**	**3.8**	**535,430.5**	**342**	**168**	**174**	**270**	**1,455,273**	**1,131,059**	**324,214**
Belgorod Province	1.1	0.2	400,633.4	6	4	2	9	53,050	46,251	6,799
Bryansk Province	0.8	0.2	196,341.9	5	4	1	14	34,540	27,917	6,623
Vladimir Province	1.0	0.2	232,630.7	3	2	1	14	33,461	28,933	4,528
Voronezh Province	1.6	0.3	304,314.2	16	11	5	15	91,775	82,100	9,675
Ivanovo Province	0.7	0.1	145,234.7	6	6	0	5	31,327	29,740	1,587
Kaluga Province	0.7	0.2	322,517.0	3	1	2	18	22,033	16,387	5,646
Kostroma Province	0.4	0.4	223,242.9	3	3	0	3	13,597	12,111	1,486

(Continued)

Table 9A.1 (Continued)

	The Share of Population (%)	The Size of the Territory. % of the Entire Territory of the Russian Federation	GRP per Capita (2014), Rouble	Number of HEIs			Number of Branches	Number of Students		
				Total	Public	Private		Total	Public	Private
Kursk Province	0.8	0.2	266,007.6	10	5	5	6	54,632	38,284	16,348
Lipetsk Province	0.8	0.1	341,454.6	6	4	2	11	24,933	20,934	3,999
Moscow Province	5.0	0.3	376,698.6	34	14	20	83	111,985	84,927	27,058
Oryol Province	0.5	0.1	234,157.4	5	5	0	6	31,943	31,626	317
Ryazan Province	0.8	0.2	261,245.2	7	4	3	10	35,552	29,868	5,684
Smolensk Province	0.7	0.3	242,907.3	7	5	2	20	26,205	19,805	6,400
Tambov Province	0.7	0.2	258,822.0	4	4	0	8	29,182	26,322	2,860
Tver Province	0.9	0.5	232,832.9	7	4	3	16	29,192	24,114	5,078
Tula Province	1.0	0.1	269,177.0	8	2	6	12	34,968	26,255	8,713
Yaroslavl Province	0.9	0.2	305,210.7	9	7	2	14	37,187	29,935	7,252

Moscow	8.4	0.01	1,053,949.8	203	83	120	6	759,711	555,550	204,161
North-western Federal District	**9.5**	**9.9**	**427,922.9**	**102**	**60**	**42**	**88**	**4,64,645**	**407,721**	**56,924**
The Republic of Karelia	0.4	1.1	293,054.1	2	2	0	6	14,311	12,370	1,941
Komi Republic	0.6	2.4	553,836.2	3	3	0	8	20,515	19,451	1,064
Arkhangelsk Province	0.8	3.4	454,828.7	4	2	2	6	22,691	18,935	3,756
Vologda Province	0.8	0.8	325,789.3	4	3	1	9	24,323	21,385	2,938
Kaliningrad Province	0.7	0.1	316,999.4	4	3	1	12	27,377	19,666	7,711
Leningrad Province	1.2	0.5	403,431.2	1	1	0	14	9,867	9,146	721
Murmansk Province	0.5	0.8	416,662.1	4	2	2	10	15,394	11,103	4,291
Novgorod Province	0.4	0.3	331,842.0	1	1	0	8	12,489	10,006	2,483
Pskov Province	0.4	0.3	185,525.8	3	3	0	8	14,365	12,731	1,634
Saint Petersburg	3.6	0.01	513,782.4	76	40	36	7	303,313	272,928	30,385
Southern Federal District	**9.6**	**2.5**	**280,342.3**	**66**	**37**	**29**	**122**	**410,207**	**360,560**	**49,647**
The Republic of Adygea	0.3	0.05	174,017.6	2	2	0	5	12,637	12,637	0
The Republic of Kalmykia	0.2	0.4	163,688.1	1	1	0	3	8,546	6,932	1,614

(Continued)

Table 9A.1 (Continued)

	The Share of Population (%)	The Size of the Territory. % of the Entire Territory of the Russian Federation	GRP per Capita (2014), Rouble	Number of HEIs			Number of Private Branches	Number of Students		
				Total	Public	Private		Total	Public	Private
Krasnodar Krai	3.7	0.4	330,100.2	26	10	16	43	130,461	108,826	21,635
Astrakhan Province	0.7	0.3	283,591.2	6	5	1	12	37,766	31,668	6,098
Volgograd Province	1.7	0.7	278,961.2	13	10	3	20	71,637	61,488	10,149
Rostov Province	2.9	0.6	235,695.9	18	9	9	39	149,160	139,009	10,151
North Caucasian Federal District	**6.6**	**1.0**	**164,905.9**	**54**	**26**	**28**	**71**	**256,937**	**217,845**	**39,092**
The Republic of Dagestan	2.1	0.3	180,824.4	18	6	12	22	70,989	60,967	10,022
The Republic of Ingushetia	0.3	0.02	113,791.2	2	1	1	2	8,862	7,418	1,444

Kabardino-Balkar Republic	**0.6**	137,437.3	4	3	1	2	17,070	14,337	2,733
Karachay-Cherkess Republic	**0.3**	147,396.9	2	2	0	7	13,125	11,094	2,031
The Republic of North Ossetia-Alania	**0.5**	179,992.7	8	5	3	3	26,094	23,477	2,617
Chechen Republic	**0.9**	104,019.2	3	3	0	1	33,121	30,700	2,421
Stavropol Krai	**1.9**	193,489.4	17	6	11	34	87,676	69,852	17,824
Volga Federal District	**20.3**	**308,508.5**	**131**	**95**	**36**	**228**	**946,023**	**823,837**	**122,186**
The Republic of Bashkortostan	**2.8**	306,771.3	11	9	2	30	114,417	101,654	12,763
Mari El Republic	**0.5**	209,488.1	3	2	1	2	19,645	16,488	3,157
The Republic of Mordovia	**0.6**	210,858.7	3	2	1	7	30,148	24,793	5,355
The Republic of Tatarstan	**2.6**	434,509.1	25	15	10	35	163,201	124,225	38,976
Udmurt Republic	**1.0**	291,287.5	7	5	2	11	51,290	44,225	7,065
Chuvash Republic	**0.8**	189,736.4	5	4	1	14	38,349	31,727	6,622
Perm Krai	**1.8**	367,086.6	12	8	4	20	66,369	59,799	6,570

(Continued)

Table 9A.1 (Continued)

	The Share of Population (%)	The Size of the Territory. % of the Entire Territory of the Russian Federation	GRP per Capita (2014), Rouble	Number of HEIs			Number of Private Branches	Number of Students		
				Total	Public	Private		Total	Public	Private
Kirov Province	0.9	0.7	191,444.5	6	4	2	8	36,202	32,139	4,063
Nizhny Novgorod Province	2.2	0.4	310,866.4	13	10	3	32	98,192	89,052	9,140
Orenburg Province	1.4	0.7	364,761.5	5	5	0	15	53,322	48,082	5,240
Penza Province	0.9	0.3	219,181.9	4	4	0	8	40,159	37,172	2,987
Samara Province	2.2	0.3	358,648.8	25	16	9	19	110,963	98,648	12,315
Saratov Province	1.7	0.6	225,374.5	7	6	1	19	84,494	78,846	5,648
Ulyanovsk Province	0.9	0.2	220,575.7	5	5	0	8	39,272	36,987	2,285
Ural Federal District	**8.4**	**10.6**	**652,935.4**	**59**	**40**	**19**	**110**	**362,126**	**328,391**	**33,735**
Kurgan Province	0.6	0.4	193,434.0	3	3	0	5	21,232	18,961	2,271
Sverdlovsk Province	3.0	1.1	384,228.1	26	14	12	39	135,370	120,743	14,627

Tyumen Province	**2.5**	8.5	1,453,073.3	7	7	0	10	65,337	63,619	1,718
In its part of Khanty-Mansi Autonomous Okrug	**1.1**	3.1	1,761,159.0	8	5	3	14	27,287	25,483	1,804
In its part of the Yamalo-Nenets Autonomous Okrug	**0.4**	4.5	2,985,310.6	0	0	0	12	2,597	1,631	9,66
Chelyabinsk Province	**2.4**	0.5	284,190.7	15	11	4	30	110,303	97,954	12,349
Siberian Federal District	**13.2**	**30.0**	**316,380.1**	**96**	**69**	**27**	**124**	**631,346**	**571,420**	**59,926**
Altai Republic	**0.1**	0.5	184,011.4	1	1	0	0	3,334	3,334	0
The Republic of Buryatia	**0.7**	2.1	189,325.7	5	4	1	9	33,574	30,791	2,783
Tyva Republic	**0.2**	1.0	149,334.8	1	1	0	2	4,990	4,593	397
The Republic of Khakassia	**0.4**	0.4	299,913.3	1	1	0	2	8,614	8,614	0
Altai Krai	**1.6**	1.0	187,587.3	10	7	3	16	60,711	51,798	8,913
Transbaikal Krai	**0.7**	2.5	209,002.5	2	2	0	5	26,996	25,868	1,128
Krasnoyarsk Krai	**2.0**	13.8	498,372.4	10	9	1	25	89,690	80,925	8,765

(Continued)

Table 9A.1 (Continued)

	The Share of Population (%)	The Size of the Territory. % of the Entire Territory of the Russian Federation	GRP per Capita (2014), Rouble	Number of HEIs			Number of Branches	Number of Students		
				Total	Public	Private		Total	Public	Private
Irkutsk Province	1.6	4.5	375,481.9	12	8	4	15	79,228	73,952	5,276
Kemerovo Province	1.9	0.6	273,825.1	8	7	1	24	61,619	56,552	5,067
Novosibirsk Province	1.9	1.0	326,867.5	22	14	8	10	110,331	100,184	10,147
Omsk Province	1.4	0.8	303,088.5	15	9	6	9	88,706	73,056	15,650
Tomsk Province	0.7	1.8	399,207.9	9	6	3	7	63,553	61,753	1,800
Far Eastern Federal District	**4.2**	**36.0**	**518,185.5**	**38**	**30**	**8**	**56**	**179,410**	**164,782**	**14,628**
The Republic of Sakha (Yakutia)	0.7	18.0	690,642.5	7	5	2	15	26,851	23,850	3,001
Kamchatka Krai	0.2	2.7	456,481.5	2	2	0	4	6,396	5,300	1,096

Primorsky Krai	1.3	1.0	332,383.3	9	7	2	15	5,4181	51,654	2,527
Khabarovsk Krai	0.9	4.6	410,190.4	12	9	3	8	55,673	52,147	3,526
Amur Province	0.6	2.1	290,398.1	4	4	0	4	19,361	17,501	1,860
Magadan Province	0.1	2.7	650,273.4	1	1	0	3	4,451	2,854	1,597
Sakhalin Province	0.3	0.5	1,620,312.5	2	1	1	3	8,889	7,868	1,021
Jewish Autonomous Province	0.1	0.2	246,449.0	1	1	0	2	3,148	3,148	0
Chukotka Autonomous Okrug	0.0	4.2	1,118,861.7	0	0	0	2	460	460	0
Crimean Federal District	**1.6**	**0.2**	**68,526.2**	**8**	**5**	**3**	**10**	**60,512**	**55,787**	**4,725**
The Republic of Crimea	1.3	0.2	73,190.1	6	4	2	5	45,360	42,578	2,782
Sevastopol	0.3	0.01	45,784.9	2	1	1	5	15,152	13,209	1,943

Source: Federal State Statistics Service, 2015.

Chapter 10

China
The 'Commanding Heights' Strategy Revisited

Rong Wang and Po Yang

INTRODUCTION: HIGHER EDUCATION IN A NON-FEDERALISM STATE

Regional higher education growth in non-federal states has not attracted sufficient attention in recent conversations over tertiary education expansion (Arum, Gamoran and Shavit 2007; Marginson 2016a) or discussions about high participation countries across the globe (Marginson 2016b). Yet, regional systems are critical pillars for tertiary development in most countries, with or without a federal system (Carnoy et al. 2013).

How do states without a constitutionally regulated division between national and subnational government of responsibility for higher education create credible incentives for local bureaucrats to provide higher learning for local residents? What strategies are commonly used to steer regional development? Are regional variations in higher education growth greater in non-federal states? Whether and how do political regimes condition the stratification of higher education embedded in its expansion? With China, the home to one of the largest systems of higher education, its experience may help to answer some of these challenging questions.

China's economic reforms in the past 35 years have generated spectacular growth (Xu 2011). However, its institutions may not be matched to this achievement. Some economists believe that 'from the viewpoint of standard wisdom, such as the Washington Consensus or the recent empirical literature of cross-country studies, Chinese institutions in government, corporate governance, law, and finance look notoriously weak' (Xu 2011, 1077). Lack of a tradition of rule by law is deeply rooted in China's governance structure. Even though China is highly decentralized economically, it is neither a *de jure* nor a *de facto* federal state. Instead, contemporary China has a regionally decentralized authoritarian system (Xu 2011), which relies heavily on the leadership of the Communist Party of China (Zhou, Chen and Li 2005).

Under its political regime, in the past three decades, China has developed a particular central–local government relationship that shares many characteristics with countries with asymmetric institutional patterns (Wei 2015). The national government has legislative powers over finance, while subnational governments have no right to raise revenues by taxing. This implies a high level of vertical fiscal imbalance, which tends to favour fiscal centralization.

The political, economic and fiscal climates have profound influences on a country's higher education development. Owing to the fact that China is not a federal state, a federal system of higher education has not been adopted in China. According to the conventional wisdom, to achieve both expansion and excellence in a national system, a large state should adopt a federal system of higher education, characterized by a clear division of tertiary responsibility between national and subnational government (Clark 1983). Local governments should be the chief providers of tertiary services with funding from local tax revenues, while the national government should steer education through a regulatory system or intergovernmental coordination. In a typical federal system of higher education, local governments are not only self-contained but also have a certain level of autonomy guaranteed by the Constitution. In theory, the division of responsibilities among various levels of government is either clearly stated in the Constitution (as in the case of competitive federalism) or there exist coordination rules set in advance (as in the case of cooperative federalism).

In sharp contrast to these 'ideal' scenarios, decentralization with or without coordination, China's central authority seems to be reluctant to delegate powers to regional governments, even though the latter are the major providers of tertiary services (Xu 2014). Instead, the approach developed has been as follows: The state has implemented a commanding heights strategy to steer its tertiary sector; the central elites has controlled the higher education institution hierarchy, a handful of selective research universities and a set of intervention measures; and, at the same time, the national government has loosened its grip on the mass of tertiary institutions and decentralized them towards local governments (Wang 2014a).

The commanding heights strategy is part of a system of political rule specific to China. Although many countries adopt some versions of social engineering policies when building their national tertiary systems (Carnoy et al. 2013), the central–regional relation in China has been organized to provide for system development in central government terms. The centralization of political, personnel and fiscal authority and the decentralization of administrative responsibilities create an asymmetry in intergovernmental relations. This power asymmetry allows the central elites to consolidate the higher education authority to the Ministry of Education and create commanding heights in this sector at the expense of subnational governments' capacity and incentives for growing regional tertiary systems. Nevertheless, since the mid-1990s, local governments have found some loopholes to escape central capture.

The commanding heights strategy is a double-edged sword. On the positive side, it facilitates the political and economic mobilization underpinning the unparalleled growth of tertiary education in China. On the negative side, it leads to a high degree of institutional differentiation between mass institutions and the world-class research universities (Altbach 2009; Carnoy et al. 2013; Yang 2014). In addition, it also leads to a large and visible variation between regions in terms of the size and structure of regional tertiary systems, college access, relative opportunities to attend elite research universities and the funding levels of higher education.

This chapter is one of the first attempts to analyse China's higher education expansion and stratification from the perspective of political economy, although numerous other studies have been devoted to these phenomena (see, for instance, Carnoy et al. 2013; Min 2004; Wang and Liu 2011). It explores the political economic dimension of regional higher education growth in a non-federal state, by analysing China's political institutions, the central-local relationship associated with the regime, the evolution of intergovernmental fiscal relations and the associated commanding heights strategy, the rise of regional stratification, and the contemporary development of China's higher education governance and the limitations of the stratification strategy. This chapter closes with a comparison between China and other large federal and unitary countries, highlighting the significance of the case of China and pointing towards directions for future investigation.

CHINA'S POLITY AND INTERGOVERNMENTAL RELATION

China's Governance Structure

State sovereignty and local autonomy are key to constitutional studies in the legal field (Zhang 2012). The constant struggle between the national and the subnational governments is a principal aspect of multilevel Chinese governance. After nearly 70 years of political development, China has a governance structure with five tiers (Xu 2011). The first tier is a central government; the second tier includes 23 provinces, 5 autonomous regions, 4 provincial-level municipalities and 2 special administrative regions; the third tier consists of 333 municipality-level units (prefecture cities); the fourth tier is comprised of 2,853 county-level units; and the bottom tier includes 40,497 town-level units, as of 2014.

In earlier economic literature, China's governance structure is modelled as a stylized multiregional governance form (M-form; Qian and Xu, 1993; Qian, Roland and Xu 2006). In the M-form hierarchy, every region is controlled by the central government politically, whereas each region not only enjoys a certain degree of autonomy but also is self-contained in its functions. However, in a recent study, Xu (2011) challenges that argument and proposes that China's fundamental institution is a regionally decentralized authoritarian (RDA hereafter) regime, which is characterized by highly centralized political and personnel controls at the national level, and a regionally decentralized administrative and economic system. Both decision making and policy implementation in the RDA regime, from national strategic issues to concrete local matters, are deeply influenced by this combination of political centralization and economic decentralization. (Xu 2011, 1082)

Within the RDA framework, the dominant role of the Communist Party of China makes China's regime essentially different from a federal system. First and foremost, it is not a federal state by constitution (Wei 2015). China's Constitution stipulates that regions have no inherent power and their power is granted by the central authority.[1] China's regime is not a *de facto* federal state either. Regional leaders are appointed by upper-level governments through the Communist Party personnel system, not by regional election (Krug and Libman 2015). In fact, this decentralized authoritarian system depends crucially on the leadership of the Party, which has substantial controls over the personnel matters of subnational governments, commands the leading economic sectors and controls the ideological apparatuses, such as education, the justice system and the mass media (Zhou et al. 2005).

Chinese-style Federalism and Local Incentive

Can an RDA state incentivize local authorities to promote local economic growth and provide public services? Although few education scholars have explored these issues, in the economics literature, local autonomy and regional behaviours are a focal point of analysis. Economists have found that economic development in large countries depends on how subnational governments perform in implementing pro-development policies (Bardhan and Mookherjee 2006).

---

[1] The People's Republic of China issued its first Constitution in 1954 and three following versions in 1975, 1978 and 1982. After the enactment of the 1982 Constitution, four amendments occurred in 1988, 1993, 1999 and 2004. Except for the first Constitution, the Common Principle of 1954, none of China's Constitutions or their amendments explicitly stipulated the scope of fiscal authority of national and subnational governments (Wei 2015, 176).

Several strands of literature on Chinese-style federalism in economic terms contribute to our understanding of China's growth and regional behaviours.[2] The first strand considers China as an example of 'Market-Preserving Federalism' (Qian and Weingast 1997). This line of literature argues that the economic decentralization was the driving force of economic growth. Jin, Qian and Weingast (2005) claim that China's fiscal contracting system provides local governments with strong fiscal incentives and, at the same time, improves horizontal distribution of budgetary spending across provinces.

The second strand of literature introduces a political dimension into the discussion. It characterizes China as a nation with decentralized economic governance plus centralized political governance (Xu 2011). The central government has control over the personnel system, whereas subnational governments run much of the economy through local institutions. The state is thus able to provide political incentives for local growth through the 'regional tournament competition', which promotes local leaders in the political system based on local economic performance such as the growth of GDP (Li and Zhou 2005).

However, recent literature criticizes this analysis by highlighting that political tournament competition can only provide incentives for heads of regional governments, and even their promotion to the very top depends relatively little on regional growth. Instead, this third strand of literature focuses on political mobilization within the Party system. Shih, Adolph and Liu (2012, 167) argue, 'Factional ties with various top leaders, educational qualifications, and provincial revenue collection played substantial roles in elite ranking, suggesting promotion systems served the immediate needs of the regime and its leaders, rather than encompassing goals like economic growth'. Empirical literature provides evidence for factional ties and their influence over economic decentralization in China (Liu et al. 2014; Shih et al. 2012).

In more recent literature, Krug and Libman (2015) further explore the conditions under which non-democratic political regimes are

---

[2] Notice that the literature we discussed is not in terms of time sequence. Our use of strand differs from 'generations' of federalism literature (for example, see Weingast 2009).

capable of making credible commitments to maintain a certain level of local autonomy and to incentivize local bureaucrats. They believe that China is capable of making credible commitment to local autonomy due to the competition between vertical elite networks and China's limited access to natural resources.

Asymmetric Institution Pattern and Vertical Fiscal Imbalance

The RDA argument emphasizes political and personnel centralization and administrative and economic decentralization in China. However, it overlooks another pivotal aspect of the central–local relation—the fiscal centralization in recent decades, which has concentrated the rights to collect and distribute revenues to the national government and transferred the responsibility for spending to subnational levels.

The fiscal relation is definitely a key part of China's multilevel governance structure. There are different ways to describe the intergovernmental fiscal relation (for instance, Zhou 2012). Here we introduce the concept of the *institutional pattern of fiscal relations between national and subnational government* to describe ways in which administrative duty and fiscal expenditure responsibility are divided between national and subnational government. This is a comprehensive yet succinct way to characterize central–regional fiscal relation, introduced by prior comparative legal studies (Wei 2007, 2015).

According to Wei (2015), the institutional pattern of fiscal relations refers to a particular combination of institutional arrangements in four areas. First, the division of public service duty and fiscal expenditure responsibility mainly describes how major administrative duties are divided between national and subnational government, and how their respective duties are financed. Second, the arrangement of fiscal allocation power is the key to a country's public finance institution. It refers the allocation of rights to fiscal gains, rights to fiscal legislation, rights to levy taxes and budgetary rights. Third, the arrangements for intergovernmental transfer indicate conditions under which upper-level governments transfer resource to lower-level governments to fulfil their expenditure duties. Fourth, coordination and dispute resolution are very important for smooth operations of a public finance system. Federal congress in Germany is the formal coordination organization, and there exist other informal coordination mechanisms between federal and state governments. These institutional arrangements are often based on a nation's constitution and history and may vary across time.

Using institutional arrangements, legal scholars are able to categorize intergovernmental fiscal relations in advanced democracies into two types—nations with a symmetric institutional pattern (such as the United States and Canada) and countries with an asymmetric institutional pattern (such as Germany and Japan). Table 10.1 summarizes the characteristics of both types of institutional patterns.

In general, countries with the symmetric institutional pattern tend to have a clearer intergovernmental division of duty and responsibility, and a higher degree of match between administrative duty and rights to fiscal gains. Also, for such countries, rights to fiscal gains coincide with rights to fiscal legislation and subnational governments tend to have a high level of fiscal autonomy and independent duties, in comparison with nations under the asymmetric institution pattern. Table 10A.1 compares the United States with Germany to illustrate differences between symmetric and asymmetric patterns. One unintended consequence of the asymmetric institutional pattern is vertical fiscal imbalance (Wei 2007, 2015). This is a measurement of imbalance in fiscal revenue and expenditure between upper and lower level of government, indicating the degree of fiscal centralization of a nation's public finance system (Rosen and Gayer 2009). It refers to the difference between a national (or subnational) government's share in total fiscal revenue and in total fiscal expenditure. A high vertical fiscal imbalance rate indicates high fiscal centralization. Recent studies show that countries with asymmetric institutional pattern have a higher degree of vertical fiscal imbalance. In year 2001, vertical fiscal imbalance rates for Germany and Japan (asymmetric patterns) were 28 per cent and 20 per cent, respectively, while the rates were 13 per cent and 7 per cent for the United States and Canada (symmetric patterns).

China's public finance system has certain features of the asymmetric system. First, the intergovernmental division of administrative duty and expenditure responsibility is ambiguous and fluctuating due to the lack

Table 10.1 *Characteristics of Symmetric and Asymmetric Institution Pattern*

	Symmetric Institution Pattern	Asymmetric Institution Pattern
Division of administrative duty	Highly consistent, duty implementation and legal supervision belong to same government	Less consistent, duty implementation and legal supervision belong to different levels of government
Match between administrative duty and rights to fiscal gains	High level of match	Low level of match
Relation between rights to fiscal gains and rights to fiscal legislation	Well adaption; both rights belong to same government	Maladaptation; rights to fiscal legislation are relatively centralized
Responsibility of subnational government	Subnational government enjoys a relatively large budgetary autonomy;	Certain limitations for subnational governments' budgetary autonomy;
	Having more independent administrative duties;	National government is accountable for subnational government debt;
	National government does not provide emergency aid when subnational governments are deeply in debt	Existing large-scale intergovernmental transfer for equalization

Source: Authors' summary based on Wei (2015).

of constitutional basis (Wei 2015). Second, the lack of constitutional provision also leads to a low degree of match between administrative duty and rights and the fiscal revenues of respective governments, generating limited fiscal autonomy. China's central government retains the exclusive authority for fiscal legislation. Local governments cannot issue their own debts without central endorsement. Lastly, the state creates large transfer programmes for regional equalization, but, for local governments, there is a high bargaining cost to obtain such transfers. The outcome is very high transaction costs, high uncertainty and rigid central control over the use of transferred grants.

According to Wei (2015), the vertical fiscal imbalance rate in China at the national level was 33 per cent in 2010, 34 per cent in 2011, 33 per cent in 2012 and 32 per cent in 2013, higher than other countries with asymmetric institutional patterns. From 1995 to date, the central fiscal transfer share of total regional fiscal expenditure has been high and fairly stable, between 40 and 50 per cent. Empirical analyses provide additional evidence of the fiscal centralization (Jing 2007; Jia and Liang 2011) at national, provincial and even local level (Jiang 2009). Vertical fiscal imbalance has detrimental effects on the provision of public services, such as access to and the quality of compulsory education (Liu and Ke 2015; Luo 2009).

Intergovernmental Relation and Higher Education Governance

Intergovernmental fiscal relations can have far-reaching impacts on a nation's higher education governance, independent of its political institutions. Not all federal states follow the same governance structure. As demonstrated in other chapters of this book, among typical federal states, nations with symmetric institutional patterns tend to follow a competitive federalism model (such as the United States and Canada), while states with asymmetric institution pattern often associate with a cooperative federalism model (such as Germany).

Under a competitive federalism model, higher education is mainly the responsibility of provincial or state governments and the federal government provides supplementary support (see the chapter on Canada). This is consistent with the clear division of administrative duty between national and subnational government implied by the symmetric pattern. Provinces or states are responsible for regional tertiary institutions' operating budgets, the approval of new institutions, quality assessment, planning and coordination and the regulation of tuition fees. They are able to fulfil these functions because of their budgetary autonomy and a good match between administrative duty and rights to fiscal revenues. Federal government often offers financial support for research and student aid (see the chapter on the United States).

In the cooperative federalism model observed in Germany, state (*Länder*) governments are in charge of higher education legislation, supervision and finance (see the chapter on Germany). In areas requiring nationwide coordination, there are two types of coordination—interstate and between federal and state governments. The areas of coordination are wide, including access and admission, accreditation, funding for research, funding for temporary policy areas and international activities. Although Germany is a federal state and higher education is the responsibility of state governments, federal–state coordination is inevitable and plays a relatively strong role. This relates to the constitutional belief in homogeneity of living conditions which requires equal access to tertiary education across regions.

Germany's asymmetric institutional pattern also calls up the coordination approach. More than 68 per cent of tax revenue is shared by federal and state governments. A high level of tax sharing creates conditions for coordination between federal and state government regarding public service provision. Indeed, federal government can utilize large-scale intergovernmental transfers for regional equalization. It provided €5 billion for Germany's higher education sector in 2014, while the state sources contributing €23.1 billion (Teichler forthcoming).

From Control-all to Commanding Heights Strategy

As mentioned earlier, China exhibits certain features of a centralized fiscal system. However, its regime is fundamentally different from a federal one. Consider policy domains such as institution and programme accreditation, standards for access and admission, quality assurance and funding for research. A cooperative federalism state deals with these domains by federal–state coordination. A competitive federalism state deals with them by decentralizing authority to lower-level governments. An authoritarian regime such as China must find alternative ways to handle the issues that align with its formula of administrative and economic decentralization combined with political centralization.

Since 1949, China has transformed from a totalitarian state to a regionally decentralized authoritarian regime (Xu 2011). The institutional arrangement for higher education has been also adjusted accordingly. In the early days, under the planned economy, China adopted a control-all strategy. The state monitored and managed every aspect of economic and social life in a military fashion. Higher education was a state apparatus for producing the human resources needed for planned accelerated industrialization. Students were provided with free education at higher education institutions which were all publicly owned and operated. What was of paramount importance to the system was that graduates of colleges, universities and three-year polytechnics were subject to direct state assignment to guaranteed jobs in the state sector.

The reforms of early 1980s stimulated a spectacular economic growth and also led to changes in how the central government manipulated the tertiary sector. The state moved from the control-all strategy to a commanding heights strategy. 'Commanding heights' was first used by Lenin as a defence of his 'New Economic Policy'. In persuading his suspicious colleagues, Lenin proclaimed at a convention in 1922 that the reforms were rather modest, and the new Soviet state would always retain its control over what he called the 'commanding heights' of the economy. By the commanding heights, Lenin referred to critical sectors that dominated economic activity such as electricity generation and heavy machinery production. In other words, the state would control the most important elements of the economy by commanding its heights and leaving the rest to the market.

Since the mid-1980s, China's central government has claimed its rights to the most important elements of its tertiary sector in two ways—directly managing the commanding heights of the institutional hierarchy and controlling the commanding heights of mechanisms of intervention (Wang 2014a). The central authority has kept control over elite research universities and key resources for higher education development, while loosening its grip on the mass of higher education institutions and decentralizing them towards local governments.

This strategy matches well with China's recent political structure. As noted, the commanding heights strategy is part of the political regime specific to China—centralized political and personnel controls at national level and a regionally decentralized administrative and economic system. It guarantees that the central elites can readily control personnel in the tertiary sector as well as the allocation of key resources within this sector such as institution and programme accreditation, research funding, student aid, enrolment quota and admission tier. Meanwhile, local governments can only operate low-tier enrolment—absorbing institutions.

EVOLUTION OF CENTRAL-LOCAL RELATION AND SECTOR STRATEGY
Changing Central-Local Relation

China's public finance system has been in flux for over six decades. The intergovernmental fiscal relation experienced several cycles of centralization and decentralization. During each cycle, the higher education governance structure changed accordingly, fulfilling the role of the tertiary sector as the human resource production unit of the state (Wang 2014a; Zhan and Chen 2013). Central government regularly adjusted its position in this sector, imposing on local governments changing incentives for regional higher education development (Wei 2014).

Some scholars divide the evolution of China's central–local fiscal relation since 1949 into three periods (Jia et al. 2008; Liu 2013). The first period was from 1949 to 1979. The fiscal structure underwent constant adjustments during this period, reflecting the dominant position and the discretionary power of the central government. Twice the national government decentralized to subnational governments part of the responsibility for administrative duty and fiscal expenditure, during the 'Great Leap Forward' (1958–1961) and the 'Cultural Revolution' (1966–1976). However, fiscal authority was never genuinely deconcentrated to regional level. In both periods, the latter still had no access to rights of fiscal legislation, rights to levy taxes and rights to budget. The political cycles alternated central and local governments' responsibilities in higher education sector. In the early days of the Republic (1949–1953), tertiary institutions were affiliated either with the central government or with one of the six regional territories. The state provided funding for all institutions. During the 'Great Leap Forward' movement, the central authority encouraged regional competition over tertiary development, which led to the first tertiary expansion in the late 1950s.

The second period was from 1979 to 1993. Between 1981 and 1992, national government adopted an economic and fiscal decentralization strategy (Xu 2011). This fiscal policy was literary translated as 'serving meals to different diners from different pots'. It represents a variation of fiscal contracting between upper- and lower-level governments. Tax revenue was divided between central and local governments at a fixed ratio and each were held accountable for balancing their budgets. On the one hand, a stronger fiscal incentive generated by this reform and measured in terms of a higher marginal revenue retention rate for regions implied faster regional economic development. On the other hand, decentralization reduced the national government's revenue share and compromised its fiscal capacity (Jia et al. 2008).

With the rising fiscal power of local governments, the major higher education governance principle was stated as 'unified leadership and decentralized administration', meaning that the central government retained political and personnel authority while provincial governments operated the majority of tertiary institutions. The fiscal contracting reform during this period guaranteed that provincial governments had sufficient fund to support regional development.

In the third period, the central government initiated a Tax Sharing Regime reform from 1993 to the early 2000s to restore its fiscal position. The reform consisted of three parts. First, it established guidelines for the division of administrative duties and responsibilities for fiscal expenditure between central and provincial governments. The national government was responsible for national security, foreign affairs and regional redistribution, whereas subnational governments provided funding for regional development and services. Second, the reform divided fiscal revenue between national and subnational government. Different tax revenues (such as value added tax and sales tax) were shared by the different levels of government. Lastly, the reform initiated a tax return regime and a regular system of intergovernmental transfer. The subsequent Income Tax Sharing Regime reform of 2002 further consolidated the revenue base for intergovernmental transfer programmes.

This reform has had many long-term impacts. It centralizes fiscal revenue to the central level but delegates many public expenditure tasks to subnational governments. After the reform, the central government's share in total fiscal revenue increased and its share in total fiscal expenditure decreased (see Figures 10.1 and 10.2).

The centralization of revenue and the decentralization of public expenditure also creates an asymmetry between national and subnational government, which fiscally compromises local authority's capacity for providing higher education services to their constituencies.

Unexpectedly, the process of fiscal centralization overlapped with the great tertiary expansion in China. This expansion was orchestrated by the state with the assistance of the aforementioned commanding heights strategy. From 1993 to 2013, the total number of higher education institutions in China increased from 1,065 to 2,491. In 2014, the majority are regional or local public colleges and universities (1,661 or 67%) or private ones (717 or 29%), with a small minority under the direct control of central government (113 or 5%). Provincial governments are mandated to provide operational budget for affiliated institutions (RMB 12,000 per student in 2010 onward, Ministry of Education and Ministry of Finance 2010). The central government provides research funding and financial aid for eligible full-time students.

Rise of Commanding Heights Strategy and Organizational Differentiation

The commanding heights form of central–regional relations is a strategy to provide regional governments enough incentives to grow their local tertiary systems while maintaining firm central control over the higher education sector. As mentioned earlier, the commanding heights strategy has two components—the commanding heights of higher education institution hierarchy and the commanding heights of the mechanisms of intervention (Wang 2014a). For central elites, the key principle is to keep core resources and selective institutions in the hands of the central government and leaving the rest to regional governments.

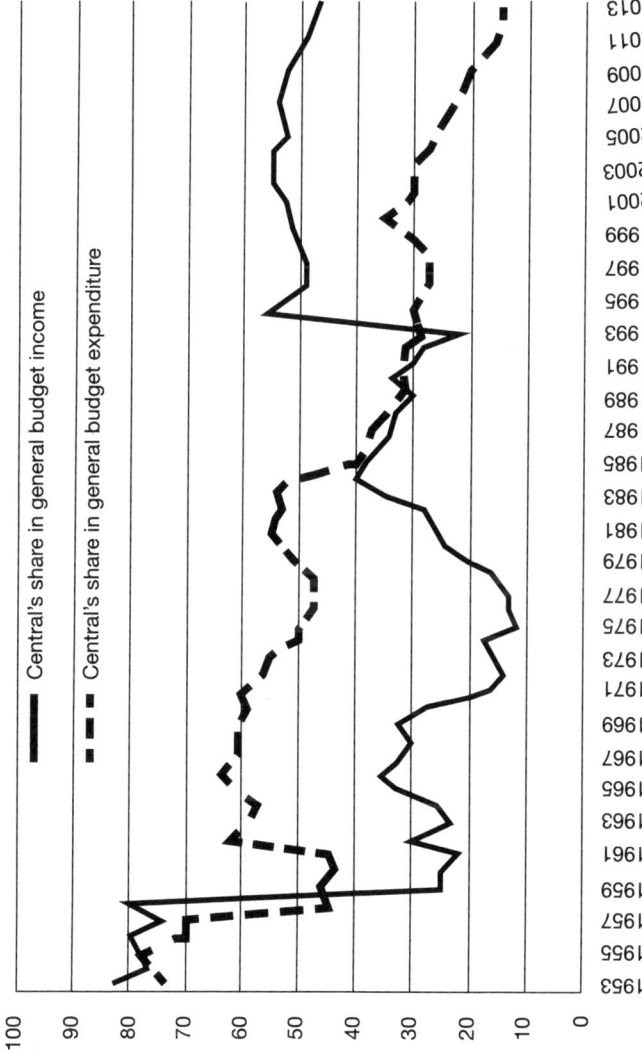

Figure 10.1 *Central Government's Revenue and Expenditure Share (1953–2013)*

Source: Authors' summary based on Wei (2015, Figures 2 and 3).

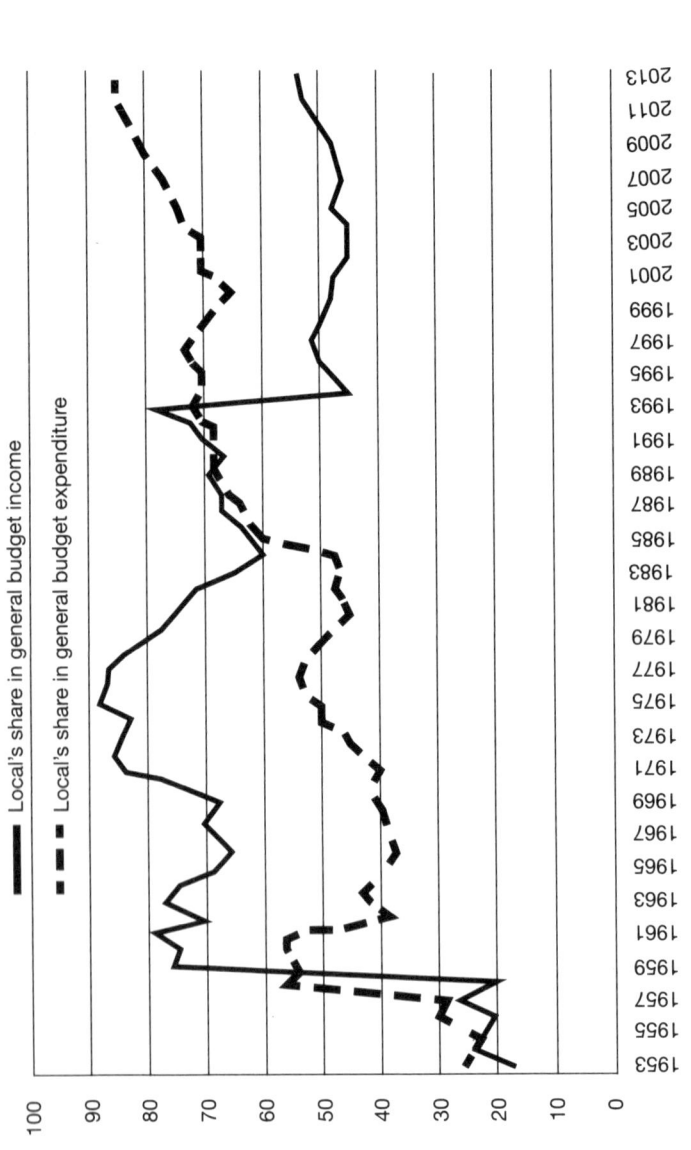

Figure 10.2 *Local Government's Revenue and Expenditure Share (1953–2013)*

Source: Authors' summary based on Wei (2015, Figures 2 and 3, p. 167).

Commanding heights of higher education institutional hierarchy

Since mid-1980s, the state has successfully implemented a series of reforms intended to create the commanding heights of institutional hierarchy. Selective public four-year institutions remain under the direct control of central authorities. These centrally managed institutions are prioritized in the overall higher education system as elite national research institutions.

Several policy measures were carried out to achieve this goal. The central government strictly controlled the enrolment growth in national universities and allowed regional universities to absorb the mass of new students coming into the system as it expanded rapidly in the late 1990s and the first decade of the 2000s. This enabled elite institutions to focus on research and graduate education and maintain their positions in the hierarchy. The launch of several national excellence initiatives, such as Project 985, Project 211 and Project 2011, enabled the state to allocate a large amount of public funding to a small group of elite universities under the umbrella of supporting the development of world-class research universities (Altbach 2009).

At the same time, to create the institutional hierarchy, the central authority decentralized its control over the mass of tertiary institutions towards local governments. A series of reforms underpinned this effort, including the localization of higher education institutions that formerly belonged to central-level line ministries; the structural streamlining of regulatory and management responsibilities to a two-tier management system, consisting of the Ministry of Education and provincial education bureaus; and a decentralization of accreditation authority for three-year vocational and professional institutions to provincial governments.

Commanding heights of mechanisms of intervention

The state also implemented the commanding heights of mechanisms of intervention, including allocation of talented students to various institutions, accreditation of majors and disciplines, accreditation of degree programmes and allocation of funding among institutional types. This maintained national control over personnel and other vital resources (Yang 2015).

Since the late 1990s, there have been many reforms to resource allocation in the tertiary sector. The state has allowed tertiary institutions more leeway in fund raising but taken measured steps in allowing private institutions to proliferate. It has developed more comprehensive rules of quality assurance, retained control over accreditation of four-year institutions and graduate programmes, developed funding regimes for various project-based initiatives, and retained its hands-on approach to personnel management—in effect, the central authority has maintained direct control over hiring and firing decisions in the universities.

Organized institutional differentiation

The direct consequence of the implementation of the commanding heights strategy has been a process of organized institutional differentiation, including administrative differentiation, financial differentiation, functional differentiation and demographic differentiation (Wang 2014b). The commanding heights strategy has enlarged the gap between institutions positioned at different tiers in the institutional hierarchy.

Administrative differentiation refers to the creation of a strict institutional hierarchy by organizational affiliation. This hierarchy determines each institution's access to high quality freshmen in the recruitment process. The most selective or high-tier institutions recruit first after the announcement of the National College Entrance Examination scores in June, and the least selective or low-tier institutions take the rest with lowest scores. According to Loyalka, Song and Wei (2012), the first or the highest tier of higher education hierarchy consists of the most selective public four-year universities, the less selective four-year public universities comprise the second tier, the third tier comprises of still less selective four-year public or private universities (often called independent colleges), and three-year vocational institutions are the fourth and lowest tier (see Figure 10.3).

In 2013, the first tier of the hierarchy includes 73 universities affiliated with the Ministry of Education and other line ministries, 112 'Project 211' institutions and some leading provincial institutions (see Table 10.2). The second tier consists of 40 institutions under other

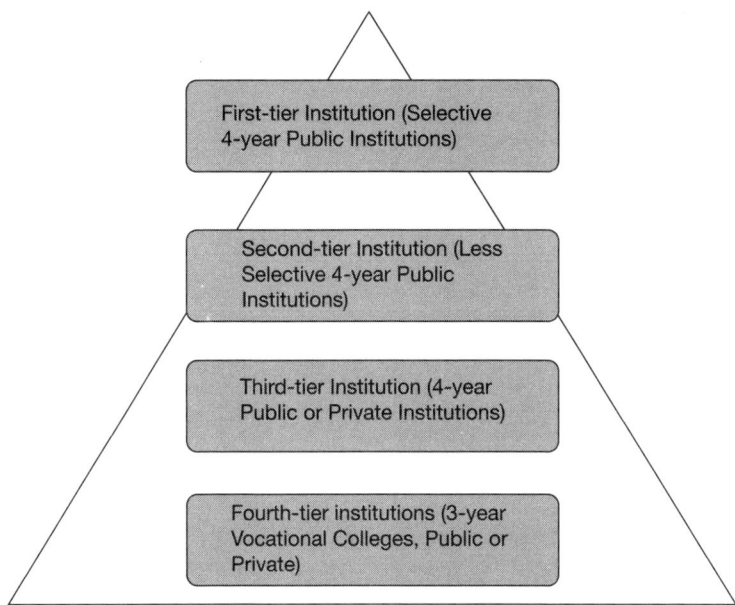

Figure 10.3 *Four Tiers of the Higher Education Hierarchy in China*
Source: Authors' summary based on Loyalka et al. (2012).

central ministries and agencies and more than 600 institutions affiliated with provincial governments. The third tier includes nearly 400 private four-year colleges, and the fourth tier consists of 325 private and 996 public three-year vocational colleges.

Another aspect of differentiation is finance. Grants for excellence initiatives such as Project 985, Project 211 and Project 2011 have enlarged the resource gap between top and bottom institutions. Figure 10.4 illustrates the difference in per student expenditure for institutions affiliated by the Ministry of Education and the regional ones. In 1998, per student expenditure for the former was 35 per cent higher than for regional institutions. Thirteen years later in 2011, the resource gap was 57 per cent.

Functional differentiation has been associated with the consolidation of power at the Ministry of Education; now the sole educational authority within central government. In addition, since the mid-1990s, the

Table 10.2 *Number of HEIs by Type and Sector (2013)*

	Total	HEIs Under Central Ministries & Agencies			HEIs Under Local Authorities				Non-State/ Private HEIs
		Total	HEIs Under MOE	HEIs Under Other Central Agencies	Total	HEIs Under Department of Education	Run by Non-education Departments	Local Enterprises	
Regular HEIs	2,491	113	73	40	1,661	1,015	598	48	717
University	1,170	110	73	37	668	601	67	41	392
Intendent College	292	—	—	—	—	—	—	—	292
Non-University Tertiary	1,321	3	—	3	993	414	531	—	325
HEIs for Adults	297	13	1	12	283	96	146	—	1

Source: Educational Statics Yearbook of China (2014).

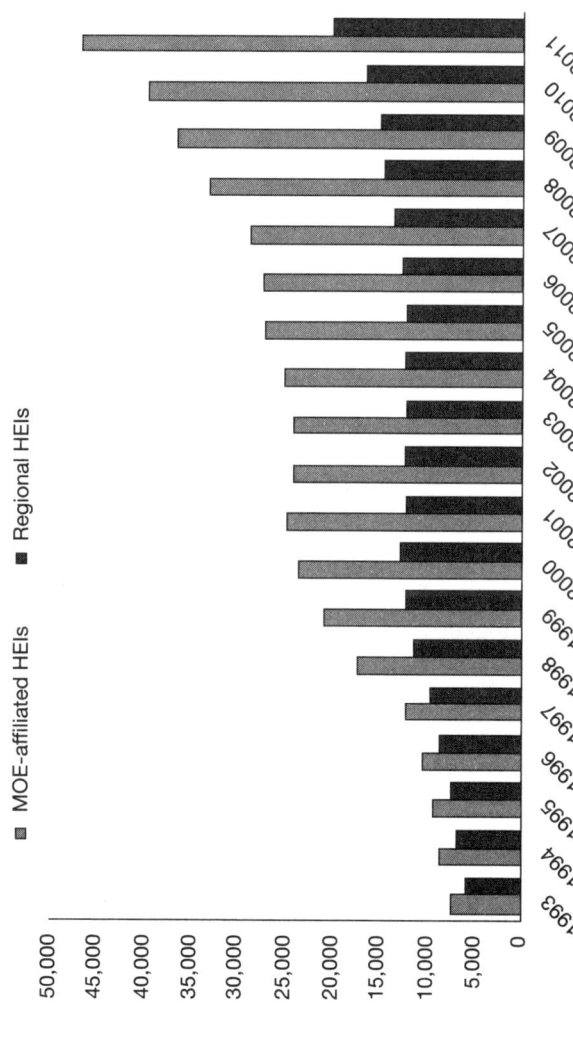

Figure 10.4 *Expenditure per Student in Centre- and Region-affiliated Institutions*

Source: Educational Statics Yearbook of China (various years); China Compendium of Statistics (1949–2008).

Ministry of Education has gained strengthened administrative authority over scientific research and development, alongside the Ministry of Science and Technology. Wang (2014b) argues that the Ministry of Education has formed a political coalition with elite institutions to advocate the construction of world-class universities (WCUs) in China. It constantly mobilizes political and social support for this. Once the project-based funding mechanism (e.g., Project 985 and Project 211) came into being, government support for individual institutions was no longer primarily determined by their own performances or routine budgetary appropriations, but it depended on the success or failure of the mobilization led by the Ministry of Education to secure and retain these huge categorical grant projects plus the collective performance of elite universities. The political coalition is the major source of support for functional differentiation.

Finally, demographic differentiation refers to the allocation of talents among tertiary institutions. China reintroduced a unified nationwide college entrance examination in 1977. Most tertiary institutions rely on this standardized test as the sole criteria for admission. Interestingly, Chinese colleges and universities cannot compete freely for talented high school graduates. Each year, the Development and Planning Division of the Ministry of Education allocates enrolment quotas for each province and, together with the Department of Education in each province, announces the recruitment tiers for public postsecondary institutions. The Ministry retains power over the allocation of one of the most sought-after resources in Chinese society—access to elite research universities. The tier system guarantees that national universities always recruit the most talented students and maintain their reputational rankings.

TERTIARY EXPANSION AND REGIONAL STRATIFICATION

The rise of the commanding heights strategy and the subsequent organizational differentiations are recent phenomena, accompanying the Fiscal Centralization Reform of the mid-1990s. If one takes a longer time horizon, it is obvious that China has experienced at least three tertiary expansions since 1949. Each of these expansions was conditioned by the central–regional relation at that time.

Those successive expansions highlight the power of the authoritarian regime to mobilize local governments to develop regional tertiary systems, politically and economically. At the same time, those expansions unavoidably reveal the limitations of the capacity of a fiscally centralized state to control regional variations in terms of provision and quality of tertiary education. In other national systems, these regional variations can be addressed either by federal-state coordination in the cooperative federalism state or by the decentralization of responsibility to lower-level government implied by the competitive federalism model.

Legacy of Three Expansions

Since 1949, three major higher education expansions occurred in China—the late 1950s, the early-1980s and the late-1990s (Yang 2014).

In the early 1950s, the national government adopted the Soviet Union model. It restructured the tertiary sector by consolidating comprehensive universities into specialized institutes, training industry-oriented talents and providing human resources for the industrialization process. Most tertiary institutions were centralized to the national government and followed a unified curriculum. However, during 'the Great Leap Forward' movement in the late-1950s, Chairman Mao decentralized the control of higher education to regional governments. The number of institutions increased from 205 in 1949 to 229 in 1957 and over 1,200 in 1960 (see Figure 10.5). Most of these institutions were affiliated to regional governments. The first wave of expansion served the national priority of an accelerated industrialization, and it was subject to the instrumental rationality prevailed at that time (Zhan and Chen 2013). It was also the result of a political competition among regional leaders encouraged by Chairman Mao under the slogan of 'promoting both central and regional incentives'.

The Cultural Revolution marked the beginning of another decentralization movement. The central government handed over nearly all its affiliated colleges and universities to local governments in 1966 and afterwards closed them down (Wang 2015). The number of institutions declined from over 1,200 in the early 1960s to around 400 in the late 1970s.

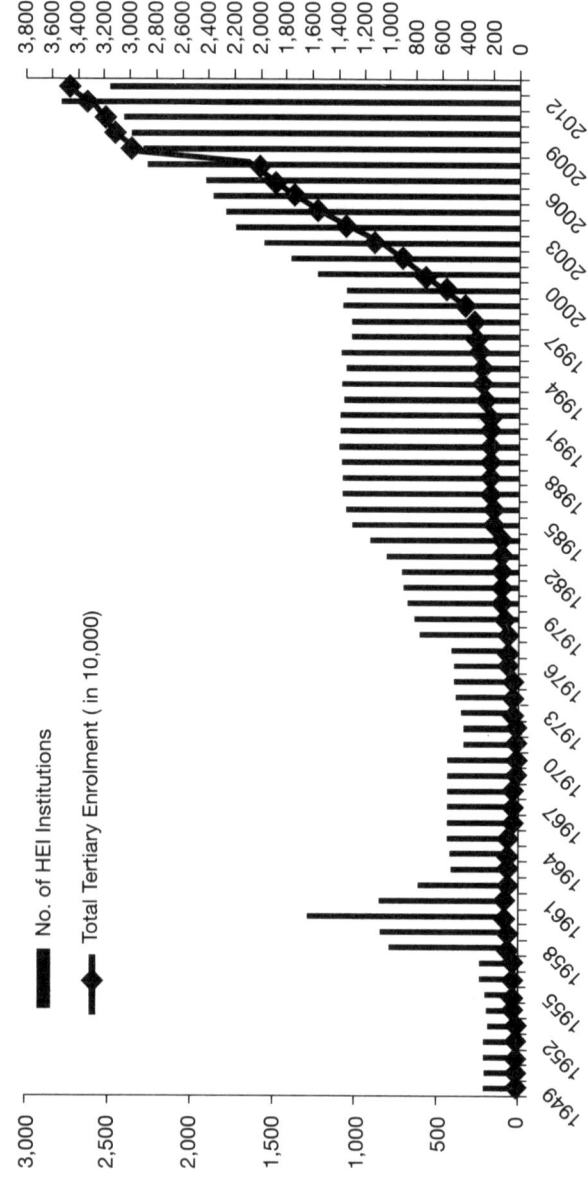

Figure 10.5 *Three Higher Education Expansions in China (1949 to Date)*

Source: Educational Statics Yearbook of China (various years); China Compendium of Statistics (1949–2008).

Their resurrection came in the second wave of expansion in the early to the mid-1980s, after the reopening of the National College Entrance Examination in 1977. The number of tertiary institutions bounced back to over 1,000 prior to the structural reforms that began in 1985. The structural reform changed the provision, governance, finance, recruitment, job placement and institutional administration of China's higher education system. Nearly 1,100 colleges and universities were operating by the mid-1990s. This second expansion was fully supported by regional governments. The fiscal decentralization policy at that time gave local leaders fiscal capacity and incentive to grow local institutions. The second wave of expansion aimed at satisfying the human resource needs of regional economic reforms (Yang 2014). Associated with the economic rationality dominant in the 1980s (Zhan and Chen 2013), it was largely financed by increased off-budget revenues generated by local governments from the profits of non-state enterprises and local state-owned enterprises (Ping 2007).

The third, latest and largest expansion occurred in the late 1990s and early 2000s. It lifted China to a mass higher education country. To stimulate domestic growth after the Asian Financial Crisis of 1997 and satisfy social demand for higher education, the state decided to provide wider access by encouraging regions to launch local institutions on a fee-paying basis. The number of colleges and universities jumped from less than 1,100 in 2000 to 2,491 in 2013. This expansion was guided by the practical rationality of the 1990s (Zhan and Chen 2013). As noted, the Tax Sharing Regime reform of 1993 fundamentally changed the incentive structure, so that higher education was defined as an administrative duty for subnational governments. Between 1998 and 2000, 196 institutions affiliated with either ministry or the central agency were transferred to the regions. Another 250 institutions affiliated to the Ministry of Education were transferred to provincial governments, under the co-sponsorship of central government and local government (Han and Guo 2011).

The majority of newly established colleges and universities are under local control. Among regular tertiary institutions, 66.7 per cent controlled by provincial or prefectural city governments. However, the growth of regional colleges and universities seems to contradict the fact that on-going fiscal centralization reform deprived local authorities of their fiscal capacity and incentive for tertiary expansion. The lack of incentive and capacity has been reconciled by the commanding heights strategy. The central authority allowed local governments more leeway in fundraising for regional expansion via private and public channels.

First, private financing was legitimized under the principle of cost sharing or cost recovery (Min 1998). The Ministry of Education had permitted local colleges and universities to charge tuitions and fees since 1997 as a part of their revenue diversification strategy. Moreover, the state had strengthened its financial aid system by the late 1990s. A large proportion of aid was provided by commercial banks via student loans (Ministry of Education 2015; Yang 2010). After 2004, student borrowing was an important revenue source for regional institutions, especially private ones.

Second, local governments' fiscal capacity was improved by the growth of off-budget revenue. Due to the increasing pressure for fiscal expenditure, their inability to form fiscal legislation and their lack of access to financial markets, China's regional governments had to find alternative funding resources. This led to a huge expansion of off-budget revenues after the mid-1990s (Fu 2010; Jia and Bai 1998; Wang and Gong 2009). Local off-budget revenue increased from RMB 291.8 billion in 1998 to RMB 606.2 billion in 2009. For 30 provincial governments, the average share of off-budget revenue in total fiscal revenue reached a historical height of 28.7 per cent in 2009 (Jiang and Xia 2012). Average local government expenditure climbed to 21–22 per cent of the value of regional GDP in 2004, which was high by international standards (Ping 2007).

A large proportion of off-budget revenue came from trading land for money, the so-called land finance policy of the past two decades (Zhou 2012), whereby local governments charge fees for land use through land department surcharges, user fees or rent collected by finance departments and a variety of fees imposed by other departments (Ping 2007).

Some provincial and prefecture city governments encourage local higher education institutions to acquire new and cheaper campuses in suburban areas by trading their original and expensive inner city sites to government. Thus, regional institutions can obtain new spaces and facilities needed for accommodating enrolment expansion, while local governments put precious inner city land up for sale and generate handsome profits. This new kind of land-grant institution is often located next to new industrial clusters created by local governments as a way to attract foreign and domestic investments. Land finance has become a popular method of regional governments' indirect financing of local higher education systems.

Higher Education Stratification from a Regional Perspective

The political nature of China's tertiary expansions and the variety of rationality behind them—the instrumental rationality of 1950s, the economic rationality of 1980s and the practical rationality of 1990s and early 2000s—have made regional stratification a defining characteristic of China's higher education expansion. The political, personnel and fiscal centralizations are mixed with economic decentralization. The central authority can stimulate regional higher education growth through the commanding heights strategy, but it cannot enforce a homogeneous standard for regional development. The previous section has demonstrated that the commanding heights strategy leads to an organized institutional differentiation. The following section provides evidence of its various impacts on regional stratification. This has many dimensions, including the size and structure of tertiary system across regions, college access across regions, the distribution of elite research universities across regions and differences in financing levels among regions.

Differences in size and structure of tertiary system

As discussed, provinces and prefecture cities are the primary service providers as well as being responsible for supervising and funding higher education. China's economic, social and cultural conditions vary substantially across regions. The widely used measurement of income inequality, the Gini coefficient for household income, was 0.479 for 2003, 0.491 for 2008 and 0.474 for 2012, according to China's National Statistics Bureau (Xinhua News Agency 2013).

The size and structure of regional tertiary systems reflect the unequal distribution of wealth (see Table 10A.2). The number of higher education institutions is high in developed regions such as Jiangsu (156), Shandong (139) and Guangdong (138), but low in less developed regions (6 in Tibet, 9 in Qinghai and 16 in Ningxia), with an average of 80 per province in 2013.

The enrolment size of regional tertiary system also varies (see Figure 10.6). Among all provinces, Tibet had the smallest system with 33,452 enrolled students in 2012, 2 per cent of the total enrolment in Jiangsu which has 1.67 million students. Many provinces enrolled more than one million students, such as Hebei, Jiangsu, Anhui, Shandong, Henan, Hubei, Hunan, Guangdong, Sichuan and Shaanxi.

Regional access to private colleges also varies substantially. Private institutions on average account for 24 per cent of institutions at provincial level. While Tianjin, Inner Mongolia, Guangxi, Guizhou and Tibet had no private universities in 2012, private colleges flourished in Shanxi (39%), Beijing (44%), Shanghai (76%) and Shandong (40%).

Among public institutions, access to academic and vocational institutions also differs by region. The average three-year vocational colleges share in the total public institutions was 53 per cent in 2013, ranging from 29 per cent in Beijing to 69 per cent in Inner Mongolia. Enrolment size by institution type shows a similar pattern (see Table 10A.3). As most high school graduates prefer to enter baccalaureate programmes in universities, 77 per cent of freshmen in Beijing enrolled in four-year universities, while only 43 per cent of freshmen were admitted to universities in Guangxi.

Differences in college access and student mobility

The varying size of provincial higher education systems definitely affects college access and student mobility. Regional college participation rates vary substantially. Figure 10.7 and Table 10A.4 illustrate that for every 100,000 residents in each province, the numbers of high school students and college students differ substantially. Nationwide, the average number of college students for every 100,000 residents were 2,488 in 2014. Beijing, Tianjin and Shanghai have far more college students than

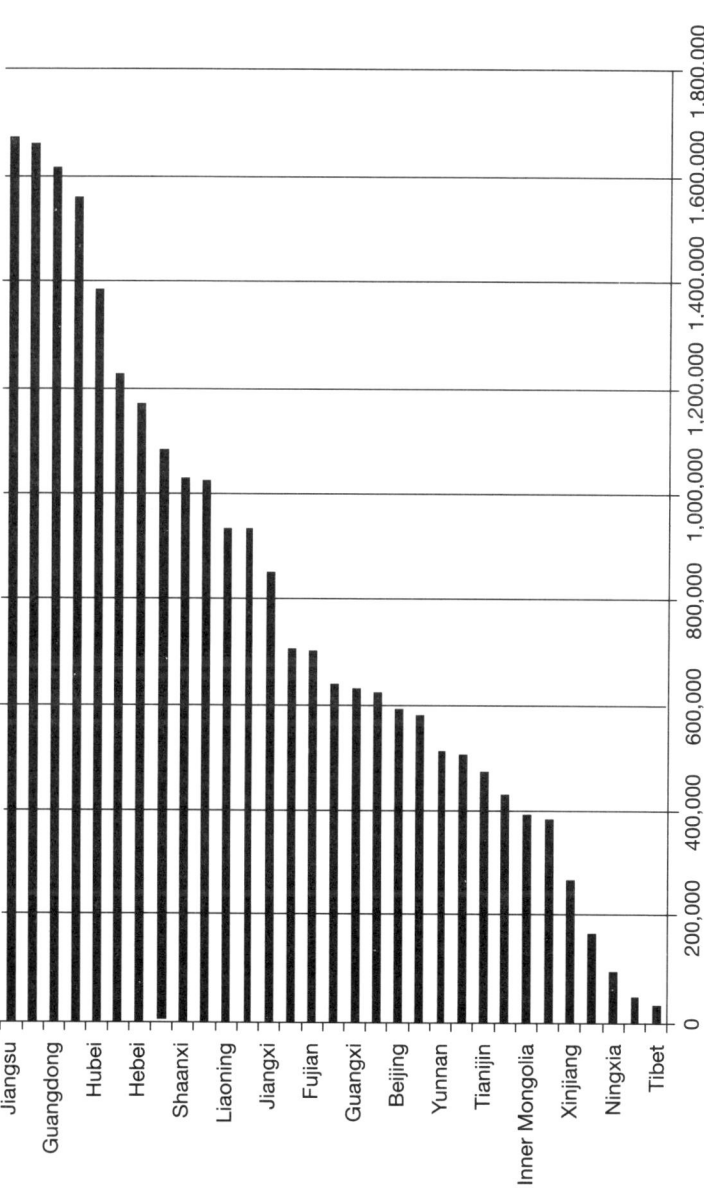

Figure 10.6 *Number of Enrolled Undergraduate Students by Region (2012)*
Source: China Statistic Yearbook 2013.

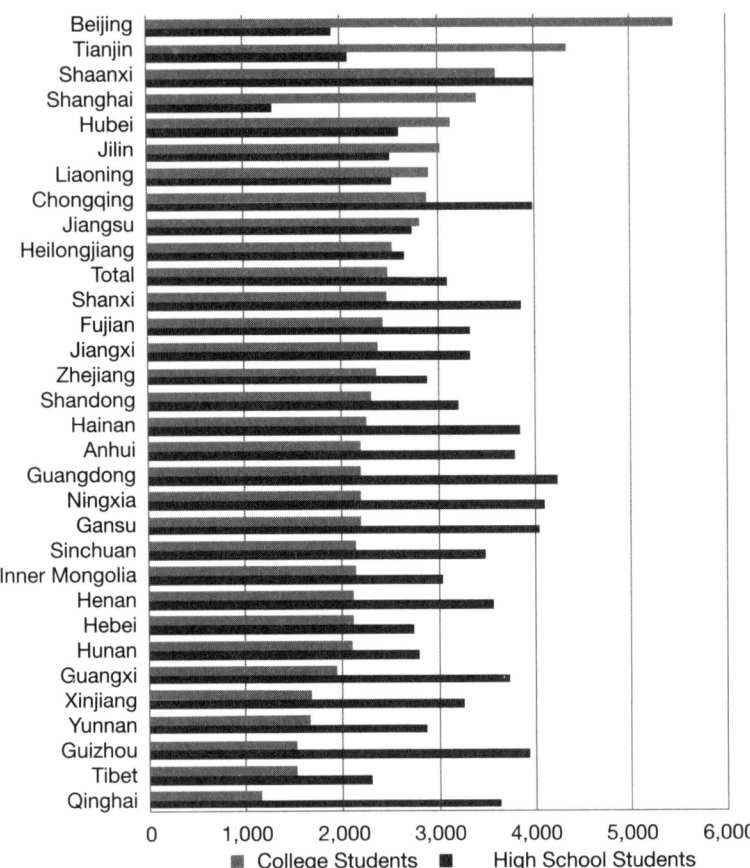

Figure 10.7 *Number of High School and College Students for Every 100,000 Residents (2014)*

Source: China Statistic Yearbook for Health and Birth Control 2015.

other regions with 5,469, 4,346 and 3,421, respectively. Table 10A.4 also reports the high school to college student ratio, another indicator of college access. The higher the ratio, the more difficult it is to attend college in the region concerned. Anhui, Henan, Shanxi, Guangdong, Guangxi, Hainan, Sichuan, Guizhou, Gansu, Qinghai, Ningxia and Xinjiang have a score of 1.5 or higher on this scale, which is translated to a lower college access for local residents.

Student mobility rates also vary across regions. Recent analysis of the distribution of vocational college students indicates that richer regions tend to absorb enrolment from other regions. Table 10A.5 shows that, on average, 82 per cent of high school graduates attended vocational colleges in their own provinces in 2008. The ratio ranged from 43.38 per cent in Tianjin, 56.54 per cent in Shanghai and 70.92 per cent in Chongqing. In less developed regions, such as Guangxi (92.43%), Anhui (92.61%), Yunnan (93.41%) and Tibet (100%), most high school graduates had to attend their regional institutions.

Distribution of elite institutions

One characteristic of China's higher education hierarchy is that classification is not based on an institution's mission, but rather a combination of institution type and sector. Unlike the Carnegie Classification (2011), which is mainly based on institutional mission and profile such as instruction, enrolment profile, size and setting, Chinese tier system reflects the selectivity of undergraduate enrolment, the highest level of degree conferred, and sector (public versus private) of institution. The tier system is heavily influenced by history and institutional affiliation. It is both a reputational hierarchy and works as an administrative tool, and it is fixed. It is almost impossible for an individual institution to move upmarket within the system.

Since 1980s, the central authority has improved research in the national universities, which have become elite research institutions.[3] There is a concentration of selective universities in certain regions, generating regional variation in access to high quality institutions. Beijing has 26 and Shanghai has 9 'Project 211' institutions, while 13 other provinces have only one such institution, two provinces have two, four provinces have three, and other four provinces have four.

---

[3] Recent data shows a very high level of overlap between national universities and Project 211 institutions—the most selective university in China (Li et al. 2012). Among 110 centrally controlled universities, 73 (66%) are affiliated to Ministry of Education. They are all designated as the Project 211 institutions. In comparison, only 39 out of 668 (5.8%) regional universities are chosen as Project 211 institutions.

Differences in financing levels

As noted, the commanding heights form of central–regional relations means that the central government plays a supplementary funding role, and provincial or prefecture city governments are the leading funders of regional institutions. Variation in the fiscal capacity of regional governments affects the funds available for local institutions (see Table 10A.6).[4] The total revenue for public higher education institutions reached RMB 43,090 million in Guangdong in 2013, 28.9 times larger than funds for colleges in Qinghai (RMB 1,491 million).

However, the amount of revenue is the same as governmental fiscal commitment. Some provinces rely more on budgetary appropriation, while others depend on private finance (see Table 10A.6). Beijing (73%), Tianjin (66%), Shanghai (68%), Inner Mongolia (67%), Guizhou (64%), Tibet (90%), Qinghai (71%), Ningxia (67%) and Xinjiang (72%) are examples of a relatively high level of budgetary appropriation. In comparison, Hebei, Liaoning, Jilin, Heilongjiang, Zhejiang, Fujian, Hubei, Guangdong, Chongqing and Shaanxi are typical tuition-dependent regions where tuitions covered more than 30 per cent of institution revenue.

The single most important indicator of regional stratification in finance is per student fiscal expenditure. Table 10A.7 provides information for 2013. The high expenditure regions include Beijing (RMB 48,071 per student per year), Tianjin (RMB 23,047), Shanghai (RMB 35,682) and Tibet (RMB 37,423). Six low expenditure regions— Anhui, Henan, Gansu, Fujian, Shandong and Heilongjiang—failed to meet the national standard set by the central government in 2010, which was RMB 12,000 per student per year by 2012.

These explicit variations in regional tertiary systems, in structure and resources, highlight the fact that the extensive use of the commanding

---

[4] Owing to the fact that intergovernmental transfer accounts for 40–50 per cent of local governments' fiscal expenditure and the difficulty to split the budgetary transfer from the central government and the revenue generated by regional governments, here we can only identify higher education institution's revenue from fiscal allocation, tuition and revenue from sales and services.

heights strategy supports a rapidly expanding higher education sector in China but also one that is increasingly stratified.

HIGHER EDUCATION GOVERNANCE AND A SYNTHESIZED FRAMEWORK

Current Higher Education Governance

The commanding heights form of central–regional relationship has shaped China's contemporary tertiary governance structure. By commanding the heights within the higher education sector, the national government can steer this sector from above, while subnational governments must run regional systems with the authorization from the central government. The canonical division of higher education responsibility was formally stated in China's Higher Education Act, 1999 (HEA 1999 hereafter), and reinforced by the National Outline for Medium- and Long-Term Educational Reform and Development (2010–2020), jointly issued by the Communist Party's Central Standing Committee and the State Council in 2010.

The 1999 Act emphasizes that the national government has the absolute authority over national higher education affairs and directly rules a small group of tertiary institutions that serve national interests. In contrast, regional governments can manage local institutions on behalf of the central authority (Articles 13 and 14, HEA 1999). For instance, Article 13 of the Act stipulates,

> The State Council shall unify its leadership and management of national higher education. Provincial, SAR, and Municipality City governments shall coordinate higher education affairs within their jurisdictions, managing regional higher education institutions entrusted by the national authority which cultivate talents mainly for regional development.

Article 14 further states that the Ministry of Education under the State Council should be responsible for national higher education affairs and manage tertiary institutions which cultivate talents for the nation and are designated by the State Council.

Based on the World Bank's analytical framework for university governance (Fielden 2008), we develop a three-dimension schema to analyse China's higher education governance. First, we divide administrative responsibilities into three categories—regulation, provision and finance. Next, we separate central and provincial governments' administrative duties for each category. The information supporting this analysis includes various educational legislation, national planning and key reform documents from the late 1990s up to the present.

Regulation

The regulation of tertiary education involves many areas. The HEA 1999 authorizes China's Ministry of Education to fulfil most administrative duties on behalf of the central government. The central government has granted this ministry the rights to set the vision and goals for the higher education system; set national higher education policies and objectives; determine the size and shape of the sector; and assess the quality of teaching and research. The Ministry of Education is able to control the most sought-after resources affecting regional system development, such as the enrolment quotas for regions and institutions.

The Ministry of Education is supposed to share certain administrative duties with other central line ministries and agencies. Inter-ministry coordination plays an important role in central regulation. To enforce its policies, the Ministry of Education often forms coalitions with other powerful players such as the Ministry of Finance, the State Council and the State Development and Reform Committee. For instance, recent tertiary policies regarding graduate student financial aid (Ministry of Finance and Ministry of Education 2013) and undergraduate instruction quality and reform (Ministry of Education and Ministry of Finance 2015) were all jointly issued by several ministries or agencies.

Meanwhile, the State Council authorizes provincial governments to regulate and coordinate regional institutions within their jurisdictions. With central authorization, the provincial Department of Education can steer educational planning, system size and structure, quality of teaching and research in its region.

Provision

Accreditation is one of the most important aspects of higher education governance. China's Ministry of Education is authorized by the central government to grant licences to new public or private four-year institutions, while provincial governments can accredit public three-year vocational colleges and private ones with authorization from the State Council (Article 29, HEA 1999). This allows the central government to control the size of the more selective tiers and balance the regional distribution of four-year institutions. It also gives regional leaders incentives to expand vocational institutions.

In matters concerning the internal governance of universities, such as approving universities' strategic plans or supporting university governance and management, the Ministry of Education only manages its affiliated institutions, the 73 national universities. Other line ministries or central agencies take care of their affiliated institutions, another 40 or so colleges and universities. At regional level, all four-year public institutions are affiliated to provincial Departments of Education. They negotiate their internal issues with regional education authorities. Many three-year vocational colleges are affiliated with prefecture city governments, so that their internal governance issues are in the hands of local authorities.

Finance

As noted, the provincial level is the prime level for running public institutions in terms of financing (Articles 29 and 60, HEA 1999). The central level provides supplementary funding focusing on research and development as well as student financial aid.

The Ministry of Education operates major national financial aid programmes, such as the National Grant Program, National Student Loan Program, Tuition Exemption Project, Temporary Assistance for College Freshmen, Graduate Student Aid Program, and Work Study Program (Yang 2010). In 2014, the total amount of financial aid for college students reached RMB 71.69 billion, which covered 40.64 million students (Ministry of Education 2015). In terms of composition, 31.21

per cent of college financial aid comes from the central government. Local government contributes another 19.93 per cent. The rest of aid comes from higher education institutions' sales and services revenue (23.84%), social funds (1.72%) and commercial banks (23.29%).

In research funding, the State Council distributes most of the basic research funding through the National Science Foundation of China and the China Academy of Science system. However, the Ministry of Education is involved in the allocation of research funds at national level. In 2013, it allocated RMB 17.29 billion for research in tertiary educa-tion institution, 2.11 per cent of the national fiscal allocation for tertiary education. The Ministry of Education has also supported national excel-lence initiatives since the mid-1990s. For instance, it invested RMB 23 billion for the first phase of Project 985, another RMB 23 billion in the second phase and more than RMB 450 billion in the third phase.

As part of the commanding heights of institutional hierarchy, the Ministry of Education provides operational budgets for the national universities. Other ministries or central agencies pay for their affiliated institutions. The Ministry of Education also uses intergovernmental transfers to support special national programmes[5] and monitors insti-tutional teaching and research performance by setting accountability criteria and conducting periodic inspections.

Provincial Departments of Education are only responsible for pro-viding operational budgets for their affiliated institutions. They also use categorical grants to support special programmes within their jurisdic-tion and monitor the performance of local institutions.

CONCLUSIONS

Commanding Heights Strategy Revisited

The commanding heights form of central–regional relation has by and large shaped the profile of China's higher education system in recent

---

[5] For instance, Ministry of Education had provided categorical grants for the construction of 100 Demonstrative National Vocational Colleges from 2006 to 2010, while these three-year colleges were affiliated to provincial, prefecture, county government or even local enterprises.

years. As mentioned earlier, the centralization of revenue and political authority and the decentralization of public expenditure responsibilities have created an asymmetry in intergovernmental relations. Central government can consolidate authority over higher education authority to the Ministry of Education and build multiple commanding heights in this sector,[6] while significantly compromising subnational governments' capacity and incentive for providing tertiary education services.

The commanding heights strategy is part of a system of political rule specific to China. By maintaining control over personnel and their mobility at all levels, the Communist Party of China can use the higher education system as a national labour bureau for privileged careers that constitute both a ruling cadre and a clientele dependent on that cadre. The party also pays special attention to social elite formation and reproduction. These are overlapping though not identical functions and in both of them higher education has a central role.

The current central–local governmental relation provides both legitimacy and functional infrastructure for the commanding heights strategy. On the one hand, the central–regional relation favours the creation of an institutional hierarchy. Fiscal asymmetry enlarges the funding gap between national universities and regional institutions, as demonstrated by Figure 10.4. The resource gap has direct implications for institutional ranking. The heavy investment from the central government in national universities allows them to pursue a costly research-intensive strategy, which rapidly improves their reputation. Thus, the commanding heights of institution hierarchy are made possible by the resource gap derived from the asymmetric central–regional relation. On the other hand, the power asymmetry legitimizes the central government's interventions in regional systems. With the support of huge intergovernmental transfers, the Ministry of Education is expected to improve quality of regional systems and equalizing resources available

---

[6] The commanding heights in China's higher education sector include (a) centralized control over allocation of talented students to various institutions through enrolment quota and the function of a rigid higher education hierarchy, (b) centralized control over institution and programme accreditation through Ministry of Education and the State Council, (c) centralized control over elite research universities and (d) centralized control over research funding through national excellence programmes managed by Ministry of Education.

for regional institutions. The commanding heights of mechanisms of intervention are thereby legitimized and accepted.

A Synthesized Framework for Regional Tertiary Development

The discussion so far reveals two limitations of the commanding heights strategy. First, it can potentially compromise subnational governments' capacity and incentive for providing tertiary education services. This refers to its 'cooling-out effect'. Second, even if this strategy can incentivize local bureaucrats, it can lead to unbalanced regional higher education developments, the 'polarization effect'.

To overcome these negative effects, it is of primary importance to discover conditions for higher education growth and development in China's regions. Those conditions shall produce sufficient incentives for local politicians to adopt pro-higher education policies, while discouraging over-supply of tertiary services.

Prior literature has focused on conditions that encourage subnational governments to implement growth-oriented economic policies, such as realistic promotion opportunities for local politicians based on their performance and allocation of residual budgetary revenues to the regional budgets (Weingast 2009). Scholars find that non-democracies are traditionally unable to uphold these conditions and decentralize the governance system (Filippov, Ordeshook and Shvetsova 2004). This dilemma is true for China's local governments who are responsible for regional tertiary systems: Higher education governance is relatively centralized and the promotion of educational bureaucratese is marginally related to their performance.

To analyse this subtle incentive question, we extend the prior Chinese-style federalism literature by arguing that although asymmetric central–regional relations may compromise local bureaucrats' incentives, sectoral and political mobilization can potentially induce local efforts. Based on this argument, we propose a synthesized framework for analysing the development of regional systems. Figure 10.8 lays out its four major elements, including consensus of the Communist Party of China elites, sectoral authority and sectoral network, local pro-higher

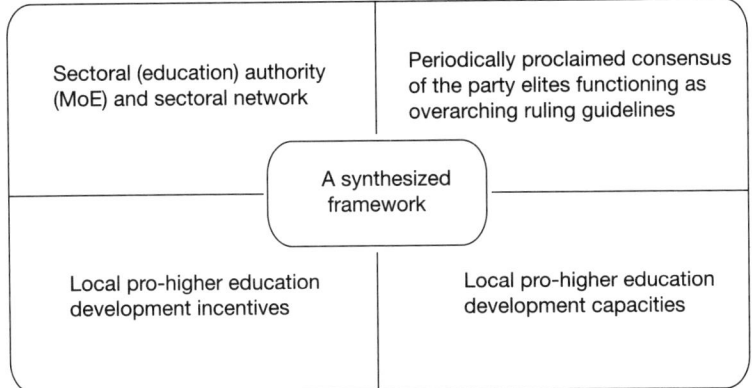

Figure 10.8 *A Synthesized Framework for Regional Tertiary Development*

Source: Authors' summary.

education development incentives, and local pro-higher education development capacities.

The first part of the framework focuses on political mobilization for regional higher education development. We hypothesize that the periodically proclaimed consensus of the Party elites can function as the overarching ruling guidelines for regional development. Political elites can push local bureaucrats to adopt pro-higher education policies through the 'campaign-style governance routine', typically observed in public policy adoption and implementation at regional level (Zhou 2012). By manipulating the fiscal relation through sizable intergovernmental transfer programmes or the use of land finance policies, the Party can easily stimulate local politicians to adopt pro-higher education policies.

The second part of the framework focuses on sectoral mobilization. The dual nature of the Ministry of Education—functioning as both line ministry and leading agency in a vertical political coalition—makes it possible to mobilize subnational governments to pursue regional growth. As noted, our earlier work indicates the Ministry of Education has successfully created a vertical network though the campaign for the construction of WCUs (Wang 2014b).

Local authorities have sectoral, political and economic incentives for tertiary development.

- *Sectoral incentives*: When regional bureaucrats are seen to improve the quality of higher education services under their jurisdiction, they advance their position in the hierarchy. The cadre ranks of institutional leaders are officially linked to the administrative ranks of institutions.
- *Political incentives*: Higher education performance indicators may be considered in decisions concerning the promotion of local governors in the Party cadre hierarchy. Hence, regional candidates for central positions may invest in local tertiary education systems.
- *Economic incentives*: Tertiary education institutions can directly contribute to regional innovation and growth, stimulating local leaders to improve regional higher education services.

Significance of the China Case

Although the stratification effect of the commanding heights strategy seem large, at world level, strategies like this have been common during periods of higher education expansion. California's Master Plan is an early example of stratification embedded in tertiary expansion (Clark 1983). Carnoy et al. (2013) observe that most of the BRIC countries introduce some kind of excellence programme, with stratifying effects.

Most large countries, federal or unitary, have expanded their tertiary systems in recent decades. They have followed a range of trajectories. Table 10.3 compares the characteristics of some large tertiary education systems.

Several observations can be made about this comparison. The dynamics of stratification may vary in different countries, depending on whether there are national universities and/or elite private universities, and whether regional universities are in the majority.

First, national government does not always directly provide higher education through national public universities. Among the six countries compared, only Russia, Japan and China have national universities. Interestingly, elite private universities are very rare worldwide. Here

Table 10.3 *Some Characteristics of Large Tertiary Education Systems*

	US	Germany	Canada	Russia	Japan	China
National Public Universities	No	No	No	Yes	Yes	Yes
Elite Private Universities	Yes	No	No	No	Yes	No
Regional HEIs as Major Public Providers	Yes	Yes	Yes	No	Yes	Yes
Binary System (with TVET as Independent System)	No	Yes	No	No	No	No

Source: Authors' summary.

they only exist in the United States and Japan. Private universities in the other four countries never earn national significance or join the elite league. Elite private universities play a much lesser role in Japan (a unitary country) than in the United States (a federal state). Moreover, higher education expansion does not necessarily lead to the growth of a diverse regional system. Russian's regional higher education institutions are not the major public providers. Russia is unusual in its retardation of growing regional systems. Finally, tertiary vocational education is often united with the academic higher education system. Only Germany has a binary system in which universities of applied sciences are an independent vocational sector.

Some of these system characteristics are related to the specific nature of the strategies of expansion. Japan and China both have national universities and a large regional university system. However, all elite universities in China are public while some are private in Japan. The lack of elite private institutions in China indicates that the central government has managed the growth and role of private colleges and universities by keeping them in the lower tiers of the hierarchy and maintaining tight accreditation standards, thus helps to maintain a politically controlled organizational field for higher education development.

The China case illustrates that in a non-federal state, it is a possible to launch a rapid higher education expansion including the quick growth of regional systems. The state is able to both build WCUs and absorb the increasing enrolment in the non-selective regional institutions, as long as the commanding heights strategy can provide local bureaucrats with enough incentives through the decentralization of administrative authority towards regional governments. The commanding heights strategy is more than a convenient higher education policy; it is part of the system of political rule of China.

Discussion and Future Research

This chapter is one of the first attempts to explain the nature of China's recent and massive higher education expansion and the associated institutional and regional stratification, from the perspective of political economy. The centre–region relation and the related stratification of higher education have been essential in shaping the national system over time. Our discussion shows that to develop a better understanding of central–local government relations in higher education it is essential to know a nation's political institutions and public finance system. Political institutions determine the division of responsibility for higher education between national and subnational governments, while the intergovernmental fiscal relation has direct effects on both the fiscal capacity of regional authorities and higher education governance.

China's case also suggests that commanding heights-type strategy has its limitations. This strategy can promote a rapid enrolment expansion in regional institutions, but it may also lead to a cooling-out effect in local politicians' incentives for tertiary development and a polarization effect in terms of considerable and increasing regional variations.

This chapter also demonstrates the importance of incentives for the growth of regional systems. In China, the combination of political and fiscal centralization with economic decentralization implies that additional political and sectoral mobilizations are needed to incentivize regional bureaucrats to focus on pro-higher education policies. However, it is still unclear under what conditions local politicians will follow beneficial policies and to what extent political and sectoral mobilization are perceived as real incentives.

Future research is needed in several areas. First, empirical analysis of the impact of the commanding heights strategy on regional variations may help us pin down the 'cooling-out effect' and the 'polarization effect'. Second, careful case studies of typical regions may provide evidence of political and sectoral mobilization within China's tertiary sector. Third, a comparative analysis with other non-democracies, such as Russia, may contribute to our understanding of whether the commanding heights form of central–regional relations is unique to former Leninist regimes, and how to make credible commitments to local bureaucrats.

REFERENCES

Altbach, P. G. 2009. 'The Giants Awake: Higher Education Systems in China and India'. *Economic and Political Weekly*, 39–51.

Arum, R., Gamoran, A., and Shavit, Y. 2007. *More Inclusion than Diversion: Expansion, Differentiation, and Market Structure in Higher Education*. In *Stratification in Higher Education: A Comparative Study*, edited by Y. Shavit, et al., 1–35. California, PA: Stanford University Press.

Bardhan, P. K., and Mookherjee, D. 2006. *Decentralization and Local Governance in Developing Countries: A Comparative Perspective*, Vol. 1. Massachusetts: The MIT Press.

Carnoy, M., Loyalka, P., Dobryakova, M., Dossani, R., Froumin, I., Kuhns, K., and Wang, R. 2013. *University Expansion in a Changing Global Economy: Triumph of the BRICs?* Stanford University Press.

Clark, B. 1983. *The Higher Education System: Academic Organization in Cross-national Perspective*. Berkeley, CA: University of California Press.

Fielden, J. 2008. 'Global Trends in University Governance'. World Bank Education Working Paper Series, Washington, DC, USA.

Filippov, M., Ordeshook, P. C., and Shvetsova, O. 2004. *Designing Federalism: A Theory of Self-sustainable Federal Institutions*. Cambridge, UK: Cambridge University Press.

Fu, Y. 2010. 'Fiscal Decentralization, Government Management and the Supply of Non-economic Public Goods'. *Economic Research* 2010 (8): 4015.

Han, G. J., and Guo, J. R. 2011. 'The Organizational Transformation of the Ownership Transferred Colleges: A case study of a University in Hubei Province'. *Education Research Monthly* 53–57 (in Chinese).

Jia, K., and Bai, J. M. 1998. 'Revenue Sources of Chinese Government and Improvement Policy Analysis'. *Economic Research*, 1998 (6): 46–54 (in Chinese).

Jia, K., and Liang, J. 2011. 'Institutional Logic for Central-local Fiscal Allocation in China'. *Fiscal Study* 2011 (1): 5–14 (in Chinese).

Jia, K., and Zhao, Q. H. et al. 2008. *30 Years of Review of China's Fiscal System Reform and Future Perspective*. Beijing, China: People's Press (in Chinese).

Jiang, K. Z., and Xia, C. M. 2012. 'The Off-budgetary Revenue Expansion and Public Goods Supply of Local Government Under Fiscal Decentralization—An Empirical Analysis Based on China Provincial Panel Data'. *Zhejing Social Science Journal* 8 (15): 222–224 (in Chinese).

Jiang, Q. 2009. 'Empirical Analysis of Vertical Fiscal Imbalance at Provincial, City and County Level in China'. *Journal of Anhui University* 2009 (3): 134–140 (in Chinese).

Jin, H., Qian, Y., and Weingast, B. R. 2005. 'Regional Decentralization and Fiscal Incentives: Federalism, Chinese Style'. *Journal of Public Economics*, 89 (9), 1719–1742.

Jing, Q. 2007. 'The Tax Sharing Regime and the Vertical Fiscal Imbalance in China: Measurement Based on Hunter Method'. *Journal of Central Finance & Economics University* 2007 (1): 13–16 (in Chinese).

Krug, B., and Libman, A. 2015. 'Commitment to Local Autonomy in Non-democracies: Russia and China Compared'. *Constitutional Political Economy* 26 (2): 221–245.

Li, H., and Zhou, L. A. 2005. 'Political Turnover and Economic Performance: The Incentive Role of Personnel Control in China'. *Journal of Public Economics* 89 (9): 1743–1762.

Li, H. B., Meng, L. S., Shi, X. Z., and Wu, B. Z. 2012. 'Does Attending Elite Colleges Pay in China?' *Journal of Comparative Economics* 40 (1): 78–88.

Liu, Y. 2013. *Public Finance*. Beijing: Peking University Press (in Chinese).

Liu, C. Q., and Ke, X. 2015. 'Impact of Vertical Fiscal Imbalance on Provincial Basic Education Service Performance Variation in China'. *Economic Issue* 2015 (1): 7–14 (in Chinese).

Liu, M. X., Zhang, D., Shih, Z. H., and Zhu, M. C. 2014. 'Power Structure of Political Elites and Sustainability of Economic Centralization in China'.

Loyalka, P., Song, Y. Q., and J. G. Wei. 2012. 'The Effects of Attending Selective College Tiers in China'. *Social Science Research* 41 (2): 287–305.

Luo, W. Q. 2009. 'Do Fiscal Decentralization and Vertical Fiscal Imbalance Affect China's Basic Education Quality?' *Journal of Tsinghua University* 24 (S1): 13–20 (in Chinese).

Marginson, S. 2016a. 'Global Stratification in Higher Education'. In *Higher Education, Stratification, and Workforce Development*, 13–34. Basel, Switzerland: Springer International Publishing.

———. (2016b). 'High Participation Systems of Higher Education'. *The Journal of Higher Education* 87 (2): 243–271.

Min, W. F. 1998. 'Essay on Theoretical Foundation of Cost Recovery Policy in Higher Education'. *Journal of Peking University (Philosophy and Social Science)* 1998 (2): 181–185 (in Chinese).

———. 2004. 'Chinese Higher Education'. In *Asian Universities: Historical Perspectives and Contemporary Challenges*, edited by P. G. Altbach and T. Umakoshi, 53–84. Baltimore, Maryland: JHU Press.

Ministry of Education and Ministry of Finance. 2010. Guidelines for Further Increasing Per Student Fiscal Allocation in Regional Four-year Institutions. Available at http://old.moe.gov.cn//publicfiles/business/htmlfiles/moe/moe_1779/201308/155147.html

———. 2015. *Guidelines for Undergraduate Instruction Reform and Teaching Quality Projects in 2014 and 2015*. Available at http://www.moe.gov.cn/jyb_xxgk/moe_1777/moe_1779/201408/t20140811_173687.html

Ministry of Education. 2015. *National Report on Student Financial Aid in 2014*. Available at http://www.moe.gov.cn/jyb_xwfb/gzdt_gzdt/s5987/201508/t20150818_200680.html

Ministry of Finance and Ministry of Education. 2013. *Temporary Regulation on National Grant for Graduate Students (No.2013.220)*. Available at http://www.moe.gov.cn/jyb_xxgk/moe_1777/moe_1779/201308/t20130812_155561.html

Ping, X. Q. 2007. 'The Trend of Expansion of China's Local Government Expenditure Scale'. *Comparative Analysis of Economic and Social Institution* 129 (1): 50–58.

Qian, Y., and Weingast, B. R. 1997. 'Federalism as a Commitment to Preserving Market Incentives'. *The Journal of Economic Perspectives* 83–92.

Qian, Y., and Xu, C. 1993. 'Why China's Economic Reforms Differ: The M-form Hierarchy and Entry/Expansion of the Non-state Sector'. *The Economics of Transition* 1 (2): 135–170.

Qian, Y., Roland, G., and Xu, C. 2006. 'Coordination and Experimentation in M-form and U-form Organizations'. *Journal of Political Economy* 114 (2): 366–402.

Rosen, H. S., and Gayer, T. 2009. *Public Finance*, 9th edition. New York, NY: McGraw-Hill Irwin.

Shih, V., Adolph, C., and Liu, M. 2012. 'Getting Ahead in the Communist Party: Explaining the Advancement of Central Committee Members in China'. *American Political Science Review* 106 (01): 166–187.

Teichler, U. forthcoming. Germany: Continuous inter-governmental negotiations. In *Higher Education in Federal Countries: A Comparative Study*, edited by M. Carnoy, I. Froumin, O. Leshukov, and S. Marginson. New Delhi: SAGE Publications.

Wang, J. L. 2015. 'The Critical Reading into Chinese Education Finance History based on CCP Convention Reports'. Unpublished Working Paper, China Institute for Education Finance Research, Beijing, China.

Wang, R. 2014a. 'The Commanding Heights: The State and Higher Education in China'. In *The Oxford Companion to the Economics of China*, edited by S. G. Fan, Ravi Kanbur, Shang-Jin Wei and Xiaobo Zhang, et al., 472–477. Oxford, UK: Oxford University Press.

———. 2014b. 'Organized Differentiation, Political Coalition and China's Higher Education'. Paper presented at the 2014 Annual Conference for Russian Higher Education Research Association, Moscow, 14–19 November.

Wang, X., and Liu, J. 2011. 'China's Higher Education Expansion and the Task of Economic Revitalization'. *Higher Education* 62 (2): 213–229.

Wang, Z. G., and Gong, L. T., 2009. 'Fiscal Decentralization and Local Government Non-tax Revenue: Based on Provincial Fiscal Data'. *World Economic Literature* 2009 (5): 17–38 (in Chinese).

Wei, J. G. 2007. 'Comparative Study on Institutional Patterns of Division of Fiscal Powers and the Choice of China'. *Law and Social Development* 78 (6): 128 (in Chinese).

———. (2014). 'Historical Evolution of China's Higher Education Finance'. Unpublished Working Paper, China Institute for Education Finance Research.

———. (2015). *On Legalization of Fiscal Relationship between the Central Government and Local Governments*. Beijing: Peking University Press (in Chinese).

Weingast, B. R. 2009. 'Second Generation Fiscal Federalism: The Implications of Fiscal Incentives'. *Journal of Urban Economics* 65 (3): 279–293.

Xinhua News Agency. 2013. 'Gini Coefficient: Which Version is More Reliable? Public or Private?' *Xinhua News Agency*. Available at http://news.xinhuanet.com/politics/2013-02/05/c_124322401.htm

Xu, C. G. 2011. 'The Fundamental Institutions of China's Reforms and Development'. *Journal of Economics Literature* 49 (4): 1076–1151.

Xu, H. X. 2014. 'Introduction to the Chinese System of Higher Education'. Unpublished Memo, National Center for Education Development Research, Chinese Ministry of Education.

Yang, P. 2010. 'Who Gets More Financial Aid in China? A Multilevel Analysis'. *International Journal of Educational Development* 30 (6): 560–569.

———. 2014. 'Chinse Higher Education in Expansion'. Paper presented at the II Summer School of Higher Education Research, National Research University-Higher School of Economics, Institute of Education Pushkin, St. Petersburg.

———. 2015. Regional Government's Fiscal Allocation for Vocational Higher Education Institutions in China. In *Chinese Education Finance Policy Consultation Report*, edited by R. Wang and J. G. Wei. Beijing, China: Education Science Publishing House (in Chinese).

Zhan, L. X., and Chen, X. F. 2013. 'Rational Perspective: Moving Out of Higher Education'. *Peking University Education Review* 2013 (1): 950125 (in Chinese).

Zhang, Q. F. 2012. *State Sovereign and Local Autonomy: Legalization of the Relationship Between the Central Government and Local Governments*. Beijing, China: China Democracy and Law Press.

Zhou, F. Z. 2012. *Yi Li Wei Li: Fiscal Relation and Local Government Behavior*. Shanghai Sanlian Press.

Zhou, H. F., Chen, Ye, and Li, Hongbin. 2005. 'Relative Performance Evaluation and the Turnover of Provincial Leaders in China'. *Economics Letters* 88 (3): 421–425.

APPENDIX

Table 10A.1 Characteristics of Symmetric and Asymmetric Systems

	Symmetric Country (United States)	Asymmetric Country (Germany)
Constitutional Structure and Government Levels	Three levels: federal government, state government and local government	Three levels: federal government, state government and local government
Division of Duty and Responsibility for Fiscal Expenditure	Federal government: macro issues, national public goods provision such as national defence, foreign affairs, R&D and pay for related affairs	'Subsidiarity principle' Federal government: national defence, foreign affairs, civil rights; federal and state jointly provide health and social welfare
	State and local government: micro issues related to local interests and pay for education, welfare, highway, police and etc.	State government is in charge of culture, education, university. Local government provides local highways, sport and etc. Each government pays for their own affairs and share the burden for joint affairs.
Rights to Fiscal Gains	Federal government relies on income tax; State government relies on sales tax; local government relies on property tax	Almost all important taxes, such as local sales tax, income tax, value added tax, tax on interests and dividends, are shared by federal and state government.

(Continued)

Table 10A.1 *(Continued)*

	Symmetric Country (United States)	Asymmetric Country (Germany)
Rights to Fiscal Legislation	Federal government has power over tax levy; state government doesn't need federal government's approval for tax levy; they can decide their own tax base, tax rate and other rules.	Federal government is in charge of tariff and proprietary activities and jointly shared legislative power with state for shared taxes; state and local government have some legislative rights for local taxes.
Rights to Fiscal (tax) Collection	Three levels of government have independent rights and agencies.	Federal and state government have independent rights and agencies. Local government cannot collect their own taxes.
Budgetary Rights	All three levels of government have rights to make their own budgets.	Federal and state government can make their own budgets, but states have very limited autonomy (68% of taxes are shared and controlled by federal government).
Intergovernmental Transfer	Federal provides grant for state and local; state provides grant for local, including general grants, categorical grants and block grants.	'Uniformity of living conditions principle' leads to Financial Equalization Law, achieved through redistribution of VAT, interstate equalization, federal supplemental grants.
Coordination for Disputes	No coordination	Federal congress is formal coordination agency, with intergovernmental councils.

Source: Authors' summary based on Wei (2015).

Table 10A.2 *Number of HEIs by Region (2013)*

Region	Regular HEIs				Adult HEIs		Other Non-Government HEIs
	Total	Of Which: HEIs Under Central Ministries & Agencies	HEIs Offering Degree Programmes	Higher Vocational Colleges	Total	Of Which: HEIs Under Central Ministries & Agencies	
Total	2,491	113	1,170	1,321	297	13	802
Beijing	89	35	63	26	24	8	69
Tianjin	55	3	29	26	14	–	–
Hebei	118	4	57	61	7	1	36
Shanxi	78	–	29	49	12	–	49
Inner Mongolia	49	–	15	34	2	–	–
Liaoning	115	5	63	52	20	2	70
Jilin	58	2	37	21	14	–	14
Heilongjiang	80	3	37	43	22	–	36
Shanghai	68	10	36	32	15	–	219
Jiangsu	156	10	74	82	9	1	–

(Continued)

Table 10A.2 (Continued)

Region	Regular HEIs				Adult HEIs		Other Non-Government HEIs
	Total	Of Which: HEIs Under Central Ministries & Agencies	HEIs Offering Degree Programmes	Higher Vocational Colleges	Total	Of Which: HEIs Under Central Ministries & Agencies	
Zhejiang	102	2	56	46	9	–	22
Anhui	117	2	44	73	6	–	7
Fujian	87	2	32	55	3	–	–
Jiangxi	92	–	40	52	8	–	23
Shandong	139	2	63	76	11	–	91
Henan	127	1	50	77	13	–	50
Hubei	123	8	67	56	14	–	19
Hunan	122	3	47	75	12	–	13
Guangdong	138	4	58	80	15	–	31

Guangxi	70	–	32	38	6	–	–
Hainan	17	–	6	11	1	–	–
Chongqing	63	2	24	39	4	–	7
Sichuan	103	6	48	55	18	1	16
Guizhou	52	–	26	26	4	–	–
Yunnan	67	–	29	38	2	–	–
Tibet	6	–	3	3	–	–	–
Shaanxi	92	6	54	38	16	–	–
Gansu	42	2	21	21	6	–	30
Qinghai	9	–	4	5	2	–	–
Ningxia	16	1	8	8	1	–	–
Xinjiang	41	–	18	23	7	–	–

Source: China Education Statistical Yearbook 2013.

Table 10A.3 *Number of Admitted, Enrolled and Graduate Students (2012)*

Region	Number of HEIs	Admitted Students					Enrolled Students	Graduate Students
		Total	Sub-Baccalaureate Number	%	Baccalaureate Number	%	Total	Total
Total	2,442	6,888,336	3,147,762	46	3,740,574	54	23,913,155	6,247,338
Beijing	89	158,602	35,951	23	122,651	77	591,243	155,233
Tianjin	55	137,223	55,948	41	81,275	59	473,114	113,034
Hebei	113	321,407	165,289	51	156,118	49	1,168,796	315,755
Shanxi	75	197,181	99,085	50	98,096	50	637,330	162,571
Inner Mongolia	48	105,629	49,412	47	56,217	53	391,434	105,054
Liaoning	112	264,385	96,223	36	168,162	64	934,078	235,984
Jilin	57	162,602	47,142	29	115,460	71	578,953	146,517
Heilongjiang	79	196,970	69,022	35	127,948	65	704,538	203,792
Shanghai	67	136,808	47,247	35	89,561	65	506,596	136,697
Jiangsu	153	435,047	194,760	45	240,287	55	1,671,173	470,254
Zhejiang	102	269,127	120,021	45	149,106	55	932,292	247,537
Anhui	118	286,246	141,866	50	144,380	50	1,023,033	265,477
Fujian	86	201,200	88,983	44	112,217	56	701,392	178,492

Jiangxi	88	237,734	116,293	49	121,441	51	851,119	232,048
Shandong	136	466,695	235,159	50	231,536	50	1,658,490	474,266
Henan	120	455,289	229,561	50	225,728	50	1,559,025	435,308
Hubei	122	402,055	185,126	46	216,929	54	1,386,086	353,014
Hunan	121	311,026	146,185	47	164,841	53	1,082,235	306,809
Guangdong	137	501,939	262,483	52	239,456	48	1,616,838	404,011
Guangxi	70	192,144	109,818	57	82,326	43	629,243	162,169
Hainan	17	49,615	23,498	47	26,117	53	168,270	40,887
Chongqing	60	192,940	82,504	43	110,436	57	623,605	137,635
Sichuan	99	364,488	183,224	50	181,264	50	1,223,680	286,756
Guizhou	49	125,093	60,263	48	64,830	52	383,815	85,285
Yunnan	66	142,753	55,090	39	87,663	61	512,178	118,944
Tibet	6	10,022	4,426	44	5,596	56	33,452	8,580
Shaanxi	91	312,776	125,946	40	186,830	60	1,026,254	265,279
Gansu	42	130,153	58,515	45	71,638	55	431,069	102,980
Qinghai	9	14,634	6,181	42	8,453	58	48,668	11,661
Ningxia	16	30,779	12,877	42	17,902	58	96,440	20,718
Xinjiang	39	75,774	39,664	52	36,110	48	268,716	64,591

Source: China Statistic Yearbook 2013.

Table 10A.4 *Number of Enrolled Students for Every 100,000 Residents (2014)*

Region	High School Students	College Students	High School to College Student Ratio
Total	3,100	2,488	1.2
Beijing	1,912	5,469	0.3
Tianjin	2,077	4,346	0.5
Hebei	2,745	2,108	1.3
Shanxi	3,872	2,474	1.6
Inner Mongolia	3,048	2,137	1.4
Liaoning	2,539	2,903	0.9
Jilin	2,513	3,033	0.8
Heilongjiang	2,658	2,529	1.1
Shanghai	1,308	3,421	0.4
Jiangsu	2,738	2,814	1.0
Zhejiang	2,887	2,363	1.2
Anhui	3,794	2,203	1.7
Fujian	3,341	2,435	1.4
Jiangxi	3,336	2,381	1.4

Shandong	3,213	2,304	1.4
Henan	3,571	2,114	1.7
Hubei	2,607	3,144	0.8
Hunan	2,797	2,106	1.3
Guangdong	4,239	2,199	1.9
Guangxi	3,727	1,939	1.9
Hainan	3,846	2,253	1.7
Chongqing	3,989	2,894	1.4
Sichuan	3,497	2,140	1.6
Guizhou	3,943	1,535	2.6
Yunnan	2,860	1,662	1.7
Tibet	2,292	1,528	1.5
Shaanxi	4,012	3,612	1.1
Gansu	4,048	2,193	1.8
Qinghai	3,638	1,162	3.1
Ningxia	4,097	2,195	1.9
Xinjiang	3,266	1,681	1.9

Source: China Statistic Yearbook for Health and Birth Control 2015.

Table 10A.5 *Mobility of Vocational College Students (2008)*

| | Per Capita GDP | Vocational Colleges | Enrolled Students | Student Origin (%) | | | | |
	RMB	Number	Number	Municipality	Eastern Region	Middle Region	Western Region	Local Resident
Shanghai	73,124	30	15,620	57.25	15.49	18.42	8.84	56.54
Beijing	63,029	22	18,615	79.97	5.05	8.59	6.39	79.13
Tianjin	55,473	26	18,946	45.73	9.37	25.18	19.73	43.38
Zhejiang	42,214	47	90,155	0.26	94.39	3.33	2.02	92.54
Jiangsu	39,622	74	153,141	0.49	91.74	5.05	2.72	87.62
Guangdong	37,589	70	175,145	0.27	94.51	3.36	1.87	93.54
Shandong	33,083	66	179,152	0.34	88.76	6.55	4.35	86.64
Inner Mongolia	32,214	26	69,545	0.17	0.97	4.57	94.29	92.79
Liaoning	31,259	41	55,420	0.41	85.38	8.76	5.45	83.17
Fujian	30,123	51	66,558	0.39	90.96	6.18	2.47	88.74
Jilin	23,514	19	33,426	1.29	6.36	84.13	8.22	74.29
Hebei	23,239	51	129,634	1.57	2.71	91.70	4.02	85.91
Heilongjiang	21,727	42	56,602	0.83	4.79	84.59	9.79	73.35
Shanxi	20,742	44	64,327	0.41	2.07	92.30	5.21	86.63

Xinjiang	19,893	21	25,637	0.45	1.55	9.14	88.86	73.07
Hubei	19,860	51	108,184	0.63	5.51	86.14	7.71	78.50
Henan	19,593	51	200,047	0.19	0.95	96.93	1.93	95.05
Shaanxi	18,246	37	86,366	0.51	1.43	8.04	90.02	81.69
Chongqing	18,025	25	38,599	70.99	3.48	8.31	17.22	70.92
Ningxia	17,892	8	13,541	0.00	0.74	3.18	96.07	89.06
Hunan	17,521	68	135,174	0.61	2.97	91.50	4.91	86.41
Qinghai	17,389	5	10,463	0.95	1.73	6.26	91.06	82.18
Hainan	17,175	9	15,339	2.92	18.10	56.67	22.31	31.49
Sichuan	15,378	47	86,598	3.38	1.25	3.44	91.93	86.50
Guangxi	14,966	38	91,326	0.20	1.13	4.33	94.35	92.43
Jiangxi	14,781	41	69,219	0.46	5.36	86.30	7.87	75.96
Anhui	14,485	60	128,383	0.31	2.58	95.46	1.64	92.61
Tibet	13,861	3	2,023	0.00	0.00	0.00	100.00	100.00
Yunnan	12,587	34	54,810	0.61	0.53	2.58	96.28	93.14
Gansu	12,110	21	59,494	0.03	0.18	0.70	99.10	97.87
Guizhou	8,824	22	42,098	0.97	2.06	4.85	92.12	87.33
National Average	22,698	37	2,293,587	8.79	20.71	32.47	38.02	81.89

Source: Wei Yi (2010) Unpublished Master Thesis. Peking University.

Table 10A.6 *Revenue from Various Sources for Regional Institutions (2013)*

Region	Total Revenue Amount	National Fiscal Allocation for Education Amount	%	Of Which: Budgetary Appropriation Amount	%	Revenue From Tuition Amount	%	Revue From Sales and Services Amount	%
Total	559,736	325,755	58	308,094	55	167,573	30	26,608	5
Beijing	20,709	16,888	82	15,054	73	2,762	13	592	3
Tianjin	13,846	9,331	67	9,185	66	3,515	25	378	3
Hebei	22,142	12,792	58	12,407	56	7,479	34	446	2
Shanxi	15,790	9,844	62	9,447	60	3,911	25	852	5
Inner Mongolia	11,011	7,796	71	7,429	67	2,471	22	272	2
Liaoning	23,630	14,227	60	13,286	56	7,255	31	571	2
Jilin	14,043	8,627	61	8,145	58	4,152	30	351	2
Heilongjiang	13,683	7,612	56	7,428	54	5,447	40	253	2
Shanghai	22,291	16,021	72	15,257	68	3,936	18	1,007	5
Jiangsu	42,523	21,805	51	19,690	46	11,582	27	4,362	10
Zhejiang	29,043	14,800	51	12,627	43	9,474	33	2,355	8
Anhui	17,660	10,228	58	9,786	55	5,597	32	513	3
Fujian	15,382	7,119	46	6,706	44	5,231	34	607	4

Jiangxi	18,244	11,129	61	10,814	59	5,275	29	572	3
Shandong	32,293	19,645	61	18,532	57	9,785	30	710	2
Henan	31,712	19,089	60	18,176	57	9,803	31	1,834	6
Hubei	25,080	12,473	50	11,682	47	9,024	36	979	4
Hunan	24,187	13,999	58	13,563	56	7,209	30	1,583	7
Guangdong	43,090	21,886	51	20,519	48	16,405	38	1,317	3
Guangxi	14,939	8,500	57	8,113	54	5,034	34	399	3
Hainan	4,200	2,527	60	2,405	57	1,394	33	132	3
Chongqing	14,278	6,825	48	6,585	46	5,119	36	1,279	9
Sichuan	23,224	12,469	54	11,996	52	7,616	33	568	2
Guizhou	9,978	6,589	66	6,426	64	2,230	22	643	6
Yunnan	14,505	8,160	56	7,960	55	4,109	28	1,367	9
Tibet	1,563	1,414	90	1,413	90	101	6	7	0
Shaanxi	21,809	11,242	52	11,046	51	7,711	35	1,421	7
Gansu	7,780	4,831	62	4,760	61	2,319	30	231	3
Qinghai	1,491	1,092	73	1,057	71	232	16	135	9
Ningxia	2,555	1,707	67	1,652	65	538	21	166	6
Xinjiang	7,057	5,087	72	4,947	70	856	12	704	10

Source: China Education Finance Statistic Yearbook 2014.

Note: Amount is in million RMB.

Table 10A.7 *Per Student Fiscal Expenditure for Regional Institutions (2013)*

Region	Budgetary Appropriation				
	Amount	Of Which: Operational Expenditure		Of Which: Basic Construction Expenditure	
		Amount	%	Amount	%
Total	14,186	13,729	97	457	3
Beijing	48,071	47,629	99	441	1
Tianjin	23,087	23,047	100	40	0
Hebei	13,135	12,904	98	231	2
Shanxi	12,073	10,942	91	1,131	9
Inner Mongolia	15,599	15,356	98	242	2
Liaoning	13,488	12,494	93	994	7
Jilin	12,909	12,852	100	57	0
Heilongjiang	11,790	11,595	98	195	2
Shanghai	35,682	30,186	85	5,496	15
Jiangsu	15,000	14,837	99	163	1
Zhejiang	13,766	13,766	100	–	–
Anhui	10,215	10,103	99	112	1
Fujian	11,295	11,202	99	93	1
Jiangxi	12,744	12,638	99	106	1
Shandong	11,700	11,546	99	154	1
Henan	10,845	10,681	98	163	2
Hubei	13,115	12,529	96	586	4
Hunan	13,184	12,995	99	189	1
Guangdong	14,894	14,186	95	707	5
Guangxi	13,774	13,382	97	392	3
Hainan	16,640	15,165	91	1,475	9
Chongqing	12,792	12,358	97	434	3
Sichuan	12,172	12,012	99	160	1

Region	Budgetary Appropriation				
	Amount	Of Which: Operational Expenditure		Of Which: Basic Construction Expenditure	
		Amount	%	Amount	%
Guizhou	15,310	14,957	98	353	2
Yunnan	13,231	12,826	97	405	3
Tibet	37,423	27,379	73	10,045	27
Shaanxi	13,364	12,935	97	429	3
Gansu	11,059	10,497	95	561	5
Qinghai	17,327	16,505	95	823	5
Ningxia	18,188	17,666	97	522	3
Xinjiang	15,897	15,372	97	525	3

Source: China Education Finance Statistic Yearbook 2014.

Note: Amount is in RMB.

About the Editors and Contributors

EDITORS

Martin Carnoy is Vida Jacks Professor of Education and Economics at Stanford University, the United States. He was trained at the University of Chicago and writes on the economic value of education and the political economy of educational policy. Much of his work is comparative and international.

Isak Froumin is Professor and Academic Supervisor at the Institute of Education, National Research University Higher School of Economics, Russia. His current key research interests are the development of higher education systems, higher education differentiation and university and school governance.

Oleg Leshukov is Research Fellow at the Laboratory for Universities Development at the Institute of Education, National Research University Higher School of Economics, Russia. His current key research interests are development of regional higher education systems and national–regional relationships in governance of higher education.

Simon Marginson is Professor of International Higher Education at the UCL Institute of Education, University College London, United Kingdom. He is also the Director of the ESEC/HEFCE Centre for Global Higher Education and Editor-in-Chief of *Higher Education*. He focuses on global and international aspects of higher education, system design and education and social inequality.

CONTRIBUTORS

Anthony Lising Antonio is Associate Professor of Education and Associate Director of the Stanford Institute for Higher Education Research at Stanford University, the United States. His research focuses on stratification and postsecondary access, racial diversity and its impact on students and institutions, student friendship networks and student development.

Lys M. V. Dantas holds a PhD in Education and is currently Professor at the Universidade Federal do Recôncavo da Bahia, Brazil. Her works involve topics in the fields of public administration and education.

Glen A. Jones is Professor of Higher Education and the Dean of the Ontario Institute for Studies in Education of the University, Toronto. His research focuses on higher education governance, systems and academic work.

Marion Lloyd is chief project coordinator for the General Directorate for Institutional Evaluation at the National Autonomous University of Mexico, Mexico. Her research focuses on comparative higher education policy, access and equity, university rankings and science and technology policies in Latin America.

C. Rose Nelson is a doctoral student at Stanford University, the United States, who studies the sociology of higher education.

Christian Noumi is a PhD candidate at the University of Toronto, Canada. His research focuses on comparative higher education. He holds an MA in Higher Education from the University of Kassel and a BA in History from the University of Yaoundé.

Imanol Ordorika is general director for institutional evaluation and a research professor at the Institute for Economic Research at the National Autonomous University of Mexico, Mexico. His work focuses on university politics and governance, international university rankings and student activist movements, among other topics.

Roberto Rodríguez-Gómez is a sociologist and full professor at the Institute of Social Research of the National Autonomous University of Mexico, Mexico. His main academic interests include comparative higher education policy, history of the university and innovation processes in university organizations.

Ulrich Teichler was Professor, from 1978 to 2013, and the Director, for many years, at the International Centre for Higher Education Research (INCHER-Kassel), the University of Kassel, Germany. He is a sociologist, who conducts research on higher education and the world of work, higher education systems, international cooperation and mobility and the academic profession.

Jandhyala B. G. Tilak, Economist of Education and former Full Professor and Vice Chancellor, National University of Educational Planning and Administration, is presently a Distinguished Professor at Council for Social Development, New Delhi, India.

Robert Evan Verhine is Full Professor of Education in the School of Education of the Universidade Federal da Bahia, Brazil. His research and publications deal with aspects related to the economics of education, comparative education and higher education evaluation.

Rong Wang is Full Professor and the Director of China Institute of Educational Finance Research, Peking University, China. Her main research interest focuses on education finance, economics of education and educational policy evaluation.

Po Yang is Associate Professor at Graduate School of Education, Peking University, China. She conducts research on economics of vocational education, higher education finance and policy evaluation.

Index